# MOVIE STAR

*A Look at the Women Who Made Hollywood*

by

## ETHAN MORDDEN

ST. MARTIN'S PRESS / NEW YORK

# Also by Ethan Mordden

*Better Foot Forward: The History of American Musical Theatre*
*Opera in the Twentieth Century*
*That Jazz!: An Idiosyncratic History of the American Twenties*
*A Guide to Orchestral Music*
*The Splendid Art of Opera*
*The American Theatre*
*The Hollywood Musical*

Design by Manny Paul

Library of Congress Cataloging in Publication Data

Mordden, Ethan
  Movie star.

  Bibliography: p.
  1. Moving-picture actors and actresses—United States—Biography.  I. Title.
PN1998.A2M555  1983      791.43′028′0922 [B]  83-302
ISBN 0-312-55049-9

Again to my parents,
still delighted, still not surprised

# Contents

*Preface*                                                          xi

*Acknowledgments*                                                  xii

*Introduction: The Star Is Born*                                   1
    FLORENCE LAWRENCE
    THEDA BARA

*1. The Silent Women*                                              11
    MAE MURRAY
    GERALDINE FARRAR
    BETTY BRONSON
    ZASU PITTS
    NAZIMOVA
    COLLEEN MOORE
    CLARA BOW
    GLORIA SWANSON

*2. The First Star and the Greatest Star*                          37
    MARY PICKFORD
    LILLIAN GISH

*3. Forward to Yesterday*                                          57
    JANET GAYNOR

*4. The Pope's Wife, the Doomed Harlot,*
*   and the Loyal Shopgirl*                          66
    NORMA SHEARER
    GRETA GARBO
    JOAN CRAWFORD

5.  *Women's Women: The Ladies*                                       93
       RUTH CHATTERTON
       ANN HARDING
       HELEN HAYES
       LYNN FONTANNE
       JEANETTE MACDONALD
       MYRNA LOY
       IRENE DUNNE
       MARGARET DUMONT
       GREER GARSON

6.  *Men's Women: The Harlots*                                        105
       MARLENE DIETRICH
       JEAN HARLOW

7.  *No One's Woman*                                                  116
       MAE WEST

8.  *Comics I*                                                        125
       MARIE DRESSLER
       CAROLE LOMBARD
       MARION DAVIES
       LUCILLE BALL
       GRACIE ALLEN
       EVE ARDEN

9.  *The Evergreen Moralist*                                          141
       KATHARINE HEPBURN

10.  *Fighters*                                                       160
       GLENDA FARRELL
       JOAN BLONDELL
       ROSALIND RUSSELL
       ALICE FAYE
       BARBARA STANWYCK

11.  *Dame Camp*                                                      182
       BETTE DAVIS

12.  *Maidens and Pinups*                                             194
       SHIRLEY TEMPLE
       DEANNA DURBIN

Judy Garland
Elizabeth Taylor
Rita Hayworth
Betty Grable
Ava Gardner

13. *The Ultimate in It*                           220
Marilyn Monroe
Jayne Mansfield
Kim Novak

14. *Comics II*                                    232
Judy Holliday
Audrey Hepburn
Madeline Kahn
Miss Piggy
Lily Tomlin
Goldie Hawn

15. *Musical Women*                                245
Doris Day
Julie Andrews
Barbra Streisand
Liza Minnelli
Bernadette Peters

16. *Persons; or, All Women Are Whores*            260
Ingrid Bergman
Raquel Welch
Bo Derek
Sally Kellerman
Diane Keaton
Jane Fonda
Meryl Streep

*A Selective Bibliography*                         285

*Index*                                            291

# *Preface*

This is a look at certain influential Hollywood actresses. It is not a feminist study, nor is it particularly concerned with the sociological impact of the roles that women have played in the movies, though this naturally comes into the picture. There have already been two superb studies in the feminist line, Marjorie Rosen's *Popcorn Venus* and Molly Haskell's *From Reverence to Rape.* Rosen and Haskell handled the subject from the script side, so to speak, examining the range of parts that have been allotted to women, assigned them. This book tacks from the casting side, treating not the range of parts but the women themselves: the images they projected, the conflict between their career plans and the expectations of the public and the money bosses, and what happened to them.

This is my own highly personal selection of actresses, those whom I see as unique for a variety of reasons. I offer no compendium of the most gifted, or the most famous, or the most "important." Readers may find their favorites neglected; but, I repeat, this is my selection, for my reasons. Write your own book.

There may be too many superlatives in the text, too much mention of the first, the most, the last. However, the book deals with superlative women, exemplary persons, and the writing is bound to reflect their eminence. Some of these women were in fact the first to play a certain character, or a familiar character in a certain way; or they were strikingly efficient about aspects of their business; or were the ones who capped an era. Why not say so?

The author wishes again to acknowledge the enthusiasm and guidance of his editor Michael Denneny, and to salute Paul Liepa's expedition; Greg Weber's eagle-eyed copy-editing; Deborah Daley's imaginative design for and Barry Gross' execution of the cover; Bill Tynes' trove of photos, which delivered up Little Mary, Colleen Moore, and Lillian Gish; Manny Paul's sumptuous design; Ina Shapiro's sharp production; Judy MacDonald's incisiveness; and, as always, the patience and tenacity of Dorothy Pittman.

*You either have It or you don't.*

—ELINOR GLYN

# MOVIE STAR

*A Look at the Women Who Made Hollywood*

# Introduction:
## *The Star Is Born*

FLORENCE LAWRENCE
THEDA BARA

*I read so many lies about myself that I
hardly know what is the truth anymore.*

—THEDA BARA

Toward the end of the first de-
cade of the twentieth century, the American motion picture was well on
its way to acculturation, prosperity, and artistic expansion. The store-
front nickelodeon was already beginning to cede to larger and more
comfortable theatres. The early audiences of immigrants, city proletariat, and sailors were soon to be joined by the middle-class and
highbrow adventurers. The documentary bits ("Electrocution of an El-
ephant") had been replaced by short stories, and inventive directors
were devising style, structure, technique—Edwin S. Porter from 1901,
D. W. Griffith from 1908, Thomas Ince from 1910. The close-up, to
show what theatre and fiction could only tell of; cross-cut editing, to
pull different parts of story into order; and the life-scaled space, to
contain story as life contains real lives—all these were in use. There
were no full-length features yet, no sound track, and no Hollywood.
But the essential qualities of film as Americans know it were placed and
developing.

Except: there were no stars.

In a way, there weren't even actors, virtually none that anyone
could name. For while the star system was ancient in the American
theatre, the first movie businessmen viewed their actors as hired employees. So, by the way, did the established theatre people. Movies were
junk and movie people junk dealers unworthy of literature, tradition,
glamour, and good timing—the elements of theatremanship. In the

theatre, they asked, "How do you read lines?" In film, they asked, "How will the camera see you?" What talent did that call for, what craft? Some Broadway producers wouldn't hire anyone who had worked in film, and unemployed actors took to giving fake names when applying for movie work. It was just as well, because movie work could hardly lead to anything notable or even steady. Its public was largely poor and illiterate, for one thing; for another, the egalitarian setup of the early film studios meant an actor might play a romantic lead in one film on Monday, do a villain bit in another film on Wednesday, and fill in with the extras in a third film on Friday. Anyway, the short films came and went so fast, how was the public to recognize or choose a favorite?

Somehow, the public did adopt favorites, nameless and elusive as they were. The public wanted to learn more about the actors, to know them: because it already knew them. The public committed the same error it commits today, associating actors with their roles. But, after all, the theatre audiences did this, too, and in theatre the story space was only being depicted. In film, the space happened as you watched. So, the public demanded to complete its acquaintance with its favorites, and there *were* movie stars. They just didn't have names.

The movie men decided to keep it that way. They were monopolists, WASPs or Germans, banded together around Thomas Alva Edison and George Eastman, who between them controlled the key patents to the movie-making and -exhibiting apparatus and the available domestic film stock. Known as the "Patents Trust," this group was determined to run film as a plain industry, the studios to be factories where workers labored, all for the same salaries. (The directors, like Griffith, got more, as would a factory manager.) No matter what its plot, characters, or special procedures, each film—strictly one-reelers, about ten minutes long—would take as much time to assemble as each other film, and each actor of a given type would be interchangeable with another. Why distinguish a few with billing and promotion? They'll just ask for more money.

If film was an industry, it was not plain but fancy. It began to find itself when one of the many independent producers, outraged at the Trust's high-handed oligarchy, seized one of the nameless stars, named her, and relaunched her as his own little gem with the sort of promotional campaign that was to become standard in the movies: imagination, exaggeration, and prevarication. The story is thrice-told. Carl Laemmle was the producer, the Independent Motion Picture Company his outfit, and the Biograph Girl his prize. The Biograph Girl! She was heroine, mother, adulteress, cowgirl, thief; as a newlywed she tried her hand at wifely virtue in the Griffith comedy *Her First Biscuits* and almost poisoned the entire Biograph stock company, including Mary Pickford in her first film role. She was popular, familiar, perhaps even beloved.

She was, it turned out, one Florence Lawrence. Tiring of Biograph's standard five dollars a day, she and her husband, Harry Salter, apparently made overtures to another Trust studio, Essanay. Trusts stick together: Essanay told Biograph, and Lawrence and Salter were fired. Laemmle, a leader of the upstart immigrant class of producers which was to take over the industry in the ensuing decades, swept Lawrence up and began to beat the drum. **"We Nail a Lie,"** cries Laemmle's advertisement, and lo, IMP's signet, a cheeky devil in eyeglasses, bears a photograph of Florence Lawrence. "The blackest and at the same time the silliest lie yet circulated by the enemies of the 'Imp,'" Laemmle went on, "was the story foisted on the public of St. Louis last week to the effect that Miss Lawrence (the 'Imp' girl, formerly known as the 'Biograph' girl) had been killed by a street car. It was a black lie because so cowardly. It was a silly lie because so easily disproved."

Indeed it was; it was never believed in the first place. No one had heard of any streetcar accident involving the Biograph girl. When Biograph got rid of an actress, it didn't bury her; it fired her and forgot her. Laemmle invented the story in the ad without even bothering to tell it somewhere first. Moreover, he then had Lawrence make a personal appearance in St. Louis and inflated what appears to have been a relatively placid meeting of star and public into the first of the great starcrash rampages by reporting it as such. They touched her! grabbed her! tore her clothes! Not only was a star born, but the whole star business, for other independents saw what it did for Lawrence and followed Laemmle's lead. They were smart. While maintaining a star system was vastly more expensive than employing an anonymous labor pool, film without stars proved unworkable. The Trust studios resisted it . . . and died.*

Another independent, William Fox, went further than Laemmle in preparing a star's PR campaign. Florence Lawrence had already been popular when she met up with Laemmle; all he had done was nudge the public in her direction. Fox *created* his first star, Theda Bara, out of nothing. Bara was the first of the movies' many PR ghosts, a creature that could be seen but wasn't real. The PR told you what to look for, and there she was. But the uninformed, or those immune to commercial suggestion, couldn't quite find her. Fox's debutante set the new style for stardom: you are what you play. She also set the style for a fast decline: if you aren't, they'll take it away from you.

Bara's career lasted from 1915 to 1919, but her PR was so densely derived that we have to backtrack nearly twenty years just to understand who she was supposed to be. It starts in 1897 with a painting by Edward Burne-Jones, "The Vampire": a woman all in white, posed

---

*By 1920, only one of the Trust firms, Vitagraph, survived. It was absorbed by Warner Brothers in 1925.

next to the drained body of her prey. Rudyard Kipling wrote a poem
in the portrait's honor:

> A fool there was and he made his prayer
> (Even as you and I!)
> To a rag and a bone and a hank of hair
> (We called her the woman who did not care)
> But the fool he called her his lady fair—
> (Even as you and I!)

A woman who did not care: this was novel. It was pop art's most basic
tenet that people cared about love relationships. The vampire, it appeared, had sex but not romance. Porter Emerson Browne made a play
of the poem, *A Fool There Was,* produced in New York in 1909 with
Katherine Kaelred in the lead. Browne attempted to capture Burne-
Jones's *Jugendstil* timelessness with a cast list of archetypes: Kaelred
played The Woman, her victim was The Husband, he had The Wife
and The Child and The Friend, and so on. No names, only wonder
and nightmarish lurkings. The husband is a diplomat. He meets the
woman on an ocean voyage and becomes her slave, ruining his marriage and career in alcoholic enchantment. The woman is no mere
femme fatale, but an eager destroyer of men. She's a sportswoman: she
hunts.

The play did good business, and William Fox saw in it the chance
to upgrade his shabby operation, Box Office Attractions, with a film
version. Now, whom to cast? It was 1914. Hollywood had been discovered, but most films were still being made in New York, and there
Fox's director Frank Powell met a distinctive-looking actress named
Theda Goodman who was having trouble getting a niche on Broadway.
Born in Cincinnati, the daughter of a tailor, Theda (formally Theodosia) was what gets called a nice Jewish girl and had one quirk, a
fascination with the occult. Something in this registered with Powell:
the vampire is of the dark world, with a magically irresistible power.
She can't do what she does on beauty or fashion or wit alone. She
*spiritualizes.* That must have appealed to Theda, and Fox couldn't afford an established name anyway, so on Powell's recommendation he
produced *A Fool There Was* (1915) with Theda as the vampire.

Sometime later, the actress admitted that the whole thing seemed
silly, but she needed work and the job was promising, with contract,
options, codicils, and plans. Given the public's interest in the "vamp,"
as the character was most frequently called, the movie might well yield
a career. But what if Theodosia Goodman, actress, became the prisoner of Theda the vamp? What if the public assumed Theodosia was a
real-life vamp? "Naturally," she observed, "all sorts of wild rumors and
weird stories about one sprang up."

They didn't spring up; Fox planted them. Fan magazines had begun to appear in 1911, not coincidentally just after the lead actors began to get name billing, and the newspapers, too, were starting to run Hollywood stories. From Fox's mouth to America's ears, the tailor's daughter was sold as the exotic horror, Theda Bara, to press and public in the first modern PR campaign. Lies, lies: she was born in the Sahara in the shadow of the Sphinx; she was French, she was Russian, she was Arabian, she was of mixed blood; she saw men die at her feet, and saw that it was good. There were so many lies that they were contradicting each other even before *A Fool There Was* opened; and, after her first press conference, which Bara gave in a dark, overheated, over-perfumed hotel room, pretending not to speak a word of English, she rushed to a window, tore off its drapery, and pulled it open, crying, "Give me air!"

She didn't get much. Fox had to keep his star under wraps for fear of losing credibility, and eventually he had to spell out the components of exotic horror in Bara's contract—no marriage, no going out unless heavily veiled and dressed for the part, no public transportation (what's a limousine for?). Because movies could be made in a matter of weeks then, Fox kept Bara busy, with nine features in 1915, nine in 1916, seven in 1917, six in 1918, and eight in 1919, not to mention the many interviews and personal appearances. She was well paid for her time, making $4,000 a week when she left Fox in late 1919, but the vamping was supposed to get her started in films, not limit her. "Five practically uninterrupted years of vamping have drawn my nerves pretty taut," she complained, though in fact she made a number of non-vamp films. Sandwiched between *The Devil's Daughter* (1915), *Carmen* (1915), *Gold and the Woman* (1916), *The Tiger Woman* (1917), *Camille* (1917), *Cleopatra* (1917), *Madame DuBarry* (1918), *Salome* (1918), and *A Woman There Was* (1919) were *The Two Orphans* (1915), *Romeo and Juliet* (1916), *Kathleen Mavourneen* (1919), and a few other such. And, contrary to legend, not all her non-vamp roles bombed out at the box office. But Bara as an actress was of little use to Fox. He had engaged her to launch a vamp cycle. This she certainly did, to such an extent that besides the Theda Bara Super Productions, Fox released a slew of cheap vamp spinoffs with Bara imitators. One of these, Betty Blythe,* might have become even bigger than Bara if she hadn't got married and run off to Europe.

But who needed Theda Bara as a poor orphan or Juliet or a col-

---

*Blythe faced the question of how closely vamping relates to sex square-on in *The Queen of Sheba* (1921), a "fall of Rome" spectacle but subtler and grander than any of Bara's vehicles. Director J. Gordon Edwards, Blake Edwards' grandfather, personally chose Blythe to succeed Bara as Fox's allvamp, and let her wear even less than Bara had worn as Cleopatra. Netting, pearls, and sandals suited Blythe to the nth, making *The Queen of Sheba* as much a man's treat as a woman's. "I wear twenty-eight costumes," Blythe reported, "and if I put them on all at once, I couldn't keep warm."

leen? It was bad for business, confusing a public that had come to expect a certain kind of entertainment from this certain star. One Juliet too many and they might give her up for good. So in the end the vamping not only started Bara but finished her as well. When her contract came up for renewal in 1919, she insisted that the vamping was over, and William Fox decided that Theda Bara was over, too. She attempted to re-establish herself on the stage in *The Blue Flame* (1920), a grotesque melodrama poured from the mold of Bara's scenarios. (In brief: an atheistic scientist invents a ray of life, resurrects his dead girlfriend Bara, and gazes on in terror as she, reborn heartless, goes on the usual vamp rampage of seductions and leechings. At length, it develops it was all a dream and the scientist learns faith in God, the only authoritative giver of life.) Al Woods, a specialist in trash genres, produced *The Blue Flame*, intending it for provincial tours to catch what was left of Bara's following, and out of town *The Blue Flame* was a smash, giving the moviegoing audience a rare chance to see a favorite in the real *and* hear her for the first time. But Bara wasn't in it for the money. This was her comeback, and she demanded that Woods take the show to New York.

That was a mistake. Bara should have realized that her fans consisted of rustic factions, mainly women, who were impressed by a worldliness that compared well with the modesty of their native farm towns and industrial villages. The northeastern intelligentsia, however, disdained her and New Yorkers in general had other things to do in cinema. Journalists in particular were gunning for Bara. Much as Rudolph Valentino, Kay Francis, Gene Autry, Shirley Temple, John Wayne, and Burt Reynolds after her, she exasperated critics unable to disenchant her following. Hardly anyone read movie reviews at the time, true—but many thousands read the New York theatre columns in 1920, and *The Blue Flame*'s first-nighters fell upon Theda Bara like the fold on the wolf. Let Heywood Broun of the *World* speak for them: "Miss Bara kept within the city ordinances, but she was not so very good, either. At the end . . . she made a speech in which she said that God had been very kind to her. Probably she referred to the fact that at no time during the course of the evening did the earth open and swallow up the authors, the star, and all the company."

New York screamed with laughter, effectively transforming Bara from a threatened species into an extinct one. Her hopes of filming *The Blue Flame* and starting all over in Hollywood in modern-dress occult melodrama were dashed, and though she kept herself listed in the casting directories as "at liberty" almost until her death in 1955, she made two last films in the mid-1920s, the latter one, *Madame Mystery* (1926), a Hal Roach burlesque of . . . Theda Bara.

The saga of Theda Bara raises questions about stardom in general and women stars in particular. How can an actress be *so* popular for a while and suddenly fall out of work? Can PR really invent stars—and, if it can, does that mean that literally anyone can be a star? Does the public believe all PR literally, or does it come to the movies just to see what the fuss is about and decide for itself? How strategic are talent and training? Is stage experience relevant or can a star learn it all before a camera? Are women's roles in film limited to what their culture allows, or can they expand the elements of intelligence and initiative in their roles and feed this new information into the culture? Are women more prone than men to be treated as articles of beauty and/or sex and therefore bound to lose their hold on the public after a period of exposure?

Theda Bara offers a good place to start, for she was one of the three or four most popular stars of her time. First of all, how well did she act? Given the stylized and fantastic nature of her stories, she seems to have been adequate, slinking down stairways, glaring at enemies, and coiling herself around her victims. She would draw jeers and giggles today—she was already doing so in her own day—but her hold on the public had more to do with Fox's PR machine than with her films. Bara playing a vamp was really an afterthought to the notion of a man killer, of a woman who did not care. There was a hint of feminism in the image, and, as the months went by and Bara became restless under the mask, interviewers found her by turns ridiculing and interpreting the image and throwing aside the tales of her foreign birth and magic powers. "For every vampire," she told them, "there are ten men of the same type, men who take everything from women—loving devotion, beauty, youth—and give nothing in return! . . . The vampire that I play is the vengeance of my sex upon its exploiters."

But why *this* woman? What did Theodosia Goodman have that persuaded Fox and his audience to let her play the archetype? She described herself as "an ordinary woman, a little tall, a little thin, with big black eyes and a face of shadows." With her long dark hair, in her period robes, she looked like a pre-Raphaelite poet on the way to her pottery wheel; in modern clothes, she looked passé. Perhaps this, more than the generally risible quality of her films, was what made her a temporary person: she was a revolutionary idea disguised to look antique. Women were intrigued by her assault on conventional morality, but her constant escapades in the historical past and her outlandish city getups kept her remote—her hat in *The Tiger Woman* looks like the offspring of the surrey with the fringe on top and the little church around the corner. At one point she claimed to be Cleopatra reincarnated, no doubt at a PR man's suggestion; the idea held on and held her back. What could Cleopatra teach women who, during Bara's five years of stardom, lived through a world war, an influenza epidemic that killed half a million Americans, and the countless convulsive little social changes that culminated in the liberating vitality of the 1920s?

For all her ambition and commentary, for her willingness to pretend to dwell in the dream and her decision to break it open, Bara was little more than a curiosity. Was she even sexy? Censors had nervous breakdowns screening her pictures, and every so often something arrestingly honest would slip through, as when, in *Gold and the Woman*, she sidles up to a hulk who has just torn his shirt sleeve in a fight and contemplatively feels his right biceps. But she had crouched gloating beside too many quivering wrecked men to be taken seriously as a vamp or a feminist.

She could still be a star: when America entered World War I, Bara personally sold millions of dollars' worth of Liberty Bonds, and one California regiment made her their honorary godmother. The sorceress of sex a godmother? Surely no one could care much one way or another about her after that. Moreover, making thirty-nine films in four years—an average for any star of Bara's vintage—insured the woman's quickly becoming obsolete in a way no modern star could, with one or two films a year at the most. One subtitle in *A Fool There Was*, "Kiss me, my fool," became one of the nation's most repeated catch phrases—this alone made Bara memorable. And she did establish a new character in movies, the unstoppable woman whose attentions destroyed men. (We'll meet interesting variations on the character in the coming pages.) But she was hopelessly dated in the way she looked and moved and even in the very sound of her name. One half expects to hear of her comb being turned up in some archeological dig. Moreover, Bara is the only major American film star whose pictures have almost entirely vanished: all but three are lost. Still, film historians will never cease to cite her, for she was, if nothing else, the first star who was entirely created: imaginary name, imaginary roles, imaginary life.

Florence Lawrence, the first star, and Theda Bara, the first invention, make good history here, for they typify the two most basic elements of stardom, the public's interest and the producer's engineering. One is spontaneous, the other developed. Florence Lawrence was the spontaneous star, virtually acclaimed by her fans, for while Laemmle did to an extent "present" her, he only did so in order to centralize her already collected following. Bara, then, was the developed star, heralded as an institution before anyone even knew who she was.

Both women also typify a hazard of stardom that will trap nearly every actress in this book, the problem of survival. It has been said that Hollywood permitted cowboys, detectives, warriors, and even romantic male leads to age well beyond the time span their roles implied, while women had to retire or go into "character" when they reached middle age. Gary Cooper, Clark Gable, Spencer Tracy, and John Wayne stayed top till they died, and Cary Grant seems to have retired at his option. But the biggest women stars found themselves displaced after a decade or so or just managed to hang on in unimportant pictures or had to reinvent themselves in some unique way. Mary Pickford's and Gloria Swanson's careers were disrupted by sound, though both had fine voices. Constance Bennett, Hollywood's top-dollar performer in 1932 at $30,000 a week, was reduced to featured bits in the 1940s. Luise Rainer won two Best Actress Oscars in a row; two years later, she was discarded. Even Joan Crawford and Bette Davis, two classic cases of the survivor, hit bad times in the early 1950s and had to make a comeback in a low-budget thriller that lampooned their old personae as masochist (Crawford) and sadist (Davis). And Garbo, in some ways the ultimate Hollywood attraction, ran out of steam after fifteen years and melted away.

The problem of survival, however, is greater than gender. All film actors, men as well as women, worked in a business precariously based on variables well out of any one person's control—audience caprice, producers' vendettas, directors' and writers' abilities. One might say that all Hollywood actors were "women": decorative accessories expected to follow orders and make nice. In the days of the Patents Trust, all artistic and many business decisions were made by directors, and in the 1920s some few players were in effect or literally their own producers—Charlie Chaplin, Buster Keaton, Douglas Fairbanks, Mary Pickford, Gloria Swanson, Lillian Gish. But studio power, developed by the independents who replaced the Trust firms, utterly controlled the industry by 1930. They even used the sound panic to impose discipline, destroying certain actors' careers as an example to the others. One can see the old spontaneous, person-scaled cinema giving way to the regimented studio system in the stories of Lawrence and Bara: the former easily won her freedom from Biograph anonymity and earned perhaps the greatest fame of her time, climaxed when Carl Laemmle gave her her own production company, Lawrence to produce and star in whatever struck her fancy, and her husband to direct. But Bara, only a few years later, was entirely the property of William Fox.

The way the two women ended their careers is also instructive. Bara, we know, was ushered out after five years; she spent her thirty-five-year retirement as a Hollywood hostess, locally admired for her gourmet dinner parties and world famous with nothing to do. Lawrence, for her part, was badly hurt in a studio fire in 1914, took two years to recover, and suffered a relapse one week into shooting her comeback entry. Five years later she tried again, but by 1921 the art and business of film had changed beyond her recognition. (She had never made a feature, nor even been in Hollywood.) Most of the people she had known were gone, and the new people were all busy with new things. A has-been at thirty-two, she played leads in a few quickies, did bits and extra work, and killed herself in 1938.

Some of Hollywood's women influenced the culture, whether as role models, fashion models, or opinion makers. Some others—like

Florence Lawrence, the conventional romantic-comic-melodramatic heroine, and Theda Bara, the foolish legend—did not. Some managed to span eras; others died with their day. Some were versatile; others were trapped by their image. Some were gifted actresses; others were personalities or technicians of genre, like the musical. Some controlled their careers, giving rather than taking orders; some managed to leave their marks without coming near to stardom. Some fit in beautifully in Hollywood, professed it, practiced it devoutly; others despised its hypocrisy.

But all had this in common: whatever latitude they enjoyed they had to wrest from the businessmen, not because they were women but because they were actors. Because they were dolls, painted, dressed, wound up, and aimed. Then how can we speak of them as influential? How could such women "make" movies, or anything else?

In this way. Because of their peculiar hazards, show biz and the movies attract all sorts of people but generally only allow the most exceptional people to push to the top, those with unique gifts, persistence, and the ability to take good advice and recognize opportunity. Such a group would naturally include those of fierce independence as well as those willing to adapt, and out of the chaotic epic of the applicants who come and go—the empty-headed starlets groomed to be the next version of the last version; actresses in search of a look; debs, moms, hick belles, maids, and other types settling into an obscure series . . . out of all this come a few extraordinary women who imitate no one, assert their own look, and reject the wrong properties either through intelligence, instinct, or good advice. These people invent themselves, without or despite studio PR, sometimes with the help of wise directors or because scriptwriters or producers see something special and plan around it. Not all actors are auteurs; but not all directors are, either. Who can say to what extent Theda Bara devised her vamp out of her imagination and to what extent she got the informing sensibility for it from her first director, Frank Powell, or her best director, Herbert Brenon, or her most frequent director, J. Gordon Edwards? In the Hollywood run by the money bosses, film is a bordello and actors are whores, from PR stills sessions to scripted talk-show jaunts, from making it for fame to doing it for money. It's interesting that while many of the key women stars broke the rules and made their own way, some others did what was necessary. This book, like the world, is only sometimes about free will.

# 1

# *The Silent Women*

MAE MURRAY
GERALDINE FARRAR
BETTY BRONSON
ZaSu PITTS
NAZIMOVA
COLLEEN MOORE
CLARA BOW
GLORIA SWANSON

*I think the auteur theory of* Cahiers du Cinéma *is crap . . . Some writers and some directors are jealous of the stars' glory and the auteur theory is just another attempt to wipe the star off the screen with words.*

—LOUISE BROOKS

*As a star you have to learn to hear what you want to hear, ignore what you have to ignore. You have to learn to take the cream and leave the milk.*

—CECIL B. DE MILLE,
to the young
Gloria Swanson

*You don't have to keep making movies to remain a star. Once you become a star, you are always a star.*

—MAE MURRAY

In the 1920s, American film enjoyed its golden age, exuberant, confident, daring, even cosmopolitan. Foreign, mainly German, directors brought with them the Freudian subtleties of expressionism; genres were refined and reinvigorated yearly; and technique, from acting through design to engineering, never stood still. Most importantly, the old one-reel village romances, thriller chases, and situation comedies had turned into a host of possible story ideas, an expansive (though admittedly very centralized) mythology on the American character, on the national style in heroism, ambition, courtship, adultery, goofing off, competing, and surviving.

There was much too much repetition and imitation, too great a willingness to say the same popular things forever. But the public seemed to like the repetition, seemed to favor certain slants on heroism or courtship. Every so often, it enjoyed a novelty—*The Homemaker* (1925), for instance, wherein a husband and wife change roles because she's more efficient at making money and he's more comfortable looking after the house and children. Or *Dancing Mothers* (1926): a wife beats her husband and daughter at their own game of selfish partying and then walks out on them. But generally Hollywood observed the received virtues in such matters. Men work; women clean and cook; society women fuss at maids and dazzle men.*

Ironically, many women held positions of some power in Hollywood at the time, as writers, editors, and directors. Of them, only Lois Weber and Dorothy Arzner are noted for a woman's viewpoint, and only Weber regularly dealt with social issues, attacking anti-semitism in *The Jew's Christmas* (1913), intolerance in *Hypocrites!* (1915), and capital punishment in *The People Vs. John Doe* (1916). But, whatever their slant, such writers as Anita Loos and Frances Marion counted among the most prominent of their profession, and Jeanie Macpherson, actress at Biograph, director at Universal (at the time a haven for gifted woman leaders), and writer for Cecil B. De Mille at Paramount, can be said to have learned more of how movies are made than most of her colleagues of either sex. Perhaps the most formidable of this group was June Mathis, nominally a writer at Metro but a studio plenipotentiary of great initiative in developing properties and personalities. (Valentino, a misconceived player till Mathis took him in hand, was only one of her discoveries.) Mathis suffered defeat on her involvement in the disastrous Italian location shooting for *Ben-Hur* (1926); yet, but for her early death from cancer, she might have recovered to become one of the best-known producers of the talkie era.

The late silent years were an age of do it yourself, youthful adventurers learning from experience. There were few traditions; convention was constantly being rerouted. It was a time when writers with ideas could push them through from treatment to editing, advising actors and directors, and an age when actors of intelligence could produce themselves. For actors with perspective about themselves and their audience, with a comprehension of what film did, it was vacation with pay. For stars, the pay seemed as limitless as the fame. However,

*Note that men, regardless of social class, basically tallied to one character while women of means and proletarian women were two different breeds. This holds true even today. Bruce Dern as aristocrat in *The Great Gatsby* is a genteel relative of Bruce Dern the hick brute of *They Shoot Horses, Don't They?* But entirely different value codes impel Meryl Streep the lawyer in *The Seduction of Joe Tynan* and Meryl Streep the coaltown daughter of *The Deer Hunter*.

for those who never caught on, the going could be bitter. Consider the case of Mae Murray, "the girl with the bee-stung lips."

Murray was a dancer. With her elegant waddle, her celebrated preening moue, and her long blond hair, she had a distinctive look. This plus her dancing made her a toast of Broadway in Ziegfield's *Follies* revues in 1908 and 1909. Murray was sharp. She took over Irene Castle's part in the Irving Berlin revue *Watch Your Step* on a few hours' notice, and she wasn't even a member of the company. But already she was showing a tendency to make odd mistakes in her personal life, eloping with a millionaire's son, living in poverty with him, and leaving him. In 1915, Murray made it to Hollywood, in care of Paramount. What does one do with a dancer who can't act? She played gamines, ladies, a tomboy, a nurse; she was *The Dream Girl* (1916), *The Plow Girl* (1916), *The Mormon Maid* (1917). No one taught her anything, Hollywood was Cabbageville after New York, and importunate men kept getting on her nerves. She undertook a second ill-advised marriage—apparently at gunpoint—and this one, too, was quickly dissolved.

But now Murray hit a lucky streak. She came to an artistic and personal understanding with Robert Z. Leonard, and in 1917 Carl Laemmle invited them to head their own unit at Universal, to choose the stories, cast them, and edit them without interference. This was just what someone like Murray needed. Developing her own projects, she could sidestep the acting challenges that she couldn't hope to meet and emphasize her dancing. Ten features, all directed by Leonard, made Murray a star and established her collaborator as the director to hire, especially for the showcasing of handsome women. Wealthy, popular, and now married, the Leonards formed their own production company, releasing through Metro. By 1925, the marriage was finished, but Metro had merged into Metro-Goldwyn-Mayer and Murray was one of its top stars at $7,500 a week. What she needed now was a big one, and MGM offered it, *The Merry Widow*. A sensation in 1907, the Lehár operetta swept the nation not only with romance and waltzes but with an array of commercial spinoffs. There were *Merry Widow* candies, *Merry Widow* hats and gloves, *Merry Widow* hairdos and cosmetics. No stage work was better known, nothing had more universal appeal.* It was Murray's main chance—a rich Ruritanian widow who spars and flirts with a prince and ends up in Maxim's in Paris dancing the "Merry Widow Waltz." With John Gilbert opposite her, Murray was assured of suave support, and, as an experienced auteur of the Murray style in cinema, she must have been planning some of the big scenes in

---

*Filming a musical as a silent was no problem, for while one did have to do without singing, the prints were released with instrumental parts synchronized to the action, arranged for everything from symphony orchestra to solo piano. *The Merry Widow* even used the original Lehár tunes.

her mind. Then she learned that the director would be Erich von Stroheim.

Remembered today as a nasty Prussian who bullied actors and spent huge sums on intricate touches of atmosphere, von Stroheim was in fact a fair man and a brilliant director. The tales of his spending were mostly PR inventions, the bullying was often provoked (by people like Murray especially), and if von Stroheim had a fault, it was his refusal, in a company town, to play the company man. Some fault. But it's true that von Stroheim would blithely outrage his employers by shooting far more footage than could possibly have been used, and, when called out for it, would turn his wicked wit on them. He is not the kind of person who does well in a place like Hollywood, especially not in a time when studio moguls are consolidating their power by humbling the more independent directors and stars. (All three of *The Merry Widow*'s principal collaborators—von Stroheim, Murray, and Gilbert— were to be destroyed by L. B. Mayer, the head of MGM.)

Moreover, he was not the kind of director who films Ruritanian romances in the typical dirndls and dew. Promising the film's producer, Irving Thalberg, that he would find some place somewhere for a Maxim's set and, of course, the all-important waltz, von Stroheim and his co-scenarist Benjamin Glazer adapted Lehár beyond recognition, though the outline of the original remains. Filling it out are bizarre new characters and grotesquerie, but at least there was Gilbert as Prince Danilo and Murray in the part of her life as Sally O'Hara, a dancer in the *Manhattan Follies* who, on tour in the Balkans, marries an ancient baron on the rebound from a failed amour with Gilbert. The baron dies on his wedding night, Sally becomes his merry widow and the holder of the biggest fortune in the kingdom, and goes off to Paris, followed by Danilo under royal order: keep the national fortune in the family. And so on.

It still sounds like an operetta on the face of it, but von Stroheim filmed it with sadists, degenerates, and semi-nudity, and got the participants in a *louche* party sequence not to act one but to *have* one. The next morning, the cleaning staff encountered what Don Ryan (who played a villainous noble's vicious adjutant) described as "a scene of wreckage that beggars description: a piano swimming in cider and broken glass; a lieutenant of the guard stretched at length beneath it. . . . One of the little whimsies of the evening had been a descent upon the sofa pillows . . . with drawn swords. An electric fan had added to the confusion." Not part of the leavings was the "white orchestra," six young men and women blindfolded, painted white, and clad in as few leaves and feathers as possible.

Here was operetta as Lehár never scored it and Murray never knew it. One can imagine what it must have been like on the set. One doesn't have to: the Murray–von Stroheim feud was the talk of the town. Von Stroheim thought Gilbert too much the "ladies' hair-dresser," but after a few rough weeks the two had a drink and made their peace. Murray and her director, however, never did come together on which film they were making, her star vehicle or his study in middle-European decadence. She complained about him to everyone she met, sent warning telegrams to the money bosses in MGM's New York office, claimed to have had to shoot her own close-ups at night in secret (impossible), and finally exploded—predictably, over the handling of the big waltz number. Murray's style was show-biz glitz: extras in ball scene discovered dancing, hubbub off camera, all turn to see and, awed, make path for !MAE MURRAY! in spectacular tight black *diamanté* gown, cut to mid-calf, topped by a superb feathered headdress and set off by the Murray pout that had captivated New York millionaires. And she goes into her dance. Zow!

Von Stroheim's approach was to play it as he played everything, for real: the widow pushes through the dancers to Danilo and they dance together, expressing their love so intently that the others pull back and watch. Von Stroheim filmed the scene his way, but Murray was so insistent that Mrs. von Stroheim, a persuasive adviser, suggested they try it Murray's way as well. The director assented, turned his back, and said, "Tell me when the damn thing is done."

"Why, you dirty Hun!" Murray screamed, according to some accounts attacking him bodily. The extras hissed her and she fled the scene in tears while von Stroheim went right to MGM executive Harry Rapf and quit. Monta Bell replaced him. But the extras demanded their original chief back and served as an intermediary force between von Stroheim and the studio. As the *Los Angeles Record* explained it, "MAE-VON SIGN PEACE." Minor incidents continued to bedevil production, but von Stroheim finished *The Merry Widow* in fourteen reels (about two and a half hours, virtually a short subject in von Stroheim's table of running times), MGM cut it to twelve reels, releasing it to critical huzzahs and smash popularity. Murray was almost the only one who didn't like it. Franz Lehár, who might have borne legitimate grievance, conducted the orchestra at the Vienna premiere.

Murray should have liked it. It's a great picture, the Gilbert-Murray waltz in particular remaining a touchstone of silent-era lyricism, the camera sweeping around the pair in a tender thrill. Not even Robert Z. Leonard set Murray off as well as von Stroheim. But then Murray was out of touch with film: all she knew was stardom. She wanted perquisites, not thematic honesty. She liked costume, not a character. She was a vain beauty with good movement and bad judgment. And now she goes to hell.

Though she was thirty-six, a perilous age for a glamour queen, she flouted her MGM contract to sign with UFA in Germany, and though she did return to Hollywood she became even more difficult to work with. She married "Prince" David Mdivani, who went through her multimillion-dollar fortune and then dumped her. She tossed a proposed script on L. B. Mayer's desk, walked out on MGM again, and ignored his admonitory cables. So Mayer drew a line through Mae Murray's name. And in this Hollywood, when Mayer canceled you, everybody canceled you.

Murray returned from Europe with her fatherless infant son; scarcely anyone wanted to touch her. She made a terrible comeback in *Peacock Alley* (1930), a talkie pathetically named after her first Metro hit (1922), and began to fade from view. But life had become a movie to Mae Murray, and she behaved like the heroine of a weepie, losing her son to foster parents; losing another comeback part to Mayer's Olympian blackball; instigating and being served with lawsuits; making headlines but no movies as she slapped faces, wearied old friends, and quarreled with prospective partners in old dance revivals; storming bookstores in 1959 to cross out mention of her given name, Marie Adrienne Koenig, in the Jane Ardmore book about her, *The Self-Enchanted;* crumpling unflattering photos of herself in New York's Museum of Modern Art stills collection when she thought no one was looking; and, for the climax, turning up dazed and homeless in St. Louis, whence the Salvation Army sent her back to Hollywood to die in the Motion Picture Country Home. Stardom didn't wreck her. She wrecked herself with stardom.

As the rest of this chapter will show, most stars are not so egotistically self-destructive as Murray. But she was more rule than exception in her solipsism that treated stardom—her own stardom—as a Kantian "thing-in-itself" rather than an existential possibility. Murray saw film stardom as an absolute; we shall see how variable it really is.

Perhaps a good antidote to Murray's sad tale is that of Geraldine Farrar, the most unlikely of movie stars. Farrar, of course, was an opera singer, one of the greatest in an era rich in greatness but poor in stagecraft. Opera stage directors were traffic cops, and music rather than theatricality ruled opera houses, so whether in sensational melodrama (such as *Zazà*), fairy tale *(Königskinder),* the exotic *(Madama Butterfly),* or Victorian sentimentalism *(Faust),* Farrar had to create her characters unaided. That she did so with such abandon is surprising, for she was *very* opera singer: ultracultivated, grand rather than gala, and rather too well spoken, almost a burlesque of a diva. She might have become famous for her acting alone, but no one in opera gets by on acting. It was her intense musicality, her method of making the characters live within the music, that made her one of the most famous women of her time, like Caruso and Callas a name familiar to millions who never hear an opera.

Well, that's nice to know; but what's she doing in film? What, especially, is one of the most respectable women in America doing in a medium that, when she entered it, had only just begun to gain a mid-dle-class audience and prestige as art?* It seems that Farrar liked the movies and producer Jesse Lasky liked Farrar's Butterfly. With her European summer canceled by World War I and his realization of what her name would do for his films, a deal was set. This meant she would work with Cecil B. De Mille, Lasky's director general, which is interesting for this book in that De Mille was instrumental in establishing character role models for women in these early years. His first films were mainly adaptations of stage melodramas, emphasizing westerns with male protagonists, but for Farrar he tackled *Carmen* (1915), one of her best stage parts. If an opera star can film a decent Carmen, you know she's good, and Farrar really made it work, dirty hair, dagger, big white Massachusetts teeth, and all. Her Met Carmens were not this passionate, but then the Met never gave her Wallace Reid for her Don José, as De Mille did.

Farrar could probably have gone on filming her opera repertory, but she didn't, though she plays a singer in *Temptation* (1916) and though *Maria Rosa* (1916), again with Reid, is a lot like *Carmen*. Maybe her film roles were a little on the operatic side, a bit rich and rhetorical; maybe that was Farrar's secret. There can be no doubt that Farrar was a great film star in the sense of giving to the industry as much as she got from it. What she brought, mainly, was dedication, professionalism, and reputation; what she got, it appears, was fun. In *Joan the Woman* (1917), yet again with Reid in De Mille's only spectacular that can truly be called beautiful, Farrar suffered the martyrdom of Joan of Arc, incidentally bedding down with mice in a prison scene and playing the stake without a double. The pile of faggots is one of the biggest ever gathered, and it must have been a grisly stunt to pull off. Yet Farrar regarded her fourteen films as a holiday from the rigors of opera.

Another impressive thing about Farrar is that she knew when to quit. She was running out of voice by 1920, and would soon leave the stage forever, so an extended film career would have been handy. But after viewing her first film for Pathé, *The Riddle: Woman* (1920), she canceled the rest of her contract and that was that. Nor would she consider remaking *Carmen* when sound came in. "Retiring in time," quoth Rossini, "requires genius, too."

Some stars weren't given the chance to retire in time, like poor Betty Bronson, who held the limelight for exactly two years. Here is a case of someone's being absolutely right for one kind of picture, only to be thrown away when that kind is, so to speak, fresh out. Bronson, a petite charmer, did extra work till she lucked into the title role in *Peter Pan* when Paramount filmed the Barrie play in 1924. In selling the film

*The event that expanded film's reputation was D. W. Griffith's *The Birth of a Nation*, which astonished and stimulated members of the leadership classes at top-price legitimate theatre bookings as well as the proletariat, already habituated to movies.

rights Barrie stipulated that Peter must be played by a woman, as he invariably was on stage—and by a newcomer, to keep the magic stirring. He also retained casting approval. Beautifully directed by Herbert Brenon, *Peter Pan* made Bronson a star, but what else do you do with someone so special? Bronson played a little Miss Fix-it in *Are Parents People?* (1925), a western heroine in *The Golden Princess* (1925), and stood still and saintly for a bit as Mary in *Ben-Hur* (1926), but not till she appeared as the heroine of Brenon's *A Kiss for Cinderella* (1926), also from Barrie, did Bronson get a follow-up to her *Peter Pan,* and in a superb film. It seems odd that a director who could bring off the virile *Beau Geste* and the jazz-age morality tales *Dancing Mothers* and *The Great Gatsby,* all in 1926, could that same year place so deftly the chaste whimsey of Barrie, but it appears he was most at home in *Peter Pan* and *A Kiss for Cinderella.* Under his tutelage Bronson became the girl of the moment.

But after the Barrie pair, Bronson fell into a foolish miscellany. She was a flapper in *Ritzy* (1927), got lost in another western and a dullish urban melodrama, *Brass Knuckles* (1927), and endured Al Jolson's second film, *The Singing Fool* (1928). This last was a huge hit, bigger even than Jolson's first, *The Jazz Singer* (1927), but with Jolson and three-year-old Davey Lee pushing a ferocious upstaging contest to a stalemate, Bronson should have stayed home. That's how careers end. Bronson made a few more talkies, returned in the late 1930s for a Gene Autry vehicle, and made an appearance in *Evel Knievel* (1971). But the fame as such died in 1927. Director William Wellman assesses it well. Bronson, he says, "played kid things beautifully." But "when she tried to be sexy she looked like a little girl that wanted to go to the bathroom." One might ask why she *had* to try to be sexy. Or why she couldn't find enough parts she was right for to sustain her for more than three years of celebrity.

What is this problem with staying power? This didn't happen in the theatre then. Once an actor achieved some recognition, he or she could count on working indefinitely. At least William Fox fully exploited Theda Bara; Paramount didn't even bother to use Bronson up before discarding her. Is this because most movie stars, unlike those of the stage, were typed so narrowly that the versatile performers kept having to re-establish themselves with a shallow audience while the unique performers made themselves too familiar to a restless audience? Did, then, the greatest stars split the difference between versatility and uniqueness, hitting a mean that expanded their individuality with just enough range to avoid repetition?

Typing was the favored procedure of the studio years, from the 1920s through the 1950s. With the experimental egalitarianism of the one-reeler stock company shattered by star salaries and star fame, and with the PR dynamic encouraging stars to behave in life as they did on the screen, versatility died out and character was fixed. Not that stars always played the same character; but they became so well known as "themselves" that every character they played simply added more data to the public's reception of that particular star's image. Think of it this way: in the early, starless one-reelers, an unsophisticated public saw the stories as stories, moral instruction, entertainment. But after Florence Lawrence was identified, the star became an inveterate element in production, and the public would now see not just a story but a story in the company of Florence Lawrence—a story, even, about her. Other stars added to this with competitive personalities—silly, heroic, wily, whatever. The stories got longer, the reports on the stars' identities more detailed. Fiction and PR became one. By the time of Theda Bara, each film amounted to two stories at once: one, the narration itself; and, two, how Bara the vamp fit into it. And in something like *Kathleen Mavourneen,* there were three stories: one, that of the film; two, that of the vamp; and, three, that of the vamp playing a sweet Irish teenager for a change. Film had lost its innocence. It was not stories anymore but the collected adventures of the actors in the stories.

Typing limited the ambitious; but secondary players—so-called characters—could derive lifetime employment from it. Think of Margaret Hamilton, a popular rural busybody, a no-nonsense maid, and a witch (in *The Wizard of Oz*). Hamilton knew from the start that her looks would limit her and made the best of it, finally asserting herself with great success on stage in the national company of the Stephen Sondheim musical *A Little Night Music,* playing a sumptuous courtesan at the end of her days. This is a lovable triumph, after decades of Characters in theatre and film.

But in a comparable instance, an actress of great power was thrust into comic bits and never allowed to escape: ZaSu Pitts. Born in 1900 in Kansas and raised in California, she entered the movies when Hollywood was just easing out of its everybody-does-everything period, roughly between Florence Lawrence and Theda Bara. Pitts had suffered a not very social childhood, as her nervous habits and odd twang made her a natural butt. Even her given name was strange, an amalgamation of her mother's two sisters' names, Eli*za* and *Su*san. Nor was she a beauty. Through persistence, having no qualification other than a wild wish to do so, she crashed the movies, taking small parts as screwy maids and sidekicks and an occasional lead as a wallflower looking for love. *Better Times* (1919) is typical: an unpopular schoolgirl who invents a mail-order romance with a famous athlete is about to be exposed when a famous athlete turns up and falls for her. This is a nice credit historically, as *Better Times'* director, King Vidor, holds an outstanding reputation for his later films *The Big Parade, The Crowd, Hallelujah,* and *Our Daily Bread,* and Pitts herself was slipping into history. By 1923 she was well known enough to play herself as one of two dozen celebrity bits in *Mary of the Movies*. But Pitts's potential as an actress was not realized till Erich von Stroheim cast her as Trina, the woman obsessed with money, in *Greed* (1924).

Talk about historical credits! *Greed* may be the only film regularly hailed as a masterpiece though only a few dozen people have ever seen it. Was it too brutal to be released as filmed, or just too long?* At least it was faithful to its source, Frank Norris' novel *McTeague,* unlike von Stroheim's *The Merry Widow,* which just succeeded *Greed* in the director's troubled two years at MGM. No, it wasn't faithful. It was fanatic. Von Stroheim filmed the book page by page where Norris set it, in San Francisco and Death Valley, making the actors live in the rooming house he used for most of the action.

Working for such a man on a project replete with the incongruous improvised villainies of life—in short, hunting realism for a realist— would challenge the most resourceful actress, and Pitts is astonishing. Her role is not an endearing one; that's the price of realism. The price of working for MGM meant that much of Norris' psychological wholeness was pruned away for the two-hour release print, but enough remains to amaze, especially of Pitts's heroine. She plays the holder of a winning lottery ticket. Married to a dentist, she refuses to share her fortune with him, preferring to live in squalor to spending as much as a nickel. He degenerates along with her, beats her to death, and runs off with her money. In the last scene, Pitts's former suitor and the dentist's former friend (Jean Hersholt) catches up with the dentist (Gibson Gowland) in the desert. The dentist kills his old rival, but as he dies the latter handcuffs himself to the killer and the camera slowly backs away from him, a long figure in 150-degree heat, a hundred miles from life, his mule dead and his water gone.

Von Stroheim called Pitts "the greatest of all tragediennes" and one wonders how many of her colleagues, of any experience, could have done what she does with the part. Her wishful, disinherited quality had made every director see her as "the girl who isn't asked out," as a cartoon of a woman, worthless without a man. But this quality is only the starting point of Pitts's Trina, and under von Stroheim's direction we see how worthless marriage is to her anyway. She has her business—carving and painting wooden figurines—and her hobby—hoarding gold. This is all she needs, though both destroy her—her paint has poisoned her and her gold has driven her mad. Pitts as a maid flapping her hands in a comical dither was what Hollywood wanted, not an actress in an honest study of how greed looks and feels. The film was admired, but moviegoers had been conditioned by society vamps, lectures on upward mobility and self-confidence, and

---

*Nine hours. Von Stroheim hoped to see it shown in two parts, but it was shredded into a two-hour feature; this short *Greed* is the one that has generally been seen. Of the original full-length *Greed,* only the PR stills and a script survive.

the eternal war of evil on good, which good wins. Anyway, what was the public to think of a film in which ZaSu Pitts was, seriously, the heroine?

Von Stroheim was to use her again for the woman leads in *The Wedding March* (1928) and *Walking Down Broadway,** but moviegoers knew her only in her cartoon version. When she played Lew Ayres' mother in the moralistically anti-war *All Quiet on the Western Front* (1930), preview audiences giggled at the very sight of her and readied themselves for comic relief. But the mother's two scenes frame the sequence in which the hero goes home on leave and outrages students at his old school with his horror of war. The last thing needed at this point was laughter. Pitts's scenes were reshot with Beryl Mercer† and Pitts was condemned to comedy for the rest of her career, which totaled forty-six years and 170 features. She made the most of it. Never anything like a star, she still became one of the most recognizable women in movies, her own trademark. She managed to play a variety of parts, from pathetic to hysterical, and she is, no question, very funny. Still, seeing Pitts in *Greed* or *The Wedding March* makes one realize what potential was wasted.

Were there *any* opportunities for real actresses in these years, for versatility, for the performer who can create a different persona each time out and to hell with the PR image? We get an interesting answer to the question in that one star of this era not only proved herself as a stage actress of great range but has been called the greatest actress of the transitional period between the nineteenth-century actor-manager and the post-Stanislafskyan naturalist. Before she came along, the theatre was run by the stars, dudes and grand dames whose constipated flamboyance shattered any possibility of artistic wholeness. After her, the way was cleared for acting that sought a union with character, with the person one was portraying rather than with the feat of portrayal itself.

Literally from its first developed reels, film had been drafting stage talent and getting overblown or static performances that cinema just could not use. A ham on stage had his Moments, but on film he was hours of mute tirade. So this particular new-style star, when she left the stage for film, was wonderful: she had naturalized the techniques. She was many things Hollywood could like—haughty, self-centered, ambitious. But she was other things as well—bold, maliciously witty, and dedicated more to art than to success. Her habit of calling herself by one name seemed fit for legend, and she became one: Nazimova.

---

*The latter film was taken away from von Stroheim, largely reshot, and released as *Hello, Sister* (1933).

† Like many films of 1930, *All Quiet* came out in a silent as well as a talkie version, as many smaller theatres had not converted to sound. The silent print, as a rule, "didn't matter"—so Pitts was left in in that one.

First name Alla, addressed as "Madame." Like most thespians of her vintage she launched her movie career by filming a stage role, in *War Brides* (1916), as a pregnant woman who attempts to organize all women against producing the next generation of battle meat in a world where war is a pastime. At that, Nazimova only agreed to do the film because Herbert Brenon proposed to direct it; she had been impressed with his *A Daughter of the Gods* (1916), a spectacular vehicle for swimmer Annette Kellerman. Nazimova got $1,000 a day for *War Brides* (for thirty days), not to mention terrific reviews, so after two more years of stage work she took her high ideals to Hollywood, where Metro paid her $13,000 a week to do a series of soap operas whose only distinction is an unusual number of dual roles for the star.

Is this suitable employment for the stalwart of Ibsen and Chekhof, prize pupil of Stanislafsky himself? *Revelation* (1918) made Nazimova an amoral artist's model who, converted to Christ, becomes a nurse and saves her lover on the battlefield. In *Eye for an Eye* (1918) she is an Arab in love with a French captain, in *Out of the Fog* (1919) an unwed mother, in *Madam Peacock* (1920) an egotistical actress who competes for men's attentions with her own daughter, abandoned years before. And she topped it all with a modern-dress *Camille* (1921), the world's champion weepie. Valentino was her Armand, fresh into his stardom but an inexperienced actor overwhelmed by Nazimova in full cry.

Nazimova knew she was wasting her gifts, but she enjoyed the star trip. On a two-lane dirt road called Sunset Boulevard she built a house so huge it later became a hotel with the addition of bungalows, dug a pool roughly in the shape of the Black Sea, christened the place the Garden of Alla, and opened it with a party that lasted two days. She experimented with drugs of pleasure, held séances, wore wild getups to soirées, and never married her actor housemate Charles Bryant, though he was more or less advertised as her husband. All of this pleased her public, who saw a connection between her roles and those of the vamps. She was a vulnerable Theda Bara, a classy Betty Blythe, a woman whose vocation is love, a woman who cares.

So there was opportunity open to a versatile actress: she could upgrade the texture of pop genres and indulge in sloth and hedonism. At length, Nazimova felt guilty and, to purge herself as an artist, personally financed two adaptations from the stage, Ibsen's *A Doll's House* (1922) and Oscar Wilde's *Salome* (1923). The Ibsen came off well, but *Salome* was a disaster, a berserk vanity production with a rumored all-gay cast and designs in the Aubrey Beardsley manner by Natacha Rambova, Valentino's wife and one of Nazimova's partners in séance, among other pleasures. Nazimova played Salome herself, an ingenue at forty-four in Art Nouveau wigs; she also wrote the scenario and directed the camera, though Bryant was given credit. Nazimova's public, bored by *A Doll's House*, booed *Salome* off the screen, and she lost everything—her Garden, her fake husband, and her movie career.

Can a great actress survive in film? Nazimova couldn't. The movies tapped a vein of intemperance in her damaging to an artist. In conventional cosmetics, she could wow an easy audience; in all-out drag, she annoyed them. For *Salome* they wanted Theda Bara, for her version was the usual Biblical spectacle. Nazimova's was perverse. After a brief return to the sort of film she had made in her heyday—*Madonna of the Streets* (1924), *The Redeeming Sin* (1925), and *My Son* (1925)—Nazimova went back to Broadway. But a name like hers is too pungent to waste, and Hollywood called her in occasionally in later years, most notably in *The Bridge of San Luis Rey* (1944) but most popularly as Tyrone Power's mother in *Blood and Sand* (1941), a remake of Valentino's bullfighter tragedy. Here was a Nazimova everybody could believe in, a doom-laden woman in black, every line a prophecy, every object an omen. If the role had a caption, it would read, "All life is the history of death." Nazimova doesn't make much of it; she seems to be doing penance.

For what? For getting typed so easily in banal sin-repentance-transfiguration parables? For not mustering her star power to do something for the screen until it was too late and wrong? But why criticize Nazimova for what she didn't do? By what law did she owe us a successful *Doll's House*? Anyway, Ibsen's play had been filmed a few years before Nazimova did it, and a third version came out a year after, so there was no service to be done for the work other than preserving the portrayal of one of its most persuasive advocates. In the end, Nazimova fell victim to a hazard peculiar to Hollywood and its public: she played one kind of thing very well until everyone was tired of it and no longer wanted to see her. In anything.

This explains why staying power is so elusive. To build a star, the businessmen must make it easy for the public to apprehend the star image, which necessitates a sameness in the roles, a sameness in production values (especially in the fashion designer), a sameness in the male co-stars (including a PR romance with one or two of them, if possible), and a correlation between the PR and the roles. Joan Crawford is a prole who fights to the top, so she plays upwardly aimed secretaries and waitresses. Katharine Hepburn is northeastern, collegiate, and Broadway, so she plays wealthy, educated, sporty women, fluent in French and sailing terminology. Even the exceptions accord with the image: when Hepburn plays a wild hillbilly, Hollywood says, "See how democratic. Bryn Mawr opens its heart to the hills."

Every silent woman I have cited, except ZaSu Pitts, was knocked down in her prime, dismissed—and Pitts was spared because she was not a star and never got exposure enough to outstay her welcome.

Florence Lawrence was forced out of film by her accident, Betty Bronson because her vehicles were not an established genre in the first place, and Mae Murray managed to get herself banned for bad attitude. But even able-bodied and agreeable players working genres of practiced effectiveness find themselves obsolete too soon. Probably the biggest reason for this is that movies follow trends in contemporary life, constantly revising the mythology of character to suit new modes of behavior. Thus, the vamp as the woman who doesn't care gives way to the flapper in the 1920s, the girl who can take care of herself.

The trend to the flapper was an imitation of life, for the post–World War I era was fascinated with youth and independent women. This was the jazz age: faking out Prohibition, flouting old-time morality, getting ahead, and taking dares. Sin, in moderation, was cute. Below the surface, the 1920s saw significant changes in American society—the collapse of the agrarian economy and concomitant expansion of the urban industrial poulation centers, the rise of organized crime, the creation of a national media network in radio that would, through recordings in the 1930s and television in the 1950s, dissolve regional cultures in a great American all-culture, and the death of rural Democratic progressivism in a decade of Republican landslides broken only by Herbert Hoover's failure to conquer the Depression. But what one mainly saw, read, or heard about was flaming sheiks and shebas doing a charleston around a vat of gin.

The movies contributed to the impression. Theda Bara's vamp laid the traces for the sexually self-willed woman who didn't have to be asked to dance. Even more crucial to the development of the New Woman were the heroines of the serials—Mary Fuller of *What Happened to Mary?* (1912), *Who Will Marry Mary?* (1912), and *Dolly of the Dailies* (1913); Kathlyn Williams of *The Adventures of Kathlyn* (1913); Helen Holmes of the extraordinarily lengthy *The Hazards of Helen* (1914–16); and especially Pearl White of, among others, *The Perils of Pauline* (1914), *The Exploits of Elaine* (1915), and *Plunder* (1923). Note that even before Theda Bara and the discovery of persona-creating PR, the serial stars often used their own names in their films, being as much as playing their roles. What they played were women who needed men only for diversion—the villains and acts of God they could handle themselves. They did almost all their own stunts, which makes viewing these serials a hair-raising experience, for they involve falls off cliffs, getting tied to lumber headed for the buzzsaw, and—the favorite—playing chicken on the tracks with a speeding train.

Not only were the serials popular. As each segment came out in one reel, they would turn up regularly with all sorts of features and thus reach a wide audience. Those who only attended westerns, or comedies, or soap operas only saw, respectively, William S. Hart, or Charlie Chaplin, or Alice Joyce. But everyone saw Pearl White. And seeing her vault over every pitfall to trap the heavy and, often very incidentally, collect a man somewhere along the way was seeing the New Woman to the life.

Strangely, the heroine serials died in the 1920s without passing this new characterological information on to the features. Instead, the athletic heroine settled into the flapper, an aggressive young woman domesticated into equal parts of fortune hunter, flirt, and homemaker-in-waiting. Flappers were seldom kidnapped and never thrown in a river; the worst they did was to live on the edge of their reputations and the best they did was marry men. In *Ella Cinders* (1926), smalltown girl Colleen Moore goes to such lengths to break into the movies that we think her success (or failure) story is what the film is about. But no. When she has succeeded and we're hoping to see her rise to the pinnacle, her strong-silent smalltown beau turns up and carries her off to the altar right in the middle of shooting. Even given the convention that women really want a husband rather than a career, this ending is a terrible letdown, for nothing in the action has led us to take this romance seriously; almost everything Moore has done has centered on getting into the movies.

The very determination to do so—the guts to go after what she wants—was typical of the Hollywood flapper, and Colleen Moore epitomized the trope. The ultimate authority on all things jazz, F. Scott Fitzgerald, himself named her The One: "I was the spark that lit up Flaming Youth," he wrote. "Colleen Moore was the torch." Yet, as with so many others, it's not clear why she went to Hollywood, why she thought acting appropriate. Some reasons are desperate: a father dies young or abandons his family, and the daughter seeks work. Some reasons are historical: the movies are looking for respectability, an audacious opera star is looking for kicks, and enter Geraldine Farrar. Some reasons are practical: in the pioneer days of the Patents Trust, a firm stuck for a leading woman applied to the model agencies. What more did they need than a good-looking woman who could move? Alice Joyce, Mabel Normand, and Anna Q. Nilsson all started this way.

But some—ZaSu Pitts, for instance—simply wanted to, and hung around, and pestered, and finally got hired and kept getting hired. No experience, no acting lessons, nothing more than a "call." That was Moore's reason. She had always wanted to act, and by luck had a big-time newspaper editor for an uncle, Walter Howey, the model for Ben Hecht and Charles MacArthur's diabolical Walter Burns in *The Front Page*. Howey had kept Chicago's censors off D. W. Griffith's back when *The Birth of a Nation* and *Intolerance* played there. Now he called in the favor. Moore went to Hollywood in 1917 with a Victorian grandma in tow and a new name—the old one was Kathleen Morrison. She knocked around for years in this part and that till she entered into type in *Flaming Youth* (1923), complete with drinking parties, midnight swims, petting, dancing, generation war, and romantic payoff. Unique because of her Dutch-boy bob, Moore was sensibly cute, a role model more likable than glamorous, and *Flaming Youth* had the right credentials. Its source was a novel by Warner Fabian, a specialist in "contemporary" fiction so trashy that no one was surprised to learn that the byline was a pseudonym; it hid a respectable author, Samuel Hopkins Adams.

Moore inherited the credentials. She was the twenties flapper: much temptation, no surrender. *The New York Times*—as usual rating the film by asking, "Is it good for you?"—noted: "The moral of this picture is to show the emptiness of the pace-killing life." Wrong. The moral of this picture is "Do everything once except have sex and you'll end up in the sheltering arms of Milton Sills." Moore is so true to her trust that she throws herself into the ocean on a yacht trip rather than submit to advances. Pearl White would have stroked for shore; Moore has to be rescued. That was the flapper.

Moore defined her in film after film. The titles almost amount to an ethic: *Flirting with Love* (1924), *We Moderns* (1925), *Naughty But Nice* (1927), *Her Wild Oat* (1927), *Happiness Ahead* (1928), *Synthetic Sin* (1928). Somewhere in the middle of it all she sharpened her talent and became quite the actress, comedienne, and dancer, going into straight drama in *So Big* (1924), pulling off adaptations of hit musicals in *Sally* (1925), *Irene* (1926), and *Oh, Kay!* (1928), and playing a *very* romantic heroine opposite Gary Cooper in a wartime soap opera, *Lilac Time* (1928). But she is most special in comedy, because rather than play it she lets it happen to her, and no one was more fetching when looking quizzical. The big set piece in *Ella Cinders* finds Moore running the gate of Gem Pictures. Chased by a guard, she ruins takes, wrecks setups, enrages a lion, is hidden by a sympathetic Harry Langdon, and makes it into film. But she hasn't *done* anything, other than be there.

Maybe that's the point. Similarly, the title cards in *Orchids and Ermine* (1927), a gold-digger comedy, stress slang and put-down, but Moore resists the smartese of the day. We don't like her hip; we like her because she isn't. *Orchids'* best scene shows Moore applying for a job as a phone operator in a hotel. At the end of a long line of applicants, Moore's the dowdy one. Ranged before her on a stairway in mink and fox, they look like showgirls in *The Nome Follies*. But who gets the job? Moore, of course. Not that she extends herself to get it. She's just there, and that was the fun of her flapper. Sure, she has the right instincts and lots of charm. But, mainly, she's looking out through wide eyes saying, "Gosh, what a busy world!" Naturally she'd get ahead. She proved so likable that almost all her vehicles made huge fortunes for her studio, First National, though nobody then or now would call them anything like great.

If Moore was the classic flapper of the mid-1920s, Clara Bow took over in the late 1920s, when the flapper turned into the "Modern" and the Charleston got manic and began to head for the flat edge of the earth. Bow was a sexy complement to Moore, with an irresistible come-hither. Bow had it all: the cute, the hot, the sweet, the jive, and a mop of red hair that succeeded Moore's bob as the crowning glory of women in fashion.

Like Moore, Bow had no preparation for her profession. Moore was a midwesterner of the upper middle class who pulled a string and found work at the end of it. Bow was a working-class Brooklynite, her father a waiter, carpenter, and such, perpetually getting fired, and her mother a psychotic who stalked into her daughter's room one night with a kitchen knife. Bow, then, had good reason to get somewhere (else). Her father helped her enter a Fame and Fortune Beauty Contest in a fan magazine, the prize to be a little PR flurry and a letter of introduction to casting directors. Clara won and got a small part in a nothing picture which was entirely cut from the release print. But someone had seen her photo in the magazine and called her in for a nice part in a decent picture, *Down to the Sea in Ships* (1923). Comically disguised as a boy in sailor's togs, she caught the public eye and was signed to a contract.

It looked a good bet, for her elfin sensuality both hit the norm for the age and beat it, and she rose faster than Moore had done, making fourteen films in 1925, some of them in the lead. One of them, *The Plastic Age,* set her in college so she could make the most of the boozing, flirting, dancing, and repenting scenes that the public loved. Her contract holder, B. P. Schulberg, dubbed her "the hottest jazz baby in films." No one else could get so much out of a wink and a nod. No one else looked so good getting in and out of clothes. No one else expressed so well the restlessness of the culture; it seemed as if Bow couldn't keep still for a moment. And no one else took the whole thing so nonchalantly.

For Clara Bow was not a career woman or a dazzle dreamer but a kid who wanted a good time; the quality that most stands out in her life is not stupidity but naiveté. Colleen Moore's film *Naughty But Nice* is something of a tease, because Moore is never really naughty. Bow was, and she got into trouble. She ran through more lovers in a year than most actresses do in a decade, talked freely about their lovemaking abilities (and apparatus), and got talked about herself. Harry Richman, Victor Fleming, Gary Cooper, Nino Martini, Donald Keith, Gilbert Roland, John Gilbert, and even the doctor who performed her appendectomy (and whose wife slapped Bow with an alienation-of-affections suit) were only the best-known of her partners.

The image of the fast woman began to haunt her. An innocent, she couldn't understand why rumor should hurt her, or what she could do to protect herself. Colleen Moore knew enough about Hollywood to

demand roles that would enlarge her range, acting parts without a note
of jazz in them. She was also smart enough to nab one of the biggest
salaries in town, $12,500 a week at her height. Bow, at hers, was mak-
ing less than $3,000, and much of that was stolen by her secretary,
Daisy De Voe. When the case went to court, De Voe fought back by
exposing her employer's personal life, and the press didn't cut a word.
Worse yet, an article over De Voe's byline appeared in *The Court Reporter* and another trial ensued—this one of the *Reporter*'s publisher for
sending obscene material through the mails. Again the papers passed
all the details on to their readers. With her notoriety, Bow could get no
sympathy, and the jury acquitted Daisy De Voe of all but one of thirty-
five counts of larceny. The judge felt bound to point out, for the public
record, that the charges had been thoroughly proved. Still Bow did not
comprehend what was happening to her. "My best friend, Daisy was,"
she said. "Why did she have to do me like that?"

Naive. But you can't hope to be thought both naughty and nice.
Bow was naughty: sensual: bad. F. Scott Fitzgerald was so impressed
with her that he reversed himself on Moore and now called Bow "the
quintessence of what the term 'flapper' signifies . . . pretty, impudent,
superbly assured, as worldly wise, briefly clad, and 'hard-berled' as possible." However, the flapper wasn't supposed to get into trouble, was
expected to stay on this side of the vamp line. Bow crossed it, and
Fitzgerald was wrong. She wasn't a flapper: she was a person who
smashed the concept of the flapper by being too honest to suit it.

The wedge that broke the mold was driven in in 1926 by an English novelist famed for what was called "sex suspense," Elinor Glyn.
Popularly known as "Madame," Glyn became a sensual arbiter in Hollywood, writing ceaselessly on allure and who had it and how to achieve
it. Snobs danced around Madame like fairy dust round about Tinker-
bell, and because so much of the movies turned on romantic opera-
tions, Madame at some point or other had to tell exactly what allure
was. She defined it as "that quality possessed by some which draws all
others with its magnetic force . . . a quality of mind as well as a physical
attraction." In short, charisma. Madame had a word for it: It. And, of
course, everyone immediately decided that It was sex appeal. Nay, says
Madame Glyn. It's more complex than simple gender chemistry. To
clear up the confusion, *Cosmopolitan* published her story "It," which explained it all: "To have 'It,' the fortunate possessor must have that
strange magnetism which attracts both sexes. . . . He or she must be
entirely unself-conscious, and full of self-confidence, indifferent to the
effect he or she is producing. . . . There must be physical attraction,
but beauty is unnecessary." And everybody thought, That's right. Sex
appeal.

Who had It? Madame considered, and decreed: Antonio Moreno,
Rex the Wild Stallion, a doorman at the Ambassador Hotel . . . and

Clara Bow. Now that we had a word for it we could talk about It, and the talk was ambiguous, tricky. In the cities, where new ware sells like hotcakes, Bow was a prize, an archon, the It Girl. But in the countryside, where the old ways die slow, Bow was harmful, a contagion, the It Girl.

Hollywood celebrated the discovery of sex appeal—excuse me, charisma—with *It* (1927), produced by Elinor Glyn, with Bow as a department store clerk out to catch the store owner, Antonio Moreno. (See how nicely it all fits together? No horse or doorman, though.) Madame even put in a brief appearance in the film to explain what It was over again to the millions who blithely knew better than Glyn what It was. The film was a smash, making Bow just about the biggest thing at Paramount; a year before she wasn't even in its top ten.

She had a nice, almost sedate part in *Wings* (1927), a blockbuster World War I buddy film with Richard Arlen and Buddy Rogers, tremendous air-battle footage, magnascope wide-screen spectacle, sentimental love and death, and top-price tickets for the road-show release. In *Hula* (1927), Bow tried a relatively nude swimming scene; in *Red Hair* (1928), from another Glyn source *(The Vicissitudes of Evangeline)*, she copped a Technicolor sequence to show the true colors. It was sheer star treatment, but the trouble was brewing, because Bow personified not so much the times as the inevitability of change, a change that took us from "pure" heroine to sexy heroine, from posing vamps to girls who had sex and liked it, from the defenseless woman to the woman who can take care of herself. Colleen Moore's flapper was a change everyone could approve of, because she really wasn't that different. She was even less aggressive than the serial heroines, a leveling off. Bow's flapper was different.

By the time sound came in and everybody had to talk, Bow was near the finish. Her heavy Brooklyn accent was a letdown, her trademark bustle and twirling and her little shticks with compacts baffled the sedentary microphones ("We'll have to take that again, Clara"), and she was exhausted and unhappy. Then in 1931 came the De Voe trial, and the gleeful gossip pretty much finished her. She married actor Rex Bell, lived with him on his Nevada ranch for a bit, made two last talkies for Fox, and retired except for a short comeback in the late 1930s running the unsuccessful It Café, plus some radio spots in the 1940s. She lived on till 1965, separated from Bell at the end, but she delivered a telling epitaph for herself back in the 1920s on the Paramount lot when journalist Whitney Bolton asked her—was he the only one who thought to do so?—what It was.

Clara replied, "I ain't real sure."

Too many actors, including those shrewder than Bow, weren't sure, weren't prepared to stay on top of anything that happened to them. What if they became, absolutely, their own producers, running every aspect of their careers? *Then* could they last as long as they wanted to? Gloria Swanson can tell us, for she not only had a great deal of power but commanded an image with enough facets to let her play a reasonably wide range of parts. But watch what happens, and try to reckon why.

Swanson, too, had no training. Moreover, she had no itch to act. One day in 1913, fifteen-year-old Gloria visited the Essanay studio in Chicago with her aunt, just to see. Someone asked the girl to fill in with a bit, and she liked and stuck with it. Charlie Chaplin was working for Essanay then, and sooner or later their paths would cross; when they did, he tested her for a slapstick sequence (he was to kick her in the behind) and told her she wouldn't do. "Thank you," she told him, "I think it's vulgar, anyway." She had already found her métier, looking ravishing and having poise. Or maybe she would sing—she had quite a voice. But she stayed with film, working for Mack Sennett at Keystone (not, it seems, as a bathing beauty). When Sennett offered to make Swanson a "second Mabel Normand," she refused to be a second any-body, and he threw her out.

Given her opinion of low comedy, the whole Sennett contract sounds an odd proposition. But she says that mastering the countless little businesses taught her timing. Cecil B. De Mille at Paramount thought so, too. He saw in her comedy shorts an "epitome of tech-nique" and put her into *Don't Change Your Husband* (1919), the first of a cycle of marital studies remembered for their luxurious "society" set-tings, dawdling bathroom scenes, dream sequences (often flashbacks to pagan days to set up for an orgy), and moral messages.

De Mille has been accused of guessing what the public wanted be-fore it knew itself, of pandering, trifling, and wallowing only to excuse himself at the last minute by warning the weak, cheering the good, and fading out. But he was a nifty storyteller, intelligible and well paced, and his emphasis on upper-class backgrounds only reflected the pub-lic's desire to use the cinema for vicarious let's-pretend games. More-over, he helped the culture move from the Victorian courtship tales of the Griffith Biographs into the post-wedding dramas of a more grown-up people with grownups' problems: not staying pure, but staying sexy; not finding the right mate but holding him or her; not rocking on a farmhouse porch but drinking in the city. De Mille was halfway from Theda Bara to Clara Bow, just far enough, and his series on society adultery was already in gear with *Old Wives for New* (1918) and *We Can't Have Everything* (1918) when he tapped Gloria Swanson for *Don't Change Your Husband.*

Why Swanson? She was short (four feet eleven), a crude actress (for tension, her nostrils flare, suggesting a very cute little cow about to charge), and rather young for the parts De Mille had in mind for her, imperious women of the world who take and do. But it worked wonderfully—their collaborations entrance today. She called him Mr. De Mille and he called her Young Fellow; and she says he did it and he said she did it: "The public, not I, made Gloria Swanson a star." The fact that he had to say it suggests that some thought otherwise.

Whoever did it, the De Mille-Swanson marital films count as one of the most appropriate of Hollywood genres, of and about the taste of the time. We must be contemporary, the moguls would cry to their staffs. Each new thing must be the next thing. The next thing when Swanson entered the picture was conspicuous consumption. The bathrooms and boudoirs weren't there for titillation so much as to revel in all the things beauty may buy to remain beautiful. The men in such films wore dinner clothes with distinction, the women were poured into silk, velvet, and fur. The subtitles, by Jeanie Macpherson, emphasized hunger where previous writers tried to de-emphasize it. And Swanson, who became the best- or at any rate the most-dressed woman of the 1920s, held the center of it all: as a wife who divorces a styleless husband, marries a playboy, and returns to her first husband when the playboy plays out in *Don't Change Your Husband;* as a fiancée with two suitors in *For Better, For Worse* (1919); as a supercilious aristo shipwrecked on an island where the butler organizes the survival tactics, orders the lords around, and captivates Swanson in *Male and Female* (1919), from Barrie's *The Admirable Crichton;* as, for a change, a dull wife whose husband divorces her and then wins her back after she fixes herself up in *Why Change Your Wife?* (1920); as, for greater change, a smalltown girl in *Something to Think About* (1920); and as the wife who patiently waits while husband Wallace Reid plays the field and at last returns—not because he needs her particularly, but because the world is dull—in *The Affairs of Anatol* (1921), from Arthur Schnitzler's play.

Not all of De Mille's sexy society films had Swanson or bathroom episodes or pagan flashbacks, but the general impression they left was of this one woman, so lavish in her appetites that only stupendous bathrooms could host her ablutions and only wild places could serve her libido.

Why Swanson? Because she accommodated the style of her films so naturally that she adopted it in her life, actually becoming more or less a clotheshorse who spent fortunes and fell in and out of marriages. "I have decided," she said sometime before this, "that when I am a star I will be every inch and every moment the star. Everyone from the studio gateman to the highest executive will know it."

Paramount did not have to shroud its star in character-creating PR, as Fox had done Theda Bara, for Swanson's persona depended not on the occult or a sexual mystery, but on the daydreams of her generation of American women. Bara was a strange woman. Swanson was basic, a distillation of the modern wife, mother, and lover, just a lot richer than her sisters. Most of her roles were designed to give her fans a chance to test their own resources of chic, passion, and boldness. What is *Male and Female* but a "what if" dream?: what if you were a British noblewoman with pots of money and beaux falling all over your feet; and you're out on your yacht lording it over this really rather devastating but arrogant butler (the best kind), as pale as the moon and solid as Big Ben; and you're shipwrecked and *he* takes over and now you know what it feels like to be possessed to the utmost; but you're resisting, so the butler quotes Henley—"I was a King in Babylon and you were a Christian Slave"—and suddenly there you all are in ancient Babylon, you in these cunning leopard skins; and you're given a choice: renounce your religion and be the king's bride or be thrown into the lion's den; you take the lion, and there you are, so real-looking it can't have been faked, getting pawed by the king of beasts and finally the island party is rescued, and you and your butler must part: you to your money and beaux and he to his duties upstairs, downstairs.

De Mille pared away the Barrie original's whimsey for a torrid romance; the lion scene is one of the hottest, meanest bits in silent film. How many actresses of the day would have done it? Swanson was a trouper, easier to work with than many, and a strong believer in what she was doing. De Mille gave her the option of leaving it out, but she knew he craved to shoot it and she went through with it, even after one of the trainers warned De Mille that it would be too dangerous if she were menstruating. She wasn't, but the question makes the whole business even more harrowing, sexy in a diabolical way. Her back was protected from the lion's paw by canvas and a loaded rifle stood at the ready, yet it remains a dire stunt for a star who wasn't an "action" type. Swanson was so shaken after the ordeal that she asked to be excused for the rest of the day. (Her father, whom she hadn't seen in five years, had just shown up for the lion episode; one wonders what he was thinking.) De Mille sat Swanson on his knee, pulled out a tray of jewelry, and told her to take her pick. Her description of the event aptly recalled the whole Swanson sensibility: "I picked out a gold-mesh evening purse with an emerald clasp and immediately felt much better."

After the De Mille pictures, Swanson took her emeralds, pagan flashbacks, and such along with her, though a series of films in the early middle 1920s directed by Allan Dwan filled out her character with horseplay and grit. If De Mille established her persona, Dwan humanized it, especially in *Zaza* (1923), a backstage tale which in various versions has flattered such divas as Réjane (on stage), Farrar (in opera), and Pauline Frederick and Claudette Colbert (in films respectively before and after Swanson). The best of this lot is *Manhandled* (1924), for which she tried running a bargain counter in Macy's and getting crushed in the Times Square–Grand Central subway shuttle preparing for a shopgirl role.

Why Swanson? Because the more they gave her to do, the more she did with it. As star, she topped them all for glamour; as person, she enjoyed herself and retained her perspective. For star credit, she made *Madame Sans-Gêne* (1925) entirely in France. For star blitz, she forged Hollywood's first alliance with nobility by bringing home as her husband the Marquis de la Falaise de la Coudraye (first name Henri; nickname Hank) and reportedly wired ahead to the west coast, "Am arriving with the marquis tomorrow please arrange ovation."

For personal reasons she underwent an abortion in Paris, a risky move in those days for someone regarded as public property. But Swanson was passing her own rules for stardom. She didn't bother to have a feud with Pola Negri when Paramount imported her from Germany, thereby lining up two superstars of a similar stripe on the same lot. Swanson rose above it, prompting Paramount to PR a feud into being by applying the First Law of Communications: news is truth.* Nor was Swanson devoted to Hollywood as place. During her Dwan period she lived and worked in New York.

When you're that big, and you do that much, a few years of career can seem like an epoch to the public, and they may tire. They welcomed Swanson with immense applause at the Los Angeles premiere of *Madame Sans-Gêne,* but she hit the nail on the ace noting that it was a climactic demonstration, a point of culmination —at the age of twenty-six. "What's left?" she asked herself. "How can I top it?"

She nearly did top it when she left Paramount to become her own producer, carefully building the atmosphere of excitement and attraction from film to film. The first, *The Love of Sunya* (1927), was standard Swanson fare. The second was ambitious, *Sadie Thompson* (1928), from W. Somerset Maugham's short story which, on Broadway as *Rain* with Jeanne Eagels in 1922, gave a startlingly sympathetic view of a prostitute nearly destroyed by a hypocritical minister. *Rain* was on the index of forbidden material drawn up by Hollywood's official censor, Will H. Hays, but Swanson worked around Hays—more precisely, right through him—and pulled off a grand show, with Lionel Barrymore in the minister's part (changed to a reformer without clerical affiliation). The film made a mint and got Swanson a Best Actress nomination in the first year of the Academy Awards (she lost).

First film ordinary, second film daring. For the third, Swanson determined to press into history with a unique project. Erich von

---

*Swanson is lucky that Negri ignored the "feud," too, for in all other things she played the definitive Hollywood Star. No sooner had she landed in town than she set up an affair with a biggie, Charlie Chaplin, kept a panther on a leash, called everyone "darling," demanded that she be called Madame Negri or Countess Dombski, sabotaged shootings with tantrums and feigned headaches, laid Chaplin aside for Valentino (more to the point), gave a smashing performance at his funeral in New York shortly before suing his estate for $15,000 (a loan), and, like Swanson, married a title, Serge Mdivani, brother of Mae Murray's David Mdivani. She could act, too.

Stroheim had devised a tale he called *The Swamp,* about an Irish orphan's adventures among debauched German nobility, and Swanson
not only bought the story but hired him to direct. She had acquired a
business partner in Joseph Kennedy (father of the president), but Kennedy remained in the east while Swanson filmed in Hollywood, and she
was thus her own and von Stroheim's boss. A lot rode on the piece,
renamed *Queen Kelly,* for shooting began in late 1928, strictly silent,
when every Hollywood studio was turning out talkies. Clearly, *Queen
Kelly* would have to be very special to compete with the novelty of
sound.

At least in terms of Swanson's part in the whole Hollywood epic,
*Queen Kelly*'s plot unravels an intriguing retrospective of who Swanson
was: first a girl, comically losing her panties when she encounters her
romantic vis-à-vis (Walter Byron); suddenly a young woman, challenged by love problems in the person of Byron's evil fiancée Queen
Regina (Seena Owen); later a mature woman in Africa who survives a
nasty forced marriage (to Tully Marshall) to close at last in Byron's
arms. All the Swanson atmosphere was carefully gathered—the sets,
the clothes, the swells—but viewed through von Stroheim's prism it
turns, bends, and shudders at its reflection. Surely Swanson is pulling
off the ultimate topper: this is in effect her own graduation pageant,
testimonial, and passion play.

But something went wrong. Von Stroheim, as usual, was shooting
far more than a two-hour film could possibly use, endlessly retaking
key scenes and, Swanson thought, overplaying the debauchery. He was
brilliant. She had hired him for his brilliance. But the early rushes of
the African sequence seemed "rank and sordid and ugly." The European scenes were wild—the wicked queen at one point strolls through
the palace naked and carrying a white cat—but at least they were
sumptuous. Now von Stroheim was getting into "an apocalyptic vision
of hell on earth." When the director began coaching Tully Marshall in
the precise art of gurgling tobacco juice onto Swanson's hand while
fitting on the engagement ring, she said, "Excuse me," left the set,
phoned Kennedy in New York and told him to come west fast, then
went home. Kennedy was obsessed with saving *Queen Kelly* (he was not
a man to accept failure lightly, or any way), but in the end neither he
nor Swanson pulled it off, because by then silent pictures were a dead
issue. Swanson went on to make a fine sound debut in *The Trespasser*
(1929) and didn't need *Queen Kelly;* Kennedy didn't know what to do
with it. (They did release it, but with an absurd tacked-on ending, and
only in Europe.)

The debacle wrecked von Stroheim's hope of surviving as a director, and while it did not hurt Swanson, something else did, something
von Stroheim understood and constantly attacked in his films: profligacy. Spending, wanting, owning, wearing. Despite her ease in di-

alogue and voluptuous singing, Swanson hit a snag in sound, because it came in simultaneously with the Depression. Suddenly the public turned against the consumption it had loved about Swanson in the 1920s, resented the mansions and beach houses and private railroad cars, and resented those who had them. Hollywood never gave up its glitz of ownership, but it gave up bragging about it, and the superstars of Swanson's day, with their hauteur and feuds, passed on. Look at Pola Negri. She was so outrageously Star that she never even won a popularity to lose. American moviegoers didn't like her, once they got to know her, and she ended up more famous off screen than on.

Most readers expect a chapter on silent stars to end with almost everyone's failing to crash the sound barrier, but reading lines and singing hurt few actors. What hurt them was style—artistic style in the revolutionary naturalism that stories-in-dialogue forced upon stories-in-pictures and cultural style in the new outlook of a public suffering the Depression. Silent Hollywood was wrong for sound pictures and wrong for what the nation wanted of its mythopoetic archetypes; and when silent Hollywood died most of its stars died, too: of new age. The old rural heroines, the brazen serial acrobats, the vamp, the flapper, the bathing adulteress—all were replaced. Much of their innocence and simplicity had to go as well, for throughout the 1920s the public kept getting headline information on just how complex and sinful Hollywood was. Within a few months of each other in 1922: the jovially silly Roscoe "Fatty" Arbuckle was accused of raping a starlet to death; adorable elfs Mabel Normand and Mary Miles Minter were implicated in the still unsolved murder of William Desmond Taylor; and the quintessential collegiate Mr. Right, Wallace Reid, died of drug addiction. Just imagine, people told each other, what *wasn't* reported.

The studios tried to placate the national outrage by hiring Will H. Hays, the former national chairman of the Republican party and briefly Warren Harding's postmaster general, to set and enforce guidelines for sanitary moviemaking. And yes, the outrage died down for a time. But it's interesting that while the Hays office did occasionally pass on proposed subject matter or interfere on matters of script or dress, Hays's main job was policing the town, checking up on what movie personnel did on the personal rather than professional level. In other words the movies consisted of people, performers, the stars. Movies weren't writing, designing, camera thrust, technique. Movies were what the stars did, twenty-four hours a day. Movies were a congeries of human style.

It was style that Hays was after, not cinema itself. Typically, his first act in office was to blacklist Fatty Arbuckle. Fatty in films was a gentle lampoon, but Fatty in life—it appeared—was a big fat dirty appetite, and that's the particular Fatty that the public took for true. Movies were a question of appearances. Not till 1933, when bluenose groups banded together to threaten a nationwide boycott, did American film suffer an all-encompassing censorship. Not till then was the public sophisticated enough to separate performer from part. But by then the true objects of the bluenose crusade—the strange people under the familiar masks—were mostly dead or dispersed.

Style constantly changes; that's the problem in Hollywood. Theda Bara the temptress; Geraldine Farrar the diva; Nazimova the thespian; Gloria Swanson the consumer; Colleen Moore the flapper; Betty Bronson the *delicata;* Clara Bow the jazz baby, in that chronological order, all caught style and lost style. Can no woman star hold it indefinitely? (In the whole eighty years of film exhibition, only one woman has done it; we'll meet her in due course.) Are the variables of stardom so unstable? Before we go on to the sound era, let's consider the roots of American womanhood as portrayed in the movies with two stars in particular. One was, by any shape of judgment, the biggest star ever. The other was, to my mind, the greatest.

# 2

# *The First Star and the Greatest Star*

MARY PICKFORD
LILLIAN GISH

*I really was that little girl.*

—MARY PICKFORD

*Don't act it; feel it!*

—D. W. GRIFFITH

It is said that stage acting is dynamic, hurling character *out* at the public through technique, imagination, and wit; and that film acting is magnetic, drawing the public *into* character through . . . well, It. To put it another way, the stage actor has to work his way into a character, impersonating an imaginary being, while the film actor plays himself, or rather doesn't play at all, just is. This is a chapter about one magnetic star and one dynamic star, and, as the previous chapter was meant to outline the structure of silent stardom—its beginnings, its possibilities, and its ends—we can take these two stars in the context of the period. For if Little Mary Pickford was the movies' most popular personality and Lillian Gish the exemplar of concentration of character, it will be interesting to see what happens to them, especially as they both start at precisely the same place and time, with D. W. Griffith in the American Biograph Studio at 11 East Fourteenth Street in the heyday of the one-reeler.

Little Mary first. She was rare stuff, a beautiful blond cherub with guts and enthusiasm, and she started so early she can scarcely be said to have had a childhood. Her family lived in Toronto. Her father, John Smith, died in an accident, leaving his widow Charlotte with three small

children, Gladys, Lottie, and baby Jack. Iron-willed Charlotte put them
all on the stage. From the first, it was Gladys who got the parts. She
looked great, thought up bits of business, and could take care of herself, which, in those days of The Road, was essential. The theatre of
that time was nothing but hardship to the actors who weren't stars or
under contract to a reputable producer; not till 1919, when Actors Eq-
uity closed the nation's theatres in a strike for recognition and minimum rights, could performers even count on getting paid. "I loathed it
all and I was lonely," she says. But by luck she happened to get
through to David Belasco just when he was looking for a little girl for
*The Warrens of Virginia* in 1907. He signed her (for thirty dollars a
week), renamed her Mary Pickford, and all her life she kept with her
the prop china doll she used in the play, so the experience must have
sat well with her.

Certainly it was refreshing to play a Broadway hit with a first-rate
company after the dingy tours, the reckless provincial audiences, and
the outdated melodramas she had known. But one wonders what she
might have picked up from Belasco, a canny hack who became famous
for plunking tradition-minded ham actors into elaborately naturalistic
settings, creating a genre at once realistic and fantastic. The naturalistic
look of Belasco was a good springboard into film, but one thing Pickford never was was ham. Belasco has a few words to say here: "She was
a hard worker, the first at rehearsals and the last to go. . . . Her features did not become strained. She was all repose—easy and graceful at
all times."

Not that Pickford had any intention of making movies—after
Broadway with Belasco? But *The Warrens of Virginia* closed and money
ran out. With four mouths to fill, Pickford needed a job and applied
for work at the studios. Essanay and Kalem turned her down, but
Griffith took her on at Biograph, where she played kids, sweethearts,
mothers, prostitutes, Indians, Mexicans; where she grinned, pouted,
wept, defied, eloped, killed, pined, prayed; where she took direction
and admired and resisted her director; and became such a popular
draw—despite Biograph's almost ideological refusal to identify any of
its players by name*—that she began to bargain for higher pay.
Higher and higher yet. She bargained well and often, after she left
Biograph, after Biograph and the Patents men went under, after the
one-reeler was retired for the two-reeler, the five-reeler, the two-hour
feature, after the whole shebang closed up the eastern branch and
moved to Hollywood, till she was getting so much that no one could
afford to give her any more and she hired herself. They say Gloria

---

*For English releases of American films the players were named, but pseudonymously.
Still, once you know a name, you know a person, whether it's the real name or not, and
American moviegoers called Pickford "the girl with the curls" and, taking a cue from a
title card, "Little Mary."

Swanson spent the second Hollywood million. Pickford made the first.

It's interesting that she started in films with Griffith after an extensive stage apprenticeship: it meant that she outranked her Biograph colleagues by training, and that combined with a strong sense of self made her a little outlaw among Griffith's flock. He was an authoritarian, friendly but remote, a southern gentleman who treasured the egalitarian *communitas* of the rustic America that had all but vanished by 1909, when Pickford joined his company. His stories were the old stories, tales of decent people defending their code against the selfish, the greedy, the amoral. His men were tall, dark, strong. His women were fair and frail. From the beginning, Pickford had no chance of fitting into the scheme; for while she had the look, she lacked the humility.

It's typical of the whole Pickford-Griffith Biograph adventure that he originally hired her to play the title role, that of a saintly vagabond kid, in his adaptation of Browning's verse play *Pippa Passes*, but eventually made it with someone else. Pickford was no saint. Rather, she was a woman of tenacity and resilience, exactly the sort to rise to the top of this open-ended business and exactly the sort who takes orders reluctantly or not at all. No one would PR this kid into quack imagery as they did that poor torrid jello Theda Bara. Nor would she attempt to run a career on Nazimovian soap opera or It girl comedies. At one point she so angered the phlegmatic Griffith that he seems actually to have hauled off and pushed her down, yet she knew enough to delight him just before she hit him for the next raise. In New Jersey (at that time the location capital of American film) playing Billy Quirk's audacious girlfriend in *They Would Elope* (1909), Pickford had to take a spill in a canoe, spilled expertly, and then, shivering in a blanket as she and Griffith rode back to town, put on her dearest face and asked for a raise.

She got it. She almost always did, though eventually she left Griffith and his various successors because she knew she was worth more than they were paying her. "Mary, sweetheart, I don't have to diet," producer Adolph Zukor told her. "Every time I talk over a new contract with you and your mother I lose ten pounds." But she was a bonanza; her pictures alone sold a studio's entire output. Exhibitors couldn't reserve certain pictures—they had to take all or none. To get Pickford's, they took all.

By the time she teamed up with Zukor in 1913 for $500 a week, the days of the anonymous stock company were nearly over, and Pickford was the main reason why. In one sense it's sad, because playing such a variety of parts brought out the best thing in Pickford, her faceted imagination. But in a more important sense, it's appropriate, for her constant heckling for better contracts points to what should have been, and for a while was, the logical outgrowth of the movies' early industrial structure: a neighborhood of auteur performers, each running his own show. Pickford didn't need more money. She needed the right to exercise final authority over her art.

Authority? Over a series of dribbling goody-nice inanities? Little Mary optimist? Little Mary dauntless cutie? Little Mary splashing around in a Fort Lee brooklet wangling extra candy from Uncle Griffith? But all this, though it sums up today's memory of Pickford's films, is not at all what Little Mary was about. Because she bought up virtually all her films and carefully supervised their distribution thereafter, few people had access to them in later years, and much of this "memory" of Little Mary has been supplied by those who weren't there in the first place.

In fact, Little Mary, as delineated in some fifty full-length features from Zukor on into talkieville, was a fighter with an instinctive sense of justice who spit on bigots and helped the weak. True, many of her most famous parts suggest sugar-cream sentimentality—*Pollyanna, Rebecca of Sunnybrook Farm, Little Annie Rooney*, and, in drag, *Little Lord Fauntleroy*.* Also true, too many of her PR photos disclose a smirking, posing creature who might have crawled out of a box of Cracker Jack. But her films in toto reveal a much richer character, one that takes in extremes of violence and no end of dirty fun. In *Tess of the Storm Country* (1914), for instance, the film that saved Zukor's foundering business and affirmed Little Mary's place as the biggest draw in narrative-action features,† she is a wild kid living among fisherfolk oppressed by bourgeois villagers led by a church deacon. There is a love plot—Tess's romance with the deacon's son—but the movie concentrates on Tess's leading her people against the village and sheltering an unwed mother. In the snow, she steals milk for the baby, is caught and punished, then says, "I have been whipped. Now can I have the milk?" In the lavish stained-glass bourgeois church she forces her way to the font to baptize the child. Everyone naturally thinks she is its mother and turns against her, but she stands up to them. Next to her, everyone's a coward or a hustler. Little Mary says, Fight the bad guys. The good guys win.

This is antique advice, suitable for a pioneer era when the good guys still had fight in them. Today everyone is a hustler and we have to sneak our good-versus-evil parables into *Star Wars, Superman*, and other science fantasy where the moral code is supposedly a cartoon. But in the 1910s, the old advices were not yet in eclipse. If Little Mary is a goody-goody, it's only because those in power are so rotten—Sunday Christians like those in *Tess;* the urchins who torture a helpless dog and the barroom toughs in *Rags* (1915); the land speculators in *Heart o' the Hills* (1919); creeps who abuse children in *Sparrows* (1926). In her pre-1920s features especially she is eternally righting wrong through

*Pickford also played the little lord's mother. In a dress.
†Only Chaplin rivaled her, and at that in episodic comic features.

force, or at least telling off snobs and deserting wealthy suitors for slum kids.

It was not thought remarkable that a woman tackle so much herself, because Little Mary came forward at the climax of an age of remarkable women, of settlers, suffragettes, and actor-managers. In the event, she was more or less producing and directing as well as performing. "The director would often just direct the crowd," her favored cameraman, Charles Rosher, reported. "She knew everything there was to know about motion pictures." A lot of them shared the acts of creation in those days; the silent era is heavy with the names of people who left acting for directing, or who wrote as well, and so on. Later on, in the mid-1920s, Little Mary found herself on location in San Francisco with a handful of extras ready to go and no sign of director Marshall Neilan, who had a habit of wandering off from time to time. "Who's in town?" Little Mary asks; someone'll fill in. A search of the likely speakeasies turned up no one, however, so Little Mary directed the scene herself. Louise Brooks, who tells the story, concludes, "Today, everyone would fall apart and no one would do anything."

It's no wonder Little Mary left Griffith early on. Not only was she unsuitable for his world view that starred the fair, frail women; she also didn't need a master to learn from. Still, she must have missed the ingenious Griffith, always concerned with character and narration, when she worked with Edwin S. Porter on *Tess of the Storm Country*. Porter, so innovative that he instituted the close-up as a function of story in *Life of an American Fireman* and *The Great Train Robbery* early in the century, was obsessed with the mechanics of filming but utterly unaware of its dramatic possibilities; and Little Mary made a point of doing *Tess* all over in 1922 with John Robertson in charge. So Pickford, for all her power in the industry, is going to have to deal with a special problem—finding a director congenial with her special qualities who can make decent pictures.

She felt she found one in Maurice Tourneur, a Frenchman as refined in his personal behavior as in his aesthetics. However, is refined what Little Mary needs? For *The Poor Little Rich Girl* (1917), the tale of a ten-year-old neglected by her parents, little Mary and scenarist Frances Marion concocted an assortment of slapstick gags that horrified Tourneur. But they make the picture, for another of Little Mary's features is her unstoppable appetite for pranks. Vachel Lindsay, one of the first highbrows to appreciate the cinema critically, dubbed her the "queen of my people," but she's more the tomboy princess. With her dad wholly dedicated to business, her mom a social butterfly, and a platoon of humorless servants to mind her, Gwendoleyn's only outlet for amusement is to get into scrapes. Yet no matter how they punish her, she cheers up and does something else, whatever's handy. When a local brat named Susie-May is brought over to play, Gwendoleyn tries to be nice, but a brat is a brat and a ruckus ensues. For penance, Gwendoleyn is ordered to give the creep her best lace dress. No way! She locks herself in her room and throws her entire wardrobe out the window, including hats and the dress she's wearing. Then she is forced to wear boy's clothes. This depresses her for maybe three seconds. One look in the mirror and she's cavorting again, enjoying the costume, playacting. Later, locked in a bathroom, she trashes the room, breaking the sink off of the wall and dancing around in the water; she also takes on some street kids in a mud fight in the garden, and is in genuine despair when the gardener breaks it up. What's money to Little Mary, the poor little rich girl? She wants only to be a "free little poor girl."

That money was unquestionably much to Pickford does nothing to subvert the fun, for as her own producer she spent plenty to make her films look like something. *The Poor Little Rich Girl*'s narrative titles are illustrated as beautifully as a child's prize storybook, the famous Tourneur design of shadows and angles is painstakingly invested; and such little touches as having the words "I hate her!" come flying out through the keyhole of Gwendoleyn's locked door during the siege of Susie-May or even the extraordinary clarity of everyone's lip movements attest to Pickford's ability to make the most of her power. Moreover, it seems that she was usually right in her disputes about company planning, promotion, and artistic questions, no matter who held the opposing opinion. Not only did Tourneur discourage her monkeyshine improvisations on the *Poor Little Rich Girl* set, but Pickford's boss, Adolph Zukor, thought the film a flop when he screened it, and made his star promise to knuckle under to her next director, Cecil B. De Mille. She had to put it in writing, in a self-deprecating telegram that De Mille did not answer. It probably unnerved him: Little Mary bound was far more the tiger than Little Mary free. Anyway, *The Poor Little Rich Girl* was a smash hit, proving that Pickford and Marion had the right ideas in the first place, and after it the actress hooked up with a most sympathetic director in Marshall Neilan.

Despite an unstable personality that would eventually alienate Pickford as well as much of Hollywood, Neilan spent freely of his Irish charm and well understood the spontaneous nature of the Little Mary technique. She was not a great rehearser; she liked to put it on its feet and bring it to life. With Neilan she did some remarkable things, starting with *Rebecca of Sunnybrook Farm* (1917), which some consider the best of Little Mary's Cinderella comedies. They all have their moments. *Rebecca* has the heroine gamely stamping up her aunt's stairs with flypaper on her shoes (to avoid muddying the carpet), unaware that the glue has picked up a strand of her aunt's knitting and every step drags out another few stitches. *Daddy Long Legs* (1917) features the famous cider sequence, wherein orphans Little Mary and Wesley Barry, denied their lunch for protesting the orphanage food, fill up on cider, stagger around, and look on in confusion as a dog laps up some of the same and stands blotto leaning against a wall. *Pollyanna* (1920), one Little Mary feature in which the charm really does cloy, contains perhaps the classic Little Mary bit, in which she kills a fly just for the fun of it. But after her early variety of parts, this concentration of Little Marys is a little wearing.

What became of the spitfire of *Tess of the Storm Country?* Pickford boldly tested her talent with Neilan in *Stella Maris* (1917) playing Unity Blake, a wretched and unattractive servant who commits murder and then suicide to make others happy. To placate her public, she also played the title role, that of a rich, beautiful, and pathetically crippled teenager who takes the happy ending, cured and wed. Even at that, Pickford had to sneak *Stella Maris* into production while Zukor's back was turned; when he bumped into her in her Unity Blake kit one day, he suffered quite some shock. With her slicked down, darkened, center-parted hair, sallow skin, and dull mouth, she was a perfect Little Horror. "Don't worry," she told Zukor. "I die before it's over."

Everyone dies. Everyone ages, too—except Little Mary. Pushing thirty, she was still playing kids, still bearing the golden curls and the unique toothy grin. Yet she had become so honcho in the industry that she and the three other biggest names banded together to form their own studio and put the Zukors and De Milles out of their careers forever. Incorporating in 1919 as United Artists, Pickford, Douglas Fairbanks, Charlie Chaplin, and D. W. Griffith in effect told Hollywood that the day of the cinema businessman, interposing himself between artists and audience, was over. From now on, film would belong to the people who made it. Who knew better than Little Mary what form her adventures should take? Who better than Fairbanks how to conceive and execute tales of athletic romance in costume or modern dress? Who could second-guess Chaplin or edit Griffith, the presiding genius of the feature film?

This is all the public Pickford. What of the person herself? In 1920, she rid herself of her long absent first husband, Owen Moore, an actor she had met at Biograph, and married Douglas Fairbanks just when their secret affair was about to become public knowledge. Pickford had feared what her fans might think, for she was a Catholic, and Fairbanks, too, was married. But the fans were thrilled. Consider the symmetry: such a little queen and his majesty the American! The pair set up house in a gala mansion that the press christened "Pickfair" and quickly became the first family of Hollywood, the people all people longed to meet. Visiting celebrities learned just how celebrated they were by whether or not they got an invitation to Pickfair, and a European tour proved that the Little Mary and Doug personae were even more potent combined than separate. From England to Russia they were mobbed and worshipped, and on their return Pickfair hummed with the glory.

Except that the two were in fact a bad match. Pickford was the compleat moviemaker: actress, businesswoman, and artist. Fairbanks was a loafer who leaped through the stunts and strolled through the slow parts. She liked solitude; he liked to party. She had fought to understand herself and control her life; he was surprisingly insecure under the confident mask and enjoyed disorder. She liked her liquor; he held it in horror. However, they erected a tight facade of domestic congeniality, and the public began to demand apotheosis: Little Mary and Doug together in film. They did finally make one, and it was the mistake of Pickford's life; but let's not get ahead of ourselves.

Now that Pickford and Fairbanks had an extra profession to maintain, entertaining at Pickfair, they made fewer pictures, one big one each a year. Time for Little Mary to grow—but a contest in *Photoplay* magazine at about this time asked readers what they wanted to see Little Mary in, and it wasn't *Joan of Arc, Camille,* or *Flaming Youth.* They asked for *Cinderella, Heidi, Alice in Wonderland.* The contest winner wrote what amounts to the brief in a class action suit against realism: "These particular roles are your greatest opportunities . . . to create and preserve an almost perfect illusion." However, the new wave of Colleen Moore and Clara Bow marked the sunset of the old good-versus-evil heroine, and Little Mary knew it. Determined to expand her character and to play someone contemporary, she imported Ernst Lubitsch from Germany to direct *Dorothy Vernon of Haddon Hall,* ancient in setting (Elizabethan) but centered on an independent young woman of some reference to the flapper. With the script ready and sets built, Lubitsch arrived and refused to do it. He said Elizabeth I and Mary Stuart, though secondary characters in the story, would overshadow the heroine. A lame excuse; still. Lubitsch suggested *Faust,* but Goethe's heroine strangles her illegitimate child and Mama Charlotte Pickford put the kibosh on that one. Finally Little Mary and Lubitsch agreed on *Rosita* (1923), stolen from *Tosca,* with Little Mary as a guitar-strumming Spanish street singer. The star hated it till the day she died. "Doors! He's a director of doors! Nothing interests him but doors!" she cried, slamming her car door in the Pickfair garage, while up in the house her brother Jack and his guests would throw on their clothes in a panic. Mary's back!

They were a wild family, and Little Mary was of the blood. However, she had discipline, and put out her best for *Rosita.* It did good business, but once it was out of release she threw it into a vault to rot.*

---

*The Berlin Film Festival programmed *Rosita* in 1967 as part of a Lubitsch salute, borrowing a print from an archive in Moscow, and the audience gave it an ovation. Despite her distaste for Lubitsch, Little Mary considered working with other European "art" directors, and actually signed papers with Josef von Sternberg after viewing his *The Salvation Hunters* (1926), a dark slum tale, privately made, which Chaplin got United Artists to release. Nothing came of the Pickford–von Sternberg project.

The following year she went ahead with *Dorothy Vernon of Haddon Hall* (1924), with Neilan directing, but the fans said, Okay, that's two; now bring out Little Mary. *Little Annie Rooney* (1925) and *Sparrows* (1926) duly followed. Okay, says Pickford, that's two; and she made *My Best Girl* (1927), as a shopgirl in love with the store owner's son, Buddy Rogers, stealing her first screen kiss. A year later, she very publicly had her hair bobbed, again agonizing over what her fans might think, and while the PR photos show her posing and mincing at her worst, the act was transitionally final. Simultaneously, silent film is over and Little Mary retires. From now on, it'll be Pickford and sound.

Is she ready for all that sound promises, all its technology and post-flapper contemporaneity? She has scarcely been able to wean her public away from Little Mary; throughout the 1920s, it has been a standoff between *her* young woman of today and *their* old-fashioned kid who fights the righteous fight. In a direct line from Bara to Swanson to Moore to Bow, movie women had developed a new line of character that conflicted with Little Mary and the Victorian spur she followed— yet here was Little Mary trying to play these antithetical parts! It was as if Griffith had gone into vaudeville with a magic act or Colleen Moore had tried opera. Their fans might take in these excursions out of loyalty, but they couldn't enjoy them.

How could Little Mary's public enjoy her as a flapper or an urban shopgirl when she represented all the traditional values and the behavior code that flappers and shopgirls overthrew? *Sparrows*—now there's a Little Mary to treasure. Griffith might have filmed it from a tale by Dickens: Little Mary protects a group of orphans brutally enslaved by a farmer and, when a kidnapped child is brought to the farm to wait out the ransom payment, leads the whole troop through treacherous swampland to safety. The film's last quarter is a Griffith-style cross-cut chase rescue, generating real suspense when the kids must clamber to safety on an insecure tree branch over a pool of alligators. At the end, the kidnapped child's father gratefully adopts not only Little Mary but the whole orphan kaboodle.

This is the mid-1920s, age of the tycoon, the gangster, and the babbitt. Yet Little Mary gets away with old-hat tricks that would have killed anyone else. *Sparrows'* title cards reveal a rustic patois remaindered from a thousand ancient melodramas; some miniature exteriors of farmhouses during a rainstorm and the climactic boat chase are badly faked; and when one of the orphans dies in a sleeping Little Mary's arms, Jesus steps out of a lamby pasture vision to take the child to heaven. In the *jazz* age?

But that's just the point. Little Mary transcended jazz. She could enthrall millions with a folkwise, Jesus-loves-me, meek-inherit-the-earth-if-they-bite-the-villain-in-the-knee fable precisely because if she didn't, then the whole country had gone to hell in a Charleston. Little

Mary was a kind of redemption from the easy-living, gold-digging heroines of the decade. If she joined them, who needed her?

Let's stop here. What has happened? A woman with prodigious organizational and artistic gifts pushed into film, became symbolically instructive as a moral force in egalitarian, Manichaean fables, took her fable into real life by becoming one of the few stars to help run not just a production unit but a whole studio, and has had one major problem: her indestructible, unvariable image. She has had another problem as well, a more mundane one: finding directors with whom she shares a rapport and who are as good at their job as she is at hers.

Funny that Pickford had that problem, because Hollywood in the 1920s was seething with inventive directors both American and foreign. Griffith had cast a spell of self-willing individuality: everyone wanted to do something special. But an actress pays for superb direction with her liberty, and this Pickford could not do. Even with Lubitsch, whom she admired (and disliked) and who was to become, as she foresaw, one of Hollywood's unique talents, Pickford at one point had to take her director aside and point out that she owned the picture from script to rushes, that he was working not only with her but for her, and that in controversy she would cast the telling vote.

Pickford's fellow Biograph player and lifelong friend Lillian Gish never had that problem. She stayed with Griffith to make some of the greatest films ever made in America, left him when their association had reached its natural end, worked with the brilliant Henry King on two foreign ventures, and became one of the biggest stars at the biggest studio, working with King Vidor and Victor Seastrom. And while Pickford made her last film in 1933 and never acted again, Gish is still active, having played a key role in Robert Altman's *A Wedding* in 1978 and made a presentation on the 1981 Academy Awards show. It is, without rival, the longest star career in history.

It began like Pickford's, with mother, fatherless sibling (Dorothy), and the regional stage. The Gishes met the Smiths on one of their tours and one day at the movies spotted Gladys in a Biograph, *Lena and the Geese* (1912). Eager to see their old friend, Lillian and Dorothy sought her out at Biograph, where Griffith beheld Lillian and saw in her all the conflicting romances of the Victorian gentleman—for mate, mother, and angel—made manifest. Blanche Sweet, another Biograph principal, observed that Griffith was so affected by Gish's beauty that he had to struggle to keep his composure. What Gish felt for Griffith, besides an epic loyalty and admiration, has never been made clear.

It was a unique collaboration, astonishingly concentrated. A generation later, Josef von Sternberg and Marlene Dietrich would duplicate this interdependent eloquence, but their films are almost entirely about Dietrich's image, whereas in his Gish films Griffith creates an entire world. Actually, he believed he was describing the world as it is, and to many he was: a world in which beastly men and gallant men vie with each other for the chance to debauch or protect women. Gish, with her rosebud mouth, tumbling locks, fragile body, and wide, seeing eyes, was the absolute Griffith heroine; but more: the ultimate Griffith star, for no other better suited his way of working. The Gish sisters folded nimbly into the Biograph stock company, so that we find them in 1912 playing the leads in their first film, *An Unseen Enemy,* as two girls terrorized by burglars; and as extras later that year in *The New York Hat,* strolling merrily through a village scene.

The New York Hat marked Mary Pickford's farewell to Griffith, as a girl pilloried by gossips because the town minister (Lionel Barrymore) has made her the present of an expensive hat. At length it is revealed that the gift is a bequest of the girl's mother, who died exhausted by a skinflint husband and wanted her daughter to enjoy a luxury. Griffith tacks on a marriage at the end for Pickford and Barrymore, but what he's really after is a sense of smalltown life, with its misers and snoops as well as its goodness. Pickford had had enough of getting locked into these increasingly well-detailed friezes of American life—plus she wanted more money. But Gish found herself in her element helping Griffith open his camera upon the world, and money was not an issue with her. She enjoyed his lengthy rehearsals, preparing a film as if it were a play, perfecting the whole thing before taking a shot, and didn't miss not having name billing. Indeed, Griffith couldn't tell Lillian from Dorothy at first, and directed *An Unseen Enemy* by the color of their hair ribbons: "Red, you hear a strange noise. Run to your sister. Blue, you're scared, too. Look toward me, where the camera is."

This appears to contradict Blanche Sweet's report on Griffith's obvious attraction to Lillian from minute one, but it is sure that at some point early in there Griffith and Lillian Gish locked eyes, and she figured heavily in his mythopoeia from then on. In a lead role in *The Birth of a Nation* (1915) Gish is already well on the way to defining the Griffith heroine* and already a surprising actress. At first you think, What's all this stuff she's doing? What's this mannerism? Then, looking more closely, you recognize the "mannerism" as the gestures of life, and it's all so natural that an actor who would get by quite nicely in some other film would look like something out of a home movie next to Gish. Certain of her bits in *The Birth of a Nation* are famous—her goodbye to her brothers as they leave to fight the Civil War on the northern side, when she worries and flirts and jokes all in a matter of a few seconds; the way she fidgets when, tending her wounded southern beau in a hospital, his mother comes in; her habit of drawing back

---

*It might help to get a fix on Gish's screen persona to consider that Tennessee Williams had her in mind when he conceived the part of Blanche duBois in *A Streetcar Named Desire,* and that Max Reinhardt was to have directed her in a film based on the life of a German woman who suffered the stigmata of the crucified Christ.

from men she likes, as if their sexual power is something she can feel and fear; or her imperious palm that breaks up hostilities between her beau and an unctuous carpetbagger.

Yet, again, Griffith is not featuring any one person but pulling the parts of a world together into a story. His actors must be this naturalistic, all of them, and this expressive, or he can't pull it off. If we are to believe in his nobility, his villainy, his world where beauty dies in a day because the rats never stop coming, that world must seem to be the true world, at least while the film is running. You can rehearse for a year, but in the end you can't act it: you must dwell in it. That was the Griffith training. That's why, when films were shorts and only a few people attended them, his films were the best films, and that's why, when he began to make full-length films, everyone in the country became a moviegoer.

That's also why Little Mary had enough of Griffith fast. She didn't want to be a part of someone else's world, nor did she regard film as morally as Griffith did. Typically, it was Gish who talked Pickford out of destroying her films. Pickford thought of them as timely art that would lose its effectiveness when fashions changed; Gish thought of them as an ageless force for community, a ritual like that of the old Greek stage. Griffith's good guys will always be on the right side if you're as good as they are, and his bad is always bad, no matter what current opinion maker is selling what particular brand of snake oil. Good is fairness. Bad is rape, stealing, murder, making business monopolies, fomenting civil disorder, and passing laws to invade other people's lives. No wonder some people find Griffith so awesome.

Can so moral a code survive a jazz age? Even as early as 1919, when Griffith joined Pickford, Fairbanks, and Chaplin in United Artists, many thought he was played out. But in *Broken Blossoms* (1919) he and Gish proved that their way was still vital—so much so that the entire film consists of a thread of story involving a helpless waif (Gish), her brutal father (Donald Crisp), and the Chinese man (Richard Barthelmess) who chastely adores her. We don't need a whole world this time. This is Griffith's cameo tragedy, his little gem. Everybody dies. Crisp beats Gish to death, and Barthelmess avenges her and kills himself. Griffith had made *Broken Blossoms* for Adolph Zukor, but when Zukor screened it he thought it insultingly depressing; and Griffith, in perhaps the only sound business deal of his life, bought the negative back from Zukor for $250,000 and took it to United Artists for their first release, as a top-price road show. It grossed millions.

Clearly, Griffith and Gish were not yet outmoded. In fact, their vision of protective man and defenseless woman reached its apex in *Way Down East* (1920), "a simple story of plain people." Its source, an old melodrama, had been a staple of second-rate regional stock but a joke in the city centers, yet Griffith paid an unheard-of $175,000 for the rights. Now he must be mad. The story is familiar: a country girl seduced by a city slicker finds shelter with good country people and love with their son; she is unmasked and thrown out into a blizzard. The son saves her from death in the icy river.

With city wags and town characters, mansions and barns, Griffith would again produce his microcosmic allegory, and with Barthelmess again paired with Gish, young American love would find its ideal representation in his sturdy grasp of events and her touching inability to cope with them. True, 1920 saw American art nearing the age that liked women who could cope and which had lost interest in rustic chivalry. Still, Griffith held an ace in the river rescue—no one filmed a suspense chase finale as well as he—and he managed to renew the old tale with that typical Griffithian commitment to what it says. For Griffith and Gish did not care about time. They cared about what they believed, about what is true, not what is successful.

In a world ruled by gruff country squires, vile seducers, and comic constables and filled out with wise, forgiving mothers and self-righteous spinster reformers, Gish as Anna Moore delivers her most fulfilled portrayal. In his opening titles, Griffith tells us that man's "greatest happiness lies in his purity and constancy." But man is fickle, and Griffith shows "the suffering caused by selfishness." His heroine is basic: "We call her 'Anna'—we might have called her Woman." No surprise then that Gish is so finely textured here: she's carrying the weight of her entire sex. *Broken Blossoms* has the most famous Gish touches—the pathetic smile she makes by forking her fingers into her upper lip, for instance, or the hysterical fit she suffers in a closet, whirling around out of control as her father breaks in to kill her. *Way Down East* doesn't dazzle that way; the world doesn't dazzle. Even Gish's most famous scene, the baptism of her dying infant, is not the aria we expect from hearing it described, but another mere fast bad moment in Anna Moore's life. Not till, exposed in her "shame," she exposes her betrayer at a populous dinner does she at last release the frustration and outrage pent up in her. It's a terrific sequence: mingled fury and tears in a back-lit close up,* then Barthelmess smashing a plate and going for the blackguard who made Gish miserable . . . then the realization that in the melee Gish has fled the house.

The ice chase follows. One thing that sets silent days apart is silent actors' willingness to take bald risks if the action called for it. They didn't do all their own stunts, not even Douglas Fairbanks. But Swanson's bout with the lion and the serial queens' acrobatics are typical, and so is the participation of Gish and Barthelmess in *Way Down East*'s finale on the ice floes, which still gets cheers today. Griffith intercut a

---

*Griffith takes his iconographic presentation of Gish too far in the *Way Down East* close-ups by filming them all against a gray background, ignoring the decor of each scene. They come off more as dreams of Gish than as details of story.

few shots of Niagara Falls, but most of the footage was shot in a blizzard at White River Junction, Vermont. It was so cold the ice on the water had to be dynamited each day to produce the plates that Gish lies on and Barthelmess leaps to and from to rescue her; the camera froze; some of the crew came down with pneumonia. And, of course, Gish thought of the last touch of realism, letting her hand trail in the water as the floes glide along. (The hand still bothers her occasionally today.)

Why did these people go through all this? Certainly not for the money. Griffith paid the lowest salaries going. Foolish as it sounds, they simply believed in what he was doing. So did the public, who made *Way Down East* a vast success and boosted Griffith back up to the eminence he held at the time of *Birth of a Nation* five years earlier.

One wonders what Mary Pickford, Griffith's fellow United Artist and Gish's close friend, thought of *Broken Blossoms* and *Way Down East*, of the Griffith-Gish collaboration in general. After all, she might have been the "Griffith Girl" if her temperament hadn't led her down her own road. Even apart from Griffith and Gish, however, Little Mary belongs to them and they to her. The three of them together encapsulate the value system of silent audiences, from city proles in the nickelodeons to fashionable New Yorkers who paid ten dollars a head to attend *Way Down East*'s first night. Griffith fixed and enforced the moral code, laying down role models for manly heroism; Little Mary and Gish complementarily shaped the ideal of womanhood, independent and sexually adult (Little Mary) and weak and unknowing (Gish). Little Mary's would seem the more adaptable prototype, especially in the 1920s, but Pickford found herself hemmed in by the expectations of an audience which suddenly had the Colleen Moore flapper to admire for grit. From Little Mary they wanted sentiment.

Gish's problem was that critics (and presumably the public; producers made that assumption) began to tire of her persona, though she brought it off flawlessly every time. Another problem was that Gish and Griffith had gone as far as they could together. Even before *Way Down East* the director had begun breaking in the next Griffith Girl, Carol Dempster. Gish made one last film with her mentor, *Orphans of the Storm* (1921), with her sister Dorothy as foster sisters caught up in the French Revolution, and then moved on—sadly, it appears, but then Griffith habitually fledged youngsters and then launched them forth from the nest onto the money and the fame. Gish needed neither. But, as she must have realized, she also didn't need Griffith.

Gish had always had a knack for picking stories ripe for film treatment; and, pulling together everything she had learned with Griffith, she starred in *The White Sister* (1923) and *Romola* (1924), for Inspiration Pictures, both directed by Henry King with advice from Gish. The heroine of *The White Sister* is an epitome of the Griffith heroine: a nun who dismisses lover Ronald Colman (whom Gish more or less "discovered" for the two films) to honor her vows, though she only took them in the first place because she mistakenly believed Colman dead. *Romola*, from George Eliot's novel set in Renaissance Florence, has more than a touch of Griffith about it, in the score by Louis F. Gottschalk (a Griffith regular) and the *Intolerance*-like detail work in the sets. Moreover, here were two propositions that Hollywood simply could not see—one heroine is a nun! and the other runs around Renaissance Florence in these gigantic snoods!—just as Hollywood couldn't see Griffith's ambitious ideas (till they made fortunes). But *The White Sister* attracted such notice when Gish premiered it in New York that Metro picked it and *Romola* up, signed Gish to a contract, and, reformed as MGM, set the wheels in motion to make her their biggest woman star.

But Gish was no Theda Bara, no Mae Murray, no Nazimova. You couldn't fool or coddle or flatter her. And look what she says: "The only time I had a personal press agent was when I . . . hired Richard Mitchell to keep my name out of the papers without hurting anyone's feelings." *Out* of the papers! Nor was Gish eager to adapt to studio methods when her own would make the art longer. Still, the MGM stint started well. For her debut Gish suggested Henri Murger's *Scènes de la Vie de Bohème*, the novel about starving artists in Paris that became Puccini's opera *La Bohème*. Gish wanted the director and stars of *The Big Parade*, a war film she had screened in rough cut. She asked for Hendrik Sartov, from the Griffith days, as cameraman, and she urged the studio to use the new panchromatic film that she had tried on *The White Sister* and *Romola*—much easier to light for and photograph on than the standard Hollywood stock. To all this, her producer, Irving Thalberg, assented.

So Gish was in effect her own Little Mary, her own Griffith, her own person: and queen of the lot. She convinced *La Bohème*'s director, King Vidor, to let her show the cast how to rehearse the entire film *before* shooting, in the Griffith manner, talked the front office into letting her play a virginal Mimi who loved but was never seen to kiss her Rodolphe, John Gilbert, and played such a convincing death scene that Vidor thought she had got carried away and really died. In the end, Gilbert (who was being built up as The Great Lover) had to kiss his Mimi, and Gish obligingly suffered the clammy retakes, but otherwise *La Bohème* (1926) shows the profit of letting Gish have her way. How many others could march into a rising, already sinfully powerful studio and have their way almost to the nth? When Griffith yelled, "Feel it!" at you every day for years, you learned to feel; this more than anything marks Gish's MGM features, because she's feeling down into the bald truth of character and most of the others are big gullible puppets. Similarly in control on *The Scarlet Letter* (1926) and *The Wind* (1928), Gish was the last actress to make a series of truly great films in Hollywood at her pleasure, without reference to what was currently popular.

Thalberg thought *The Wind* dreary. Its tale of a gentle Virginian maiden whose marriage tragically disintegrates in the unstable Texas climate built up to a rape attack, detailed her murder of the rapist and her ensuing madness as the wind blows away the sand with which she covered his body and seems to jerk him back to life to terrorize her all over again. Thalberg plunked a happy ending onto it—the man who comes into the house at the end is not the dead rapist but Gish's rough-hewn husband (Lars Hanson)—proving that independence is finite. Furthermore, a pair of MGM features that Gish neglected to plan herself did not come off well. Still, while MGM believed her hot enough to take her advice in order to release her pictures, she managed, quite smoothly, to make totally satisfying films, something Mary Pickford did at this time with some difficulty. No public clamored for a Little Lillian, no Lubitsch marred Gish's sense of self, no lingering identity as a big spender will threaten her in the hard times just around the corner, as it will Gloria Swanson.

What makes a star? More exactly, what gives a star power? Little Mary's favorite director, Marshall Neilan, ticked off "The Six Great Essentials" for women stars in a *Photoplay* article: beauty, personality, charm, temperament, style, and the ability to wear clothes. Neilan did not require these as a whole. Rather, the ideal star emphasized one above the others. For examples, he cited Pickford for personality, Swanson for the clothes, and so on. Lists like these are shallow and misleading, but so were many perceptions about stardom in 1922, when Neilan unveiled his recipe, and virtually all stars of the day covered all six points nicely. (True, Pickford's roles put her into rags and pinafores more often than not, and Gish counted the dress parade as the least absorbing essential of acting. Still, they both filled gowns nicely when asked to.) If one must choose one thing that set Pickford and Gish apart from others it was Pickford's lovability and Gish's concentration, but the closest thing on Neilan's list to either element—thinking grandly, now—is temperament, and for that Neilan cited Norma Talmadge.

Who?

The most remote of the biggest silent names, unknown to today's young movie buffs, who have at least caught a clip of vamping Bara in some retrospective or checked out Nazimova's *Salome* curio, Norma Talmadge is virtually never seen, and when mentioned she is usually dismissed as a soap opera conceit who couldn't act. Yet she spans the silent years, from the freewheeling Patents Trust days right into the front end of studio power and the talkie, and in many ways is the most representative of all stars.

Like Pickford, Gish, and countless others she entered film young as the breadwinner for a fatherless family. Like Pickford she had a stage mother; like Gish she had a sister also in films. Like most stars she worked with great directors (like Herbert Brenon and Allan Dwan), okay directors (Frank Borzage and Clarence Brown), and hacks (Sam Taylor). Without stage experience, Talmadge wandered into the one-reeler at the age of thirteen, grew up playing everything, worked for D. W. Griffith,* and married mogul Joseph M. Schenck, who made her the star of the kind of films which historians and critics neglect and which fans and buffs savor: stunning costumes, romance, suffering, and the heroine's sad, sad yearning gaze off into somewhere. Her co-workers liked her, the public adored her, she made a fortune, her films rotted away in vaults, and who now knows what she was?

Who knew then? For here was the apogee of the banal. Talmadge had beauty and the ability to wear clothes, but she had the personality of melting sherbet and the style of a pizza waitress. Temperament? *Farrar* had temperament. *Nazimova* had temperament. *Negri* had temperament. Talmadge had hairdos. Yet she is central. Her popularity tells us so. She stands at the crossroads of parts that were to prove key for decades: her *New Moon* (1919) was remade by Grace Moore,* her *Smilin' Through* (1922) by Norma Shearer and Jeanette MacDonald, her *Secrets* (1924) and *Kiki* (1926) by Pickford, her *Camille* (1927) followed Nazimova's and preceded Garbo's, her *Dubarry, Woman of Passion* (1930) succeeded versions by Bara and Negri. There may well be only one Great Essential for stardom: to be in the right place at the right time.

Maybe no one can avoid being typed, if only because anyone who is worth noticing has character, and character is what "type" is, from role to role. But to survive for more than an era, a star must avoid being what one might call typed by time: limited to one role useful to the culture in one age and not useful thereafter. Swanson's clothes-horse and Colleen Moore's flapper, for instance, were trapped by their eras, which is why they couldn't work much beyond 1929, when the era turned over. Sound didn't hurt them; history did, transformation, from jazz into Depression.

We left Little Mary and Lillian Gish at the plateau of 1929—Wall Street or the sound track, depending on how you read it—and it will be interesting to see how these two key characters weather the changed times. Pickford has less to worry about, as she owns her work. Gish, at MGM, is vulnerable. How long can a PR-resistant woman stay famous in this increasingly PR-devoted era? How long will Mayer and Thal-

---

*Talmadge appeared in Griffith productions, but none was directed by Griffith himself. She watched him put *Intolerance* together, however, and her sister Constance played the Mountain Girl in its Babylonian episode.

*Moore's *New Moon* (1930), with Lawrence Tibbett, was supposedly an adaptation of the Romberg-Hammerstein Broadway operetta, but it followed the Talmadge scenario. A third *New Moon*, with Jeanette MacDonald and Nelson Eddy, in 1940, reverted to the Broadway plot and also retained more of the Romberg score.

berg permit their prima donna to tell *them* what *she* wants? What's this business about rehearsing films as if they were plays?

Throw her out! Mess her up so the competition won't grab her. Use sound—maybe she'll talk funny. Give her the worst director in Hollywood. Make her sing, make her charleston. Throw them all out, that bunch who thought they owned Hollywood! Swanson, Chaplin, Pickford, Fairbanks, Talmadge, the united schmartists. This is the age of the studio, producer power. Fit in or get out.

Possibly Gish noticed the change in the air when Thalberg offered to invent a romantic scandal for her, to focus public sympathy on her. She may simply have longed to try the stage again. She may have heard about Mayer's plans to sabotage John Gilbert's career to make an example of him (if we're willing to mash our own biggest star, at a cost of millions of dollars, then there's no one we can't mash, and they'll all know it) and left Hollywood in horror at the kind of people she was dealing with. She had grown close to the viciously witty theatre critic George Jean Nathan, who hated the movies; perhaps he talked her into heading for Broadway. Whatever her reasons, Gish left on her own initiative. But, though she didn't know it, she was in the process of being edged out at MGM, and out of Hollywood altogether.

Her time had come; that simple. It had taken a very heavy decade to do it, but the very world that Griffith had used to create the American film—film as the American collection of heroic and romantic sagas and film as industry—was gone by 1929. Gish and Little Mary had to go with it. So, tragically, did Griffith, who made two clumsy talkies and was definitively pastured while his successors set to rewriting the sagas. Griffith's—and Gish's and Pickford's—models for fine men and courageous or holy women were renovated for a post–jazz age America; and no one, not filmmakers and not filmgoers, wanted to give the old hands a chance to take part. How different talkies will be from silents!—and not only, not even mainly, because of the dialogue. It's the characters that mark the major changes, changes that were under way throughout the 1920s, when Little Mary was still the biggest thing in cinema and when Gish, through the presentation of her commitment, could play nun and harlot, then Renaissance dame and industrial-age slavey, and make us accept them all as variants on one all-basic vision of womanly wisdom and beauty and balance. Virtually behind their backs, movies turned around, as the culture did. And suddenly Griffith was out and Pickford was out and Gish was out; and the men were a little dirty or cowardly or selfish, and the women were a little stupid or cowardly or trivial. Okay, our mythology could use a little naturalism, and naturalism dissipates heroism and wisdom. But it's sad for the heroes.

One can understand how easily studio power toppled Griffith and Gish. The director had hopelessly overextended himself in his business dealings, never to come out from under the debts he assumed in making *Intolerance* in 1915. And Gish, as a Hollywood dissenter, would go quietly. But how could Little Mary have gone down, with her millions of fans and her share of United Artists? Share? Those who were there recall the UA board meetings as being largely a tug of war between businessmen who had no grasp of film and Pickford, who had forgot more about film and business than anyone will learn. Chaplin was as ignorant of business strategy as Griffith, and Fairbanks was a jerk. It was Pickford who made the studio make sense. They'd all talk, and she'd listen, then she'd cut in with "No, gentlemen, I don't agree," and proceed to demolish all that had been said with the logic of experience and vision.

Which suggests that Little Mary should have been the one woman to weather the timechange. But she didn't. Having, she thought, prepared the way for a Big Mary in *Dorothy Vernon* and *My Best Girl*, she played the heroine of a southern middle-class tragedy in *Coquette* (1929), winning the first talkie Oscar as Best Actress. Great. But the public had been clamoring for a Doug and Mary picture, remember? She pulled off a walk-on dream lady in Fairbanks' *The Gaucho* (1927), not unlike Elizabeth Taylor's Helen of Troy in Richard Burton's *Doctor Faustus,* but in 1929 the Fairbankses went all the way in *The Taming of the Shrew,* directed by Sam Taylor.

If they had to do a film together, this was a good choice. Petruchio would provide Fairbanks with his brash rogue shtick, and Katherine would test Little Mary with a new part. He could only be Fairbanks and she liked a test, so it should have worked. Instead, it killed her. Taylor, one of Hollywood's worst drudges, was Fairbanks' man, and he colluded with the increasingly unsure actor at Pickford's expense. The set was run along Fairbanks lines, with late starts each day, no retakes, plenty of time out for exercise sessions or snowing visiting VIPs or just loafing, and Pickford had no help from either man. The film looks good, but it's a disaster and Pickford knew it. Fairbanks sounds like a potato chip talking, Taylor's edition of Shakespeare is illiterate, and Pickford flounders. One longs for Lubitsch.

Little Mary's fans didn't want Shakespeare in the first place, and they must have been thinking, Who needs this? Where's our righter of wrongs? Where's our comic? This is what went wrong with Little Mary's four sound films: the contemporary Mary is not what her following wanted, and the few moments of the old fighting, comic Mary are wrong for the 1930s. And the oddest thing of all is: she knew this. But, like her characters, she thought of a solution and applied it. She would film a story that exploits the Little Mary heroine yet is timeless, working with her most sympathetic director, Marshall Neilan. A sound plan. But alcohol had dulled Neilan's brain; and the subject, Norma Talmadge's *Secrets,* the story of a pioneer couple, didn't seem timeless so much as historical. At some point late in the production, Pickford took stock, realized it couldn't work, and closed the production down. She was so angry she burned the negative.

Nothing else she tried worked, either. Nothing flopped, precisely, but she needed a smash. *Kiki* (1931), a Parisian backstager directed by the relentless Sam Taylor, was more Big Mary, and her second try at *Secrets* (1933), this time with a fine director, Frank Borzage, and Leslie Howard as her husband, opened just after Franklin Roosevelt's bank holiday, when nobody was in a movie mood. And that was the end of Little Mary.

Gish went back to the stage, but Pickford stayed put at Pickfair. Her marriage to Fairbanks was ailing; from *The Taming of the Shrew* on, their ability to tolerate each other's incompatible qualities was blunted, and at length Fairbanks' affair with Lady Sylvia Ashley, much touted in the press, made reconciliation impossible. Pickford divorced Fairbanks and married Buddy Rogers, her co-star in *My Best Girl* and, all things considered, a better consort for America's Sweetheart than Fairbanks. Rogers was America's Boyfriend, Fairbanks America's Big Man on Campus, his ego constantly chafing against the wide reaches of his girl's celebrity. Mary and Buddy remained active in Hollywood doings, and in the mid-1930s she proposed to try a radio show, *Parties at Pickfair,* in a variety format like that of Louella Parsons' *Hollywood Hotel.* But Parsons discouraged great stars from appearing, and such was her power that this in effect canceled Pickford's show.

That was the new Hollywood: jackals owned it. No wonder Little Mary ended up a bedridden recluse sipping gin. Griffith, too, drank his wretched life away. But Gish, the most formidable of actresses, stayed so busy and vital that eventually Hollywood needed her all over again. She shall return, some chapters hence.

# 3

# *Forward to Yesterday*

JANET GAYNOR

*What do you mean "comeback"? I was always on top!*
—JANET GAYNOR
at the time of *A Star is Born*

If the most efficient way to gain stardom is by representing something important to the culture at a given time, that's also the most efficient way to secure one's own obsolescence. Probably the biggest challenge to Hollywood's big names was the switch from silence to sound; but one star not only didn't adapt to the new styles in talkie storytelling but actually got more old-fashioned in some ways. Even as she made the ritual obeisances to the new god sound, singing and dancing inexpertly in musicals, she kept turning up in rural settings to ratify the old virtues. Her colleagues of the 1930s wrestled with new codes of chivalry on city streets, and so did she, when she had to. But she made it so fresh that she became the second-biggest box-office star in 1931, held it for two years, then rose to first place in 1934. It was as if she were making silents that developed sound tracks and modern patina through some lab process, leaving her untainted, a Biograph girl dwelling in the future. How could she get away with it?

Simple. She got her contemporary roles out of the way early on, *before* talkies. Thus, her talkie privileges assured, she went on to make the good old films while everyone else scrambled around trying to be newfangled.

She was Janet Gaynor. Philadelphia-born, named Laura Gainor, and raised in Chicago and Los Angeles, she started in movies in true twenties style, as an extra. The screen test was already established as an audition rite, and Gaynor got hers at Fox in 1926, getting a nice part in *The Johnstown Flood* with George O'Brien. Winfield Sheehan, William Fox's vice-president, happened to be looking for a sweet kid to raise to stardom, and Janet was surely it, a petite brunette with a rustic flush to her cheek. Sheehan paid her $100 a week, sent flowers to her dressing room every day, and plonked her into a spate of sweetheart parts. It all paid off in *Seventh Heaven* (1927), directed by Frank Borzage for extremes of tenderness and horror, the love story as adventure.

The setting is Paris. Gaynor is Diane, a helpless orphan bullied by a vicious sister; Charles Farrell is Chico, a sewer cleaner who finds her in the street and takes her to live with him in a seventh-floor walkup, from the gutter up to heaven via some elaborate crane shots of the stairways as the loving couple go up and down. The picture made a fortune for Fox and reputations for Gaynor and Farrell, and is still loved today; for while there is nothing distinctive about the plot, the Parisian atmosphere, or the theme song, "[I'm in heaven when I see you smile, my] Diane,"* Gaynor's waif has reserves of great spirit. In the end she is savage when she turns on her sister—audiences clap and cheer—and is nearly hysterical when Farrell, whom she thought dead on the battlefield, suddenly turns up, blind and more in need of her than ever. It's every girl's dream, maybe. Or some girls' dream. No, it's a crazy soap opera of no import whatsoever, but it holds you.

The two leads became stars together and blended so nicely that Sheehan reunited them in film after film, loving it when the fans begged the pair to marry for true as they did in each movie. As early as the second Gaynor-Farrell opus, *Street Angel* (1928), the studio stuck close to *Seventh Heaven,* not exactly remaking it but bringing Borzage back in as director and let us say referring to the original in many certain ways. For a few years, Gaynor and Farrell became *the* Hollywood duo, just good friends in life but absolute guaranteed chemistry on the screen. Why? Jeanette MacDonald and Maurice Chevalier were much sexier, Joan Crawford and Clark Gable almost outrageously involved with each other, Katharine Hepburn and Cary Grant far more deft in mating rituals. But Gaynor and Farrell were unique in that they were both waifs. He is as soft as she, as easily cowed, and does his courting at length, with a host of little-boy glances at her for help. In an age of It, these two observed the ancient innocences.

On the verge of sound, Gaynor was a big star, a studio product, looking good. But by chance she falls out of pop nostalgia and into art history here, for in between *Seventh Heaven* and *Street Angel* Fox released an extraordinary film that has been listed among the few greatest silents; some critics call it the greatest film ever made. And Gaynor is very much in it.

A farmer becomes infatuated with a city woman who is in the country for a holiday. He neglects his work and family and even agrees to the city woman's suggestion that he kill his wife, sell his farm, and

*We're edging into sound already. Though talkies were not to come forth in any number for two years, many films, especially those of Fox and Warner Brothers, were made available in sound prints, with musical and noise-effect tracks synchronized to the action.

come with her to the city. On the edge of the act, however, he suffers an assault of conscience, totally repents his adultery, and reclaims his marriage in a joyful spree with his wife in town. But on their way back to the farm she dies in an accident—exactly the "accident" the husband was originally going to arrange for her.

This is the outline of Hermann Sudermann's story *The Trip to Tilsit,* which, with the addition of a happy ending, was the source of this celebrated film. It was made to upgrade William Fox's reputation for sharp practice and crass packaging: he sent to Europe for prestige, importing the expressionist director F. W. Murnau from Berlin to hand him carte blanche. You make the art; I'll pay the bills. True, Sudermann's tale suggests soap opera. But the chiaroscuro precision that made Murnau's *Nosferatu* (1922) so scary, *The Last Laugh* (1924) so touching, and *Faust* (1926) epic now turned schmaltz into a rhapsodically elemental fable of almost insane commitment to itself. After all, soap opera's fault is its stupid routine; this films tells it as if it had not been told before. Murnau's pictorial drive polarizes the narrative into enlightening thematic battles—man versus woman, marriage versus adultery, earth versus water, country versus city, human scheming versus acts of nature. His characters are archetypal—the Man, his Wife, the Woman from the City. His sets are unplaceable, ranging from a Grimm Brothers village to a newsreel-true city with American cars and European buses.* All this keeps the film timeless, gives it the persuasion of myth and the familiarity of a classic.

The film is called *Sunrise,* and in 1927 it failed. Few were in the mood for eternal verities then, and coming out just after *Seventh Heaven* it disappointed Gaynor's just-gathered following, for as the poor little wife she runs a pallid third place to George O'Brien as the Man or Margaret Livingston as the Woman from the City. The studio had wanted Farrell opposite Gaynor, but Murnau needed someone sturdy in the part. O'Brien was not a great actor, but the almost Swansonesque beauty of his face contrasted neatly with his spectacular physique, giving his action scenes real menace and making his kissing close-ups among the most erotic in film. Clearly, Murnau meant to make *Sunrise* the ultimate marital parable, casting the most distinctive actors in the most generalized sort of parts. Livingston's vamp is a shocker, an updated Bara dressed à la mode, smoking the sensualist's cigarette and devouring men for fun. At one point she even shimmies, the last of the big-time jazzbo vamps.

Gaynor, too, is something special, a woman so pure in tone that she came off chaste even after playing a street angel. Here in *Sunrise* she is colorless in her blond hair, pulled back taut and limp, dowdy in

---

*Fox nearly had a heart attack when he saw the cost breakdowns; prestige cost him more than he had planned to spend. To his credit—little else is—he spent it anyway and retained Murnau, who died in an auto accident in 1931.

her dress-up clothes for the expedition to the city, complete with the rube's ludicrous Sunday hat, two generations out of style. But Gaynor was not a star whose costumes mattered. Like Little Mary and Lillian Gish she represented not things to do but a person to be: a morality. Something clean in Gaynor burst through the PR and the sentimentalistic plots of her films to present a sisterly good nature so broad she could play madonnas and whores without shifting gears. True, her street angels are really just madonnas in a tight dress; we scarcely believe the shocking facts even when the narration is clear about them. Still, Gaynor made more friends in the shabby *Seventh Heaven* and *Street Angel* than in the righteous, ecstatic *Sunrise*. Moreover, in 1928 she won the first Best Actress Oscar ever given, for all three roles, beating down Gloria Swanson and Louise Dresser.

This is significant. The Academy Awards were not designed, and have never been treated, as awards of merit but as tokens of recognition in the industry. A Best award, whether for acting, directing, or anything else, goes not for the most inventive or inspiring or fulfilled achievement but to the person the Academy* wishes to honor, for any number of reasons. Best Picture awards have recognized innovation (*Marty, Midnight Cowboy*) but at other times have simply bowed in awe to a huge capital outlay (*Ben-Hur*). Best Director awards have singled out journeyman technicians (Victor Fleming) and newcomers who promise to be famous (Mike Nichols) as well as the singularly gifted (John Ford). As for the acting citations, these have gone to the talented and the mediocre, to freaks and to straights, to company regulars and repentant outlaws, to the recently deceased as a memento, and to people who missed out a year or two before, by way of apology.

Giving the first Best Actress to Gaynor was the film colony's way of putting a seal of approval on her as a principal figure in the corporation. This was prescient, for Gaynor virtually led the attempt to connect stardom from silents to talkies. Something in her reaches far back into the American past, into the Little Mary morality, the child in the woman, the cutup in the tragedy. Something else in her promoted the new urban Cinderellas, complete with acceptable speaking voice and an artless fluency in dialogue. Gaynor encompassed two contradistinctive ages, something few stars have managed to do. And Gaynor's era, late 1920s to mid-1930s, was the hardest to maintain, for silence was rapt fantasy and sound was almost intellectually naturalistic, two wholly different cinemas. Pickford herself couldn't hack it, but Gaynor updated

*The Academy of Motion Picture Arts and Sciences was founded in 1927 as a forum for institutional, educational, and diplomatic activities among filmmakers of all vocations. Quickly politicized, it suffered divisive controversies in the 1930s and has never commanded universal respect even from its members. However, Americans love an awards night, and ever since the Oscar ceremonies were first broadcast complete in 1945, the public has taken them with some seriousness.

Little Mary, even unto remaking several of Pickford's films (not as many, though, as Fox wanted).*

No doubt the twelve-film partnership with Charles Farrell contributed a great deal to Gaynor's eminence. The moviegoer of the sound years couldn't believe anymore in the self-sufficiency of a Little Mary or in the perfect chastity of a Gish. As a willing girlfriend, Gaynor drew on their force while rehabilitating it for a less credulous age. But the best thing about Gaynor, among many opinions, was her indifference to the showier aspects of stardom, the glamour of a Swanson or a Constance Bennett. In 1931, *Photoplay* ran an article entitled "Charm? No! No! You Must Have Glamour," holding up Marlene Dietrich "of the heavy-lidded, inscrutable eyes"; Joan Crawford, "the exponent of the younger generation"; Lilyan Tashman; Elissa Landi; Lil Dagover; and the revamped Norma Shearer with her "madcap method of living" as the paradigms of heroine. The author, Katherine Albert, noted that "nice girls" like Betty Bronson, Mary Philbin, Colleen Moore, and of course Little Mary and Gish, were gone. Albert reckoned that typing comes and goes in waves—"sweet girls, vamps, sweet girls again, and now glamour."

She had to admit that Gaynor was the "amazing exception," but not long after 1931 many of the glamour favorites were gone or in deep trouble. Elissa Landi? Lil Dagover? Even their names are dead. Glamour, being by nature tied to fashion, is a pedestal that constantly gets pushed around, often suddenly. In 1937, trying to keep her footing, Constance Bennett appeared in a bizarre color short called *Daily Beauty Rituals,* in which the goddess welcomes us into her boudoir, demonstrates about three tons of cream and paint, hassles her maid, and kisses her little boy off to school. I don't know how this was greeted in its youth, but at a recent screening the audience came near to rending its garments laughing at the sight of Bennett's internal contradictions accidentally pushed to the fore. She rises from bed *already* salved to the pores, her meticulous toilette makes her look like a cracked fresco, and the entire attempt at cinema verité is overgone even for hype.

Next to this, Gaynor is a rose in Sharon. Even admitting—she readily did so—that she wasn't right for musicals, she put out like a trouper on *Sunny Side Up* (1929), as a tenement lass who wins a Southampton beau (Farrell). Gaynor is good for the city, even New York, because she lends it the even temper and resilient backbone of the pasture; and naturally in Southampton she shows us how to deal with snobs. Farrell's treble tones made him a bust in sound, but Gaynor brought off her songs, though a tearful third reprise of "[I'm a dreamer] Aren't We All?" gets a little grandiose. Farrell was no judge

*Gaynor almost played the Gish part in a remake of *Way Down East* with Henry Fonda, but refused. Rochelle Hudson took over.

of roles, taking what the studio offered him, whereas Gaynor was astute, pulling seven months of suspension rather than kill her career in bad-risk films.

Of course, by 1930 anything Gaynor made made money, so why worry about quality? Gaynor finally came to terms with Fox, but her pictures really didn't improve much; they're the kind that only aficionados see today. There were the Little Mary retreads, *Daddy Long Legs* (1931) and *Tess of the Storm Country* (1932), beguiling rural tales like *State Fair* (1933), in which Gaynor played daughter to Fox's other surefire draw, Will Rogers, and even a loanout to MGM, *Small Town Girl* (1936). By then Darryl Zanuck had taken over the troubled Fox empire. He bridled at Gaynor's high salary and set her free, a millionaire at thirty-one and possibly the first woman to be replaced by an infant, Shirley Temple, who took over the Little Mary remake business at Fox, doing *Daddy Long Legs* yet again, with songs, as *Curly Top* in 1935.

But this is not the end. If *Sunrise* marked Gaynor's only experience in eternal art, she had yet to make a pop classic, the kind of movie that gets revived for buffs rather than critics. *State Fair* is sometimes mentioned in this context, but it has no great following, despite the participation of such experts in the bumpkin style as Lew Ayres, Frank Craven, Doro Merande, and director Henry King. No, Gaynor's big one is *A Star Is Born* (1937), the first of three films by that title and in some ways the best. Gaynor's successors, Judy Garland and Barbra Streisand, had strong musical numbers to help them summon character; Gaynor had only her instincts as the rural girl who crashes Hollywood by marrying a male star whose career dives as hers builds. The tale suggests several real-life sources, and Hollywood old-timers disagree on whose story it might be. William Wellman, who directed *A Star Is Born,* says the man was John Bowers, a second-rank silent star who drowned himself in the Pacific when talkies exposed his unspeakable voice. This is more or less what happens in the film. Fredric March, as Gaynor's husband, hugs his wife, calls to her—"I just wanted to take one more look"—and strides into the dark ocean to die.

Hollywood voodoo says movies about movies are bad luck, but everything went well on this one. It was produced by David O. Selznick, so self-willed in his approach to moviemaking that he had had to leave Paramount for RKO, RKO for MGM, and MGM to found his own studio, Selznick International. When Selznick made a film, it was calculated and improved and shot and reshot. His opening titles alone looked better than some producers' entire films, and for *A Star Is Born* he used Technicolor, tricky and expensive at the time. This was a superb credit for Gaynor, a peak to reach after the letdown of her losing her queen's crown at Fox—and heaven knows Selznick could give her the champion production that her former studio couldn't afford.

While we're talking stardom, we should keep in mind that Hollywood's definition of the word "star" was a personality appealing enough to carry virtually any picture, someone to pull in an audience regardless of who directed, wrote, or designed the feature; no matter how familiar or offbeat the subject matter; as long as studio PR kept the face on view and the characterological image in note; and only as long as that face and image stayed current. Nowadays, we think of a star as an actor with a lot of cultural pull—a biggie—but from Florence Lawrence on, a star was simply any actor with drawing power—a regular. Gaynor at Fox was a top-rank regular in a number of genres whose films were more or less competently turned out. In *A Star Is Born,* however, she grew big, expanding in the best role she ever had but also—mainly—playing *the* role in *the* Hollywood saga.

Probably few people in town liked the idea of *A Star Is Born,* or of any film about winning and losing among themselves. Films about Hollywood are not bad luck; they are dangerous. Either they must explore the corruption and silliness or must lie at length, for there is little that is truly exhilarating or noble or even nice about the place. But Selznick saw the tale as a romance. Hollywood in Little Mary's youth was a kindergarten, everyone in his twenties; by 1937 it was approaching middle age. Selznick himself represented the second generation of producing Selznicks.* Hollywood, to him, was dynastic, heroic, epic. He was so attracted to this rise-and-fall story that he had proposed something very much like it during his first rock-bottom job in Hollywood, at MGM. At Paramount shortly thereafter, he brought it up again, in a treatment written by Adela Rogers St. Johns entitled *The Truth About Hollywood* and planned as a vehicle for Clara Bow. Paramount said no. How was it to put out anything like a truth about Hollywood when almost all the major scandals of the 1920s had involved Paramount stars, from Wallace Reid to Bow herself?

St. Johns gives yet another real-life source for *A Star Is Born,* adding a layer to its texture of *à clef* allusions: Colleen Moore and her director-husband John McCormick, who became an alcoholic, ruining their marriage and, worse, her career by demanding, in the last worried days before talk, that any new Moore contract also include him. The plot was taking on the qualities of a book of legends, and finally Selznick got it all on film in 1932 at RKO as *What Price Hollywood?*—directed by George Cukor, with our old friend Constance Bennett as the waitress who makes it and Lowell Sherman as her *protecteur,* a director who drinks too hard, slides into the gutter, and shoots himself. Now the allusions really proliferated: Sherman modeled his portrayal on

---

*His father, Lewis Selznick, had been cruelly beaten out by his competitors and died a wrecked man. It is not clear how Selznick regarded those of his colleagues who had parts in this, but Lewis' other son, Myron, became an actor's agent precisely for the purpose of avenging his father by negotiating studio-breaking fees for his clients.

John Barrymore, another great talent who imploded on booze and other fun, Gregory Ratoff modeled his producer on Samuel Goldwyn, and bystanders recalled lines or incidents that were snapped up into the script.

Why Selznick felt he had to remake the film only five years later is easy to tell if one views *What Price Hollywood?* in the context of the *Photoplay* article on how glamour supposedly replaced charm. Maybe it had; maybe it hadn't. Either way, much of that glamour is bitter and crummy, made of too much money or of hard-boiled dames like Bennett who, as role models, were about as useful as sequins. Their roles showed them off well, made them elegant, but they gave no spectator a perspective on his or her experiences in life, which is what the movies had been doing from the beginning and would have to continue to do if they were to survive. *What Price Hollywood?* with Bennett is gritty despite Selznick's romanticism; it's like *Daily Beauty Rituals* with wit and a tragic ending.

Typically, when Selznick planned *A Star Is Born,* he made sure the thing would glow. Now the story sounds like a gung-ho work-ethic theme, spelled out by a lovable gruff grandmother, that connects Hollywood to the old west, a place won by the pioneer elect. The Technicolor of course adds a warmth that the black-and-white *What Price Hollywood?* lacked; and in casting, Selznick considered sweet, plucky youngsters for the girl—Margaret Sullavan and Elizabeth Bergner, besides Gaynor—and he hired the cleanest profile in town, that of Fredric March, for the director. (Everyone in Hollywood knew that the part was virtually written for John Barrymore, but that was exactly the problem: by 1937 he was a sodden washout, and would have edged *A Star Is Born* out of romance into documentary. March had played a canny imitation of Barrymore in *The Royal Family of Broadway* in 1930, however, so it's close enough.)

But let us not get too sweet and clean. Luckily, the film's sugar content is cut by a satiric screenplay credited to Dorothy Parker, her sometimes husband Alan Campbell, and Robert Carson—and by director Wellman, a tough character who enjoyed pointing up Hollywood's inanities and horrors. Selznick, like it or not, had to use him, for *A Star Is Born* was in fact Wellman's idea* and technically not a remake of *What Price Hollywood?* RKO decided it was and proposed to sue for plagiarism, but no one was able to find enough details in common to support the case. *What Price Hollywood?* and *A Star Is Born* are the same forest, but each has different trees. The biggest difference of all lies in

---

*Working with Carson on the original draft, Wellman, too, included episodes based on actual events. The scene in which a judge tells off March, arrested for drunkenness, is shot right out of Wellman's life, and it's said that March's accidental slapping of Gaynor while haranguing the audience at an Oscar banquet occurred to a couple of tertiary celebrity at the Coconut Grove. The whole film is poured from a caldron of lore.

the latter's tone, typified in Gaynor's big-tyke charm. You must, the film says, be unspoiled to make it; and you must stay unspoiled to keep on making it (which is why the director goes down: success made him lazy). You don't have to be particularly talented, but you must work. You must—at any rate might—be Janet Gaynor.

Hollywood loved *A Star Is Born*. Oscar nominations flowed freely, but it was such a rich season that voting split every which way, for *The Life of Emila Zola, Stage Door, Dead End, Captains Courageous, The Good Earth, The Awful Truth*, and grand people: Spencer Tracy, Paul Muni, Garbo, Barbara Stanwyck, Luise Rainer, and Leo McCarey, among others. Wellman and Carson won for Best Original Screenplay, giving official industry sanction to the collapse of RKO's court case and affirming the valentine atmosphere. Sure, *A Star Is Born* gives us the producer's yes-people, the gummy PR lout, the grabby mobs of fans, the terror of a screen test, with makeup artists groaning over the landscape of a starlet's face. And we do watch Fredric March crumble into bits. But we also get the lush lawns and pools, the glowing marquees, the cement footprints, the good wishes of one's colleagues, and of course the grandmother, May Robson, who sends Gaynor to Hollywood in the first place and heartens her to stay and fight it out when stardom seems more a chore than a luxury.

Interestingly, Gaynor, who pretty much played herself in *A Star Is Born*, felt oppressed by stardom just when she had reaffirmed it. After two more films in 1938, *Three Loves Has Nancy* and *The Young in Heart*, she married the costume designer Gilbert Adrian and quit. Nearly two decades later, she kindled PR fires by returning in a mother role in *Bernardine* (1957), and more than two decades after that she made her Broadway debut in *Harold and Maude*. But at heart it all ended for her with *A Star Is Born*. When stage stars go, they take everything with them. James O'Neill, Mrs. Fiske, the Lunts, and Katharine Cornell, for instance, have left us nothing (though all deposited a part or two on film in moments of blunder). But film stars are always with us in revival houses and on television, and in Gaynor's case it is *Sunrise* and *A Star Is Born* that live on. An odd couple, that: one of America's most admired pieces of Cinema and one of its pop classics, with Gaynor as an abused wife in both. Had she no glamour to offset the charm? None, except the glamour of stardom. Her clothes in *State Fair* and *Sunny Side Up* might have been borrowed from some animal, her matings with Charles Farrell were too winsome to have allure, and her studio didn't know how to project glamour in the first place. She was the American kid, a barnyard Cinderella, an urchin; her *Daddy Long Legs* actually manages to feel less sexy than Little Mary's. But then Mary, curls and pranks notwithstanding, was a woman. Gaynor was . . . young. They liked them young. Look who replaced her at Fox: a four-year-old.

# 4

# *The Pope's Wife, the Doomed Harlot, and the Loyal Shopgirl*

NORMA SHEARER
GRETA GARBO
JOAN CRAWFORD

*The Shearer and Crawford pictures had to end in a church, but the public seemed to enjoy watching Garbo die.*

—J. ROBERT RUBIN
MGM's legal adviser

In the late 1920s, Paramount was the king studio, with such a wide variety of characters that even its bread-and-butter programmers had a unique flavor. Paramount also made an impressive transition into sound in 1929, coming out with some very deft musicals in the Lubitsch-Chevalier series. But by then Paramount was in serious money trouble. Industry leadership passed on to the studio that could afford the top stars, the most proficient production machinery, and the grandest promotion: Metro-Goldwyn-Mayer.

MGM earned its status not only in the quality of its films but in the power it exercised. Louis B. Mayer, its chief, has already figured in this narrative as a holder of fanatical grudges, and his executive producer, Irving Thalberg, commanded universal awe for his front-office diplomacy and expertise in curing ailing scripts or direction. Budd Schulberg, growing up absurd in wonderland, likened Thalberg to a Pope of the film world.

Elsewhere in Hollywood, the old guard was falling away. Universal's Carl Laemmle had lost his grip on public taste except in horror pictures, William Fox was in wicked legal trouble—he actually did time—and no one at Paramount was sure from one week to the next who was in charge. But MGM maintained its trim, and set out its stars like jewels in flawless settings. The studio had one problem: there were more MGM stars than there were first-rate pictures to give them, and they all had to make a semi-dud every so often just to keep working. The one exception to this rule was Norma Shearer. She was sleeping with the boss.

Shearer, in a familiar story, came into films with a sister because the family needed money. Pickford, Gish, Talmadge—the list of such cases is endless. But most of these who became famous had something special, looks or It, if not personality or acting talent. Shearer, according to her many detractors, had nothing, not even Norma Talmadge's gluey dissipation. F. Scott Fitzgerald gave Shearer a lead part in his story *Crazy Sunday* as one Stella Walker, but even he couldn't make her interesting. She must have had something, for her following was large and her films still draw today. What was it?

Her beauty is in dispute. She is said to have been cross-eyed, though she doesn't seem so on screen. Going back to Marshall Neilan's list of Great Essentials, Shearer can certainly claim the ability to wear clothes, becoming something of a Swanson in the way women studied her wardrobe. Here MGM was invaluable; no other studio dressed its stars with such elegance, not only in film after film but in scene after scene. It was not just the top studio that Shearer had in her corner, but the top studio's top filmmaker, Irving Thalberg, and never was stardom regulated so astutely by a *protecteur*. William Fox invented Theda Bara, but he couldn't guide her. Little Mary invented herself, and with all her power she still couldn't make the public like her in the roles she liked. But under Thalberg's direction Norma Shearer became for many the prestige star of Hollywood, more admirable than Dietrich, more ladylike than Garbo, more versatile than Hepburn. Given that she was in fact none of these things, how did Thalberg manage it?

He tuned in on Shearer early in the 1920s, when he was still at Universal; and when he became Mayer's vice-president in 1923 he took Shearer along with him. (When they first met she took him for an office boy.) It was too soon for him to do much for her, so he kept her working in small safe parts for the experience. But when Mayer's company re-formed and merged into Metro-Goldwyn-Mayer, Shearer played the lead, with Lon Chaney and John Gilbert, in the new firm's first feature, *He Who Gets Slapped* (1925). It was a fancy part for

Shearer, that of a circus bareback rider loved by a hero, a sympathetic grotesque, and a villain, and told in highly poetic terms by director Victor Seastrom. (The film's source was a Russian play, the sort of thing the Theatre Guild liked to put on, with lots of symbolism direly lit.)

The following years were Shearer's building period, mostly in unimportant romantic melodramas—backstagers and smalltowners, with the odd society romp here and there. Throughout, Shearer and Thalberg were no Trilby and Svengali. They seldom saw each other on the lot, and only occasionally dated, when his major inamoratas—Peggy Hopkins Joyce, Constance Talmadge; and Rosabelle Laemmle—were unavailable. (Shearer dubbed herself "Irving's spare tire.") There was another woman in the picture, Thalberg's widowed mother, Henrietta, who took a stern view of all of the above, even of sweet little Rosabelle, a sort of girl-next-door from Thalberg's Universal days, when Thalberg was a prodigy and she the boss's daughter. But in the end Henrietta had to get along with Shearer, for in the summer of 1927 Thalberg married her, in a quiet ceremony at the Thalberg house—a Jewish ceremony, by the way. It was a company affair. Mayer served as best man, and Shearer's brother Douglas, MGM's chief sound engineer, gave the bride away. Henrietta looks miserable in the wedding pictures, but Louella Parsons wrote a nice review and thought Shearer "gave her most realistic performance."

Better performances were to come, though Mrs. Thalberg may have been Norma's best part. In her new position as the Pope's wife she was obviously going to get the treatment, and it began with *The Student Prince* (1927), Ernst Lubitsch's adaptation of the Romberg operetta, with Ramon Novarro, a very hot property at the time, as the young noble who goes off to Heidelberg, falls in love with waitress Shearer, and finally leaves her to tend to his kingdom. Besides being an MGM triple-A production (Lubitsch, no less!), *The Student Prince* gave Shearer a chance to play sweet, something some of the MGM staff thought she didn't have it in her to play. They were wrong. The film was a hit, as was Shearer's talkie debut, *The Trial of Mary Dugan* (1929), from Ann Harding's Broadway smash. Thalberg took such care with this one that he had the cast rehearse the whole thing before shooting, Gish-style.

*The Student Prince* was Shearer sweet, *Mary Dugan* Shearer tense, and to wrap it up she did the balcony scene from Shakespeare's *Romeo and Juliet* with John Gilbert in *The Hollywood Revue of 1929*, one of the all-star variety shows that all the studios turned out in the first months of sound. Shakespeare matched the sweet and the tense with the grand. The two actors may be an embarrassment, especially when they repeat the scene in slang ("Julie, baby, you're the mocha in my java"); but with Lubitsch, a Broadway hit, and Shakespeare pointing the way, the shape of the Thalberg plan is clear. Put her in class, coach her to class, and dress her for class. She'll persuade the millions that she is class.

She did. At the time of *The Student Prince*, the big MGM women were Garbo and Gish. By 1931, when Thalberg felt the sweetness and class had registered strongly enough to allow Shearer to go into a Talmadge phase playing worldly sybarites who suffer and repent, the big MGM women were Garbo, Crawford . . . and Shearer; choose your preferred order. With Garbo to tackle the sexy-erotic parts and Crawford for the proles, Shearer played Good Women, with just enough erring to make the good enticing; and her rare Bad Women always saw the light like a hymn coming thro' the rye.

She was a mixture of sweetheart and vamp, then, but mainly a wife, and not just Thalberg's. Garbo was earth mother and Crawford a jazz baby; someone had to run a household. That in itself is a form of class, given Hollywood's value system. Shearer's image as a lady was so potent that Clark Gable's career first took wing when he slapped her around in *A Free Soul* (1931). Gable had menaced other stars, but they were tough customers themselves, like Crawford and Stanwyck. If he could manhandle *Shearer,* you knew he was the goods.*

Was she the goods, though? She was utterly overparted in Noël Coward's *Private Lives* (1931), with Robert Montgomery, and in Eugene O'Neill's *Strange Interlude* (1932), with Gable again. The overall impression people carried away was of a specialist in highbrow cinema, and MGM billed her as "the first lady of the screen." But, egad, these were roles played on stage by Gertrude Lawrence and Lynn Fontanne! Even the ridiculously mawkish *Smilin' Through* (1932), with Fredric March and Leslie Howard, had once belonged to Jane Cowl, another Broadway heavyweight. To moviegoers, however, they were Shearer parts, and such was her aura that they could forgive *Strange Interlude*'s heroine having an illegitimate child. Shearer made it almost respectable.

Even more respectable was Shearer's one-picture-a-year schedule, each new release fairly described as "awaited" and a grand gesture of noblesse oblige. She had won an Oscar in 1930, and now she was getting nominated for every other part—for *The Barretts of Wimpole Street* (1934), for *Romeo and Juliet* (1936), and *Marie Antoinette* (1938). She didn't win for any of them, but then she wasn't all that popular in town anymore. The nominations might be read as recognition of Thalberg's ingenuity. Thalberg's wife should have succeeded Mary Pickford as Hollywood's social majesty, but Thalberg's delicate health and long working hours precluded any Pickfairish agenda. Still, if Shearer didn't give all that many parties, she attended plenty, and constantly got into

---

*This Lady Norma thing took a boomerang turn, though, when folks began to think of her as highfalutin. MGM's PR gang eventually had to send out shots of Shearer riding a roller coaster just to put her feet back on earth, as it were.

scrapes over dress regulations. For the 1936 Mayfair Ball, a white-tie operation, chairman Carole Lombard decreed white dresses for the women. Jeanette MacDonald turned up in mauve, but that's almost white; Shearer, however, wore red, inspiring vigorous commentary from Lombard on Shearer's taste in clothes and the offer, from the "Mexican Spitfire," Lupe Velez, loyal to Lombard, that she slit Shearer's throat with the stiletto she habitually carried in her garter. In another part of the forest, Shearer wore a gigantic Louis XVI gown to an American-themed soiree at Marion Davies' Santa Monica beach house. Davies ordered her to take it off, and Hedda Hopper helpfully told Shearer it was rude to wear a French costume in the presence of Davies' lover, William Randolph Hearst, who had recently been asked to leave France.

Perhaps Shearer was trying the gown out as a dry run for her performance in *Marie Antoinette,* which Thalberg had been planning for five years as the ultimate Shearer vehicle: Norma as wife (to Robert Morley), sweetheart (of Tyrone Power), and empress (of France). She was better in *The Barretts of Wimpole Street,* where she let vicious father Charles Laughton and ardent swain Fredric March do all the work; and she looks great in *Romeo and Juliet* with Leslie Howard. There were murmurs that at thirty-six Shearer was too old for Juliet; but in fact most of the celebrated stage Juliets were considerably older before they dropped the part, and a youthful one (even given the upcloseness of film) would have been unthinkably out of tradition.

Shearer had grown so grand that conventional criticism no longer applied to her work. She was Dame Norma, the Katharine Cornell of the screen, a reputation disguised as an actress. Thalberg died in 1936, however, and Shearer's fortunes took a turn. *Marie Antoinette* went into production without the Thalberg touches of care and patience. The director, W. S. (One Take) Van Dyke, was reported to have been promised a sum for every day he was under schedule when shooting was finished. The writing on the wall spelled out, "Mayer Takes Revenge."

Relations between L. B. and Thalberg had been rocky for some time, the former resenting the latter's renown as the industry's producing champ. Worse yet, the Pope was hardly buried before there was talk of a sainthood, and Mayer was feeling dangerously helpless. You can hate and distress a living nemesis, but what do you do to a dead one?

Try rumbling his widow. Mayer moved slowly; Shearer's contract had five films yet to go. The first two are typical Shearer class entries, both Broadway hits, including another Fontanne part, *Idiot's Delight* (1939) and *The Women* (1940). Gable partnered her in *Idiot's Delight;* in Alfred Lunt's role as a cheesy cabaret hoofer Gable was more at home than Shearer was as Fontanne's pseudo-Russian playgirl. For some reason she tried to look and act exactly as Fontanne had done on stage, and comes off like a big stick of Tangee doing a corn dance.

But *The Women* found Shearer in her element as a patient wronged wife, though she had a hard time holding center screen against Rosalind Russell, Joan Crawford, Paulette Goddard, and—in a bit as a rich Reno regular—Mary Boland, who cries *"L'amour! L'amour!"* and orders incessant "wee drinkies." (There are no men in *The Women*, but at least there's a gay, cynical about love and forever in it.) Perhaps Shearer's heavy competition was Mayer's idea. Certainly Crawford, in the role she was raised to play as a man-eating moocher, was meant to steal *The Women*, for hers is the standout part.

But Shearer's fans were agog, for here at last was their idol stripped to her essence. Gone were the Elizabethan robes and the Louis XVI coiffeurs, gone the O'Neill and Coward, gone the Fontanne wig. It was Norma the town-and-country wife in her most convincing performance. For once, she's terrific, so comfortable in the dialogue and the day-to-day situations that one realizes how much was lost in her costume romances and melodramas. Here is one star who can really project the radiant contentment of a housewife, can define the idea of a happy marriage, and does it entirely by playing to servants and child. (Her husband, of course, never appears.) If Shearer had played more than one Mary Haines—tolerating bitchy friends; admiring her wise mother; confronting a spoiler with logic that won't hold; slipping down into divorce; and at last fighting for and retaking her man—Shearer might have been the unforgettable woman in film, the true wife.

Feminists are revolted by *The Women*'s philosophy (from the Broadway original by Clare Boothe Luce) but some of its lines, as adapted by Anita Loos and Jane Murfin, ring true today. "You can't trust any man," states a fashion clerk, and a model rejoins, "What else have we to give?" Or, from Paulette Goddard: "A woman's compromised the day she's born." Rosalind Russell says of Shearer, "Did you ever know such a housewife?" No one did, not even Thalberg—no one's this sublime. But we see at last what Shearer represented to America's women, in costume and out: the reasonable wife/mother that all aspire to be or know.

Shearer should have stopped there. Obviously, she was destined to reign in retirement as a village grandee and, despite *The Women*'s success, she knew her position was insecure. Three pointless films followed, then Shearer threw in the towel. Was she missed? Was Theda Bara missed or Little Mary or Colleen Moore or Janet Gaynor? Thalberg's canny schedule of roles for his wife, establishing her sweetness, developing this in tandem with some sensuality, combining this with a virtuous swank, kept her invulnerable to contemporary trends. And when she had to be modern, in *Idiot's Delight* and *The Women*, she could be. Yet two years later she was finished. *Was* she missed? She was irreplaceable; everyone in this book was. But they didn't stop making movies when she retired.

This same mysterious finish will shade the ends of the other two in MGM's Big Three, but with them other factors are involved. With Shearer it may have been industry politics. Mayer wanted her out and no one else in Hollywood wanted her in badly enough to flout him. There were reports in the mid-1940s that Shearer had signed with an independent company, but no footage was shot. Like many other retirees, she remained active on the Hollywood social circuit, presumably wearing red gowns to countless white balls till illness overtook her. But as actress the Pope's widow was displaced in 1942, by orders of an overwhelming pontificate.

> *Why do they want me to sign a contract*
> *for five years when I haven't even*
> *finished my first picture?*
>
> —GARBO
> in 1925

> *I feel so sorry for you.*
>
> —GARBO
> to a mob of fans, in 1931

> *You daughters of joy are always so*
> *gloomy. Why is that?*
>
> —RUTH GORDON
> to Garbo, in *Two-Faced*
> *Woman*

Greta Garbo's regime at MGM almost exactly coincided with Norma Shearer's, but no one guided Garbo. Nor did she share Shearer's variety of parts. "They don't have a type like me out here," she wrote to a friend back in Sweden not long after she arrived in Hollywood in 1925. But once they determined what type she was, they ran it over and over till it stuck in the projector and the public blacked out. "They" was not a consortium of image makers agreed on what Garbo was, but simply a succession of writers and directors who let Garbo be. What Garbo was, only Garbo knew.

She is often written about, yet the enigma has yet to be cracked. She is called the greatest actress the movies produced, and as often called a mere mechanic in love poses, sin grimaces, and kiss panels. She was still at her prime when she got out, but she stayed out. Intense on camera, she was limp and heedless in life; some actually thought her boring outside of her fame. No doubt her enigma is what has made the best of her films endlessly entrancing, for most of them are not very good films in general, and she left only a few performances worthy of her reputation.

It would seem that the Garbo riddles paradoxically enlighten the viewer: the less you are sure of about her, the more intimately you associate with her, for her mystery is so highly charged that it acts as its own information. By stripping away everything in her life but her performances, she—alone among Hollywood's stars—could be known solely, and therefore absolutely, through her characters. Her lines have passed into memory as things *she* said ("I want to be alone," for example), and her plots of adultery and death became the most believed fictions going. Her melancholy was so persuasive that when she appeared at the start of *Wild Orchids* (1929) laughing happily and easily, some part of the public insisted that MGM must have used a double.

Garbo did in fact have a guide like Shearer's Thalberg, but only at first. She came to MGM from Europe with director Mauritz Stiller as a package deal at Stiller's demand. He met her as a slightly plump student at the Academy of Stockholm's Royal Dramatic Theatre, renamed her,* coached her, and brought her to stardom in *Gösta Berling's Saga* (1924) and, on loan to Pabst in Berlin, *Die Freudlose Gasse* (1925). As she says, they didn't have a type like her in America, and MGM wasn't sure how to handle her when the two of them arrived. Stiller knew, but with the trouble they had been having with headstrong directors, Mayer and Thalberg thought it prudent to separate the two to keep them off balance. The self-willed, slow-moving Stiller was not to stay long in Hollywood, anyway, and Garbo didn't expect to last either when she saw her first American film, *The Torrent* (1926), in which she played about seven different parts.

It wasn't planned that way. *The Torrent,* from a Blasco-Ibáñez novel, presented Garbo as a village girl who becomes a legendary opera singer and courtesan, La Brunna. Neither scenarist Dorothy Farnum nor director Monta Bell knew what they had on their hands in Garbo, and, as if holding an audition, or staging a revue, turned her character around every reel or so. Somewhere in *The Torrent* are pieces of the Garbo to be, with her fatalistic vamp here, her worldly beauty there, her neurotic prima donna in between.

Garbo was miserable in Hollywood. She was baffled by the climate, couldn't speak the language, and mistrusted Mayer's nagging efforts to sign her to a long-term contract at low wages. Worse yet was the PR

*Her given and family names, Greta Gustafsson, are too well known to figure in a trivia question. However, collectors of arcana should make note of Stiller's early projection for a Garbo pseudonym, which he hoped would suggest all European nationalities at once: Mona Gabor. It sounds Hungarian to me.

people's bewilderment. PR stills, candid and posed, informal and dressy, were a given in building a star. But what is Garbo informal? When is she candid? The dressy shots were a cinch, for while she went around in clothes a goblin wouldn't die in, she wore sensational gowns with style. But the candids . . . well, those Swedes are outdoors types, right? They had her swimming, they snapped her with animals, they put her into uniform to pose with the USC track team. Garbo had to go along with it, but she noticed that Lillian Gish, then reigning as MGM's prestige star, never had to submit to such dishonor. Garbo resolved to become famous if only because fame would give her the power to make films and skip the et cetera.

The hardest blow of all was her segregation from Stiller, who was assigned to direct her second film, *The Temptress* (1926) but was replaced early on by Fred Niblo. Stiller had no trouble reading the Garbo persona; Niblo was trapped between wanting to let her show him how it went and not being able to follow it when she did. But MGM caught on to her quality quickly enough, if vaguely, and by the most basic Hollywood logic: foreign women are sexy women. Like Pola Negri, Marlene Dietrich, Hedy Lamarr, and Sophia Loren, Garbo played vamp. But times had changed since the days of the freewilling women who did not care. *Sunrise*'s Woman From the City in 1927 would mark the end of the remorseless hedonist, and the downfall of Clara Bow would serve as a warning. The sensualist must pay with suffering, even death.

Death suited Garbo, because she earned it with love scenes of astonishing commitment. Perhaps it helped that on her third American film, *Flesh and the Devil* (1927) she was truly involved with her co-star, John Gilbert. The two would embarrass the entire set by continuing their lovemaking long after the camera had ceased rolling. Already, Garbo is unique, not only as an actress but as a star. Gish, also unique, didn't so much break the rules as work around them. Shearer, unique by special position, obeyed the rules until she didn't have to, much. Crawford, as we shall see, thrived on them: the rules were her structure. Garbo shattered them. Nothing would have made MGM—and John Gilbert—happier than to see Gilbert and Garbo married, for the fans loved a true romance. In late 1926, when director King Vidor married actress Eleanor Boardman at Marion Davies' place, Garbo was expected to join with Gilbert as a second nuptial couple. She never showed. Gilbert went crazy. A few months later, he talked her into eloping with him; this time she turned up but wouldn't go through with it and ran away and hid. However, *Flesh and the Devil* survives to document their passionate attachment—their horizontal love duets, with Garbo as top man; or the famous church scene in which the camera pans down a line of worshippers taking communion and Garbo takes the cup to turn it around so she can drink from the spot Gilbert's lips have touched. The film is so hot that MGM had no choice but to kill Garbo off at the end and give Gilbert to another, less fraught woman in a tacked-on happy end.

*Flesh and the Devil,* a smash, established Garbo in style, and in many ways laid down the pattern for all her films: she is caught between two men, one her husband; she belongs to but does not entirely care for the luxurious society of balls and jewelry; she takes an almost male lead in love relationships; she cannot help herself; and she suffers. Now we know Garbo, as much as we ever will, for when her box-office take began to slip in the late 1930s and she stepped out of this pattern in her last two films, we know less about her than before. Or, better, we know irrelevant things.

What MGM knew was that Garbo was a sure bet, and here begins another little chapter in the saga of stardom, the contract war. Having worked and lived with Gilbert, one of the highest-paid actors in the business, Garbo realized how cheaply she had been selling herself, and demanded a raise from $600 to $5,000 a week. (For good reason, she also rejected *Women Love Diamonds,* on which she was about to start working.) Mayer screamed and wept; you don't get to be head of MGM without knowing how to manipulate people. But Garbo was something new in Mayer's office, the rule shatterer. She said, "I think I go home," and left. Mayer placed her on suspension and, as the weeks went by, hit her with admonitory letters and threatening telegrams. More weeks went by. Silence from Garbo. Meanwhile, *Flesh and the Devil* opened to its amazed reviews and record-breaking grosses and someone at MGM said, "Settle this thing *now!*" What if she means not just "I think I go home to my rented house with no furniture and a Swedish couple who run the whole place on a hundred dollars a week" but "I think I go home to Sweden and I don't come back"?

MGM gave in, to ride the Garbo-Gilbert wave with a modern-dress adaptation of *Anna Karenina,* providentially retitled so the marquees could proclaim "Greta Garbo and John Gilbert in *Love.*" At the age of twenty-two, she took precedence over the screen's biggest male name, and sailed on through the rest of the silent years with ease. Now she could say no to the PR teams and the press; she could order her sets closed to all except key personnel; she could disrupt Hollywood's social policy by refusing invitations or turning up uninvited, throwing a terrific gloom over everyone; and still, when the cameras weren't turning, there was nobody there. "Roll 'em!"—and untellable miseries would seep out of her, or insane joys, as when in *A Woman of Affairs* (1929) she staggers out of a hospital bed, sees a vase brimming with roses, a gift of her lover Gilbert, and clutches them, pets them as if they were Gilbert himself. Then she sees Gilbert, and wafts herself into his arms.

"I don't want much," she tells him by title card. "Only you." Then, "Cut!" and the life would drain out of her and she'd slump without a word toward her dressing room.

Much is made of the way she looked, of William Daniels' photography and Adrian's designs and her spectacular face. Still, it's how she sounded that enabled her to inaugurate her talkie years not only unimpaired in attraction but improved. Here was one silent actor whose voice accurately told what audiences had imagined they had heard in the silents. The great Gilbert went down in drunken despair when naturalistic talkies exposed his florid romantic style to ridicule, but Garbo had always acted naturalistically.

Still, if only because of her accent and her difficulty with English, MGM waited as long as it could, making the last Garbo silent, *The Kiss* (1929), when every other actor on the lot had already leaped into talkies. They hedged the bet, too, by giving her *Anna Christie* (1930), from O'Neill's play about a Swedish-American prostitute trying to settle down with a sailor despite her disgust for men. Garbo was even more anxious than her employers about acting in English, but MGM simultaneously made a German-language *Anna Christie* on the same sets with a different director and supporting cast.

Garbo needn't have worried. In the role, the accent was appropriate, and her first line, to a bartender, "Gimme a whiskey, ginger ale on the side—and don't be stingy, baby," gave off a throaty contralto that beautifully complemented the person. The film itself isn't very good, despite excellent casting. Charles Bickford as the sailor, George F. Marion as Anna's father, and Marie Dressler as the father's girlfriend go for it all the way, but their work suffers from the uneven rhythms of the early talkie. There are too many odd silences, too much static camera work, and Garbo wasn't as ready as her colleagues for the in-and-out of dialogue acting. It's no different in *Romance* (1930), from a dilapidated stage snuffler not unlike *Rain* but with an opera singer instead of a prostitute and New York instead of the tropics.

But in *Susan Lenox: Her Fall and Rise* (1931) Garbo made speech a tool of her highly concentrated mimesis. It is one of her best performances, unfortunately in one of her worst films, crudely scripted, poorly directed, sloppily edited, and with Chaikofsky's *Romeo and Juliet* love music soaring out at the most inopportune moments. Worst of all, opposite Garbo as the architect who nearly destroys himself with love for her is Clark Gable, at the time still a mere comer (his name in the opening credits falls under the title) with too little experience to stand up to Garbo's exhaustive naturalism. Other than from Adrian and cameraman Daniels, Garbo got no support on *Susan Lenox*.

Too bad; the film had possibilities. Based on a popular novel by David Graham Philips, it tells of an orphaned Swedish-American girl who runs away into a world of uncontrollable appetites. Her dour uncle sets it up for us in the first scene, putting the prude's curse on the Garbos of the world: "[Her mother] was pretty, too, and what did it bring her but disgrace?" An attractive woman is a sensual woman is a temptation, man bait—at least in an MGM film, which was family fare as a rule. How different it might have been if Garbo had managed to escape from MGM to Paramount (as, by the way, Stiller did), where men and women were equal partners in the sport of sexuality.

Garbo's uncle betroths her to a neighbor, who tries to rape her. See? Beauty leads to disgrace. Garbo flees, is taken in by Gable, but must again flee her searching uncle and fiancé. She leaps onto a train, only to blunder into a car filled with circus freaks. The *Fall* of the title begins here, for by the time Gable catches up with Garbo, engagement ring at the ready, she is a prisoner of the circus manager, another of the film's numerous exploiters, who are different from Gable in that they don't want to marry and don't have love-idol looks. MGM hadn't intended to say it, but as *Susan Lenox* progresses the feeling we get is that all men are exploiters—not sinners, like Garbo, but bad men, crooks. Even Gable won't listen to Garbo's explanation, throws away the ring, and calls her names. Now she sees it. "I'd always hated men till I met you," she tells him, and her mouth hardens as she adds, "From now on, it'll be different!"

She sleeps around for money, and the *Rise* begins. Now Garbo too, is an exploiter, but the worst exploiter of all is MGM, which in this and other films gave Garbo so little to work with in text and casting that she couldn't do her best work. An actor in her style of instinctive whole-person realism needs penetrating writing and elaborated characters to bring a part to life. A shallow script and obtuse fellow players queer her procedure. So it is here in *Susan Lenox*. A second-rate actor, a "personality" (as Gable was at this point in his career), can coast over the lines, relying on magnetism. A first-rate actor can present little more than what is in the material supplied. Sure, Garbo brings in wonderful touches in the open spaces between the lines, as in the nervously radiant ways she fidgets around Gable at the end of their first meeting, when he is leaving for a business trip. But this is a talkie, and it must speak; and when it speaks it's dumb.

Anyway, *Susan Lenox*'s plot deteriorates into a back and forth between Gable's attempt to escape Garbo's spell and her helpless pursuit of him. Toward the end she finds him in some tropical rathole looking like dirty work at the crossroads, unshaven and ill. Gable says he's made of "hate, booze, insects, damp rot, and sweat" and it's her fault. But Garbo patiently reasons it out for them. Separate, they're cripples; together, they're straight. "I'll make you believe in me," she insists at the fadeout.

"They don't have a type like me out here." How right that was. No one in Hollywood acted with such nuanced precision—indeed, the

American stage was only just formulating comparable acting technique in Lee Strasberg's coaching of the Group Theatre, and even the Stanislafsky-trained Nazimova was as devoted to the Big Moments of the old glamour stage as she was to life-scaled characterization. For all its polish, MGM seldom met Garbo on her own level, as it did Shearer: polish was all Shearer really needed. This is perhaps why Garbo's detractors don't see what Garbo's supporters see: the work of an actress who relied on architectonics too sensitive for studio-factory screenplay and direction.

MGM couldn't challenge Garbo's craft, so it concentrated on designing her clothes and reflecting gems in her eyes. With its circus sideshow and *Rain*-derived bar, *Susan Lenox* gave us a Garbo cut off from many of the components of her exotic allure, so MGM carefully reshaped the alien idol in her next film, *Mata Hari* (1932). Here Garbo's ambiguity and contradictions are raised to the utmost degree, as a woman in a man's job (as spy), a woman of no patriotic loyalty (she lives in France, works for Germany, and carries hints of an Eastern background), a woman who uses men and then inadvertently allows herself to be used, a woman of calculation and impulse, of passivity and impetuosity, a woman of disguises who suddenly emits the most direct statements about herself. This was the Garbo everyone adored, who could make more or less the same movie over and over because her momentous impenetrability kept them from feeling finished when they were over. In each film, she longs for death yet struggles when it comes; she knows that romance is fatal and resists it in so many little gasps of revulsion or fear that we never can see the point at which she gives in to it; and she can kill, yet the merest twinge of menace depresses her. Her whole MGM career—once arrived in America, she worked for no other studio—floated on these puzzles, still unresolved. No wonder they haven't stopped talking about her four decades after she retired. You have to keep going to Garbo's films to find out how the first one ended.

She is not all fatalist. When breaking taboos she is witty, as if offending tribal values is her only fun. She really does enjoy Mata Hari's lascivious dance performed before a statue of Siva; and seducing Ramon Novarro, a naive, mother-loving lieutenant in the Russian Imperial Air Force, is child's play. "I love you as one adores sacred things," Novarro tells her, but she treats him as Bara vamp might have done in their night together, in a room lit by an icon of the Madonna. Novarro's mother made him promise to keep it always illuminated, so naturally Garbo wants him to put it out. He refuses.

"I'm going," she tells him. And she will, too.

"Forgive me," he whispers, as if in church. Lights out. And the next morning as she leaves, she relights the icon with a sardonic smile.

Garbo's stardom makes a hash of Marshall Neilan's list of star qualities, for her essential quality was that she had none. She doesn't even know who she is in *As You Desire Me* (1932), as a cabaret singer suffering amnesia; and the last lingering shot of *Queen Christina* (1933) shows absolutely nothing: Garbo's face. It is the most expressive face in film, yet here, with Garbo playing the Swedish queen who abdicates for love and then loses her lover, it is intently empty, to serve the most enticingly incomplete of all her fadeouts. "Think of nothing," director Rouben Mamoulian told her, "I want your face to be a blank sheet of paper. I want the writing to be done by every member of the audience."* Earlier in the film she has topped this with an extraordinary ballet in the room in which she has been startled by romance. With her Spanish lover watching, she walks through their tavern bedroom caressing its furnishings. The bureau, the mirror, the spinning wheel, the bedclothes. One is mesmerized.

"What are you doing?" her lover asks.

"Memorizing this room. In the future, in my memory, I shall live a great deal in this room." She hugs the room, embraces it. And tells him, "The Lord must have felt like this when he created the living world."

John Gilbert played the Spaniard in *Queen Christina* at Garbo's insistence. She had first approved Laurence Olivier, but the two could mix no chemistry in their rehearsals. An icy Garbo would decimate a Garbo film; insouciance was one quality this woman must never project. "At the touch of my hand," Olivier recalled, "Garbo became frigid. I could feel the sudden tautness of her." Mamoulian gave them a break and sent them off to talk and get used to each other. Back on the set, still nothing. Inscrutable Garbo gave no explanation, but, as her contract empowered her to do, she effected a replacement—Gilbert, almost totally destroyed by his succession of talkie disasters and only one year away from death.

Mayer must have been seething at the affront to his revenge plot, and in any case Gilbert was little more than a walking shadow. But his magic still told for Garbo. "'Now I Help You,' Says Garbo to Gilbert," crowed *Photoplay*, typically eager to smooth over the rotten heart of Hollywood for the blissful fans. Forget Garbo's remoteness, forget the rumors of the studio arrangement for Gilbert's downfall. Gilbert was nice to Garbo on *Flesh and the Devil* six years before and now Garbo is nice to Gilbert. "Who will say," the article concludes, "that royalty knows no gratitude—or that Garbo lacks warm human feeling?" An accompanying photo shows the two shaking hands and beaming at each other.

We know there was more to this than *Photoplay* can tell, at the very

---

*Josef von Sternberg secured a comparable effect from Marlene Dietrich at the end of *Morocco* by asking his star to count backwards from twenty-five.

least a tumultuous love affair. Chivalry is complex. Perhaps Garbo was also concerned about the level of collaboration MGM had supplied her with on her previous seventeen films. Norma Shearer, who had first call on everyone for her pictures, worked in these early talkie years with the likes of Sidney Franklin, Robert Z. Leonard, Clarence Brown, George Fitzmaurice, and Edmund Goulding, decent *routiniers,* seldom if ever keen. MGM was simply not a great studio for directors; keen directors were too self-willed to suit the paternalistic MGM factory. True, George Cukor and Ernst Lubitsch both flourished there, and it should be said that Goulding's best pictures are wonderfully brought off. But Paramount, Warner Brothers, and Columbia (for Frank Capra, if no one else) are the studios that gave their directors creative play. Even as MGM's unique property, Garbo had to make do with only okay leadership.

Art direction and wardrobe design were of course luxurious, and her co-stars numbered among the top rank. Gilbert appeared with her three times in their heyday as a silent team, and Lars Hanson in *The Divine Woman* and John Barrymore in *Grand Hotel* partnered her well. But too often she was married to men like Lewis Stone and bedded with boys like Lew Ayres. (Shearer, by contrast, ran through the studio contract list from Gable to Leslie Howard without having to worry about whether her screen lovers would match her energy. If anything, they had to play down for her.) Rouben Mamoulian, at the time of *Queen Christina* a big item in Hollywood for *Applause, Love Me Tonight, Dr. Jekyll and Mr. Hyde,* and the just-released *Song of Songs* (with Marlene Dietrich), was the first great director Garbo got to work with. Perhaps she wanted Gilbert around not only to give him a break but to assure herself of an adequate partner.

In the event, Gilbert's performance does not matter much. *Queen Christina* is Garbo's most soloistic vehicle, made of pictures of loneliness and alienation. These, too, add to the Garbo riddles. How can a woman so isolated become so involved with her love partners? Even as Anna Karenina (1935), in her second version of the part, she is alone, not because Fredric March isn't really with her—he isn't, but that's not why. Here, at the height of her abilities as the screen's most absorbing romantic, Garbo pulls along on her own steam, acting as much despite as with her fellows. Scenarists were writing lines that Garbo "might" herself have said: "I shall die a bachelor" *(Queen Christina),* or "One day I shall find myself alone" *(Anna Karenina),* or "I am not afraid of anything except being bored" *(Camille),* or "I knew I was too happy" *(Camille).* Even the other players have caught the drift. In *Anna Karenina,* her mother tells her, "You, my dear, have the divine gift of silence"; at the end, after she has killed herself in despair over March's rejection, a friend tells him, like a fan consoling a fan, "It was fate. She was doomed."

Her loneliness was a sometime thing. Reporters delighted in spying on Garbo in the company of conductor Leopold Stokowski, and the public thrilled to gaffes that were bound to result from Garbo's dedication to privacy, such as the day Louella Parsons of the *Los Angeles Examiner* told of the Garbo-Stokowski wedding plans while Sidney Skolsky, also of the *Examiner*, told there were none. (Skolsky was correct, and Parsons had him bumped out of his job. A few weeks after, Skolsky ran into Parsons in a restaurant and bit her arm.)

Moreover, since losing the guidance of Mauritz Stiller when he returned to Sweden in 1927, Garbo had acquired other advisers, so she was not totally on her own. Writers Mercedes de Acosta and Salka Viertel drummed up ideas for new roles, the latter with some certain bearing on the Garbo case, having played the Marie Dressler part in the German-language *Anna Christie* and co-authored screenplays for a number of Garbo's films. Both women favored the heavy European chamber epics Garbo had already done to death, but how many more times was MGM to film the same story in the same setting?

After *Anna Karenina* came *Camille* (1936), with Robert Taylor very adequate as Armand—no puppy can fail in that role—and the extremely purposive direction of George Cukor backing up the familiar Garbo doings: a little polka in a party scene, nibbly kisses in her first love scene with Taylor, suspense when her bill-paying baron sadistically makes her miss a crucial rendezvous with Taylor, suggestions that Taylor is both the last in a humdrum series and "the romance of my life," faintings, the opera of gloves and gossip, ardor, bill collectors, country air, despair, Paris flats, she knew she was too happy. Cukor gives the film a lot of personality by following the escapades of Garbo's demimonde circle. Olympe (Lenore Ulric) dances a can-can, Prudence (Laura Hope Crews, the virginal Miss Pittypat of *Gone With the Wind*) smokes a cigar and chatters as she empties the dying Garbo's purse of its last pennies, Gaston (Rex O'Malley) is gay, and the atmosphere is rich. For once we have more than Garbo to fascinate us. Cukor later observed that she was born to play the part, and so she surely was, all her parts. They were all Camille, though, all—in Cukor's words—"the author of her own misery"; and after *Camille* she needed something different. She was the highest-paid contractee in town at $275,000 a picture and almost certainly the most prestigious actor in film. But while her costume settings and epoch-defying Lilith protected her from the perils of contemporaneity, her unanswered questions were about to tire the audience. Was she never to come to earth?

Well, that's a goddess for you. Since 1933, Garbo had been making one film a year, like Shearer, but *Conquest* (1937), with Charles Boyer as Napoleon and Garbo as his mistress, was hardly the kind of standout production that Shearer could count on. *Conquest* can't have done all that well, either, as MGM paid Garbo only $125,000 for her next film.

But at last she got the odd item her catalogue had so long needed, something fleet and droll to split the difference between her customary extremes of sacred and profane. Something *sensible*. With Lubitsch directing, Melvyn Douglas and Ina Claire in support, and, hallelujah, contemporary Paris for venue, Garbo had the rare chance to fill out her profile with a little banter as a Soviet hardliner who softens in love with a suave Parisian.

The film was hard to name. MGM tried and rejected, among others, *We Want to Be Alone, A Kiss From Moscow, Time Out for Love,* and *A Kiss in the Dark* before settling on the name of Garbo's character, *Ninotchka*. The Slavic nickname is just right, for its informality conveys the film's sense of mischief, of letting Garbo have a little fun for once. As she strides into view, on a mission to sell disputed Tsarist jewelry that former Grand Duchess Ina Claire is after, she is coldly doctrinaire, everything politicized, from the sights of Paris to sex. In a restaurant she asks for raw beets and carrots. "Madame," the waiter tells her, "this is a restaurant, not a meadow." Morosely chewing real food, she is joined by Melvyn Douglas, who, involved in some badinage, loses his balance and takes a tumble, chair and all. And Garbo laughs.

Laughs? She roars. MGM thought enough of the moment to base *Ninotchka*'s PR on it, and it's fair, for it remains, on multiple viewings, one of her most endearing turns. Some critics have called the film a mean burlesque, but Ninotchka is just the latest version of Garbo's unique woman. She has been this dour before, this absorbed before, and the love scene finds her, as before, taking a strong lead. Touring the technical achievements of Paris, she meets Douglas, lets him serve as her guide, and visits his apartment for an instructive expedition into the bourgeois habitat. When they're settled in, he kisses her. "Again," she orders. He obeys. Some talk. Then she kisses him, literally taking him as she always took her men. And when he says, "Again," it comes out like a sigh. Later, when she melts from commissar into a woman in love, she is more than ever like Anna Karenina and Camille. If this is burlesque, all of Garbo is burlesque. It is certainly her most consistent performance and remains by far the best-made film she appeared in. No, it didn't answer any of the Garbo riddles. It's a holiday.

Sadly, the process of divesting the goddess of her remote kismet fantasy went too far in the succeeding *Two-Faced Woman* (1941), a cross between *The Guardsman* and *Dr. Jekyll and Mr. Hyde*. With the hefty European market closed to American film, MGM determined to Americanize Garbo, strapping her into skis, sloshing her into a pool, teaching her to rumba. And her persona was broken up into two parts, a cool number from the snow country and a lady of the New York nightclubs. They are the same woman: Garbo marries big-time magazine editor Melvyn Douglas, finds him openly scornful of her independence, and pursues him to New York to toy with him as her "twin sister." Though Cukor was in charge, the product is slick and unfair, like a penance assigned Garbo for her years of rule busting. Actually, she's quite adept in the rumba sequence, introducing a new dance she dubs the "chicachoca" and so igniting the nitery that Constance Bennett, Douglas' old flame, engages Garbo in a confrontation in the powder room.

"What kind of woman *are* you?" Bennett cries.

"Honest."

Bennett almost hits her. Then: "You made me lose my poise. For that I shall never forgive you."

Garbo doesn't lose hers, but she can't have been comfortable in a witless sex comedy, and the public didn't buy it. *Ninotchka*'s "Garbo laughs!" was enticing (though it was by no means the first time); but "Garbo dances the rumba!" sounded inane. Now she pulled back. Of the millions she had made she had spent about $1.35 and invested the rest, so there was no financial pressure to work. She thought over the possibilities—a film about Bernhardt, about Madame Curie (Greer Garson took that one), a film of Shaw's *St. Joan* (the backing collapsed), of Chekhof's *The Cherry Orchard,* of Tennessee Williams' *A Streetcar Named Desire.* The years went by. In 1950, she said, "I'm sort of drifting."

She never made another film; that too adds to the legend. To neglect the alleged rewards of fame by not even showing up to claim them is fascinating, if only because it's so unusual in an egocentric business. But to quit, even while one is behind, is unthinkable. Not since Farrar had an actress shown herself so heedless of Hollywood, not even staying behind as they all did to give dinners and attend premieres; not even listening, I bet, to the Garbo natter that began to rev up all over again in the late 1950s when Old Movies came into their own. "Always the vomp I am," she had complained, somewhere between *Flesh and the Devil* and *Susan Lenox.* Yet her legend is sacred, not profane, the memory of a saint of sensuality, chaste because she was invulnerable to the corruptions of stardom, the hustling, the whoring, the Mae Murray megalomania. "What kind of woman *are* you?" she is asked, and answers, "Honest."

> *Without discipline what is life?*
>
> —JOAN CRAWFORD

> *Crawford was a warrior.*
>
> —FAYE DUNAWAY

Garbo disdained the system and Shearer married it. Joan Crawford thrived on it. No one was more enthusiastic about cooperating with the

PR photographers, no one more interested in what the fans actually said in those letters, no one more ready to learn from a production staff willing to teach, no one happier to take a producer's fatherly advice, and no one worked harder. She was, largely, what she showed on screen, a ballsy woman, crazed to be liked, admired, and loved. She was as well an intelligent woman who profited from experience, so when her days as a studio hotshot seemed about to end, she engineered her own comeback, and did it so skillfully that it won her the awe of the entire film industry. Her story has the fixings for a gala saga—*A Star Is Born* and *The Rich Little Poor Girl* and *Gentlemen Marry Brunettes* all in one—except it begins sadly and ends bitterly and now, with the wide popularity of *Mommie Dearest,* book and film, seems ready to turn into something like *Jaws.*

In an important way Joan Crawford is one of stardom's tragic figures, because she was one of the few who knew exactly how it worked and what it meant, yet even she could not master it. Like Little Mary, Crawford knew how to build the toy and how to repair it but not how to keep it from breaking down. Louella Parsons said, "Joan Crawford manufactured herself," and Crawford said, "You manufacture toys. You don't manufacture stars." Nevertheless, there are procedures for stardom, and Crawford learned them. She lived through Hollywood's mid-prime talkie glamour days and saw them all crash, the men dead and the women abandoned or betrayed by bad pictures. Even as convinced fans called her the greatest of movie stars, the definition of kind, even as writers told of her climb to the summit, even as drag queens did Mildred Pierce into their mirrors, in the opulent, pathetic homage of the loser to the winner . . . she was dying alone in despair. Joan Crawford broke down.

It's quite a tale. Lucille Fay LeSueur, nickname Billie, Texas girl, broken home, a loveless mother and a worthless brother. Like Mae Murray, she came into film as a dancer, hitting MGM just after Shearer did and simultaneously with Garbo, along with the usual carload of $50-a-week starlets, most of whom would be dropped after six months, would hang on looking for extra work, and would eventually vanish. But this one had good luck, catching some eye and getting the treatment, class B. There were small parts and leads in lesser films. There was a Let's-Rename-Lucille contest in *Movie World.* ("Joan Arden" won, but there already was one; back to the entries; eureka! "Joan Crawford," plain yet tinged with fancy; perfect!) There was a lead in a fine picture, *Sally, Irene and Mary* (1925), with Constance Bennett and Sally O'Neil as three showgirls on stage and in love. Crawford was put into all sorts of films. She did a Harry Langdon comedy on loan at First National, a costume melodrama, a Lon Chaney thriller, romances with John Gilbert and Ramon Novarro, a William Haines society comedy, the silent adaptation of the operetta *Rose-Marie* (1928), a Tim McCoy western. She hit pay dirt in one of the last of the jazz-age silents, *Our Dancing Daughters* (1928).

This was another of the threesome films that Hollywood made and remade throughout the studio era, but Crawford is unquestionably the star, and her dancing is a big deal. The film's very first shot presents the Crawford legs already stepping as she dresses in a triple mirror; and the famous scene at the local yacht club shows her hearing the band, getting the rhythm, shaking her wild young head, and, as she throws off her skirt, breaking into a charleston. The scene says as much about egotism and sex in the 1920s as John Travolta's disco turn did in the 1970s in *Saturday Night Fever*. *Our Dancing Daughters* placed Joan Crawford.

As Diana Medford, she's wild and self-centered only on the surface. She drinks a toast "to myself" and wants it known that she's "Diana the Dangerous" but in fact she's steadfast among friends, fair to enemies, and, like Colleen Moore, virtuous in the Victorian sense. All the girls are mad about Johnny Mack Brown, former college football hero and heir to millions, so of course Diana the Dangerous will play him for a kiss. But when he responds and takes her in his arms like a caveman in a dinner jacket, her face registers real surprise. Nor will Crawford attempt to steal him away from Anita Page, though Page only married Brown for his money and is obviously cheating on him. (MGM can fix it; drunken Page tumbles down the yacht club stairway to her death; and when Crawford returns from a two-year stay abroad, she and Brown clinch for the fadeout.)

Diana Medford's code of values stirred the women in the audience. Here was a "Modern" who had all the fun without sacrificing the old morality. In the age of Clara Bow, this was . . . quaint, yet somehow progressive. Crawford's two co-stars in *Our Dancing Daughters,* Page and Dorothy Sebastian, fell by the wayside in due course, but Crawford the Dangerous sped onward.

And upward: by learning. Edmund Goulding, director of *Sally, Irene and Mary,* warned her not to exhaust the audience by overacting. A cameraman told her to lose weight to show off her cheekbones. William Haines advised her to date at the right places to get mentions in the columns. L. B. Mayer ordered her never to appear in public out of star regalia. She herself figured out that introducing herself to all the assistants on the set would pay off, and she forced herself, despite natural terror, to face the press with a front of self-assurance. Learn it, then do it. *Make* it work.

One thing she couldn't learn her way out of was feeling like a peasant among gentry. No other business in history threw together people of such disparate backgrounds as Hollywood did. Aristocrat, bourgeois, and proletarian crossed paths every other minute, working, socializing, and making love under the eye of some of the most crass men ever to hold power (the producers), with only a thin border class of he-men and aesthetes (the directors) to keep the whole thing amiable. Accordingly, Crawford made her first two marriages with men completely out of her cultural ken, one a preppie juvenile who was virtually Hollywood royalty and the other an intellectual with art-theatre leanings and leftist politics. Typically, she made the effort to live up to their standards, to affect their tastes. It was hard labor.

This was why Crawford and Clark Gable got on so well together for so long, sexually and personally. They were both nowhere kids who had made it with the heavies, and could cheer each other up with the earthy truths of their common experience when the *fantaisie* of film threatened to engulf them. Why Crawford never married Gable is a mystery—unless it was because they were too much alike—but it is notable that she was the one whom he went to for solace the night he learned of Carole Lombard's death. In any case, given her outsider's feelings, her first marriage was a lulu—to the scion of Pickfair, Douglas Fairbanks, Jr.

Junior had all the points his father resented not having: he was tall, suave by instinct, almost entirely Aryan (Senior was part Jewish), and at ease with big men (Senior wanted to kill them, or at least best them with some athletic stunt). Many people viewed the marriage as a logical extension of the roles Crawford played, a dream of a fadeout. To their discredit, Little Mary and Senior tried to discourage the match, fearing ridicule if their Anglophile resonance were cut with Crawford's hard-baked American grit. Imagine the girl at Pickfair! She'll drink from the fingerbowl, wipe her nose on the drapes! They "would cheerfully have poisoned me before the wedding if they'd had a chance," Joan recalled. But to the fans it was the Cinderella hour. Crawford, however much the society gem in *Our Dancing Daughters*, was the quintessential American shopgirl, and her marrying Douglas Fairbanks, Jr., was making the dream true.

Thousands relished every tidbit of gossip about the engagement. But *Photoplay* was not able to tell its readers of Crawford's tortures at Pickfair, the afternoons spent knitting while the boys went off somewhere and Little Mary stumbled up to her nappy, or the dinners with the intimidating varieties of forks to sort out and Little Mary's little eyes taking in every move you make. Douglas and Joan married in June of 1929, after she had successfully hurdled sound; and by the time it ended, in 1933, Crawford had grown from a fledgling open to anything and doing everything well enough to a pro who knew her strengths from her weaknesses. The PR people could still get anything out of her—her head blooming out of a rose, a Ziegfeldian showgirl pose, anything—and she was still answering her fan mail in longhand, sending out hundreds of cards, thanking people, keeping a list. She was also growing artistically. She weathered her first big failure, Sadie

Thompson in *Rain* (1932)—Crawford might be a loose woman but her hard-worked cover poise forbade her playing one—and scored her first big achievement, the stenographer Flaemmchen in *Grand Hotel* (1932).

No film belongs more to the old golden Hollywood than this collage of star turns checking into and out of an Art Deco hotel in Berlin: Garbo as a manic-depressive ballerina, John Barrymore as a jewel thief, Wallace Beery as a coarse businessman, Lionel Barrymore as a terminally ill clerk on a spree, and Lewis Stone as a doctor with a hideous scar ruining half his face. "Grand Hotel," he intones at the start. "People coming, going. Nothing ever happens." Plenty happens. For one thing, Crawford gives a better performance than Garbo. True, this is one of Garbo's most praised portrayals, including her signature "I want to be alone," delivered in a tutu and simply, with no epic reverberations. (We add those.) But she jumps from the manic to the depressive too readily, while Crawford shines it out so smoothly the film might almost be a documentary.

She's all over the picture, too, flirting with John Barrymore, perking up Lionel, working for and loathing Beery; and throughout she's as comfortably natural as she was back in her first films when she put all her effort into dancing you into belief. She has no scene with Garbo, yet it was said that she had stolen some of Garbo's airs. Ridiculous. Two more different kinds of actress there never were. Edmund Goulding might have been less than Garbo needed as a director, but he was right up Crawford's alley, and *Grand Hotel* is his best job. Sure, everyone's in a different style; that's what all-star casts are for. Garbo invents her own genre, John Barrymore is high comedy, Lionel is weepie, Beery (the only one who attempts an accent) is thud-and-blunder melodrama, Stone is austere and military, and Crawford, in superb Adrian outfits, is from life. It's the best thing she ever did.

Riding out the embarrassment of *Rain,* Crawford entered a new phase, as superstar, a force in the culture. Her broad-shouldered *Letty Lynton* (1932) dresses revolutionized women's fashions; her second marriage, to Franchot Tone, showed an almost intellectual maturity; and she was now graciously giving advice to youngsters instead of needing it herself. Best of all, she felt so secure in her persona that she dared challenge it by playing the villain in *The Women.* Crystal Allen is the inversion of the usual Crawford heroine, a girl from the wrong side of the tracks who gets ahead not through fair play and steady work but through cheating and lazing around in bathtubs. But the fans enjoyed the ruse, and there were charming stories of sound-stage snarling between Crawford and Shearer. All was well.

But just as the start of the 1940s signaled the end of the Shearer and Garbo reigns, time was chasing Crawford—Hollywood time, the history of youth. New people were always coming along, and it was easier to type them straight out than to think of something new for the veterans. (Look what happened to Garbo in *Two-Faced Woman.*) Shearer and Garbo drifted away. But Crawford did everything with a take-no-prisoners determination, and to break with MGM was momentous for her. All her loyalties lay in that place, all the manufacturing or whatever it was that devised Joan Crawford. There are two versions of what happened. Either Mayer pushed her out, or she asked for her freedom. However it happened, she went to Warner Brothers in 1943 and sat down to wait for the right script, as long as it took. Make it work.

It took two years, but it was worth it: *Mildred Pierce* (1945). This one launched another era for Crawford, in a new persona as a stiff, angry woman slapping men around in stupid, turgid films about possessiveness and vengeance. The MGM Crawford was lithe and spunky, above all *warm*. The Warners Crawford is carved ice. But it didn't hurt her career. On the contrary, *Mildred Pierce*, which set her new type, is her most famous film.

Based on a novel by James Cain, it feels somewhat like Joan's own story as she might have told it, with a hard rise to power (from waitress to restaurateur), an ungrateful daughter, a weak husband, and an exploitive boyfriend. The film is compelling, an apotheosis of Crawford's MGM Cinderellas in the dark disquiet of Warners *film noir*. A murder mystery—who killed Zachary Scott?—it has its surprises, and the violence of the scenes between Crawford and her older daughter, Ann Blyth, are horrifying, climaxing in Crawford's "Get out of here before I kill you!" Yet she is willing to take the murder rap for Blyth. She's still a sport, still loyal. But the toughness of the real-life Crawford is spilling out.

It did so on the sound stages as well as on screen. Crawford still courted the grips and put total trust in the director, but she was increasingly quarreling with her friends and turning on her younger rivals. A third marriage, too, was failing. Worst of all, the proud Hollywood that she had grown up in had fallen apart. The studios were still operating, many of the old-time moguls still running them. But the glory was gone. People weren't dressing up anymore, the fans weren't fun to write to, stars were dying off, and the new movies were drab, Crawford's most of all. At MGM she had danced with Fred Astaire, joked with Robert Montgomery, made love to Gable, *acted* with John Barrymore and Fredric March. At Warner Brothers she got David Brian and Steve Cochran. Say *who*? *Mildred Pierce* mummified her. And she was aging. Her cooch dance in *Flamingo Road* (1949) is unflattering. Her casually barbed "shut up" to friends and foes alike in *The Damned Don't Cry* (1950) is silly. Her fast burn is a riot; enter pursuing a bear. Her imperial housewife in *Harriet Craig* (1950) is prosaic, correct but without the desperation that Rosalind Russell brought to the same part in *Craig's Wife* (1936).

Crawford had turned into Mildred Pierce, probably because so much was riding on that role and so much came from it. She had single-handedly pulled herself back on top, copped an Oscar—Hollywood loves nothing as much as a comeback—and become famous all over. But by the 1950s Crawford was a freelancer, almost a has-been, taking anything offered her.

Her inability to cope with reduced eminence exploded on the set of *Johnny Guitar* (1954), an unusual western made by Republic, a small studio that the MGM Crawford wouldn't have thrown her garbage out in. Directed by the cult favorite Nicholas Ray in Republic's own Trucolor (the world's first camp technology) and taking in Sterling Hayden, Mercedes McCambridge, Scott Brady, and John Carradine, *Johnny Guitar* is no cheaporama quickie. But Crawford was at her unprofessional worst during production, picking a fight with McCambridge and willfully, helplessly turning it into a feud. "You know how some people don't hit it off with each other? That's the way it was with us," she told an interviewer on the set. Oh, come on. It was Mildred Pierce bashing out at the disloyal world. Think of it: one of MGM's big three, superior to Shearer and "her three expressions" and second only to Garbo (but Joan had more fan clubs): the great Joan Crawford demoted to a poverty-row programmer!

It's not a bad credit, for Ray has a way of taking in all the clichés of genre as if he had never met them before, and Crawford is well cast as the owner of a gambling saloon in wild Arizona, living in a man's world by men's rules. She's still pushy and unyielding, but that kind of behavior is what westerns are about. "Never seen a woman who was more like a man," says one of her employees. "Looks like one, acts like one, and sometimes makes me feel I'm not." McCambridge plays her archenemy, a sexually introverted rancher who hates Crawford out of neurotic jealousy and finally organizes a lynch party to get rid of her. With two feuds in action, one in the plot and one in life, the press had a grand old time. Reporters hoping for a Scene took lines down from the script and quoted them as if they were backstage encounters.

Not that Crawford was no longer capable of bearing herself with generosity. But she was too much the star now, demanding a certain temperature on the set (it was low; the unwary caught colds), certain co-stars, certain changes in each script. She played a woman so vicious and destructive in *Queen Bee* (1955) that John Ireland could only arrange for a happy ending by killing them both in a car crash. Sad to say, the 1950s found this Mildred Crawford as easy to believe in as moviegoers in 1928 found gallant Diana Medford of *Our Dancing Daughters*. Young Joan was a revelry, a little off center. One never knew

what she would do next. Old Joan was the same in every film, the
tough broad who grabs love. It became a routine, and writers preparing her scripts parsed her into shtick like puzzle makers working the
jigsaw. Take *Female on the Beach* (1955), with Crawford as a lonely rich
woman involved with beachboy Jeff Chandler, who may be trying to
kill her. We get Crawford cool:

CHANDLER: People like me.
CRAWFORD: Not everybody.

Crawford sarcastic:

I'd like to ask you to stay and have a drink—but I'm afraid you might
    accept.

Crawford angry:

You're about as friendly as a suction pump!

and Crawford in rut, visiting Chandler on his boat:

CHANDLER: (as she leans in for a kiss) You'll get grease on you.
CRAWFORD: Will I? (She takes him; they break.)
CHANDLER: See, I was right. I left a mark on you.
CRAWFORD: You'd leave a mark on me anyway.

The gallantry was gone, and so was the stardom. By the early 1960s,
Crawford was, as they say, not bankable. No one wanted to do anything
with her at all.

    This is a familiar tale, the official truism of this book. They come,
they are seen, they are given the world, they are dropped. Bette Davis
was in a comparable position by then, and when director Robert Aldrich got the idea of using Crawford and Davis in a *guignol* about two
has-been actress sisters, no studio would touch it, not even on a minus-
cule budget. Finally Aldrich talked Seven Arts, a Warner subsidiary,
into going ahead with *Whatever Happened to Baby Jane?* (1962), and of
course the film cleaned up. With Mildred Pierce and Jezebel on the
same set, the press made even more of the fighting than they had done
on *Johnny Guitar,* though this time there was no fighting. Crawford
even submitted to playing the weaker sister, a cripple at the mercy of
murderous Baby Bette. With Davis taking all the best lines and weirdo
bits and with the film's final shots going to Davis' black-comic mad
scene on a beach, Davis was sure to get the reviews. But perhaps acting
with one of the biggies of her own generation heartened Crawford,

proved that the filmtown Oz she had so loved was still available for a visit.

*Mildred Pierce,* Crawford's first comeback film, had recreated Crawford the star. *Baby Jane* created Crawford the stooge of camp horror. Her four last pictures, though she took them seriously, as she took everything, were quack thrillers, cheap and sleazy. In *Strait Jacket* (1964) she is suspected of being an axe murderess. When it turns out that she is innocent, the audience loses interest in the picture: she *should* be an axe murderess, given the tone of the productions she is involved with. Off screen, she got better work as an executive of Pepsi-Cola, a job which came with her fourth and favorite husband, Alfred Steele. Crawford had faded out of the American limelight, but internationally she was still a honcho. With her on his arm, Steele was able to open up numerous foreign markets for his product. As always, Crawford applied herself to the new task, learned about it, made it work. But when Steele died, new comers in the corporation began to ease her out of the boardroom just as Mayer may have done with Shearer after Thalberg's death.

At least Crawford outlasted her two partners of the MGM Big Three, and by some thirty years; and her fame outlasted her life. She is better known now than ever, but as what? An imperious grande dame of tawdry films who, when no one was looking, abused her two older children and paid lifelong blackmail to the owner of the negative of a stag film she is supposed to have made in about 1918. The truth in these matters will never be known; besides, Crawford is legend: truth is irrelevant.

How much finer is the memory of Garbo. Even Shearer is well spoken of except by critics who don't like her performances. It's tempting to ask where Crawford went wrong in her career choices. Should she have gone freelance in 1943 instead of signing with Warners? Could she have found a nicer film than *Mildred Pierce,* something to broaden rather than narrow her range (which was never broad to begin with)? Should she have gone into television work in the early 1950s, when any film star who was willing to do so could write his or her own ticket?

These options were unthinkable for someone trapped in the rhythm of the studio. MGM stars were like children, all important decisions made for them. How could such people suddenly run their own careers? And what star balanced between status and ruin could turn down a script as right as *Mildred Pierce* was for Crawford? Weak scripts stopped Shearer; hesitation buried Garbo. And early television, with its live audiences and bad name in Hollywood, would have both scared and shamed Crawford. When she did at last try it, she was terrible.

Yes, she had the drive to succeed, the willingness to pay success's prices, and the intelligence to pick The Script when it most counted. But when she left MGM she lost a father, L. B. Mayer, who lavished paternal encouragement on those who begged him for guidance and who reserved special honors for those who followed it against their own inclinations. Joan was one who did, and one of the few who defended him for life against his critics. *Loyalty.* That was her great quality, her vulnerability, and it showed while she was at MGM, when she had people to be loyal to; and it flickered at Warner Brothers, when she was cut off from those people; and it died when the studios released their contractees and she got fewer and fewer offers. She had been loyal to the industry and got nothing in the end and finished up an alcoholic recluse afraid to go out in public and show them what failure looks like. Who can blame her? When she and Rosalind Russell co-hosted a party in honor of John Springer's book *They Had Faces Then,* the newspapers printed the most rotten pictures a photographer could snap, Russell's face bloated from the antibiotics she was taking for arthritis and Crawford looking like a roc. "If that's how I look," said Crawford, "they won't see me again."

They didn't. She died in 1971, of unemployment.

# 5

# Women's
# Women:
# The Ladies

RUTH CHATTERTON
ANN HARDING
HELEN HAYES
LYNN FONTANNE
JEANETTE MACDONALD
MYRNA LOY
IRENE DUNNE
MARGARET DUMONT
GREER GARSON

*If [Greer Garson] were not so suffocated
and immobilized by Metro's image of
her—and, I'm afraid, half-persuaded of
it herself—I could imagine her as a very
good Lady Macbeth.*

—JAMES AGEE

*Irene Dunne makes being good more
fun.*

—ADELA ROGERS ST. JOHNS

"Society ladies," as role models for the nation's womanhood in dress and deportment, were a staple of silent film. The talkies revolutionized the casting of such parts, for, with the microphone turned on, actresses had to talk smart as well as look it. After hearing the bleats and twangs of star after star in preliminary sound tests, panicky producers sent to New York for stage veterans. At least they could talk.

Many of them talked too well, in the Grand Manner of the James O'Neill and Mrs. Fiske era that was dying hard. Rural moviegoers found their refined diction snobby, and the first two years of sound production were a chaos of arrivals and departures, with new draftees pushing off of trains as their very recent predecessors pushed back on, crying for Times Square.

A few hung on, making the 1930s a holiday of sophisticated urban wives with style to spare. But unlike the Swanson-De Mille shows of the early post–World War I years, the talkie equivalents were not big trend setters. De Mille was lavish and Swanson all the candy; their successors were mired in melodramas with too much true confession, blackmail, and murder and too little fun. The De Mille plan was satire and entertainment, revelry and piety; he mixed a rich brew to divert just about every kind of moviegoer. But the dreary Ladies of the early talkies were shallow and dull, and only some women went to such films.

Ruth Chatterton was their principal victim. A light of Broadway, she came to Hollywood in 1925 with her husband, Ralph Forbes. He had the offers, so she busied herself with stage work on the coast, discovering to her bewilderment that Californians attended the theatre only for talent scouting; and hers wasn't. She was about to give up when Warner Brothers, Fox, and Paramount began seriously to consider going all out for sound. Her lustrous voice made her a shoo-in. In 1928 Paramount signed her and plunked her into a trio of vapid films, but on loan to MGM she starred in the third of Hollywood's five versions of *Madame X* (1929) and was made. As the faithless wife who pays and declines and weeps and is at length defended in a murder trial by (unbeknownst to him!) her own son, Chatterton had a fine entry in classic weepie style, and used plenty of the voice that tells us that there's soul under all that bad judgment.

However, the rest of her Paramount films were awful. Depression sensitivities kept Hollywood from overdoing the society atmosphere of spend, spend in the De Mille-Swanson manner; but if you can't satirize that world view what's the point of doing society films at all? Chatterton was so unhappy with Paramount that when Warner Brothers offered her a million dollars for two years' work, she signed with them while her Paramount contract still had almost a year to run, raising eyebrows all over town. And then her Warners films were as poor as the Paramounts.

Some people get brittle when they play sophisticated; Chatterton gets humid. "Sex attraction and sex congeniality are two entirely different things," she says in *The Rich Are Always with Us* (1932), as a woman who knows of both but will always make the socially appropriate choice. In this picture, that would be George Brent, a writer who is eternally shooing women out of his study so he can work. "I came," Chatterton tells him, "to find out whether writers make love out of fun or curiosity." Brent and Chatterton made love out of passion, but they were such stiff players that their offscreen romance, which culminated in marriage, doesn't come through on screen. Chatterton made one decent picture, for Goldwyn, *Dodsworth* (1936), with Walter Huston, from Sinclair Lewis' novel. It's the only Chatterton film that a revival house can fill up for.

Not so good. They hire a lady to play ladies and stick her in garbage. Better treated than Chatterton but as seldom seen today is Ann Harding, for some buffs the most engaging lady of all. Her straight blond hair, parted in the center with chance wisps floating about, gave an angelic look to her many wayward wives, and she was a superb actress. Originally an Army brat, one Dorothy Gatley, she made it up through the ranks from stock to Broadway over the objections of General Gatley, who vilified the "painted face" exposed to the "gaping public." It was a splendid face; it gave the whole woman amazing grace. A breakthrough success as the heroine of *The Trial of Mary Dugan* on Broadway in 1927 led Harding to Hollywood—not, unfortunately, to preserve her Mary (MGM bought it for Norma Shearer), but in another stage adaptation, *Paris Bound* (1929), Philip Barry's cautionary study of divorce. She also filmed Barry's *Holiday* (1930) in the role Katharine Hepburn played in the better-known remake, riding on the strong influence that Broadway exercised on the early talkies. Hollywood needed the work of writers like Barry and actors like Harding, for it was poor in literacy and dialogue delivery. Unlike Chatterton, trapped in gooey soapers, Harding made more than a few Broadway transformations, though *The Girl of the Golden West* (1931) and *East Lynne* (1931), both from old melodramas, scarcely began to tap her reserves of technique.

She awed reviewers. Again and again they puzzled over her looks. She seemed unmoviestarish, transcendentally glamorous; they kept talking about her hair and her voice. Actually, it was all of her at once, not physical qualities but her abilities that set her apart. She got better films than Ruth Chatterton and better co-stars, like Clive Brook, Leslie Howard, Laurence Olivier, Robert Montgomery, and William Powell. She knew how to use her parts better than Norma Shearer, who played very similar roles, and she was a better judge of material than Kay Francis, another of this group, who was so indiscriminate in accepting assignments that she ended up in many of the parts that Ruth Chatterton turned down.

With all this going for her, Harding should have had a fine career, but by the mid-1930s she was out of work. Too many weepies between the good films had subdued her aura. Sadly, her RKO contract kept her from returning to New York to play the lead in the original production of Eugene O'Neill's *Mourning Becomes Electra* (the author himself wanted her), so Harding was doubly cheated. The movies never quite abandoned her; she made a quiet comeback in the early 1940s and sailed gracefully on into the 1950s. But it is too bad that Norma Shearer and Harding couldn't have traded places. Harding would have made MGM's *Strange Interlude* and *Private Lives* eternally interesting; and Shearer, in RKO's *The Life of Vergie Winters, Enchanted April,* and *The Lady Consents,* would have been entirely suitable.

Maybe Harding should simply have stayed on Broadway. Others of her colleagues did so without a qualm. Despite continual pressure from the studios, the first ladies of Broadway made few films. Katharine Cornell laughed out loud at the notion of a movie. Jane Cowl respected the old division between film and stage folk; they were one thing and she was another. (She crossed over, however, in the 1940s.) Ethel Barrymore enjoyed visiting on the coast with her brothers Lionel and John—and made one picture with them, *Rasputin and the Empress* (1932)—but she thought everyone in Hollywood a toad and didn't linger (though she, too, returned in the 1940s, when her stage career broke down). Helen Hayes made nine films during the 1930s (plus one cameo bit in the 1940s), but she only went to Hollywood because her husband, Charles MacArthur, found screenwriting a bonanza cinch.

Like most stage actors, Hayes found that having to burp out her parts in short takes hurt her sense of continuity, but she got the hang of screen procedure well enough to win an Oscar on her first effort, *The Sin of Madelon Claudet* (1931). She kept good company; Ronald Colman played her husband in *Arrowsmith* (1932) and Gary Cooper was the American soldier who impregnates her and weeps as she dies in childbirth in *A Farewell to Arms* (1932). At this stage of her life, Hayes looked like a fastidious combination of Jean Arthur and Claudette Colbert, and as Ernest Hemingway's nurse she seems to get a lot out of doing little. Her death scene, to the strains of the Liebestod from Wagner's *Tristan und Isolde*, is outstanding, but Hayes just didn't like film. By 1935 she had had it. "I don't think I am very good in the pictures," she announced, "and I have a beautiful dream that I'm elegant on the stage."

Most elegant of all was Lynn Fontanne, who tried talkies once with her husband Alfred Lunt. Once was enough. Every studio retained at least one stage actress for prestige and the odd role that only she could play, but MGM gravitated to prestige and special events as a matter of course. Irving Thalberg met with the Lunts while he and Shearer were on their way to Europe, convincing them to entrust their Broadway hit *The Guardsman* to celluloid. Neither of them seems to have had the remotest idea of how films were made (though Lunt had made several silents), and they somehow got the impression that they were to film *The Guardsman* exactly as it had been staged, with the camera approximating the view from F 110, the way thespians of 1910 made *Macbeth* and such. Nor did they know how to get around Hollywood. They didn't even have a pass to get through MGM's front gate, and when the doorman stopped them they just went back to their rented home in Westwood.

Most importantly, they were unprepared for the erratic eye of the camera. A favorite Broadway story tells how Fontanne attended a screening of the first day's rushes and staggered home to Lunt in glum amazement. "Alfred!" she cries. "I'm terrible in it, simply terrible! I can't possibly go on with the film!"

"How was I?" Lunt asks.

"You're charming," she tells him, "simply charming. The voice is in tune, the timing is perfect, and you're *so* handsome. I think you should change your makeup a little because it looks as if you have no lips. But *I'm* impossible. Fat, clumsy, loud, sullen, and my eyes look like tiny holes in a sheet."

A pause. Lynn snuffles, Lunt considers.

"What should we do, Alfred?" she goes on. "Can we give them back their money and give up? Can we start shooting it from the beginning? I just don't see how I can continue."

And Lunt says, "No lips, eh?"

Most jarring to these stage people was the Hollywood practice of previewing films to test audience reaction, often without addressing a particular sort of film to the appropriate audience. *The Guardsman* (1932), a Continental boudoir romp, was previewed at a theatre filled with sailors and their dates and of course they hated it. Thalberg was reading the comment cards to the Lunts when Fontanne cut him off in a fury. *The Guardsman* was a fine play, she told him, and neither she nor Lunt was interested in the criticism of morons. He would find an audience for *The Guardsman*—possibly not in San Bernardino, but certainly in other places.

Fontanne was wrong. *The Guardsman* got some good reviews in highbrow places but did poor business: the audience for this grade of art had already seen it on stage. Not long after *The Guardsman*, Thalberg offered the Lunts a million dollars, sure they could still make a go of it. But he would not yield them the artistic control they demanded, and the Lunts never tried the movies again except for a bit in *Stage Door Canteen* (1943). They undoubtedly made the right decision, for Hollywood had few directors capable of handling the Lunts (Lubitsch might have managed it); and as far as ladies go, Fontanne probably went too far in the movies. She had a way of making the genteel feel brazen.

Hollywood wanted gentility from ladies, or it wanted no ladies at all. A good find, then, was Jeanette MacDonald, another of those who arrived in Hollywood at the call of sound. A comedienne and dancer as well as singer, MacDonald exemplifies the studio process in her two very distinct phases of stardom. At Paramount she was sexy and arch. At MGM she turned into a matron. The earlier Paramount films are the ones that catch the critic's eye, for they are made lithe by Ernst Lubitsch and Rouben Mamoulian to exploit rhythm and melody as the foundation of sound film. But the MGM series, a batch of operettas as lithe as a cowbell, were far more popular with moviegoers—and still are.

The difference between the two MacDonalds directly corresponds to the difference between Hollywood before the Hays production code was strictly enforced (in 1934) and after. Remember, when Hays first came to Hollywood he patrolled the activities of stars more than the moral content of their films. But a tendency to freedom in the early 1930s inspired another national outcry, and this time the Hays people put the scripts under scrutiny. Thus, while for Paramount MacDonald courted Maurice Chevalier *en négligé* and sang "[Don't make me wait] Love Me Tonight" with him, at MGM MacDonald met Nelson Eddy out of doors with a coat on and sang zi-zi-zi-zi-zing-zing. Paramount's were boudoir operettas, the kind of thing the Lunts might have done if they could sing. MGM's were family pictures, and its ladies toed the line. Let Ruth Chatterton lurk in the shadows watching husband Adolphe Menjou kiss his mistress Claire Dodd in *Journal of a Crime* (1934); let Chatterton's great eyes bulge and close; let her kill Dodd, and ache, and repent. That's easy for her to do—she was with Warner Brothers. At MGM—and then at every studio from 1934 on—ladies didn't lurk or kill. It rather cramped Ruth Chatterton's style.

Did the public need the ladies at all? Aside from the splendid artistry of MacDonald's early musicals and the undeniable pleasure of her later ones, what was the purpose of the persona? To teach Americans transatlantic elocution-class vowels? As role models? Surely not that. Most of the ladies were up to the mascara line in dark deeds. As fashion models, then? Garbo wore the most striking clothes in the movies, but—if she could be classified—was definitely not a "lady." A close second was Joan Crawford, also not a lady. Did the lady have a purpose?

Yes. She made possible one of the American film's unique contributions to art history, screwball comedy.

This term is often misused. Some apply it to all comedy of the 1930s, or to comedy set in an upper-class milieu, or to anything with Carole Lombard in it. Let's be precise: screwball comedy is literate farce that (1) emphasizes wit, charm, and good looks as the great American virtues; (2) urges idiosyncratic goofing around as the great American pastime; and (3) usually mates a wealthy woman with a fortuneless man. The literacy provides scripts rich in wordplay and fleet fun, and the farce provides intricate plotting and crazy personnel who help defeat the genre's biggest enemy: pompous logicians.

There's something of a cheat in all of this, for screwball comedy seems unable to do without money even as it says money doesn't matter. Screwball comedy distrusts plutocrats; but where does a working person get the wherewithal for goofing around? And what's madcap in a nightclub can seem boorish in a tenement. So all the screwballers produce rich people, both likable and not, to sponsor the parties and scavenger hunts and country weekends. And nearly all the screwball heroines have to be heiresses so the hero can prove his mettle by taming her, protecting her, liberating her, or coming out of his bourgeois flat damn into the live-it-up ballet.

With grand clothes to wear, clever comments to make, and pranks to commit, the screwball heroines were assured of grateful parts. You needed timing, spirit, and a distinctive look; and the few who had them entered the annals. (It's no accident that the Hollywood women most admired by the cognoscenti of the revival-house circuits all made at least one or two prominent screwballers.) Ironically, the form derived from the stage. Just as Hollywood had to borrow high-toned stage actors to get the talkie off to a proper start, Hollywood also looted the stage for high-toned scripts; and some of these—those of Philip Barry especially—already contained many of the salient properties of the screwball world view. Barry made the confrontation of stuffy aristos and vital bohemians an obsession, and the Hollywood adaptations of *Holiday* and *The Animal Kingdom* in 1930 and 1932 discovered screwball territory for film. This makes Ann Harding, heroine of both, provisionally the first of the screwball heroines. Barry had no farce in him, but Noël Coward had plenty, and Ernst Lubitsch's version of Coward's *Design for Living* in 1933, with Miriam Hopkins, Gary Cooper, and Fredric March in the parts Coward wrote for the Lunts and himself, settled the territory and called for followers. True, Ben Hecht wrote an entirely new script in Americanese, the play's wicked sex triangle was squared off, and audiences didn't like it. But the fertile land kept promising to pay off if only someone would till it properly; and in 1934 the first of the classic screwballers arrived, with immediate and huge success, *The Thin Man*.

Myrna Loy was its heroine, and she wins the palm as the first heroine of screwball. She lacks the perverseness of Katharine Hepburn in *Bringing Up Baby* and the abandon of Carole Lombard, two more essential screwball heroines. Rather, Loy, as detective William Powell's wife, retains all the established lady virtues while enjoying the color and action and even the peril of the underworld, thereby rooting the screwball heroine in the mode of bohemian patrician. She wears great wild clothes and can never be more than mildly ruffled. At the film's famous climactic dinner party during which Powell will unmask the killer (one of the guests), Loy tells a servant, "Will you serve the nuts?" Then, taking in her table of crooks and molls, she adds, "I mean, will you serve the guests the nuts?" But one senses that she thinks she was right the first time.

Adapted from Dashiell Hammett's novel, *The Thin Man** could have been merely a thriller. But it sought flair as much as suspense and became something special, a salute to the American love of adventure. Everyone wants one, says screwball comedy, not just the outlaw. At one point a thug breaks into Loy and Powell's bedroom with a gun. The

---

*Contrary to popular belief, the "thin man" of the title isn't William Powell, but the prime suspect in a murder case.

police turn up at the front door and the thug is about to shoot when Powell pulls off a complex defensive maneuver, neutralizing the thug but taking a bullet in the arm. Unfortunately, Powell has had to deck Loy to keep her out of the bullet's way, and she's terribly disappointed when she comes to and realizes that she missed the action. Life is such a *stunt!*

Some were born to screwball comedy—Hepburn and Lombard, certainly. Some achieved it—Constance Bennett, benignly tizzied in *Topper* (1937), in which she and Cary Grant spend most of the time as ghosts. Loy had it thrust upon her. She had made some fifty films from 1925 without establishing a personality. Familiar to moviegoers as various ethnic exotics—she stole the operetta *The Desert Song* (1929) from lovers and comics alike as Azuri, a treacherous Algerian—Loy played a wide variety of parts, crossing many paths. She turns up as one of Joan Crawford's fellow showgirls in *Pretty Ladies* (1925), as Jeanette Mac-Donald's man-crazed cousin in *Love Me Tonight* (1932), as rival to Irene Dunne in *Consolation Marriage* (1931) and to Ann Harding in *The Animal Kingdom*. Loy was everywhere and nowhere, for though she never stopped working, she never made herself indispensable.

Until *The Thin Man*. In its wake, every studio tried to mount an imitation of MGM's hit, which was sure to spawn a lucrative series, but to everyone's surprise it developed that the all-purpose replaceable Loy was unique. No one else could capture that urbane zing, that elated insouciance. She was always thrilled and never shocked—just the mode of behavior that screwball comedy needed. After *The Thin Man*, Loy became an official treasure. Some would say that MGM's Big Three should count Loy as a Fourth, and in 1938, when columnist Ed Sullivan held a big public contest to determine who were the king and queen of Hollywood, the winners were Clark Gable . . . and Myrna Loy.

From the mid-1930s on into the late 1940s, with Powell in and out of *Thin Man* follow-ups and finally with Cary Grant and Melvyn Douglas in *Mr. Blandings Builds His Dream House* (1948), Loy held the front ranks in comedy, also playing a standout avatar of the American homemaker in *The Best Years of Our Lives* (1946) as Fredric March's patient wife. Later films were less inveigling, and Loy was eased into supporting parts; but at least she exercised good sense, staying away from what she called the "psychotic, disintegrating old bags" that some of her co-evals played.

Comparably useful in screwball comedy was Irene Dunne, perhaps the ace lady of all. She, too, made soap operas at first, but they were better than Chatterton's and Harding's; some of them are classics of the kind. She herself thinks *Back Street* (1932) trash, but this tale of a woman who spends her life as a married man's kept floozy has endured through two remakes (with Margaret Sullavan and Susan Hayward); and *Magnificent Obsession* (1935) really does draw one into its love hash when doctor Robert Taylor blinds Dunne in a car accident and then restores her sight.

Dunne was versatile. She made her film debut in a musical, followed it up with an epic western, and used another western and more musicals to get out of the soap opera rut in the mid-1930s. Nor was she just any singer. Her soprano had the arching line necessary to put over "Why Was I Born?" "Smoke Gets in Your Eyes," "Yesterdays," "Lovely to Look At," "You Are Love," and "The Folks Who Live on the Hill" in her four mid-decade musicals, all with Jerome Kern scores; but she seems a little put out by the hokum, high jinks, production numbers, and other commotions of the form. In *Roberta* (1953) she has to play the love plot with Randolph Scott and make room for Fred Astaire and Ginger Rogers and Astaire's jazz band, and every so often she gives a look that says, "Who are these people?" Surely that's why Dunne is arresting in screwball comedy. She's so *lady* that when she becomes antic it's like a Quaker going to war: take it *very* seriously.

*Joy of Living* (1938), then, was a kind of *aria d'obbligo* for Dunne, a ritual set piece in which a proper woman learns how to have fun. Dunne is a musical comedy star with parasitical relations; Douglas Fairbanks, Jr., the unconventional millionaire who introduces her to such sport as beer guzzling, roller skating, imitating Donald Duck, staying out till all hours, and waking up with a man in her room. "One of the most professional women I've known," said Fairbanks of Dunne years later. "Everything she does is carefully thought out." Yet her most positive accomplishment is her spontaneity; otherwise how could a tale of coming out and getting the rhythm play? *Joy of Living* is about spontaneity. It tells Americans to use it or acquire it; all the screwball comedies did, and that's why Dunne came in so handy in the 1930s. She is believable in these matters, honestly afraid of Fairbanks when he first presses his attentions on her; sardonically dismissive when she realizes that, if a pest, he's at least a gentleman; and captivating when she takes his lessons in unwinding, adopting his Donald Duck noises with a disarmingly juicy punctilio, American prim running wild.

The lady trope is very thirties, for it was developed as a result of the institution of sound and was canceled as a result of World War II, when patriotic teamwork and a need for women in hard-labor jobs previously exclusive to men called for more proletarian heroines like Betty Grable. It has been suggested that the emphasis on well-spoken, well-tailored, attractive bluebloods was Hollywood's attempt to calm Depression fever by domesticating the Depression's bête noire, the rich (whose profligate Wall Streeting was blamed for the collapse of the economy). But if the objective was conciliatory, why did it create such a dangerous genre? Screwball comedy, at heart, advocates joyriding, aimless vacations, shocking novels, anarchy. Its mascot is a wire-haired terrier, impedient, headstrong, and utterly without whimsey; its secret desire is to do a back flip; and its greatest achievement is Katharine Hepburn's destruction of a museum's prize reconstruction of a dinosaur skeleton in *Bringing Up Baby*.

Perhaps, then, the use of knightly heroines tamed the anarchy? No: the screwball heroine is the agent who unleashes the upheaval, the revolutionary. The lady character became so liberated that she no longer bore any resemblance to the lady of tradition, and virtually killed her off. Margaret Dumont, the perpetual butt of Marx Brothers riot, may have been the last of her kind, the supernova of dowagers. Like ZaSu Pitts, she was not a star but has a star's resonance, with her marble bust and blue-book names. She's Mrs. Potter in *The Cocoanuts* (1929), Mrs. Teasdale in *Duck Soup* (1933), Mrs. Claypool in *A Night at the Opera* (1935), Mrs. Upjohn in *A Day at the Races* (1937), Mrs. Dukesbury in *At the Circus* (1939) and not once the whole time does she truly understand what the boys are up to. As Mrs. Rittenhouse in *Animal Crackers* (1930) she welcomes Groucho as the explorer Captain Spaulding to her baronial house party, telling the guests what a fearless adventurer he is. "Sez you!" Groucho sneers. Chico, hired to play piano, barges in and asks her, "Where's the dining room?" Harpo keeps putting his thigh in her hand. Yet in film after film she turns to jelly when Groucho flirts with her, though his love talk is spiced with facetiae and insults. The joke is kept crisp by the Brothers' penchant for improvisation and the certainty that Dumont, in life as in character, doesn't get it. In *Duck Soup* Groucho tells her, "I'm fighting for your honor, which is more than you ever did." Later, off camera, she asked him what that meant.

In a way Dumont was not the last but the most, for toward the end of the 1930s L. B. Mayer signed the woman he hoped would prove to be the most regal of heroines, Greer Garson. The Irish actress, trained in rural repertory and West End galas, was expected to sound the note of Class, and she did. She had the motherhood Garbo lacked, the propriety Crawford lacked, the acting skills Shearer lacked, better diction than all three put together; and Hollywood was duly awed, nominating her for seven Best Actress Oscars. She only won once, for *Mrs. Miniver* in 1942, perhaps because she took so long to blush and weep and thank everybody that it was feared that two such demonstrations might discourage future attendance at Oscar evenings.

*Mrs. Miniver* was the role that Shearer turned down because she didn't want to play the mother of a grown child. Garson didn't exercise the star's vanity about age, but on the other hand she wouldn't do anything she thought vulgar. She was willing to sing and dance in *Random Harvest* (1942), but refused to perform a musical comedy sketch in the revue *The Ziegfeld Follies* (1946) called "A Great Lady Has an Interview," in which Garson was to sing the praises of Madame Crematone, inventor of the safety pin. It's an appalling five minutes and a blot on the memory of Judy Garland, who filled in for Garson.

Knowing when to say no: that's class. Looking as good with Clark Gable as with Laurence Olivier, Ronald Colman, and Walter Pidgeon is more class. Almost any woman who carries herself with authority suits the polished actor, but a non-acting but experienced personality who just breathes authenticity—like Gable—can be a challenge. In *Pride and Prejudice* (1940), opposite Olivier's Darcy, Garson is a formidable Elizabeth Bennett, maybe a little coy but superbly Janeite in attack. Similarly, as the woman in *Random Harvest* (1942) whom Colman marries, forgets under amnesia, and marries again, Garson is at her ease; she could have done it one-handed. But for Gable's first film after his return from war service—"Gable's back and Garson's got him!" read the ads, to Gable's mortification—Garson plays a closed librarian who opens up after exposure to a life-loving sailor, and suddenly Garson had to work hard.

The picture is called *Adventure* (1946), and while it definitely favors hanging loose and taking chances, it also recommends the ties of a love match. *Adventure* has a bad reputation, but it's fine entertainment. There's nothing in it that one hasn't seen elsewhere. Her sidekick (Joan Blondell) is an easygoing kid of fierce loyalty; his sidekick (Thomas Mitchell) is an Irish boozer who can't resist telling the truth to liars; Gable will mary Garson, leave her, and, after suffering, come back for good; and so on. But it's beautifully handled, sharp when it's angry and serene when it melts. Garson and Gable meet when he blunders into her library, and she isn't about to play any games with the likes of him. "The nearest bar," she tells him with a smile, "is just down the street. You can't miss it." But in minutes they're tense and confrontational. Later, in a bar with Gable and Blondell, Garson seethes with what she hopes is disgust for Gable (we know it isn't) and puts on an act when his sailor friends come in. Dancing, she tells them, "I'm all warmed up and ready to take off . . . I fly on high octane."

It's absurd because she can't quite get that Irish mouth around "octane"—it comes out "okh-teyhn"—but it's apt because the film is about Garson's making a gentleman out of the rough-hewn Gable while he makes a sport out of her. This is typical of its time. With the war over and the 1930s forgotten, the lady is for taming and being tamed in fifty-fifty partnerships, with the provocative excesses of screwball comedy retired forever.

If it had to happen, at least Garson and Gable make a fair team, especially in a farewell scene midway through the picture. Gable's boat is pulling out, and to keep talking to him Garson has to run along the quay, dodging bales and ropes as dockworkers look on. Gable had bought her a mad hat, and now, as the sorrow of their impending separation threatens to knock us out, Garson goes for a light relief by tossing the hat to Gable. But he misses it and it drops into the deep as all the dockworkers groan: a sad, gritty, reckless, disappointed, wonderful moment. It's something like the last thirty seconds of screwball impulsiveness the movies were to know.

# 6

# *Men's Women: The Harlots*

MARLENE DIETRICH
JEAN HARLOW

*Drop your voice an octave and don't lisp
. . . count to six and look at that lamp as
if you could no longer live without it.*

—JOSEF VON STERNBERG
directing Marlene Dietrich


*I don't know why everyone made such a
monster of Jean Harlow. She was a kind
and amusing child.*

—ROBERT TAYLOR


The ladies taught style: how to take life with grace. The harlots taught attitude: what to think of men. Both types were adaptable, with rich potential in melodrama, costume pageant, or comedy. But there were fewer harlots, because the culture was not as happy with them as it had been with the vamps in the preceding generation. As it was, the harlot didn't even last out the 1930s.

It's rude to call them harlots, but the word describes the image they projected. They weren't vamps; vamps were creatures of habit, modeling sensuality, dressing in it, like clothes. The harlot had sensuality by nature, like skin. That, at least, was the theory of Josef von Sternberg, who created the harlot in seven films starring Marlene Dietrich.

Dietrich was an unusual choice, a cultivated woman who was headed for a career as a violinist till a wrist injury turned her to the stage and who then played all sorts of roles in the great days of Berlin's post–World War I theatre. She was as well a devoted mother and a private person, not the kind who would be content in a place like Hollywood. (She has lived most of her life in Paris.) Nor was she thought to have a photogenic face—a nose problem or something; ridiculous, the face is ingenious.

But this is to know the facts, the whole hindsight background. When Dietrich first appeared on American screens, she was von Sternberg's invention, a device whose plans were kept secret. It was claimed that she had done nothing till she met the director, then became everything. Extraordinary loyalty led each of them to credit the other with all the genius, though in his autobiography von Sternberg called her his "puppet" and claimed to have controlled "the depth of her thoughts." Moreover, on the set this notoriously difficult director brutally abused the Dietrich he created and was mad about, murmuring, "You hideous cow," in German as he made her repeat a line, a gesture, a wink over and over and over, the inspired, insufferable creep. The hideous cow helped place him in the catalogues of twentieth-century art, backed him up when everyone in Hollywood was finished with him, and defends him to this day. They got so close that in 1931 von Sternberg's wife, Riza, hit Dietrich with a suit for libel and alienation of affections. And what it was all about was this amazing female who was made of sex. All kinds.

It's fascinating to contemplate the creature Dietrich might have been on film had she started in the tolerant 1970s rather than in the 1920s, for no other woman sensualist of the screen has seemed more amused by the prospect of bisexuality, if only to put a little satire in her cabaret scenes or to provide a comic intermission during her films' throbbing affairs and kiss wounds and sex crises. Her first picture with von Sternberg presented a heroine impervious to romance, succeeding von Sternberg films introduced vulnerability, her last von Sternberg opus reaffirmed the cold front, and the sum was seven films that fascinate revival buffs but which either flopped or made too little money, considering Dietrich's celebrity. The harlot is not a choice demon in the American consciousness.

Von Sternberg was a master in making the *look* of pictures *feel* like something, but he was too foreign for local tastes. The first Dietrich–von Sternberg collaboration, *The Blue Angel* (1929), came out in both German and (eventually) English versions, but there was never a more "foreign" film. For one thing, while it's a sound film, there's a lot of silence. An early sequence shows us a typical morning in the life of a schoolteacher (Emil Jannings) in near-pantomime. Even in the classroom we hear little. We know enough just by seeing him: fat, orderly, pedantic. His students show us how the world regards him, as a clown. And sure enough, the teacher who loves rank and decorum more than anything will become a stooge virtually on one look from Dietrich.

Femme fatale. We've had them by the carload—Bara, whose power was magic; Livingston, conventional pawn in *Sunrise*'s age-old fable of connubial solidarity; Shearer, the class star out on a slum tour; Garbo, the native of a cold world who keeps turning to the sun like a plant; Crawford, who knew how to handle herself. Dietrich was something new in the line, the woman who does not care but does not believe in magic, either. She may look upon a man, and he'll crumble, and she'll shrug. To see Dietrich in *The Blue Angel* is to understand why cultures set up codes of taboo; this movie celebrates the Dionysian urge to anarchy in Dietrich's nonchalance, for her sexuality could blow a town apart. If a pedant can go crazy for her, who's safe?

Von Sternberg doesn't need the glamour of MGM to place his jewel. Dietrich is Lola-Lola, star of a touring variety show, as sleazy as they come. Sauerkraut and liverwurst vendors wander through the house crying their wares, the chorus girls smoke and hang out when they're not actively performing, and they turn a spotlight on the men in the audience when they are, as if to make an alternate show out of the degradation beauty makes of men. Imagine what they see.

We don't have to; von Sternberg has made a whole movie out of it. Dietrich sings "Ich Bin die Fesche Lola" (I'm Fancy Lola) and "Ein Richtiger Mann" (Tonight I'm Looking for a Man),* but she looks wildly uncommitted to anything, as if she were in some other song somewhere else. She continues not to care when the professor becomes her slave, when the next slave turns up to replace him, when the professor literally goes mad in humiliation. "Ich Bin von Kopf bis Fuss," Lola-Lola's big number, which became, as "Falling in Love Again," Dietrich's theme song, tells all men what they're up against—not a committed devourer (like Bara) but a natural force who "can't help it." She pets and tortures Jannings, as in her dressing room early in their affair, when she blows face powder all over him and then strokes his beard. Her power knows no limits, turning Jannings from a pompous drudge into a mincing stagedoor fop when she sings "Falling in Love Again," her superb legs crossed on a chair. At their wedding party, in a scene worthy of von Stroheim, she has him crowing idiotically to her clucking hen imitation. As the years pass, he becomes cabaret baggage, touring with her company and finally playing his hometown in overstated clown makeup.

Theda Bara could have used such a skillful image of wrecked manhood: her victims just lay there in suits. But Dietrich's victim, crowing as he had at his wedding, goes berserk backstage and staggers off to his old schoolroom to collapse at his desk. It's a brilliant, disgusting film, a little shop of horrors run with Continental finesse, and it closes with a last reminder of who Dietrich is. There's Lola-Lola on her chair singing "Falling in Love Again" in dark sequins and a floppy hat. She grins

---

*This song in particular has resonance: it's the one Helmut Berger used in his drag act in Visconti's film *The Damned*.

at us, looking this way and that. She'll be in love again soon, can't help it.

Who is she? In *Morocco* (1930) she is again a cabaret sport, in *Dishonored* (1931) a spy, in *Shanghai Express* (1932) a prostitute, in *Blonde Venus* (1932) a housewife who had been in cabaret, in *The Scarlet Empress* (1934) Catherine the Great of Russia, in *The Devil Is a Woman* (1935) again a cabaret singer. Like Garbo, she was usually European, too exotic to be believed as an American; but unlike Garbo she made her American entree in distinctively European-looking films. Paramount, which signed her in a tizzy after viewing a rough cut of *The Blue Angel,* was the only studio that actually liked weird directors; von Sternberg was the champ of weird. Stop the projector during a medium shot in any of his films and you'll see a crammed picture, every piece in it doing something. Graffiti, toys, masks, light fixtures, bowls of things: the sets are alive. Too bad Garbo never worked with von Sternberg; but then Garbo was a "good" harlot, one who repented or died the death, sometimes (preferably) both. Garbo never closed a film blithely proclaiming, "Can't help it."

However. Dietrich couldn't have sustained even a short career in America remaining impervious to romance, and in her second picture, *Morocco,* it's Gary Cooper who's the harlot and Dietrich the one who goes to hell. In *Dishonored,* too, she is undone by love, and in *Shanghai Express* one feels she would be if Clive Brook didn't take her in his arms at the fadeout and forgive her for offering herself to villain Warner Oland to keep Oland from cutting out Brook's eyes.

All right, Brook didn't catch all the details; all he knows is Dietrich would have gone off with Oland if Anna May Wong hadn't, for good reasons of her own, stabbed Oland to death. Still, the men in these Dietrich films! These unenlightened Britons or self-righteous schoolmasters or aged boulevardiers! Only Cooper, in Dietrich's von Sternberg series, can match her for unquestioning sensual abandon, for falling in and getting caught, can't help it. As *Morocco* draws to a close, patient, ultra-rich Adolphe Menjou is ready to marry Dietrich, no questions asked; but she stares at the camp followers trailing after men as Cooper's Foreign Legion troop marches off into the desert, takes silent leave of Menjou, kicks off her shoes, and trudges after Cooper as the sandy wind sweeps across the screen.

She does care, after all. When she and Brook meet up in *Shanghai Express* and he asks her how long it has been since they parted, she answers, "Five years and four weeks," precisely. She had to stay afloat in that time. How? Well, she tells him calmly, "It took a lot of men to change my name to Shanghai Lily." And each of them, no doubt, saw something different in her. Oland sees integrity. "A man is a fool to trust any woman," he observes to Dietrich, "but I believe a word of honor would mean something to you." If Dietrich is a harlot, the word loses its meaning—an honorable whore? But that's just it. With Dietrich in charge of the character, the old distinction that puts women of sensuality on one side of a heavy line and good women in the other dissolves, for Dietrich embodies so many honorable qualities that the distinction is no longer operable. She is a female version of the Douglas Fairbanks hero: chivalrous, bold, and sexy. No wonder most of the men in her films come off as pantywaists; no wonder only Cooper can equal her: because he's chivalrous, bold, and sexy, too.

Given von Sternberg's talent and Dietrich's notoriety, their films did not do as well as they should have. Americans liked her; they didn't like her pictures. As of *The Devil Is a Woman* the collaboration broke up, and with the most insidious film yet. As Concha, Dietrich returns to the impervious persona of Lola-Lola, forever joking and loving and vanishing and returning. Lionel Atwill and Cesar Romero battle for her through the action, but in the end no one can ever have her; Concha is so capricious that even her lies are lies.

It's a classic modern story, popular as Pierre Louÿs' novel *The Woman and the Puppet,* as Riccardo Zandonai's opera *Conchita,* and in numerous film versions, most recently Luis Buñuel's *That Obscure Object of Desire.* It's classic for men, at least, who see something epic in the notion of a woman who can only love in doublespeak. (Buñuel actually had two different actresses play the one part.) Students of Hollywood image making must see this film,* not only for von Sternberg's picturetelling and the diversion of watching Dietrich run through Travis Banton's collection of lacy mantillas, but to consider how crucial the foreign Venus was to the expansion of the American movie. Apparently there were things that no native woman star could dare. Who besides Garbo or Negri could have brought off these von Sternberg parts? Crawford, Hepburn, Davis, Stanwyck, Chatterton, Francis? If there had been no foreign love goddesses—harlots, let's face it—the movies would have lacked an erotic component, would have been inarticulate and artificial, too chaste to convey a sense of life as lived.

Yet with Garbo already established, Hollywood did not need von Sternberg's Dietrich, and set to renovating her. Out went the wantonness, the ambiguity. The sexuality never left her, of course, but it becomes a reverberation, an echo of Lola-Lola. In *The Garden of Allah* (1936), Dietrich has been so cleaned up that the other parts of the film have to supply her stuff. Tilly Losch, in a small role as a dancer, lends the smiling eroticism, the Arabian desert (Yuma, Arizona, in fact) pro-

---

*It isn't easy. The Spanish government was so offended by the use of a Spanish setting for Dietrich's carryings-on that it demanded the film be withdrawn, threatening to ban all Paramount films if the studio refused. Some films have been lost through negligence, but this one was discarded, the negative burned with due ceremony before the Spanish ambassador in Washington, D.C. Private prints survive, however, and the film gets around.

vides an air of fatalism and barbaric grandeur, and co-star Charles Boyer brings in a hint of mystery as a monk who flees his order and takes up with Dietrich.

*The Garden of Allah* is a Selznick picture, and we expect something special. But except for the Technicolor this is an abysmal piece, wrecked by a dull, thudding script that screams at every turn of plot. Dietrich even looks different. After all the calculated von Sternberg lighting, it's interesting to see her in the clear for once; but we first spot her in church (praying to the Madonna!), and this, for one of the century's great free women, is a bad start. Worse yet, when Dietrich hears about a certain monk who broke his vows, she cries, "How *howwible!*" Oh, please. Earlier, as if trying to remind us of what she was even as the whole film denies it, a priest says of Dietrich, "You have come to a place of fire—and I think that you are made of fire." Wrong. The von Sternberg Dietrich was made of fire (and ice). This Dietrich is made of soap flakes.

By the time she made *Destry Rides Again* in 1939, Dietrich had found a middle level between the two extremes. As Frenchy, a saloon girl of the old west, Dietrich finally undid the damage von Sternberg had done to her—if seven superb films in a row is damage. Hollywood reckoned it was. Selznick felt Dietrich needed softening, and Joe Pasternak, the Universal producer who put *Destry* on, felt she needed vitality. Von Sternberg had turned her into a "mannequin in a shop window" when she was "tough, down-to-earth, real." In *Destry* she belts out "[See what] The Boys in the Back Woom [will have]," engages Una Merkel in a crashemup saloon fight, lies and cheats for bad guy Brian Donlevy, resents and resists good guy James Stewart, and at length takes a bullet aimed at Stewart, dying in his arms. Lola-Lola was officially over.

The reclamation was continued in three more adventures from Universal with John Wayne, the last two with Randolph Scott as well: *Seven Sinners* (1940), *The Spoilers* (1942), and *Pittsburgh* (1942). "Daddy, buy me that," Dietrich whispered to director Tay Garnett when she first clapped eyes on Wayne in the Universal commissary. The two made a splendid pair on both sides of the camera. With Stewart, Wayne, Scott, and such others as Bruce Cabot, Fred MacMurray, and Edward G. Robinson to play with, Dietrich was acclimatized, became American by citizenship and company and style.

The harlot period was over. We could no longer watch her eyes for the flicker of insight into what women see in men, not in straight-forward action romances like *Seven Sinners,* in which cabaret artiste Dietrich meets, loves, and leaves Navy lieutenant Wayne rather than ruin his future. As Bijou, Dietrich hasn't lost her pepper. "Ooh! The Navy!" she breathes, spotting some uniforms playing pool. But she's more a tough charmer than an enchantress now, closer to Crawford than

Garbo. When she sings "That Man's in the Navy" and we reflect that the swaggering tune is by Frederick Hollander, the man who as Friedrich Holländer composed her sulky *Blue Angel* tunes, we see how far Dietrich has come. The elements remain, but reformed. Touring the theatres of war to entertain the troops during World War II, charging along with Allied forces into Belsen concentration camp to find her sister, and becoming a grandmother in 1948 significantly enriched the woman's profile. She had been harlot, mysterious; then love goddess, merely sublime, and the pants and tuxedo jackets and the ape suit (for a number in *Blonde Venus,* "Hot Voodoo") and the trouble with Mrs. von Sternberg seemed appropriate. But this was a woman who made a contribution to the morale of the war effort in dangerous places, a German Army officer's daughter who defied Hitler's orders that she abandon the "Jew films" in Hollywood and come home.

They kept trying to compare Dietrich with Garbo, but the two have little in common. A biographer of Garbo has nothing to report that anyone knows of, whereas Dietrich's life is crowded with public events, and keeps on going long after Garbo closed hers away for good. The two did touch common base in the early 1930s, as harlots. But with Garbo one sees what men see with such wonder; while with Dietrich one sees, through *her* eyes, the stupid men. Both launched their eminence as the protégées of imaginative Jewish directors, both were unequivocal in their disgust for anti-Semitism,* both loved and sympathized with John Gilbert, Dietrich wangling for him the lead in *Desire* (1936), which he lost to Gary Cooper when he suffered a seizure during a tennis game, just as Garbo put him into *Queen Christina.*

But what's the point of comparing them when Dietrich's stardom grew most acute just when Garbo's receded into the abstract of retirement? Besides, Garbo was Hollywood's institutional Pirandellian, the exemplar of the play-yourself school (whether she wanted to be or not; the public saw it that way). Dietrich, once the public got used to her, was regarded separately from her roles. Harlots aren't grandmothers, don't bake to a T or sign up with the USO or tell their fellow Germans that Hitler wasn't the only Nazi in Germany. This separation of actress and parts became so distinct that Dietrich could play the one thing she never could be mistaken for, a self-serving Nazi sycophant, in Billy Wilder's vicious comedy *A Foreign Affair* (1948).

Set (and partially filmed) in the ruins of Berlin, *A Foreign Affair* follows a congressional committee's investigation of morale among American soldiers. A triangle develops around congresswoman Jean Arthur, Sergeant John Lund, and cabaret singer Dietrich, Lund's lover and, Arthur suspects, a woman with strong ties to the fallen Reich.

---

*There's a tale—it could be true—that Garbo considered visiting Hitler for the purpose of killing him.

Dietrich is coy when she needs to be ("What does it matter, a woman's politics? Women pick out whatever's in fashion and change it like a spwing hat"), bitchy when she wants to be (she tells Arthur, "What a cuwious way to do your hair—or, wather, not to do it"), and, it turns out, as brutal an opportunist as there ever was. Arthur's suspicions are correct and Dietrich is unmasked. But Wilder's black comedy yields to our delight in the real-life Dietrich at the end. As she is taken away by two MP's to some official fate, a colonel sardonically sends two backup MP's to watch her guards and a third MP to watch them. "That ought to do it," the last man observes. But we think not.

Dietrich also turned in a more serious study in a comparable setting in Stanley Kramer's *Judgment at Nuremberg* (1961), and traced an enticing cameo in *Around the World in Eighty Days* (1956), looking more a granddaughter than a grandmother. But these postwar years found her leaning more to the concert stage than the movies. By then her dossier was so complexly derived that her harlot mystique is only a story in a vast collection. Yet Lola-Lola remains her best-known part and von Sternberg's best-known creation.

Von Sternberg is crucial in comprehending the Hollywood harlot, for she was made by men, not women. Women stars conceived, wrote, and produced their own material, but not often, and none of them directed her own films in these years. So the men who owned the movies also, ultimately, controlled the movies' attitudes; and even Little Mary and Lillian Gish had to answer to a Zukor, a Griffith, a Neilan, a Vidor.

There is a story. The identity of one of its two characters depends on who tells the tale, but the other of the two is always L. B. Mayer. It seems that an actor or someone (John Gilbert or Erich von Stroheim in the most prevalent versions) happened to be speaking of film, and what's in it; and of life, and what's in *that*. And this fellow calls some woman a whore.

Reddening, Mayer resents the allusion.

Coolly, the man replies that all women are whores.

"Your mother," offers Mayer, "was a woman."

"And she," says the man, "was the biggest whore of them all."

Whereupon Mayer fetches this man a blow that sends him heels over head.

A family man, that Mayer, a gent. Yet on occasions he was as fluent in crude generalization as anyone, and he was willing to share in the profits made by MGM's harlot, Jean Harlow. From Dietrich, the devil as a woman, we move to Harlow, the woman as a baby.

Harlow was the American view of the type, with no exotic mystery, no tuxedo numbers, no nuanced lighting, no free-floating Continental bric-a-brac. She was studio property, playing uninhibited women on the make for Chester Morris, James Cagney, Spencer Tracy, or Clark

Gable, with heiress or secretary parts spliced in here and there. As Shanghai Lily on the Shanghai Express, Marlene Dietrich is ironic with Clive Brook and satiric with other passengers; in *China Seas* (1935) Harlow is China Doll, frank about herself and frank with her fellow passengers. "It's China Doll!" she cries, gliding into the picture, "the gal that drives men mad!" and she immediately lets everyone know where they stand with her. She's tolerant of villain Wallace Beery, openly resentful of her high-toned rival Rosalind Russell, and wildly in love with Clark Gable. She set off a national craze for platinum blond hair, merrily went around on camera without underwear, had a bad brush with scandal in the suicide of her third husband, offered a working definition of non-acting but actionable magnetism ("That girl's so bad," Irving Thalberg observed, "she might just be good"), and died horribly young of a brain disease caused by an infected kidney. It reads as a not untypical Hollywood saga. Its major oddity is that a woman so openly sensual was not hunted from the screen by a puritan coalition; perhaps her good nature projected so well her public couldn't hold anything against her.

But over the years since her death in 1936, Harlow has become the target of every journalist looking for a cheap cultural lay. Her co-workers recall a sweet kid; they all called her "Baby." Her legend, however, features a rank slut bullied by her mother and stepfather and beaten by an impotent husband. She teamed all too well with aggressive men—only Crawford brought as much out of Gable in love scenes—and made too many films with titles like *Bombshell* and *Red Headed Woman*. Too, her most famous role today is that of Kitty Packard, the screaming, devious idiot wife of robber baron Wallace Beery in *Dinner at Eight* (1933). Rather than credit George Cukor's coaching of Harlow, who makes Kitty an amusing takeoff on manipulative gold digging, an unattuned public simply takes her at face value. After all, wasn't it Harlow who first verbalized that cliché of seduction, "Pardon me while I slip into something more comfortable," in *Hell's Angels* (1930)?

All women are whores. Whether they believed this or not, most if not all Hollywood producers actively recruited and developed actresses to specialize in harlot parts, so each little age has its sex symbol, each one telling something about her time in how far she is encouraged to go. Theda Bara made sex a magic, for the 1910s weren't prepared to deal with it in any other way. Garbo suffered for it, Crawford tried to control it, Dietrich toyed with it. But Harlow was at ease with it, and the successive holders of her contract, Howard Hughes and MGM, exploited that notion.

Harlow was the new kind of blonde, the fair woman who acted like a dark one, worldly and appetitive. In *Platinum Blonde* (1931) she nearly breaks Robert Williams' manhood with her socialite money power, sending him into Loretta Young's arms. Mean woman. Yet in

*Three Wise Girls* (1932) she is a poor girl hurt when her rich fiancé mistakenly thinks she has cheated on him. Sweet woman, almost innocent. Then comes *Red Headed Woman* (1932), and Harlow is a lascivious crook, alternatively using her body and a gun to get what she wants, and it isn't true romance. Rat woman.

She was a kaleidoscope of harlot parts, turning the pattern with each new film, tacking from sweet to rat and back to sweet. The rat was an act. She fascinated the public, appealed to the imagination of the eye; but to producers she was a commodity. If all women are whores, all men are whoremongers. Harlow seemed stupid and sloppy, so her bosses didn't have to respect her. James Whale, dialogue coach on *Hell's Angels,* called her a "pig," Mayer dubbed her "the freak whore," and some reviewers were only a little more polite, ridiculing a lack of acting talent that they forgave in many of Harlow's colleagues.

Some women are whores—that would appear to be the industry's operating rule. Certainly neither Hughes nor MGM treated Harlow as anything else. The predatory vamps were gone (except for Mae West, and West spoofed the figure). So there was room, a need, for a fun-loving sexpot. Oddly, the Harlow that most of today's moviegoers are likely to encounter is not a sex star but a comedienne—the fiancée who keeps chasing after Spencer Tracy in her bridal gown in *Libeled Lady* (1936), for instance. She took her career with a sense of humor, and this gave a lift to her many molls and slatterns. Sometimes the exigencies of playing all the kinds of parts there were overextended her. When it was her turn to play a showgirl in a musical, *Reckless* (1935), producer David O. Selznick scrapped most of the Jerome Kern–Oscar Hammerstein score but left in one huge production number and some additional backstage foofoo. Harlow was dubbed by a singer and doubled by a dancer, but she had to do some of it and doesn't look comfortable. Nor can it have been fun to play a woman whose husband commits suicide. The part was modeled on Libby Holman, but echoes of the Jean Harlow–Paul Bern marriage and his mysterious suicide are easy to hear.

It's still a baffling case, the more so because Bern's butler, when he found the body, called MGM, not the police. L. B. Mayer produced the investigation as surely as any movie, and the facts have been endlessly shuffled in the decades since, to no clear ending. The most likely explanation ties Bern to a secret "other" wife, Dorothy Millette, who may have threatened blackmail; the official MGM text, that Bern was impotent or something comparable, is probably fictitious. Still, it's a lively story, and no one with a taste for dancing around in someone else's tragedy has been able to leave it alone.

Unfortunately, Bern's suicide in 1932 kicked off the prevailing view of Harlow as the movies' harlot stooge, a sideshow curiosity of sex and scandal—as Mayer said, a freak whore. Her very sudden death in

1937 at the age of twenty-six stoked the fires, and much of the nation turned out to see her last film, *Saratoga,* completed with a clumsy use of doubles hiding under hats and behind binoculars, and including some shots of Harlow obviously ill. At her death, MGM announced that it would not finish the film because of the pain her passing caused her co-workers, a bitter pain, because she had died in agony: her mother, a Christian Scientist, had refused to call in a doctor. Worse yet were the stupid rumors that she died in a bungled abortion operation or from alcoholism. Public interest in Harlow grew so thick that MGM changed its mind about *Saratoga,* rushing it through stopgap completion and releasing it just two weeks later. Come see Harlow! Absolutely guaranteed last farewell performance!

She became an object, one of the stars known not for who she was—what she *feels* like on screen—but for the sign under her side-show booth: Queen Harlot. This false and offensive image held on when the 1940s looked for "nicer" sex stars and became relevant again in the 1950s when Marilyn Monroe became famous. In the 1960s, a lubricious biography and two disgusting films on Harlow's life, all three wallowing in Paul Bern's suicide, kept the legend hot. By now, the damage done to the woman is complete.

Unlike Dietrich, who was able to live down her reputation by a change of film style and admirable works, Harlow was trapped by journalists, PR campaigns, screenwriters, producers, and early death. She was typed and junked. Anyway, Dietrich's harlots were not what most Americans think of as tramps. An American tramp has a runny nose and a foul mouth; Dietrich sauntered through those von Sternberg fantasies like the Devil going up and down in the Book of Job: with elegance. The devil is a woman.

And some women are whores. L. B. Mayer says so.

# 7

# No One's Woman

MAE WEST

*A little bit spicy, but not too raw, you know what I mean?*

—MAE WEST
in *She Done Him Wrong*

*In my day a woman with hair like that didn't come out in the daytime.*

—ELIZABETH PATTERSON
in *Go West, Young Man*

She once said, "It wasn't what I did but how I did it." It was what she did. She kept her body covered, prohibited drinking, profanity, and other gestures of earthy license, and seemed so detached, so commentative, that audiences couldn't take her stories seriously. Yet she was the most erotic event in commercial film till porn left the underground in the mid-1960s. She was also the first drag queen with a national following, the most auteur-minded star since Little Mary and Lillian Gish, and one of the nation's universally recognized celebrities. Yet her early Broadway musicals are totally forgotten, her radio and television work was limited, and she made only twelve feature films over a period of forty-six years.

She was a last hurrah from a dead culture, strictly pre-talkies in look and vaudeville style. Brooklyn-born, she gravitated to the stage, working variety and Broadway with an act that preceded, coevally improved upon, and later referred back to Theda Bara's vamp. When Bara was arch and lowering, West came right out and purred, "Let's have a time." Bara was an archetype of woman, an expressionistic conceit, a euphemism. Mae was sex.

Even before she got to Hollywood she had perfected her act, and it was to remain unchanged for the rest of her life, nearly ninety years in all. There was the motion. In *Sometime* (1918), an Ed Wynn musical with music by Rudolf Friml, she introduced the "Shimmy Shawabble," adapted from a black dance she picked up in Chicago. There was the cool defiance of or perfunctory surrender to bluenose repressiveness. When her shimmy was denounced, "I just told them it was some kind of Polish folk dance." There were the costumes, florid and about two decades out of date. There were the noises—cooings, hehs, uhms, and the strange blues-derived wail she uses in musical numbers. There was the authorship, West writing and staging her stage vehicles herself. And there was the vanity—Mae as character and Mae as person are both devoted to Mae the image. She's not selfish. In the plots, she often helps out underdogs and in life she could be very loyal to people the Hollywood gentry wouldn't spit on. She was just wild about Mae.

Paramount, a studio in great Depression, was wild about her featured part in *Night After Night* (1932), about a speakeasy owner (George Raft) trying to improve himself culturally. Constance Cummings plays a ritzy girl he hopes to appeal to, Wynne Gibson his cast-off flame, Alison Skipworth his tutor in gentility, and West barges in and busts the place wide open as Maudie Triplett, all-around expert in romance, beauty, and other hotcha. "Goodness, what beautiful diamonds!" cries a hatcheck girl as West saunters into Raft's club. "Goodness had nothin' to do with it, dearie," says West.

She wrote her own lines, coached director Archie Mayo in lining up the tracking shots to catch her can-can promenades, and, according to Raft, "stole everything but the cameras." Paramount immediately saw West vehicles as a way out of bankruptcy. The studio offered her $25,000 for the rights to her Broadway hit *Diamond Lil* and $100,000 salary to play the lead. $75,000 more for production costs and the whole piece was in the can. Retitled *She Done Him Wrong* (1933), the picture earned $2,000,000 in its first months of release.

Note the role change in the title from the traditional *"he done her* wrong." A woman is in charge throughout: runs the plot, initiates the love interest, protects the innocent, and kills the villain. This sounds a lot like Little Mary, but besides the enormous difference in tone between Pickford and West there is also Pickford's reliance on the monogamous mating code. West is most outraging not in her suggestive jokes but in her promiscuity, all the more shocking in *She Done Him Wrong*'s period decor, that of the 1890s, when women didn't even have the vote. Cary Grant, her love interest in the film, plays a detective disguised as a Salvation Army cadet; naturally, he falls for and attempts to reform West. But this courtship amounts to his education in womanly independence. First, there's the aggressor:

WEST: Why don't you come up sometime an' see me? I'm home every evening.
GRANT: I'm busy every evening.

WEST: What are you tryin' to do, insult me?
GRANT: I've met your kind before.
WEST: Come up. I'll tell your fortune. You can be had.

Then there's the exploiter, the gold digger who sells and buys. Says Mae, "Diamonds is my career." Has she no values, no morality, no religion? WEST: "You know, it was a toss-up whether I'd go in for diamonds or sing in the choir. The choir lost."
Has she no spirituality?

WEST: Maybe I ain't got no soul.
GRANT: Oh yes, you have, but you keep it hidden under a mask. . . .
          Haven't you ever met a man who could make you happy?
WEST: Sure, lots of times.

And there's the liberated person, utterly content with free choice. At the fadeout, Grant, revealed as The Hawk, a federal agent, handcuffs West.

WEST: Are those absolutely necessary? You know, I wasn't born with them.
GRANT: A lot of men would have been safer if you were.
WEST: I don't know. Hands ain't everything.

He stows her in a paddy wagon only to slip a wedding ring on her finger. He thinks he has landed her, but we know better:

WEST: (Eyeing Grant and purring) Dark and handsome . . .
GRANT: You bad girl.
WEST: You'll find out.

The Hollywood harlot as type was distinguished from other women by rootlessness and her refusal to admit that she is as dependent upon men as any wife. Some women in the audience resented such a lifestyle; some men resented this take-the-money-and-run attitude. In *Shanghai Express*, Dietrich's character is described as a "coaster"; and right-thinking, straight-talking Clive Brook asks what a coaster is. The answer—"a woman who lives by her wits along the China coast"—evoked gasps of shock (and some laughter) in theatres all over America.

A harlot, then, is a woman who *thinks* she's free. Most of Dietrich's and Harlow's harlot roles conform to the plan. But West's never did. This made her pictures truly revolutionary. *I'm No Angel* (1933), with West as a lion tamer (she did the big scene without a double, in a cage surrounded by riflemen) and Grant again as a socialite she sues for breach of promise, does end on a rather conventional love-is-marriage fadeout. But West is polygamous at heart, and the moments that create the strongest impression are not those in which she shows how strongly she has fallen for Grant, but those in which she is cynical about sex or hungry for it. *I'm No Angel*'s opening sequence, with West as carny dancer Tira (pronounced *Tie*-ra), is basic Mae. She sings "They Call Me Sister Honky-Tonk," does her shimmy (one of the few downright arousing stunts in her films), surveys the crowd for a bankable date, asks "Am I making myself clear now?" and sashays off murmuring with a nasty bite, "Suckers!" It was because of scenes like that that professional do-gooders rose up and castrated the movies, imposing a censorship that didn't give way for over thirty years.

They murdered Mae especially. With the Hays production code dusted off, amended, and strictly enforced from 1934 on, there was little that West did that she could still do. She had dealt with censorship on Broadway in the 1920s, several times facing court action and once doing a short term in the pokey. But in New York it was her subject matter that had the prudes screaming, her views of the homosexual milieu and ultralascivious men. In Hollywood, it was West's style that came under ban, her put-downs of the received virtues, her easy riding, her shimmy.

At first she tried to work around the Code. But with a Hays minion right on the set making every take a scrimmage for power, it couldn't have been fun. There were title changes: *It Ain't No Sin* became *Belle of the Nineties* (1934) and *How Am I Doin'?* became *Goin' to Town* (1935). There were ideological appeasements: in *Klondike Annie* (1936), West nurses a dying nun, dons her habit, and carries on her good work, preaching, "Any time you take religion as a joke, the laugh's on you." Happily, much of the true West remained. In *Go West, Young Man* (1936), West is Mavis Arden, a movie star stranded in the Pennsylvania outback. She vamps yokel Randolph Scott, thrills local ingenues, and scandalizes conservatives. Observes Aunt Kate (Elizabeth Patterson) of a bygone day: "They had It all right, but they didn't photograph it and put it to music." Working on Scott, West pulls out the whole do—perfume, gown, come-hither hums, even a song. But Scott is slow to arouse. "Perfume's a lovely thing," he tells her. "But you know they make it out of the darnedest things? Horses' hooves, potato peelings, coal tar . . ." West replies, "I always say, science is golden."

She's in fettle, using the innocence of the American village to stave off national horror at her revolution. Rather than capitulate entirely to the censors, she simply tossed out the carnival side shows, Bowery saloons, hustlers, and crooks that she habitually used as background. Thus she hoped to frame a more acceptable charade while keeping her personal style unchanged. Pastoral, West seems almost middle class. She doesn't even score with Scott. Dancing with him when they're alone, she beats time on his waist and concludes her pitch: "I've missed the thing that counts most—a tender, honest love." At last Scott turns on. "Your eyes are like the water in Miller's pond," he whispers. But Aunt Kate blunders in to hear a radio program, and West gives it up. "I must be going," she says. "I'm usually in bed at this hour." And Aunt Kate snaps back, "This must be one of your off nights."

Actually, West's career was in big trouble. She couldn't stay cooped up in wide open spaces; once was enough. Her world is that of the city, of the smart money and the troublemakers and the rabble. But rural America was still in reaction against the ethnic face that the urban 1920s had turned to the culture, the Jewish vaudevillians, Irish politicians, and black musicians. A New York Catholic had actually run for President in 1928, as the Democratic candidate. Not only was West's act itself too ribald for most tastes; her entourage was objectionable. When West went back to the little old New York setting for her eighth and last Paramount picture, *Every Day's a Holiday* (1938), she was bucking a decade's accumulation of anti–New York rage and made a neat target for the backlash.

The film isn't good. Even reviewers in New York, West's hometown and her place of strongest support, were tired of her routine. And while appearing on Edgar Bergen's radio show, she again baited the righteous in a Garden of Eden sketch with her delivery of the line, "Would you, honey, like to try this apple sometime?" The storm reached its zenith just as *Every Day's a Holiday* came out to face a Bible Belt boycott, and for extra measure West was banned from the airwaves. Performers weren't even allowed to mention her name. When West insisted that Paramount let her film a biography of Catherine the Great, in Technicolor, only a few years after von Sternberg and Dietrich lost the studio a fortune on *The Scarlet Empress* on the same subject, Paramount gave up on West. She was without a contract until Universal approached her with what seems like a dream idea: Mae West and W. C. Fields in *My Little Chickadee* (1940), the con woman versus the con man, to her script with his interpolations.

Buffs adore the film, a western in which shoot-'em-up conventions are mixed with typical West and Field turns. West leads off (as she did in the billing), opening the story by getting thrown out of a frontier town. "Are you showing contempt of this court?" her judge thunders. "No," she replies. "I'm doin' my best to hide it." The scene is from life: the Catholic Legion of Decency and the Hays Office hunting West from Hollywood, telling her not to come back till she's "respectable and married."

Never. She does marry Fields, it's true, but he is unable to consummate the union. Their first scene together, on a train, is true delight. Margaret Hamilton is on hand as that staple of the Westian world, the crusading prude, and Fields pumps her for information on West. "I can't say anything good about her!" avers Hamilton. "I can see what's good," Fields growls. "Tell me the rest."

The meeting is classic, each performer doing his own stuff yet blending into mutual burlesque:

FIELDS: May I present my card?
WEST: (Reading) "Novelties and notions." What kinda notions ya got?
FIELDS: You'd be surprised. Some are old. Some are new.

For extra fun, they close the film with a tradeoff of their signature lines:

FIELDS: You must come up an' see me sometime.
WEST: I'll do that, my little chickadee.

When they play without each other, Fields comes off best, because his character has range enough to play to or around anyone. Cuthbert J. Twillie is a type awkwardly at home anywhere, while West's Flower Belle Lee, like her Lady Lou, Tira, Ruby Carter, Peaches O'Day, and the rest, can only play to adoring males, frigid female detractors, or amused black maids. There just isn't any other kind in her act.

Yet for all its limitations, Mae's act has endured. She made three films after *My Little Chickadee,* all flops seen by few. She turned up very rarely on television. She was active on the nightclub circuit, but this was cut off by 1960. Recently she died.

Who has done less than Mae—yet whose legend is bigger than hers? Obviously, something in her act caught the national imagination and has held it regardless of contemporary trend. Why? What's in the act?

Ego dominated it. The absolute auteur, West picked most of her projects, always wrote her own lines, if not the whole script, and turned down any offer that didn't promise her full control. (Once she went against her better judgment, on the Columbia musical *The Heat's On* in 1943. It virtually finished her film career.) Here was a smart professional. But the ego runs wild in the stories, too, making her films vanity productions. She was forty by the time she made her first movie and sports the hourglass figure of a dead age, yet every man is crazy about her. She tells us she's the greatest in lines that read at least partly as self-spoof, but she also has men of all ages telling us the same thing and they're supposed to mean it. It sounds a little cracked after a while.

Trying to decide what's serious and what's burlesque in West is tricky, because it all comes off in one slow glide. Each of her films has a song or two, warbled in a patently negroid light soprano, and in subject matter and performance technique they complement the image. But if one heard them out of context, not knowing who was singing, they would be thought ridiculous. Similarly, her bad grammar and whimsical one-liners ("Beulah, peel me a grape") work well in the act but are meaningless outside it. The act is an essence, one thing, like a sheet of glass. It doesn't parse easily.

West's no-nonsense preference for sex over romance sets her apart, and her implication that promiscuity is her natural condition and not a plot gimmick is of course what made her so controversial. She could not be forgiven her trespasses, because she wasn't making a mistake: she was taking her choice. Undercutting this, however, is her odd idea of what constitutes good romantic casting. Typically, she is mainly concerned with two men in each film, one an older robust type and the other a pretty boy. Yet her toughs are horrors and the boys more oily than pretty. If the eroticism is for real, why doesn't West find more authentic partners in hot? Only with Cary Grant* and Randolph Scott do we feel that West is meeting a standard. At least Gilbert Roland, in a small part in *She Done Him Wrong,* prompts a classic moment in her style of "I'll do it serious and you'll think it's funny" role playing, when she stands transfixed eyeing Roland and maid Louise Beavers pops in to announce, "Your bath is ready, Miss Lou." Says Mae, "You take it. I'm indisposed."

But her other leading men are simply not attractive. And aren't these sex comedies, i.e., *about* attraction? Edward Arnold, Ralf Harolde, William B. Davidson, Roger Pryor, Paul Cavanaugh, Victor McLaglen, Warren William, Edmund Lowe, Dick Foran, and the rest of her pickups are dismal as love interests, and as a convict who jumps prison to resume an old affair with West in *She Done Him Wrong,* Owen Moore is grotesque. He is obviously drunk, barely able to stand up, and speaks as if his mouth were full of pebbles. Moore had been a dynamic leading man for Griffith at Biograph, so irresistible that Little Mary became his secret bride when Mama Charlotte Pickford opposed the match. But years of alcoholism and failure crushed Moore, and while he was the worst possible choice for West by 1933, he is, the drunkenness aside, not that much more unsuitable than most of his fellow West admirers.

Why the inappropriate casting? Was West afraid of looking too old next to a real idol? Obviously not, as she used the very young Cary Grant twice. What's stranger yet is that when she hit the nightclubs in the 1950s she used as backup a troupe of bodybuilders in briefs. From one extreme of mostly lackluster partners she moved to another extreme of men as sex objects, characterless brutes who posed, flexed,

---

*West claims to have discovered Grant strolling through the Paramount lot, but he was already established when they met. Her claims, however, are not disingenuous. The West ego kept her from seeing other people's films, so she was probably unaware that Grant was already a leading man.

and, according to West's PR, fought for first rights to Mae behind the scenes.

One sometimes hears of men in past epochs who spent their public hours dressed and made up as women; and it was sometimes said of West that she must be a man in a costume. Certainly she was the first Hollywood star to exploit the gay sensibility. For that, in the end, is what her act was based on and what made her revolutionary. But much of it is hidden, encoded. Consider this exchange with socialite Kent Taylor in *I'm No Angel:*

WEST: I like a sophisticated man to take me out.
TAYLOR: Well, I'm not really sophisticated.
WEST: You're not really out yet, either.

"Sophisticated," in the 1930s, was in-group argot for "apparently straight, but open to suggestion," and "out" (of the closet) was in use then, too. As the first playwright to deal with the underground gay scene, in *The Drag* (which closed out of town, in 1927), West knew the terms. So is this a salute to the fraternity from a sympathetic outsider, or more of her burlesque? Most of West's shtick—the "look 'em over" stares, the come-on hints, the double meanings, the "you can be had" philosophy—is just the gay style exposed to the outsider.

It made her unique. But more: it made her character believable. Other women played aggressive (Jean Harlow, for example). Other women joked sardonically about love (Eve Arden). Other women vamped (Garbo? No, say Dietrich. Garbo moped, and men read that at their pleasure). But West does it all and changes each part of it. It's raunch elegance, and it says that no woman is a whore. When West does her stuff, that double standard that holds that man is man but a woman is either a sweetheart or a vamp falls away to nothing, for the very term "whore" is dishonest, and West is if anything more honest even than Garbo. She was also discreet, keeping her private life private. No one knows what she did with her free time.

True, she let her act down in later years, making the atrocious *Myra Breckinridge* (1970), from Gore Vidal's novel. Throwing elegance behind her, she played a talent agent in a series of heavy-handed se- duction scenes, at one point telling a Vietnam veteran who explains that he can unscrew his artificial arm and leg, "Well, come up an' see me some time and I'll show you how to screw your head off." (The sequence was deleted from the release print.) Her last film, *Sextette* (1978), more of the same, was so awful it never went into general release.

The bad deal at the end of the career is another of stardom's clichés. Crawford, too, finished off in garbage. But the X-rated *Myra* and the embarrassing *Sextette* did not damage the image of West's act. Her legend stands intact. The vamp who never undressed, the Circe who mostly charmed ogres, the obscenity who kept it clean, the paradox who never felt like a riddle, was a great influence on the culture, as a transitional figure between Victorian morality and an imagined libertarian utopia. Her predecessor Theda Bara made some stabs at translating her persona into an ideology, but West never did. And had West been acclaimed as a moralist—as a hero for her subversion of authoritarianism—she would probably have dismissed it as a joke, a stunt. An act. "I just," she once said, "suggest."

# 8

# Comics I

MARIE DRESSLER
CAROLE LOMBARD
MARION DAVIES
LUCILLE BALL
GRACIE ALLEN
EVE ARDEN

*Oh, Mother, Godfrey loves me—he put me in the shower!*

—CAROLE LOMBARD
to Alice Brady, in *My Man Godfrey*

Hollywood's major male comics tended to favor one of two type possibilities. Either they were droll farceurs like Robert Montgomery or Cary Grant or they were wimp crazies like Eddie Cantor and Danny Kaye. There was seldom anything between the two extremes: romantic verbal artists or non-romantic slapstick artists.

It was different for the comediennes. They came in all types and shapes, some of them developing unique characters which would then be imitated by younger actresses or consulted by writers stuck for psychology. Perhaps no one better proves the range of Hollywood's women comics than Marie Dressler, for she became the nation's number one box-office star despite physical equipment that should, according to the rules, have relegated her to self-spoofing bits in other people's films.

Dressler had undergone a rise and fall before she hit it big in films. She trained in vaudeville, the most cosmopolitan of America's popular art spaces, where anyone with some great or minor gift could make it on some level. Vaudeville took in everything from Shakespeare to animal acts: there was a part for everybody. Looks didn't matter much in the variety show, because whatever one performer lacked someone else on the bill might supply. This was important to Dressler, who called her autobiography *The Life Story of an Ugly Duckling* and termed herself "too homely for a prima donna and too big for a soubrette." She could carry a tune, play amusingly wretched piano, and lampoon a dated classic to its knees. Her great specialty was her expression of outrage, boredom, or assorted other means of dissent when her fellow characters got pretentious or stupid. She touched a universal nerve there.

Everyone knows a few people who are always getting away with nonsense; no one ever got away with it on a stage with Dressler.

So she rose from vaudeville to Broadway, playing leads in musicals even before the nineteenth century was finished. She played heroines at times, though slapstick prevailed over romance, as in her biggest success, *Tillie's Nightmare* (1910). Mack Sennett filmed the show as *Tillie's Punctured Romance* (1914) with Charlie Chaplin and Mabel Normand in support, but *Tillie* follow-ups did not do well and Dressler returned to the stage. She might have forgot the cinema and reigned on Broadway but for her enthusiastic participation in the 1919 actors' strike that closed most of the country's theatres for five weeks in late summer. The strike won actors minimum rights that were long overdue, but some producers gave in so bitterly that they singled out a few of the ringleaders for special revenge. Many stars and featured players were too useful to lose; a few of the let us say unusual talents could be blackballed with little loss of revenue. Dressler was unusual, and suddenly found herself out of work, the star of her own little Depression in the middle of the booming 1920s.

She was reportedly on the verge of taking a job as a housekeeper in a Long Island mansion when Frances Marion interceded for her at MGM. Dressler had befriended Marion years before when Marion was an inexperienced reporter and Dressler top copy. Now Marion was a successful scenarist with access to the crucial ears. She talked them into starring Dressler, at a handsome salary, in *The Callahans and the Murphys* (1927), one of those "bellicose, lovable Irish" comedies and something Marion had thought up specifically for Dressler's style. With Polly Moran seconding Dressler's looks of suspicion and dispute, the silent was a hit. Irish groups angrily forced MGM to withdraw it—but Dressler had proved herself. Other parts followed at intervals, then Dressler went, overnight, from unusual to indispensable. For it turned out that she was even better in talkie comedy than in silent: the voice exactly matched the character. While she looked you over, she told you off, and there was simply no one else around who did it as well.

She could also play the folks who need telling off, as in *The Vagabond Lover* (1929), Rudy Vallee's debut vehicle, a disaster. Vallee was hopelessly unready for acting, and director Marshall Neilan, used to the self-starting talents of the silent days, could do nothing for him. Vallee's line readings make Nelson Eddy an Olivier by comparison; even the songs don't interest him. Comparably poor is Sally Blane, Vallee's love interest, and the story, about the extremely minor adventures of Vallee's band, the Connecticut Yankees, is the kind that keeps saying "Yay! Let's go!" and never moves. So the whole seventy minutes is up for grabs. Dressler grabs it. As Blane's flighty society aunt, Dressler fondles her hair, pampers her handkerchief, embellishes every other word with a fume or a giggle, and piles triple-take upon double-take.

It's nothing but shtick, but it's priceless, a comic style for sound as worthy as Chaplin's was for silence.

Dressler made five films in 1929, the first year of regular sound production, running from lot to lot. She was inimitable, so every studio needed her. Yet she remained unusual in that strange way of hers, so no studio needed her exclusively, with the promotion and salary that entails. She was put into *Anna Christie* (1930) as the girlfriend of Garbo's father, and that changed everything. MGM tied Dressler down and gloried in her.

In *Anna Christie,* Garbo tells Dressler, "You're me forty years from now," and Dressler's Marthy is indeed an old wreck, scratching herself, flapping and crackling her hands hither and yon, cadging drinks like crazy. It's a funny performance, but funny from life, not from jokes. Given only two sequences, one of them rather brief, Dressler walks off with the picture. George Marion, Jr., who had already played Anna's father in the silent version of O'Neill's play with Blanche Sweet, and Charles Bickford—as Anna's lover—are both fine, and Garbo is Garbo. But Dressler was drawing on that fund of skeptical horse sense she had amassed in the decades of stage work, and you just can't bother with anyone else when she's in view. Unlike most movie actors, she always played to an imaginary audience, gauging the house, timing the laughs, mugging for the balcony, yet observing character.

She was *theatrical,* and it shouldn't have worked in film, but it did; see her for yourself. Perhaps too many of her MGM vehicles which followed *Anna Christie,* mainly farces with Polly Moran or sentimental marital comedies with Wallace Beery, emphasized Dressler the comic over Dressler the actress. But they made fortunes, and it's difficult to turn down wealth and fame after a lifetime of dues-paying that almost ended in nowhere. And Dressler did leave one imperishable performance, in *Dinner at Eight* (1933).

Like *Grand Hotel,* this was an MGM all-star production, adapted from a gala Broadway hit, with John and Lionel Barrymore, Wallace Beery, Jean Harlow, Billie Burke, and Dressler in the leads. Few would call either of the two films great except in a golden-age Hollywood sense, but they are diverting, and capture a distinct mid-Depression hunger for luxury that is sociologically instructive. Lionel Barrymore is the last in a line of merchant shippers, whose business is tottering, about to be swallowed by up-from-the-gutter tycoon Wallace Beery, Dressler is an actress of robust grandeur who will inadvertently ruin Barrymore by selling off her holdings in his company, John Barrymore is a faded Shakespearean who must get a part or die, Jean Harlow is Beery's wife, and Burke as Lionel's wife ties it all together by inviting the whole crowd to a dressy dinner. Like *Grand Hotel, Dinner at Eight* preens over its collage of unlikely people, of old and new wealth, of grace and vulgarity, of tradition and innovation, of success and failure.

And again like *Grand Hotel, Dinner at Eight* sports so many different forms of acting that one might use it in a seminar on style.

With George Cukor in charge, the styles are made to blend—the hams are toned down or at least shadowed, the naturalists egged on, and everybody is up to mischief. The film is filled with it, in fact, especially in the fetching brawls between Beery and Harlow and Barrymore's touching portrayal of a third-rate actor trying to put on front and hustle a last drink at the same time. Still, Dressler is the one most vividly recalled. Despite her knockabout comedies, MGM was touting her as a grand old stage institution, so she takes top billing and comes on so hambola she threatens to rock the film off its delicate balance. But, again, her choices are so right that they carry her through. The film closes on a classic choice, as Dressler and Harlow are walking in to Burke's dinner. Harlow, wanting to do as Romans do in this ritzy environment, offers conversation. She opens by saying that she has been reading an interesting book, and the shock of this staggers Dressler as if an earthquake had struck. Too much? Well, it's very funny, not because Dressler is so big and shaky, but because she puns physically on her grandeur. Harlow goes on to report that this book predicts that machines will replace every profession.

Dressler gives Harlow the once-over through her lorgnette. "My dear," she says, "that's something *you* need never worry about!" The end.

Dressler's end, too, came soon, and in this story the fiendish L. B. Mayer turns up in a different light. Dressler was dying of cancer, and, according to Samuel Marx, then MGM's story editor, Mayer kept the truth from her, trying to convince her with the help of her doctor that she was recuperating. Mayer had Marx supply him with story ideas for Dressler vehicles and had the PR people feed cover items to the press. But people usually can tell when they're dying, and Mayer must have known that Dressler would see through the ruses unless a stunt could turn it all around. He got his chance just before he was about to take a European vacation: Dressler had been invited to take part in a benefit show back east, and Mayer, playing the money-grabbing producer, refused to let her accept, telling her that she would have to stay handy to begin work on her next picture. No benefit. Dressler told him off and threw him out of her room. She died while he was in Europe.

Dressler's extraordinary prominence in a business that sometimes seems like a big romance comic book points to some latitude in the casting of comediennes. Perhaps the notion of a funny woman subverts the tyranny of the love story, opening it up to off-center possibilities. On the other hand, one of Hollywood's most popular comediennes was without question a stunner: Carole Lombard. She was so noticeable that director Allan Dwan pulled her into a small part in *A Perfect Crime* when she was thirteen. He just couldn't resist her.

She came of what used to be called good family: Scotch and English stock, *molto* ancestors, name Jane Peters. But, in the old Hollywood convention, she came of a broken home, a great source for movieland adolescent extras. For some years after Dwan tapped her, she worked the back lots, nearly losing the whole career potential when a car accident in 1926 cut her face badly; in time the resulting scar faded. But, to keep her mind off it, Lombard's mother enlisted her with Mack Sennett, and at the ultra-comic studio the girl learned business that would aid her later. Swanson, we recall, came out of this same training ground, and Swanson, too, profited from hanging around comic masters. It was the closest thing Hollywood had to vaudeville: when you weren't in front of the camera yourself you watched the veterans taking and giving the ancient indignities.

However, the studios didn't see Lombard as a comic. When she landed a contract at Paramount, she was trained for romance and put through the standard paces—city melodrama, society romp, even a singing part in *Safety in Numbers* (1930), in which she delivers "[Young man] You Appeal to Me," a trivial flirtation tune that she tries, unsuccessfully, to act her way through. Every now and then, she tosses a look of Pirandellian helplessness into the camera, as if saying, "The studio made me do this." But in film what you do is what you are. It comprehends no Pirandello paradox, no riddles on what is reality. Reality is what's seen.

Lombard, at the time, was seen to be captivating, and that was enough. She was rising in the industry, marrying the very coming William Powell, whose specialty was Suave and Worldly. Maybe he overdid it. Some witnesses accused him of playing his parts off screen, and with far less witty dialogue than MGM's writers could give him. "The son of a bitch is acting," Lombard supposedly said, "even when he takes his pajamas off." After two years they divorced, and by then Lombard was coming along nicely herself. She arrived fully in *Twentieth Century* (1934), Howard Hawks's version of the stage play about a battling stage director and his former protégée, a Hollywood name he hopes to drag back to Broadway. "I just turned them loose," Hawks recalled years later. Lombard came onto the set tentative, careful, and completely wrong. This was screwball city, needing a breathless tempo and all-out loving-baiting-seething jazz from the two leads, Lombard and John Barrymore. Lombard was so unready for the style that Barrymore was holding his nose—on camera—behind her back.

So Hawks introduced Lombard to screwball. He naturalized it for her—Barrymore's character is insulting you, provoking you. What would you do if he tried it off the set? "I'd kick him right in the groin." Well, use it, Hawks tells her, and the next take was splendid, gamey and vital. "This girl," Barrymore remarked, "is absolutely marvelous."

She was a romantic heroine trained in comedy, and *Twentieth*

*Century* pulled the training and her natural charm into focus. Now Lombard was a star and she knew what she did best, comedy. But Paramount kept putting her into the wrong kind of film—a Shirley Temple programmer called *Now and Forever* (1934), *Lady by Choice* (1934), *The Gay Bride* (1934), *Rumba* (1935), and so on. At least she's good when the script isn't a disaster. *Lady by Choice,* on loan to Columbia, is decent, though a mere followup to *Lady for a Day,* in which May Robson had played a bag lady converted into a dowager to impress a daughter she hasn't seen in years. Lombard, in the sequel, plays a crusty fan dancer who adopts a mother out of an old women's home for purposes of PR; naturally, the two hit it off directly because both are square shooters. They're not sentimental, either. "I don't know anything about charity," Lombard announces early in the action. "I never got any and I never handed out any." But sentimentality creeps in after a bit, with Robson playing the wisdom of her wasted life against Lombard's youthful zeal. As with Garbo and Dressler in *Anna Christie,* they're two versions of the same profession—and Robson is determined to spare Lombard ending up the way Robson has. It's Hollywood corn, extenuated by Robson's toughness and Lombard's likability. When she hunts a nice playboy for his money, she falls for him—so naturally when he proposes she has to turn him down, now respecting him too much to use him.

That sort of behavior kept Lombard noteworthy through her many insipid pictures; luckily, every so often she got a comedy and became a top star all over. In 1934 it was *Twentieth Century.* In 1936 it was *My Man Godfrey,* with ex-husband Powell as a "forgotten man" whom Lombard picks up in a trash dump on a scavenger hunt and who stays on as butler to her family. Money has ruined them. Father Eugene Pallette pays the bills but can't keep order or respect. Mother Alice Brady is selfish and trivial. Sister Gail Patrick is vicious. But money can't ruin Lombard. Heiress though she be, she is utterly at odds with the schools, clubs, and mansions of her set. She doesn't even understand or like scavenger hunts, at the time the pet mischief of America's patrician sillies and the ideal device with which to open the most politicized of the screwballers.

Written by Morrie Riskind and directed by Gregory la Cava, *My Man Godfrey* is the deftest skirmish in the class war, using plot turns (butler Powell is revealed as an aristocrat in hiding), epigrams (says Powell at one point, "The difference between a tramp and a rich man is a decent job"), and slapstick (Mischa Auer as Alice Brady's artistic protégé-in-residence imitates a gorilla) to send its satire home. And this is bitter satire, for under the apparent message that "all the classes come together in harmony," so characteristic of screwball, is a lurking disgust for the rich and a disbelief that they can ever live in harmony with anything. But the film's best feature is Lombard, mitigating the irresponsibility that keys the "madcap" screwball heroine with her genuine good nature. Loy takes screwball for granted, and Hepburn uses it as a weapon, but Lombard eyes it askance and tries to beat it back. Furthermore, she has the moxie to go after Powell at the end and win him over, since it comes down to that. A woman to like and admire.

In 1934, *Twentieth Century;* in 1936, *My Man Godfrey.* In 1937 it was *Nothing Sacred,* and in this third classic screwballer Lombard's succession of comic innocents, romantic sophisticates, and city and rural slickers reaches a summit. Ben Hecht's script satirizes opportunism in the newspaper "human interest" feature, with Lombard as a New England girl believed to be dying of radium poisoning and Fredric March as a reporter who falls in love with her while exploiting her fate. Nearly everyone in the film is detestable, from the city hustlers to the country eccentrics who, when March comes up to check on the story, stonewall and insult him. (One tyke rushes out of a front yard without warning to bite him on the leg.)

Lombard is not only the heroine of the story, but the reason why we can enjoy the film's cynical world view: she's nice. In a plain black dress with a lace collar she looks bewildered, unpolished (she was turning twenty-nine at the time), and completely suggestible. She has the uncanny knack of taking on the sentiments of those around her, whether or not she agrees with them. It's a form of vulnerability. Sorrow makes her glum, humor cheers her, confusion unnerves her. Mystery fascinates her, as a wrapped present might. When she realizes she isn't dying at all, she plans to fake a suicide to save the general honor. Then she thinks of all the fun she'll miss. "They'll hold the funeral without me!" she sobs; she wants to be there. Later, when March has her riled, she's ready to mix it up like a champ. "Oo, I *hate* you!" she cries. "Let me hit you just once!" In the end, the city cannot corrupt her, and she stays nice. In the anarchy of screwball, she represents beauty and a conscience, Hollywood's two favorite things.

Her public took her at the scripts' word, balancing *Nothing Sacred* with *Twentieth Century* and *My Man Godfrey.* Altogether, she was turbulent, sensible, and friendly, and as such she became so agreeable that a number of indifferent or downright poor films couldn't hurt her. She was lightly symbolic of an American type, unspoiled and sporty. Her friends knew a foul-mouthed, devilish character given to outrageous practical jokes. (On *Nothing Sacred,* irritated at March's amorous advances, she invited him for a drink in her dressing room—after donning a rubber dildo.) Obviously, the public knew little of such details; what they caught was what she showed on screen, or said in an occasional pronouncement, as when she reported she was happy to pay some two-thirds of her income in 1938 to the government for its services: "I really think I got my money's worth."

Lombard grew so popular, so trustworthy, that in early 1939 a relatively shocking article in *Photoplay* called "Hollywood's Unmarried

Husbands and Wives" did not hurt Lombard's standing in its revelation that she and Clark Gable were openly carrying on an affair. "All Clark and Carole did," said *Photoplay*, "was strike up a Hollywood twosome. Nobody said, 'I do!'" Citing as well such couples as Barbara Stanwyck and Robert Taylor, Constance Bennett and Gilbert Roland, and William Powell and the recently deceased Jean Harlow, the article was the first genuinely racy exposé ever attempted by a prestigious movie magazine. Its tone is cool yet it clearly intended to jolt the reader. However, there was no popular attack on Lombard and Gable for their affair, for this was the choice coupling of the era as much as that of Little Mary and Doug was two decades earlier.

Note the change in woman type. Fairbanks and Gable were both athletic, affable, and audacious. But where Little Mary was a moralist, helping herself and others in a world of good guys and bad guys, Lombard was an absurdist, trying to get along in a mad world of indistinctly drawn battle lines. Still, when the goods massed up against the bads in World War II, Lombard was relevant to the cause, raising many millions of dollars in war bonds. While on one such tour in early 1942 she died in a plane crash, throwing the country into mourning.

Gable, behind his closed doors, was inconsolable, brooding in something like a coma, not eating, leaving her rooms exactly as she left them. But others less closely associated with Lombard seemed unusually shaken or solemn. President Roosevelt sent Gable a telegram of condolence and awarded Lombard a medal for having been "killed in action in defense of her country," homeowners who flew the flag dropped it to half-mast, and numerous small businesses halted proceedings for the day or observed a minute of silence. At least one journalist thought all this a matter of carrying praise too far: Elmer Davis complained on the radio that "the death of a movie actress [has been treated as] more important than the death of fifteen Army fliers in the same incident." Davis raised a valid point, but discounted the intimate impression that Lombard and other movie actors had made on the public. The fifteen fliers, sad to say, were anonymously tragic, while Lombard was someone one had met at merry parties, in boardinghouse parlors, and in hotel bedrooms.

It's a cliché to say that we feel we know movie stars because we've accompanied them on so many trips; but it's the operating phenomenon of Hollywood movies, the You Are There—or, better, the They Are Here—that actualizes fiction. Lombard's adventures began as inventions, but in the end they became a matter of public record. Thus, her early death sealed her biography in her most vivid films, mainly her classic screwball triptych, *Twentieth Century, My Man Godfrey,* and *Nothing Sacred.*

Looks are everything in film, some might say, but they didn't hurt

Marie Dressler and they couldn't limit Carole Lombard. Perhaps come-diennes have more latitude than straight romantic leads or "charac-ters." Comedy is, after all, the richest of forms, natural and fantastic at once. (Think of W. C. Fields and the Marx Brothers.) Certainly, the invention of screwball comedy did much to broaden the American per-ception of women (men, too).

Still, some people can see only one thing. Marion Davies may have been one of Hollywood's most engaging comics—witty, game, and a sharp observer of people. Her imitations were terrific. But William Randolph Hearst, the newspaper publisher who became Davies' lover and artistic backer in 1918, saw her only as a storybook heroine, wher-ever possible in fairytale clothes and fairyland settings.

Davies was loving, loyal, and a good sport; Hearst had extraordi-nary media power besides a vast fortune. So Davies made the films Hearst wanted her to make, and Hearst could pressure the studios into hosting and releasing his projects, for to anger Hearst meant bad press from his columnists (including Louella Parsons) at the least and maybe, at worst, a full-scale exposé of lubricity and wickedness among movie people. Hearst's Cosmopolitan Productions, housed in succession at Paramount, then MGM, then Warner Brothers, enjoyed a tense accep-tance in the industry, for the threat of Hearst's power was a canker gnawing at the pride of otherwise independent moguls, and most Cos-mopolitan pictures did minor business or less anyway. It seems that Davies was just not as popular with moviegoers as she was with Hearst.

The intermediary energy that kept peace between Hearst and the studios was Davies herself. Her charm was sure and her goodness cata-logued in countless acts of charity both public and private.* Davies also gave spectacular parties, and Hollywood loves a top-line bash. Even eastern artists, by personal and political inclinations foes of Hearst's power as well as of how he used it, would attend dinners at San Sim-eon, the Hearst pleasure dome.

It was two of those easterners, Orson Welles and Herman Man-kiewicz, who established the view of Davies as a plutocrat's talentless girlfriend, in *Citizen Kane* (1941). The film's protagonist, Charles Foster Kane, was unmistakably modeled on Hearst, and at one point he ar-ranges for his unhappy wife, Susan Alexander Kane, to star in an oper-atic extravaganza at the Chicago Opera House. She is a ghastly singer, so terrible she scarcely has a right to be in the audience, much less on

*Let one example suffice. When Fatty Arbuckle was finally acquitted of his sensa-tionalized murder rap—by the third jury, no less—he was nonetheless sacrificed to the public's call for a cleaner Hollywood. Will Hays virtually reversed the court's verdict in banning Arbuckle, and no studio would touch him. Davies, with Hearst's influence be-hind her, hired Arbuckle to direct her silent version of the Victor Herbert musical *The Red Mill* (1927) under a pseudonym.

stage. And if Hearst is Kane, then Susan Alexander is Marion Davies.

RKO made *Citizen Kane*, Mankiewicz wrote it, Welles directed it and played Kane, and even before they had wrapped the film Hearst and certain Hollywood powers were attempting to prevent its release. Bookings were blocked, the Hearst papers threatened to sabotage future RKO releases, and even worse swindles were perpetrated. The film did come out and to excellent reviews, but the wasters had done their work, and *Citizen Kane* simply dissolved, not to reappear till the 1950s, with Hearst dead and his empire a ruin. Now, of course, it is a regular event in revival houses, in college film courses, and on television; its eloquent commentary and biting entertainment are as telling today as ever. (No, more telling, for the times were behind it when it was made and needed four decades to catch up.) But it has left one unfortunate impression, that Marion Davies was Susan Alexander.

This is unfair. First of all, however Mankiewicz and Welles meant their character in the *à clef* sense, there was a much closer model for Susan Alexander than Davies, Ganna Walska, who did sing opera, sang it in Chicago and badly, and was the protégée of a plutocrat, Robert McCormick. Many of the people who managed to catch *Citizen Kane* on its original release assumed that Susan was Walska, for her grungy season in Chicago was notorious on a national scale. Furthermore, while Davies was certainly uncomfortable in lacy parts, she was a gifted comedienne.

It would seem that she just didn't care that much about stardom to cultivate the intricacies of typing. Why extend yourself in nonsense like *When Knighthood Was in Flower* (1922) or *Beverly of Graustark* (1926)? Give Davies a modern-dress comedy, perhaps a burlesque of the nonsense itself, with a Hollywood setting, real faces for the camera to pan along in a commissary shot—Chaplin, Fairbanks, Mae Murray, William S. Hart—and a chance for Davies as Peggy Pepper to spot Marion Davies and make a disparaging face. That's *Show People* (1928), directed by King Vidor and Davies' best film.

Even in her element of harum-scarum comedy, Davies didn't extend herself. Working on one of her films meant arriving at the crack of eleven o'clock in the morning to the strains of her personal band playing Kern, Porter, and Berlin, socializing while the techies planned a shot, then repairing to the luncheon table for two or three hours of gambol. Some time that afternoon, four or five inches of film would go into the can. A picture that would normally be completed in four weeks would take six months with Davies in it; but so what? Hearst made it worth Hollywood's while. When he decided that Davies parts were going to Norma Shearer, he moved Cosmopolitan from MGM to Warner Brothers, but that studio was not in gear for a Marion Davies. Everything at Warners happened fast, faster, yesterday, and even

Hearst's gratitude was not worth subverting the Warners schedule. Davies made four films for Warners, then quit the movies.

In the end, Davies was unique not for her movie work but her movie play: her leisure. Today, she is more famous because of someone else's film—*Citizen Kane*—than for any of her own. But then Davies didn't need stardom. Others we have met up with did need it. To Mae Murray, stardom was flattery, to Little Mary a moralistic mandate, to Mae West a living. To Marion Davies it was a hobby you take up to make a friend happy. Her real vocation comprised parties, spoofs, and acts of philanthropy. Maybe Davies, with motivation and better management, might have been a devastating comic with a string of revival house favorites. Or maybe she was too pretty for fun, with her Lillian Gish mouth and Little Mary nose and curls.

Should a bombshell play comedy? No one thought Lucille Ball should; yet she ended up one of the nation's foremost comic stylists. With her husband, Desi Arnaz, and cohorts Vivian Vance and William Frawley, Lucille Ball virtually invented the television sitcom in *I Love Lucy* on a plan for slapstick naturalism: staying employed, moving, forgetting anniversaries, and having a baby, exaggerated by Lucy's cries, looks of horror, and pratfalls.

"The fur flies," tells *TV Guide*, describing a typical episode, "when Lucy's borrowed mink coat is stolen." Indeed, the fur flies. Yet when she began, Ball was a showpiece, just standing there and looking great. As one of the Goldwyn Girls she can be spotted in moments of the Eddie Cantor musicals *Roman Scandals* (1933) and *Kid Millions* (1934), and though she copped a few tiny speaking parts, she remained little more than a mannequin till she played a lead in Dorothy Arzner's *Dance, Girl, Dance* (1940) as a burlesque dancer. This was to prove a standard part for Ball. But while she had the figure and the fake dummy face such roles needed, she lacked a singing voice and became one of the most frequently dubbed singers in Hollywood. Ironically, she brought greater distinction to more serious parts. In *The Big Street* (1942), produced by Damon Runyon, Ball is a hard-edged Broadway type crippled by a gangster and befriended by busboy Henry Fonda. It's an unlikable part, loaded with good comebacks but small in heart. "A girl's best friend is a dollar," she says. She also breaks one of Hollywood stardom's most basic rules: don't die. *The Big Street* is not a film for most tastes, clearly. Yet, without reaching to show us the nice actress underneath the character, Ball is compelling.

As a reward, MGM signed her, gave her Norma Shearer's dressing room, and perfected a subtler dye of red for her hair. But MGM pushed her back into her burlesque queen role in *DuBarry Was a Lady* (1943), from an Ethel Merman–Bert Lahr show with a Cole Porter score. Incomparably smutty, it told how washroom slavey Lahr dreams that he's Louis XV and Merman's his ungettable lady; MGM threw out the cast, most of the songs, and all of the script. There's not much left besides the plot premise, plus Red Skelton for jest, Gene Kelly for love, and a squeaky clean atmosphere at war with the reason for doing the piece in the first place. (It was conceived as a vehicle for Mae West.) An MGM Cole Porter show is not unlike the Anita Bryant critical edition of William Burroughs. Everything's missing.

Ball got few opportunities in the 1940s to build on the tart persona she had worked out at RKO in the 1930s. She plays a wonderful drunk scene in *Easy to Wed* (1946), a remake of *Libeled Lady* with Ball in Jean Harlow's part, but nothing she did really registered, and Ball spent most of the late 1940s in stage and radio work. Fortune turned around for Ball when husband Arnaz dreamed up *I Love Lucy,* incorporated with his wife as Desilu Productions, wisely retained control of the episodes for future use, and provided Ball with a laboratory for the invention of a unique character. Originally the two were to have played themselves, but somewhere along the way they turned into Lucy and Ricky Ricardo, he a struggling bandleader and she a housewife eternally trying to crash show business (usually behind Ricky's back). What was strange about Lucy was not the devious intricacy of her schemes, but the amount of *physical* antics she indulged in. Ball revived the emphatic slapstick of Marie Dressler and Polly Moran, dead for twenty years, and reinvented it as a plausible comic mode even for a handsome heroine. Till then it was reserved for the "characters." So specially conceived was this television Lucy that her fans, viewing her old RKO's and MGM's, are bewildered and disappointed. The Ball they love is not to be found.

Ball's Lucy made an impressive crossover in type, liberating our popular arts of prefabricated role projection by that much more. Some critics might find Lucy Ricardo's commotions a questionable artistic advance, and it is true that in later years, after she parted company with Arnaz, Ball became something of a wax model of herself. In the 1930s she was a brash clotheshorse, in the 1950s a raucous bourgeoise. Thereafter, except for her Lucyesque stint in the stage musical *Wildcat* (1961), she was the grand old dame of American comedy. Terrific: only she had lost her sense of humor. In *Critic's Choice* (1963), she plays opposite Bob Hope in a classic possibility—critic's wife writes bad play. But, for starters, Hope is absurd as "the most important writer on the theatre." Hope is wily-silly, a fantastick, not an opinion maker in the arts. (Henry Fonda played the role in the Broadway original.) But if Hope can have dignity, then so will Lucy—except not only isn't she funny, she can't act anymore, either. An early crucial scene finds Hope having to tell Ball that he thinks her play is terrible. She wants him to like it. He wishes he could. But her script has no action, no theme, no characterization, and he tells her so, straight out. Ball snaps back,

"How was the typing?" The line is right, but Ball gives it nothing, no flip, no crack, no personality.

Worse yet was her stint as the grand old dame of American *musical* comedy, in *Mame* (1974). Photographed behind enough gauze to outfit twenty hospitals and doing everything in a kind of breathless slow motion, Ball is not remotely the madcap whom Rosalind Russell and Angela Lansbury made so treasurable, and it is unsettling to see a comic master turn so completely against her specialties. Is it because rough comedy, in recent decades, has become suspect? Lucy Ricardo was a burlesque of the upwardly mobile middle class in that her ambitious dreams were foolish and she only got into trouble. Had our attitudes changed so much since the 1950s that we could no longer laugh at her in the same way? Or had Ball simply decided to go for dignity as a diva?

Whichever Lucille Ball one prefers, it is noteworthy that she negotiated several changes in identity, one to take her from bit player to lead, another to take her into stardom, and still another when she evolved into an institution. However, her near contemporary and at times near fellow type Gracie Allen achieved greatness through consistency. Both women were screwball types, but Allen's was largely a verbal presentation, dependent on her practiced routines rather than on whatever a writer or studio hoped to throw her way. Both women are most famous as half of a duo, Ball with Arnaz and Allen with George Burns. But while Ball began as a solo and played but one film with Arnaz, *Too Many Girls* (1940), before they definitively teamed for *I Love Lucy*, Gracie was half of Burns and Allen as early as 1922, at the rock bottom of vaudeville in Newark, New Jersey.

It took a while for Burns and Allen to find their métier. At first Allen was straight man to Burns's jokes on this or that subject. But her delivery was so charmingly weird that he became the straight man, his subject exasperation at her illogical world view. (Later, pioneering the television sitcom along with Ball and Arnaz, Burns dropped the exasperation and played it sardonic, which was even more fun.) George fed Gracie questions, mainly about her bizarre relations, and her answers won over the audience. "There was nothing sexy about Gracie," Burns explains, "no big bust or anything like that. She was just a dainty, nice, darling Irish girl with blue-black hair and a quick delivery and great, great style."

The style was episodic, ideal for a variety show stand-up act, not for stories. Still, the conversational interchange made them a useful attraction in talkies, and they came to Hollywood in 1932. Paramount bagged them—typically, for this was the lot with the most visionary investment in comedy, Vaudeville West. W. C. Fields, the Marx Brothers, and Mae West headlined at Paramount, and while their pictures did highly variable business from smash to bomb, today these films are the study and

delight of every serious buff of American comedy. Some comedians, like Carole Lombard or Cary Grant, were actors, who bloomed in story. Others, like Paramount's group, came fully equipped, just turn them loose. Lombard can vary from movie star to dissident aristo to farmgirl to tell us who she is. Burns and Allen remain Burns and Allen: on campus in *College Humor* (1933), on a desert island in *We're Not Dressing* (1933), amid the Wodehousian country weekenders of *A Damsel in Distress* (1937). Too often, they were flipped as comic makeweights into otherwise dullish films, but they dominate *Six of a Kind* (1934), as passengers irritating Mary Boland and Charles Ruggles' cross-country motor trip. Here we meet Gracie in her truth, aimless yet tenacious and impervious to criticism. "You can't hurt her feelings," Boland cries. "We can try," suggests Ruggles. Don't bother. She'll only pull out her strange relatives, such as the niece with three feet. George asks how this is possible. Well, her brother wrote her that Gracie wouldn't recognize her niece—since the last time they met, "she's grown another foot." This is Gracie doodling. But she has a persuasive lunacy on tap as well. Surprising Boland and Ruggles sparking—this is a married couple, now—she cries out, "I saw you!" And they leap apart!

Like Ball, Allen became an American institution, something for the folklore, but she retired in 1959 and died of a heart attack in 1964 and so missed out on the revered phase of fame. Speaking strictly of film, hers was not a huge career. She and Burns made ten films together, then she made three without him, the last in 1944. And the television series is elusive. Like Ball, however, Allen is well remembered, especially by critics who ask why their humor depended so much on self-me-spoof jokes and other degrading material. Why must Gracie be dumb? Why must Lucy be loud? A misogynist slant can sometimes be inferred. Yet Ball and Allen both created their own acts. Besides, they were relatively free from self-mockery, for comedians. There were women comics who made extreme self-put-down a regular feature; next to them Lucy is a doily and Gracie a scientist. Consider Judy Canova, Republic's hillbilly star, who capitalized on her lack of physical appeal and fluke singing voice. Her numbers were country tuned to opera with cadenzas and high notes, and her jokes were mainly about her looks. For instance: "Now, I been to the zoo. Yes, my daddy took me to the zoo when I was five years old. But they rejected me." Or Martha Raye—her looks, especially her sizable mouth, supplied the content of most of the jokes in her films. In *The Big Broadcast of 1938* (1937) she shatters mirrors with a look, and, when she embraces a man, he screams, "I've been kissed by a tunnel!"

The men comics worked on their fear of violence and competition: of men. Some women comics worked on their fear of romance: of men. Most notable in this group was Eve Arden. Not a star, she nonetheless created a type in her name, a flip professional woman less lucky but

wiser than other women. She could never get what she wanted, and knew it wouldn't be worth anything if she got it. In *Mildred Pierce,* as the restaurant hostess who gives Joan Crawford her first job on her rise in the food business, Arden dubs herself "the big sister type" and offers a toast "to the men we have loved—the stinkers."

Arden seldom got a chance to do more than that. She's a wisecracker who doesn't go out on dates, no matter what she plays—a fashion magazine editor in *Cover Girl* (1944), a hero of the Russian army in *The Doughgirls* (1944), a department store owner's secretary in *One Touch of Venus* (1948). As early as *Stage Door* in 1937, she is the only one of the woman principals who isn't really in the story. Katharine Hepburn lands a plum lead on Broadway, Andrea Leeds kills herself, Lucille Ball has buffoonish dates with butter-and-egg men, Constance Collier lives on dreams of a comeback, Ann Miller dances, Gail Patrick sells her body, Ginger Rogers spars with Hepburn and flirts with a producer. Arden, though noticeable, is just part of the locale, petting her cat and leading the rowdy bitchery. When at the end one of the girls gets married, it is Ball (to Jack Carson), typically, and when she grows misty at her exit, it is Arden, just as typically, who throws in a parting jest: "Say, you should weep—it's the first job you've had in a year."

Like Ball and Allen, Arden is best known for a television character, the heroine of *Our Miss Brooks,* another of those patiently ironical women who somehow miss out on a lot of alleged fun. Miss Brooks is a schoolteacher, and, given that all television in the early 1950s was witless farce, she is surrounded by craziness that she keeps seeing and not believing: a gaseous principal, a Don Juan gym teacher, a dimwitted landlady, twitty students, and, the icing on the cake, a sexless biology teacher for her "boyfriend." How can a character who seems as sensible as Arden was in her films get so cartoony and vapid as her Miss Brooks does? Perhaps it's because in films Arden always worked a different temperamental wavelength than her colleagues did. She is tighter than they, moving fast so the insults don't have time to land. When she meets up with Crawford in *Mildred Pierce,* the tightness nearly strangles, because Crawford too moves at that speed. But these two are playing, in this film, with suave or would-be suave men like Zachary Scott and Jack Carson. Try to move that tension into the laugh-tracked vacuum of television and it falls apart.

Dressler was a ham, Davies miscast, Lombard a heroistic role model, Ball a fatale turned housewife, Allen a zany, and Arden a wallflower. There's more life in those skimpy descriptions than a comparable list of male comics would furnish, but then the 1930s was a rich era for women in the movies. Many actresses were limited by typing, true, but so were many men. Ruth Chatterton's errant wives were the most fictional of diversions, substitutionary adventures for women playing let's pretend; yes, yes. But one cannot say this of Dressler's parts, or Lombard's, or even Ball's. The elasticity of comedy, the grab-bag nature of its tricks and timing, makes it the sport of individuals as a rule. Great tragedians are often rather alike; great comics are always unique.

In certain cultures at certain times, women were made central in symbolistic mythmaking. The nineteenth-century German Romantics' obsession with redemptive mother-virgins is a case in point, and Hollywood in the 1930s might be another. There were influential male characters at this time as well, like the urban gangster who evolved into the G-man and finally into the private eye: from company man to team leader to loner, a typical American equation. But consider the personal metaphysics of Lombard, all the information one gathers from the romances, fights, and intrigues in her stories. Just listing the variations would take a book in itself, and some of them are extremely fanciful, like the mock brawl she has with Fredric March in *Nothing Sacred,* which starts as a ruse to make Lombard seem ill and develops into a metaphor for sexual love-war. Such scenes explain why the nation was so saddened by her early death: through her special parts, and through her special way with ordinary parts, Lombard had made herself instructively unorthodox. In a society too often bullied by mediocrity, she was a redemptive maverick.

Screwball was a message disguised as a style, and Lombard's vitality clues one in to the message. It wasn't an easy one for many people to take, and the screwball comedies eventually began to bomb, and by the wartime 1940s their urgency toward idiosyncratic self-determination ran counter to the prevailing community effort toward survival and they died. But the individuality that sparked them still glows, and comedy is potent: it makes individuality look easy.

# 9

# *The Evergreen Moralist*

KATHARINE HEPBURN

*Katharine Hepburn's popularity has never waned because people know (magically, intuitively) that she stands for something, even if many of them have no clear idea what that something is. They recognize that in a time of dangerous conformity, and the fear of being different, here is one who stands up gallantly to the killing wave.*

—GARSON KANIN

*I think my big virtue is my common sense.*

—KATHARINE HEPBURN

A young woman of sound New England family decides to become an actress. With unconventional looks, no training, and no polish, she attempts to make Broadway, suffers a number of minor disasters, finally catches a toehold, and from it leaps to Hollywood. She lands at a studio that is in need of a "prestige" star—someone Different who talks well—and, though her lack of experience continually humiliates her, her Difference gives her edge enough to excuse the poor films and exhilarate the good ones. Seven years later, with a smash Broadway hit behind her, she shifts studios, does the film version of the play, and begins to win over a broad following. The press, with whom she never cooperated, no longer assaults her. The industry, which regarded her as a curiosity, suddenly sees her as an idol. The fashionables, who once laughed at her, imitate her.

And the public, suspicious of her in the past, finds her irresistible, especially in her partnership with a certain male star who exactly complements her. They become the Lunts of film; but the Lunts were sly and mercurial whereas these two are open and solid. At length, the man passes on, much mourned, and she enters a new period, that of the freelancer of no set type or genre. Most movie survivors coast through their last working years; this woman takes dares. She risks unsuitable parts, yet suffers few failures. She does not tire. It is more and more and more—stage work, independent "little" films, studio projects, a Broadway musical. Now, some fifty years after she began, the received opinion that she looks odd, can't act, and puts on airs has evolved somewhat: her looks, acting, and attitude are dynamite. And lo, she has swept the field in competition. She is bigger than Pickford, has more admirers than Gish, outlasted Crawford and Garbo, proved more versatile than Davis, and made more worthwhile films than anyone. She is Hollywood's supreme woman star.

F. Scott Fitzgerald said, "There are no second acts in American lives," and at first Katharine Hepburn seemed on her way to proving that rule. She could act, but had no line, no organization. In Hollywood, she was still struggling with stage technique (putting out) when she needed something less studied (letting the audience make the effort to come in). Though her debut film instantly made her a star, succeeding vehicles were often not well made or too offbeat for a national public,* and her refusal to cater to or even tolerate the Hollywood press corps alienated the midpoint people in charge of bringing actors and audiences together. "Is Hepburn Killing Her Own Career?" *Photoplay* cried in 1935, grumbling about her "eccentricities" and "poses"—in other words, her privacy. They forgave Garbo for keeping to herself, because "Garbo is sincere in her extreme desire for seclusion." Hepburn was sincere, too, and *Photoplay* knew it, but it and the other fanzines couldn't bear to see such fertile territory for snooping and tattling go uncultivated. One Garbo was okay; her colorful manner of insuring privacy was copy in itself. But to let any other star block them out was to encourage subversion and to lose readers.

Hepburn was interesting, everybody agreed, possibly also tricky, remote. But it turns out that Hepburn was so unlike everyone who had come to Hollywood that on hindsight we can call it inevitable that she succeeded. For starters, her family background was unconventional, relishing nonconformity and controversy. Her physician father and feminist mother raised six children in Hartford, Connecticut, on a mixture of austerity and cultivation, discouraging weakness on one hand

---

*It should be emphasized that, from her first Broadway success in 1932 on, Hepburn had a huge New York following for stage and film work alike. When midwestern or southern exhibitors were reluctant to show her films in the 1930s, Radio City Music Hall booked them and liked it, the offbeat ones included.

while encouraging drives toward self-fulfillment on the other. In this home, a cold was a faux pas, a cold shower a treat, and a good tennis game a practical necessity. So Katharine Houghton* Hepburn, born in 1909,† got every chance to try things. Her father had her privately tutored, leaving her with much free time in which to develop her athletic bent, and she became an all-around champion. They called them "tomboys" then. She also staged shows in the backyard with neighborhood kids. For *Beauty and the Beast* (Kate, eleven, played Beast), she charged a hefty admission, recruited a huge cast to swell the gallery with mothers, and donated the proceeds to the Navajo Indians. Even then, she was public-spirited in her private way.

She never retired from the athletic field, nor did she lose her interest in theatre. Of all American professions it best suited a self-assured and distinctive-looking woman who was inwardly unsure of herself and out of touch with her more conventionally derived coevals, those girls of the proms. Imagine young Hepburn at a prom, twitting the beaux the way she twits Cary Grant at a posh restaurant in *Bringing Up Baby*. But she went through certain motions of her age and class, such as attending Bryn Mawr College, her mother's alma mater, where Hepburn extended herself mainly in theatricals.

When she decided to try the stage professionally, her father opposed her. Two of Hepburn's early films, *Morning Glory* and *Stage Door*, deal with the troubles attendant upon getting into the theatre, and they suggest what Hepburn must have been like in those first days alone in New York: enthusiastic, aggressive, raw, desperately eager for success, and deadly honest. True, *Morning Glory* gives us a dreamy ingenue who waits demurely in a producer's anteroom, and *Stage Door* presents a more pragmatic apprentice who charges arrogantly in and tells a producer off. (This proves, if proof is needed, that Hepburn plays character, not Hepburn.) The *Stage Door* Hepburn doesn't even care to learn her trade. "I think coaching's a waste of time," she says. What's acting, anyway? Just a matter of "common sense." The *Morning Glory* Hepburn is more respectful of tradition. Yet the two very different women share something with the real Hepburn: the awkward radiance of the convinced go-getter who hasn't yet had the chance to take it, and secretly feels that she may have to do so on a fluke.

It must have seemed so to young Hepburn in and around Broadway in the late 1920s, for though she managed to wangle parts, they were repeatedly fired out of her hands. The American theatre, in that time, had just reached the climax of its golden age. New York still counted a pride of playhouses, theatre people, and habitual playgoers,

---

*All six Hepburn kids had Houghton as a middle name, one clue to the combination of order and oddity that ruled the household.

†The year 1907 is often given as her birthdate, but she says it's 1909. She ought to know.

but other big theatre centers like Chicago had closed down their show shops one by one, dismissed the staff, and did halfhearted business in a fading light. Movies and radio had murdered vaudeville and were in the process of murdering the road tour. Even where theatre survived, it became more an industry and less a community, so that staple of Hollywood's backstagers, the producer's waiting room where unemployed actors wait for a job, became another place on the map of Hollywood fantasy, something that felt quite real in film but couldn't be found in life.

Into the last of these offices Hepburn came; no experience, just will. She got jobs and lost them. Twice she was fired during out-of-town tryouts, and once she made it to Broadway in a fast flop. Though she was coaching with one of the best-known acting teachers, Frances Robinson-Duff, Hepburn didn't know much about how the stage worked. When the flop's closing notice was posted (on opening night), Hepburn was taken aback: "I didn't realize that these shows folded up. I thought they sort of opened and then went on indefinitely." She tried marriage with the same blithe spirit, making her socialite husband change his name from Ludlow Ogden Smith to Ogden Lowell (Kate Smith? Never!), getting bored with the whole thing in two months, and separating on the best of terms without bothering to divorce.

How Different is she? Every paragraph in her biography marks an unusual person: an insistence on doing all things her way, rather than submit to the rule of those in power. An impetuosity that defies the careful moves of the dedicated careerist. A viewpoint that doesn't so much attack as simply not know the conventions. A stimulating family environment that by turns sheltered, nursed, and invigorated her, where others had frightful stage mothers, conniving stepfathers, or parasites. Jean Harlow's mother killed her with religious mysticism. Mary Astor's father lost her job after job with his horning in. Joan Crawford's mother and brother showed up when she had made it and lived off her thereafter. But Hepburn could look forward to each return to Hartford as sustenance.

Single again, Hepburn stormed Broadway anew without success. On one job, she was hired, fired, rehired, fired again, and hired again; and despite her good potential for sophisticated comedy, she was tossed out of Philip Barry's *The Animal Kingdom*. How was such bad luck possible? She was raw, a little strange, and had no sense of stage teamwork, of playing to and with rather than merely near her colleagues. When she finally made a hit, it was for her figure, in *The Warrior's Husband* (1932), a one-joke farce about life among the Amazons with a great deal of bare leg. An RKO scout caught the show, she made a test in New York, and was hired, for the role of John Barrymore's daughter in *A Bill of Divorcement* (1932), under George Cukor's direction.

Cukor was to direct Hepburn in eight pictures, all of them rated among her best, so his opinion of the RKO neophyte is one to get. "She was gifted at that time," he recalled much, much later, "and had the originality that she has and the force, but . . . she had clumsiness and she certainly had never been acting in front of a camera. . . . The first day she was required to look at her father [Barrymore], who had returned from the hospital, and she looked at him with this infinite compassion, and then her eyes filled with tears, and Jack Barrymore winked at me. He said, 'She's okay.'"

Actually, matters between Hepburn and Barrymore became less matey after he made the (for him) obligatory dressing-room pass and she batted it right out of the park. He had invited her for a private rehearsal of a scene, suddenly threw off his dressing gown and presented himself to her in glorious living color. He advanced, she retreated, and they ended against the wall, where she cried, "No, no. Please. It's impossible. I can't!"

"Why not?" he asked, his vanity roaring.

"My father doesn't want me to have any babies!"

This was a historic rebuff for Barrymore. Women didn't often turn down a tumble with the king of grand old matinee-idol, classic-repertory, Shakespearean finesse. But Hepburn wants what *she* wants. Barrymore was right the first time: She's okay.

If only Hollywood in general had seen it that way; not that it matters much now. The RKO chiefs took her, she says, as "a cross between a horse and a monkey," and folks who met her on the lot found her affected. But Cukor, at least, saw the delicacy under her awkwardness and determined to smooth her out. He nearly did. *A Bill of Divorcement* definitely reveals, listed fourth in the credits with a misspelled name, a rough talent; but the stuff of stardom, the ability to distill universals in a unique way, is there. Barrymore's daughter is an Ann Harding part, moderately drastic and extremely tender, and if Hepburn is as interesting for her poor moments as her inspired ones, she caught on fast. *Christopher Strong* (1933), a dull film with Hepburn as an airplane pilot who kills herself to protect her married lover from scandal, was badly written and, inevitably, badly acted. But the succeeding *Morning Glory* (1933) allows for a more spontaneous Hepburn, drawing on reserves of enthusiasm and commitment. And—the same only more so—as the tomboy Jo in *Little Women* (1933) she triumphed. "Hepburn was born to play the role," says Cukor. Of course: a New England nonconformist. Jo is Hepburn in hoop skirts. It was also Hepburn's first film of the old-fashioned kind that they used to make silent, with a fatherless family, a death in it, plenty of boyfriends, and a ton of snow. Typically, *Little Women* was the picture that do-gooders seized upon when assaulting the morality of the movies. "Why should there be Mae West," the question ran, "when they can make films like *Little Women?*" One might reply that if they're going to make films like *Little Women,* then there *must* be Mae West. However, with Spring Byington, Joan Bennett, Frances Dee, and Jean Parker as the rest of Hepburn's family, *Little Women* did seem like a refreshing rebuttal to West's carnival fairgrounds and lion's den.

Hepburn's next picture, *The Little Minister* (1934), put her in a Betty Bronson role right out of James Barrie, as a noblewoman who lives a double life, masquerading as an elfin gypsy. Luckily the action concentrates on the gypsy in the woman, for this is the more effective Hepburn, nimble, irreverent, politicized, gallant. She does a lot of racing off. Courting shy Scotch minister John Beal—he's so proper that she must take the lead—she is maidenly yet unorthodox:

BEAL: Can a man like a woman against her will?
HEPBURN: Of course he can. That's the very nicest way to be liked.

But when the courtship moves into lovemaking, she is startled:

BEAL: I've never kissed a woman before.
HEPBURN: (fearfully) Before what?

Hepburn is both lady and gypsy, not only in this film. This is Kate the real, regal and wild, haughty with those who intrude on her but willing, at the 1973 *Candide* revival, to leap out of the audience onto a stage bed to luxuriate drolly. She is innocent: innocent of conventional technique, innocent of Hollywood sex mores, innocent enough to play the essential Louisa May Alcott heroine.

But Hepburn was hardly one to please a moral majority. She satirized the PR routine by giving reporters bizarre answers to their banal questions, and dressed for herself, not for fans. A photographer once snapped her without warning, and the Hepburn he caught is no one's idea of Hollywoodland game playing. There she is: in slacks and a fur coat, holding a tennis racket (in its frame) in front of her face. Public places, to her, were enemy territory. Who did she think she was? She didn't even come to pick up her Oscar for *Morning Glory!* How the fanzines fumed.

Hepburn was a lone ranger, resisting, resisting. Interviews with her in recent years have revealed that her arrogance was a shy person's cover, her adjustment procedure. But in Hollywood in the 1930s, few got close enough to see through the act, and Hepburn was indicted for hubris, for not joining the company town. It's amazing they didn't freeze her out, because her RKO films didn't do all that well on the whole. This, too, amazes, for no other star has left such an interesting body of work. Gable, Garbo, Cooper, Gish, Davis, Grant, Crawford—

they all have their bombs, films so putrid that even fanatics get quiet when they are mentioned. But Hepburn is so interesting that even her soap operas and costume messes are worth viewing today. Take *Break of Hearts* (1935), a weepie with Charles Boyer that anyone might have played. And with anyone else, the risible business would have died long ago.

*Break of Hearts* proposes Hepburn as a musician entranced by brusque, temperamental conductor Boyer. He's the kind who tells the orchestra, "All correspondence school players will kindly leave the stage—also those who play by ear." Hepburn's close-ups capture the musician's involvement with art; Kate has kulcha. She has poise, too, which is why her weepie works. Her honesty redeems the clichés of the genre, even unto the scene in which she overhears gossip of her husband's adultery in a restaurant powder room. Even unto the scene in which she catches him in the act and must put on a brave smile. Even unto the scene in which she phones for a reconciliation and learns that he has left for Europe, even unto his public humiliation of her and subsequent collapse. Of course Hepburn stands by him; this is not the point. What is central here is her command of character, her eloquent pictures. Without having become fully adept as an actress, she has become representative of herself, a one-time type.

Not surprisingly, RKO wanted to star Hepburn as Joan of Arc, one hero in for another. It was to be an all-out effort, in Technicolor, and the surviving visual test reveals a barbaric, ecstatic Hepburn, hair cut short, holding her sword aloft against the wind. It looks fine, but the studio wanted Shaw's *Saint Joan* for their text and couldn't get the rights, so instead she played a smalltown social climber in an adaptation of Booth Tarkington's *Alice Adams* (1935). It was her first great performance, and remains one of her four or five most winning achievements.

"She not only had no technique," said *Alice Adams'* director George Stevens, "she didn't seem to want any." But the rawness is gone—or is she reconciled to playing raw women? Alice is a poor girl who aspires to bourgeois reputation; some viewers might find this unsympathetic. But Hepburn so beautifully suffers the heroine's many humiliations at the hands of her fellow citizens and graceless family that one is too busy understanding, liking, and rooting for her to consider her pursuit of the leading local heir (Fred MacMurray) as anything but true romance. Furthermore, her loyalty to her unsuccessful father (Fred Stone) in the face of her mother's heckling is chivalrous. If Hepburn had no technique, then she must have devised something very much like it, for even now the film stuns with its petty, enclosed naturalism. The big dance at the country club, where Alice works so hard to be gay and elegant and only turns herself into a more avid species of wall-flower; the famous set piece of the American family dinner, with Mac-

Murray as the prize guest and Hattie McDaniel as a sour pickup maid; Alice's long-delayed, heartrending sobbing scene after this dinner, which Stevens demanded and she refused to attempt until suddenly it just happened; and her despairing "Gee whiz!"—these are treasurable moments.

They are not the first of the Hepburn memorabilia. *Morning Glory* has her Shakespearean recitations at a Broadway party and her "I'm not afraid, I'm not afraid . . . why should I be afraid?" *Little Women* is a virtual vaudeville of Hepburn specialties. But her great moments in *Alice Adams* are the first such that belong to a film that has no weaknesses. The rest of it is every bit as good as the highlights.

Stardom might be hollow for vapid beauties, who do nothing but genre pictures. But the oddballs live a dangerous stardom, a stimulating but untamable one: who knows what odd projects they'll throw at you? Hepburn *made* herself notable. "Round, soft looks were the style," she recalls, and she was bony; caricaturists reveled in her jaw. She *made* them admire. But she couldn't make the bad pictures work, and of her first eight films, only *Little Women* was a big hit outside of New York. A nonconformist inspires nonconformist pictures, true; but wasn't *Sylvia Scarlett* (1936) past the pale, with its too-too script and Hepburn in boy's clothes? A cult film now, and true delight for the adventurous, it set a new precedent for bomb in its day. Still even Hepburn's less risky films weren't taking as they should—*Mary of Scotland* (1936), for instance. The source was outlandish, Maxwell Anderson's slow-moving verse play which Helen Hayes did on Broadway. But the show was entirely revamped, the poetry translated into English, so to speak, by Dudley Nichols, the action opened up into scenes of splendor and chase in castles, peasant huts, and forests, and John Ford brought in to find the pageantry in Scottish patriotism and English power playing. There are bagpipes and drums, courtly intrigues by wild characters, grand costumes, and an assortment of accents from the largely British cast on one side, Hepburn on another, and Fredric March as her lover Bothwell on a third.

Ford does some wonderful things, as one might expect. In one scene, the Scotch mob sings Mary's praises to the tune of "Loch Lomond" and then hums as Mary delivers a pep talk from a window, heartened by their devotion. "I'll find a way to win!" she promises, and a tenor solo peaks the musical action, keyed to a close-up of Mary, rapt in her ruff. Later, Ford handles her trial for treason by shooting from above the judges, high on their dais, to show their power dwarfing the heroine; he also shoots them from below, to see through Mary's eyes. There is thematic substance here, too, when, in the big confrontation between Mary and Elizabeth (Florence Eldridge, superbly bitter and ruthless), Mary asks if a woman can hold supreme power and still be a woman. Elizabeth says Mary threw away her kingdom for love; Mary calls Elizabeth's life "a magnificent failure." Her final march to the scaffold is impressive.

But the public didn't come; nor were they eager to see Hepburn as a Victorian feminist crusader, complete with illegitimate child, in *A Woman Rebels* (1936). Nor was she getting much mileage out of the fanzines, bless her heart: if you wanted to know whom Hepburn was dating, you had to wait decades to read the biographies. To spring out of her rut of flop movies, Hepburn and RKO decided an excursion to the stage would prove salubrious, but a *Jane Eyre* for the Theatre Guild suffered a long tryout tour and died without risking a New York booking. The production made a nice profit, but the notion itself was dated; plays from English novels had fallen out of fashion in the 1920s. Coincidentally, the talkies inherited the concern, more effectively capturing the motion covered in several hundred pages of fiction than the stage could. Hepburn herself helped to prove this in *Little Women*, a film that almost never stands still from its first view of Kate as Jo springing across a snow-covered yard. Anyway, Hepburn was miscast as Jane Eyre, the classic passive Gothic heroine. Her Jo brought out her best instincts and whetted public taste for an admirable eccentric who goes out and *does* things.

Accordingly, RKO lined up more appropriate roles for Hepburn's return—no more costumes. Their first idea was *The Mad Miss Manton*, a screwball mystery with Hepburn as the leader of some Park Avenue debs caught between a disapproving detective and a murderer. Hepburn never played it. Instead, she went into *Stage Door* (1937), revealing an unexploited gift for the style that would carry her on to top stardom in the next decade, comedy. *Stage Door* takes us to the Footlights Club, where young women with theatrical ambitions wait for The Break. Hepburn gets it, in the part Andrea Leeds was counting on, but Hepburn is rotten till Leeds's suicide shocks her into giving a moving performance, just in time for opening night.

This is, of course, movie hooey. One doesn't pick up technique simply by suffering an emotional crisis. But up to the finale, *Stage Door* is a delight, full of fast jabs about who has talent or charm or wit and who doesn't. When millionaire's daughter Hepburn first marches into the Footlights Club, everyone's against her, especially roommate Ginger Rogers. Their breathless verbal scrimmage on their first night together is High Sass (Rogers: "I must take my bath." Hepburn: "That might help."), and their eventual commiserating alliance touching when Rogers, who had attacked Hepburn for "stealing" Leeds's part, melts into tears at Hepburn's dazed, contrite curtain speech and enters Hepburn's dressing room wordlessly to embrace her.

RKO entirely threw out the Edna Ferber–George S. Kaufman

stage original—it seems the studio only wanted to use the title—and this is all to the good, as the play was earnest and dull.* The film *Stage Door* is earnest and funny, with the balance of bitter and sweet that waiting to make it on Broadway needs; and since Hepburn already has the earnest under her belt, she gets a chance to try the funny. She does this not through manipulative lunacy, not through timing or "business," but through icy aplomb and a sharp report, as if her wisecracks were stones she bites out of a wall to toss in hostile faces. She's not having fun; she means it; she's like a straight man for a chorus of comics.

No wonder she's serious. The experience of reliving her difficult first days in New York must have been, as the Chinese put it, interesting. Her biographer Gary Carey has pointed out the uncanny correlations between *Stage Door* and Hepburn's stage days: the father who doesn't approve but pays the bills, the mildewed grande dame coach, the bad-tempered director, the casting of an ingenue in a lead role that she is not ready to play, and Hepburn's "rich, overbearing, and overconfident" character itself are all in the movie. Even the play-within-the-film, *Enchanted April*—the one in which Hepburn intones her most quoted line, "The calla lilies are in bloom again"—resembles *The Lake*, Hepburn's Broadway bomb of 1933. Hepburn's character announces, "If I can act I want the world to know it; if I can't, I want to know it," something she must have said herself at some point. And Andrea Leeds, befriending Hepburn, sounds a historical note when she tells her, "They'll get to understand you after a while."†

*Stage Door* was a hit, and RKO put Hepburn into another comedy, *Bringing Up Baby* (1938). Here, suddenly, Hepburn *does* use manipulative lunacy, up, down, and across the yin-yang. *Bringing Up Baby* is screwball in full baroque, a glorious sunburst before the star burns out. Baby is a tame leopard and Hepburn an heiress chasing paleontologist Cary Grant, who is in danger of being fossilized by a stuffy fiancée. The plot macguffin is a brontosaurus clavicle, stolen by the indispensable screwball terrier, and the oddball assistants include a very untame leopard who is mistaken for Baby, Hepburn's aunt, a fatuous dinner guest, an even more fatuous psychiatrist, and the usual befuddled officials. If Carole Lombard is screwball's ragamuffin and Irene Dunne its first lady, Hepburn is its king, because she runs the show. The whole film is: Hepburn traps Grant.

It's amusing to compare Dunne and Hepburn in their respective

---

*Kaufman liked it the way it was. After seeing the film, he remarked that they should have called it *Screen Door*.

†One allusion to Hepburn's Broadway past that *Stage Door* neglected was her firing incidents. *Morning Glory* included one, but the sequence was cut from the release prints and one must listen hard for Hepburn's one allusion to it, in the greasy-spoon scene with C. Aubrey Smith.

screwball forays with Grant, because the two women do the same things so differently. In *The Awful Truth* (1937), Dunne and Grant start married, part, and reconvene; in *Bringing Up Baby* Hepburn and Grant meet, have a wild adventure, and end up a couple. *The Awful Truth*, right from its opening credits over doily settings, emphasizes elegance, with a lot of white tie and brandy and cigars; *Baby* is more suburban, tweedy, and all farce. Still, screwball is screwball, and there are common elements. There's the canine, of course, Mr. Smith in *The Awful Truth* and George in *Bringing Up Baby*. There are the dull fiancés to be discouraged. There's the heroine's bait-the-cops scene, to tease Grant, and the masquerade, Hepburn as a mobster ("Swinging-Door Susie") and Dunne impersonating Grant's raucous sister to shock his prospective blue-book in-laws.

Above all, there are the two women's disparate approaches to screwball. Dunne will put you down with a gesture; Hepburn will steal your car. Dunne is usually trying to get out of scrapes; Hepburn instigates them. Dunne deals with what's there; Hepburn invents. Dunne, when hurt, hides her feelings; Hepburn can't. The two of them touch base briefly in *The Awful Truth* when Dunne, pulling the sister stunt, imitates Hepburn's voice, but they are entirely unalike, especially in their relationships with Grant. With Dunne, Grant is masterful, her equal; but Hepburn baffles and mashes him. He stutters, can't seem to get out a simple declarative sentence, while she says three things at once, verbal rape; his "Oh, dear!" and her "Jeepers!" outline their respective characters like Restoration theatre character names.

It's much smoother over at *The Awful Truth*, though, push come to shove, Dunne is not above mashing Grant—but ever so lightly. As Grant's "sister" Dunne shows up in the ritziest house in town looking like Sadie Thompson's shower curtain, cries, "Don't anybody leave this room—I've lost my purse!" and goes into a sleazy song and dance. She has such style that she doesn't use the sleaze, just indicates where it would come. Yet she makes her point. With Hepburn, satire calls not for elegance but energy. God knows what she might have done if she got to confront her rival, as Dunne does, but at least she can bop Grant's prime potential philanthropist on the bean with a rock. And at the end of the film, when she visits Grant in his museum and he cringes atop a huge brontosaurus reconstruction, you know she's going to find some way to pull the thing apart.

*Bringing Up Baby* was a commercial flop. Screwball comedy never really mustered a wide following; the popular screwballers, like *It Happened One Night* and *The Thin Man*, weren't all that screwball. They enjoyed mischief, but drew the line at anarchy. The committed screwballers were subversive, and, like *My Man Godfrey, Bringing Up Baby* had to wait decades to become a classic by critical fiat and the enthusiasm of audiences at revival houses. In fact, *Baby*'s failure more or less prompted the famous "box-office poison" list of stars whom the Independent Theater Owners of America rated as bad news in film. The list named some of the biggest stars—Dietrich, Crawford, Garbo, West, and Hepburn, for instance—who had had a bad film or two of late. Though basically trade gossip, it was heavily publicized and did some damage. For Hepburn's next film, RKO offered her a role in *Mother Carey's Chickens*, not a title one but nonetheless a dumb part in a dumb movie. She had to buy herself out of her contract, and tried Columbia on a one-picture deal in a remake of *Holiday* (1938) in the Ann Harding part. But this did Hepburn no good, despite the collaboration of Cary Grant and George Cukor. Few people wanted to see *Holiday* the first time around and fewer came now.

So, temporarily, Hepburn's new career as a comedienne died, and she again sought regeneration with a Broadway hit. This time it would have to be something peculiar to Hepburn, nothing less than a smash with good movie potential so she could play the lead on film and retake Hollywood. Smartly, she stayed with comedy. *Stage Door* was proletarian (with a rich Hepburn), *Bringing Up Baby* upper middle class, and *Holiday* very upper. The new play would be uppermost. Philip Barry, author of the original stage *Holiday*, wrote the new piece specifically for Hepburn; like her he had hit a losing period and needed a recuperative sensation. Hepburn worked with Barry on the script, and it is likely that without her he might have turned out another of the gossamer light comedies about the bohemian streak in the moneyed elite that had made him famous and limited his audience.* No, this one had to go over *broad*.

The scheme started well. Barry had the right setting (the Philadelphia Main Line), a tasty plot hitch (the press descends upon a tart debutante as she is about to marry), and an ace debutante (Hepburn). But he kept writing himself into corners in the story's subplots and he wasn't coming to grips with the heroine. Who was she? What did she represent? Barry, one of the copyright holders on the type, had never thought much about it; in certain ways, Ann Harding and Hepburn, in their respective readings of the heroine of *Holiday*, worked harder to comprehend what these eccentric patricians were made of than Barry did when he made them.

So the actress, with her expert knowledge of the Barry heroine, instructed the playwright. She stood before him, presented herself. "See me as if you were seeing me for the first time," she tells him. The look, the voice, the intonation, the stance, the walk, the famous clipped "yah" for yes. "Who am I? No, look hard! *Understand* me! What am I afraid of, what do I need, what forces informed me? *There* is your play.

---

*Barry also wrote strange semi-fantasies about lost truth seekers, but the "Barry crowd" didn't care for them, and no other public would patronize him.

You just find that woman where she stands in the world, surround her with one man she detests (and doesn't know it), one man she likes (and doesn't think she should), and one man she loves (and hasn't succeeded in loving—so far—because she doesn't know how). She's a perfect woman; damn it, she's too perfect. She must come down to earth. And by the end of the evening she rejects the first man, befriends the second, and marries the third. And, Mr. Barry, there's your play."

That story isn't even apocryphal. I made it up. But *se non è vero, è ben trovato;* it could have happened, because in the end the Barry–Hepburn comeback vehicle does accomplish all this. Hidden in its plot is a kind of analysis of Hepburn's image, of her magisterial, efficient, quirky serenity and her high standards, which few but Hepburn could meet. Her morals, like herself, are beautiful. But they sting. Note the name Barry gave to Hepburn's character, Tracy Lord: half madcap, half goddess. A goddess is hard to meet. So, by the play's end, she has undergone a ritual humiliation and become humanized. It's a neat package, containing the most Hepburn of all Hepburn roles and tied up in a perfect title: *The Philadelphia Story.* Happy ending, the show was a standing-room-only Broadway smash. And, happy beginning, guess who had bought the film rights to the play? Yah.

Some might say that Hepburn's film career in the 1930s rose and fell because she was uppity, demanding, self-willing. Rubbish. She was not uppity but private; she was demanding because if she hadn't been they would have turned her into Kay Francis; and self-will is a virtue, not a fault. Her career suffered because: one, she was the first of her kind, and, two, RKO gave her mostly rotten projects (like *Christopher Strong* or *Break of Hearts)* or superb projects that couldn't appeal to a general audience (like *Sylvia Scarlett* or *Bringing Up Baby).* In *Stage Door,* producer Adolphe Menjou asks a departing theatregoer how he liked *Enchanted April,* in which Hepburn has just triumphed. "A little heavy," the man replies, "but the girl's good." That sums up Hepburn's RKO period.

Now it changes. Moviegoers have, as Leeds predicted, got to understand Hepburn. All she needs to turn into box-office sugar is a spate of good films. *The Philadelphia Story* (1940) at MGM is a fine way to start, though this was strictly a one-picture deal. Donald Ogden Stewart sharpened Barry's script, George Cukor directed, and Cary Grant, James Stewart, and Ruth Hussey took over the roles originated by Joseph Cotten, Van Heflin, and Shirley Booth. When Hepburn next came across a fetching property, she went to L. B. Mayer with it, and he not only took it on her terms but signed her to a contract as well. Hepburn was bankable.

The property was *Woman of the Year* (1942), the film that introduced her to Spencer Tracy and reinvented her in the movies. The hotshot, stagy Hepburn of the RKO 1930s was suddenly gone; she was mannered before, streamlined now. When she and Tracy first met, she opined that he was a little short for her. "Don't worry," said Joseph Mankiewicz, *Woman of the Year*'s producer, "he'll cut you down to size." But that wasn't it. "I think he simplified me," she said in a television interview with Barbara Walters in 1981. "Just *do* it. Just *do* it."

They joined an honorable line of romantic teams—Garbo and Gilbert, Crawford and Gable, Gaynor and Farrell, Powell and Loy, Astaire and Rogers—in nine films over twenty-five years, their chemistry flavored not with erotic interaction, aroused innocence, joie de vivre, or terpsichore, but with the directness of their opinions. They play sensible people candidly. Hepburn's other MGM films are oddities, like *Dragon Seed* (1944), in which she plays a Chinese peasant guerrilla, or *Undercurrent* (1946) in which her husband, Robert Taylor, turns out to be a psychopath. But the Hepburn-Tracy teamings are either first-rate comedies or melodramas made interesting by the conspiracy of their performances.

Because they are sensible, they are competitive: neither wants to walk behind the other. Sometimes the competing goes too far, as when, at the close of *Woman of the Year*, he sits at the kitchen table and smugly watches her fudge every detail of that great American production, breakfast; or when, in *Adam's Rib* (1949), she humiliates him publicly by having a mountainous woman lift him in the air to prove a point. Generally, however, the contest is fair and keen, two equals expressing the paradox of romance between equals: who gives in first? In *Woman of the Year* he's a sportswriter and she's a cultural reporter; in *State of the Union* (1948) he's an idealistic hero type being rushed by politicians who want to make him a presidential candidate and she's his even more idealistic wife; in *Adam's Rib* they're married lawyers pitted on opposite sides in Judy Holliday's trial for attempted murder. Each time, one or the other must give way, because the other one's just a little more sensible. That was part of their charm.

Their teaming made them copy, whether they liked it or not. They ignored it. But there it was: she was unmarried and he was complexly close to and separated from his wife, yet reports had it that Hepburn and Tracy were as involved in life as on screen. This, ironically, made Hepburn not objectionable but accessible. It was her first known Hollywood romance. And because the Hepburn-Tracy chemistry featured camaraderie rather than heat, it never told on their privacy, never dared the moviegoer to approve or disapprove. When Ingrid Bergman left her husband to live with Roberto Rossellini and conceive his illegitimate child, Americans banned her from their lives. But Hepburn and Tracy didn't come off as an *amour*.

Take *Pat and Mike* (1952), the final event in Hepburn's MGM contract, at the sunset of the studio period, when the studios began to release their stables of headliners and everyone went freelance. Cukor is in charge, Garson Kanin and Ruth Gordon, friends of both stars, have written the script for them, and the stars are fresh in trim, as if they had yet to meet for the first time—as if we didn't know about them. With Garbo and Gilbert, Gaynor and Farrell, and the other golden-age partners, the team magic was based on our advance relish of how the stars would function together. But Hepburn and Tracy are so chastely earthy they surprise us. In *Woman of the Year* they came together from different backgrounds. In *Adam's Rib,* they shared a background. In *Pat and Mike,* they manage to come from different backgrounds in the same world.

Hepburn is Pat, an athlete, sensible past the edge of rudeness. Right at the top, in a golf game, she tells off a partner a little too free with advice—"If you could possibly lift the needle from that long-playing record you've got in your face!"—and tees off some eight or ten balls with perfect drive.

Tracy is Mike, a sports promoter in a *Guys and Dolls* striped suit and dark shirt, who becomes Hepburn's manager. He knows sports, but nothing else. Hearing that Hepburn spent some years at Pacific Tech, he asks, "What'sa matter? You couldn't pass?" On the contrary, she was teaching. Well, he'll take her anyway. "Nicely packed," he notes of her as she walks away into a discreet ass shot in skirt and sweater. Then the classic line, as he leans over a water fountain: "Not much meat on her, but what's there is cherce."

Their partnership, of course, forms the bulk of the film, with its sparring and jesting. ("Don't forget to throw me over your shoulder and burp me after lunch," Hepburn remarks dryly when Tracy outlines her training regimen.) We have known since *Woman of the Year* that they come to mutual terms by factoring their divisive components of cynicism and challenge, but in *Pat and Mike* there is a third person to get out of the way first, Hepburn's fiancé, William Ching, a playboy type. Ching isn't just a threat to Tracy; he's a threat to Hepburn, with his reckless male glamour. She can't play her best when Ching is around, and Cukor uses this surrealistically at a crucial tennis match. When Ching arrives in the stands with some giggling women, Hepburn starts blowing her shots. The ball wobbles as if in a cartoon, Hepburn's racket appears tiny against her opponent's huge smasher, and the sound track magnifies the enemy strokes while Hepburn's come off as blips. Chings begin to surround Hepburn. The referee, the public— everyone is Ching. Hepburn faints.

In the end, she conquers her fear of Ching by conquering her need of him; she needs Tracy, a man on her terms. Maybe he needs her more, for it is Hepburn who saves him when he is menaced by gangsters Charles Bronson and George Matthews, pushing them around like nobody's business. Few other men gave Hepburn so much to counter so joyously—perhaps only Humphrey Bogart in *The African*

*Queen* (1951), Cary Grant in their earlier comedies, and Peter O'Toole in *The Lion in Winter* much later—and she does seem at her best as a loving adversary. But there's so much of her now, so crisply projected, that she could play with anyone and make art of cardboard.

"I always feel that I'm a sort of amateur actor," she said in 1981. "I don't know why." Yet she was succeeding in tricky roles, like that of Clara Schumann in *Song of Love* (1947), with Paul Henried as Robert Schumann and Robert Walker as Johannes Brahms. In the 1930s, Hepburn played a queen, an aviatrix, a feminist, a boy (sort of, in *Sylvia Scarlett)*, and they all seem a bit off, for in the RKO years you can take the girl out of Bryn Mawr but you can't take the Bryn Mawr out of the girl. But now she's neater, regular, simple. Just *do* it. Her Clara Schumann has dignity and soul, no stunt in it anywhere. *Song of Love*'s script tells us that Brahms is the man she loves while her husband Robert is the man she admires, and for a woman of such nuanced sensibility this is no quandary, no Hollywood "triangle." It's a case of the star making more sense than the film.

Gifted actors who have made it often turn crazy under the combined pressures of exposure and competition; they're so busy hating criticism and defending themselves from intruders that they turn paranoid. But Hepburn never went Star in the first place, never incorporated into queen bee and retinue. She is too bizarre to be sage, but she is wise, sometimes heedlessly agreeable. In the 1930s she was curt with her co-workers, but backstage stories of the later Hepburn tell of charity and loyalty. She insisted that Judy Holliday be cast in a featured part in *Adam's Rib* specifically to get her the lead in the film version of *Born Yesterday,* which she had played on Broadway but which Columbia's Harry Cohn was determined to film with almost anyone else. Furthermore, she had Cukor focus interest on Holliday in an important scene, reducing herself to stand-in status. Later, she was definitely sympathetic to Montgomery Clift on the set of *Suddenly, Last Summer* (1959), though Clift infuriated everyone else with his deranged bungling, director Joseph Mankiewicz in particular. When shooting ended, Hepburn strode up to Mankiewicz, got his assurance that their collaboration was officially over, and spat. At his feet, in one version; in his face, in another.

Hepburn's colleagues spent their third decade of stardom either as institutions or relics. (Joan Crawford was both; Bette Davis was a relic and became an institution.) Hepburn was sheer institution, for the roles she accepted in the 1950s emphasized her moon-eyed aggressiveness. She was both too gentle and too winning to slide into relic status, and her films were hits, *and* she played her age, which made her timeless: an institution. She enacted many a spinster, in *Summertime* (1955), on holiday in Venice; in *The Rainmaker* (1956), her imagination whetted and her beauty invited out by con man Burt Lancaster; in *The Desk Set*

(1957), again with Tracy and again in competition—she's head of an office brain pool and he's supposed to replace them with machines. She played formidable mothers as well, the monster matriarch out to destroy niece Elizabeth Taylor with a lobotomy in *Suddenly, Last Summer* because Taylor knows the ugly truth about Hepburn's late son; the drug-addicted Mrs. Tyrone, modeled on Eugene O'Neill's mother, in *Long Day's Journey into Night* (1962); and Queen Eleanor of France and England in *The Lion in Winter* (1968). While her coevals of the old Hollywood scrabbled for work, Hepburn took the plums.

They began to call her a survivor. "I'm revered," she commented, "rather like an old building." True, she was sixty when she made the last of the Tracy teamings, *Guess Who's Coming to Dinner?* (1967), the guest being the black fiancé of Hepburn and Tracy's daughter Katharine Houghton (Hepburn's real-life niece). It was inevitable that someone would do such a film, and many thought it came off well, but today it seems as frivolous as it was well intentioned. Its easy-listening theme song heard over the opening credits ("You've got to give a little . . . that's the story of, that's the glory of love") would be insipid in a Doris Day sex comedy. Its careful use of "colored" and "Negro" (the stars' reactionary black maid uses "nigger") was dated before the film was made. Katharine Houghton, in her screen debut, gives a truly terrible performance. And the use of Sidney Poitier as the fiancé—a much-honored, several-times-published doctor, magna cum laude from Johns Hopkins—subverts the film's apparent subject, white racism. If director Stanley Kramer had really wanted to test his characters, he would have made the fiancé a mechanic or schoolteacher and cast an actor less "acceptable" to lily-white tastes than Poitier.

One wonders if Hepburn would have made the film in that case: how radical is she? Her and Tracy's characters in *Guess Who's Coming to Dinner?* are old-time middle-road *New Republic* liberals; on Tracy's desk is a framed photograph of Franklin Roosevelt rather than, say, Trotsky or Warren Beatty, and of course we recall that both Hepburn and Tracy treated the red-purging of the McCarthy years with disgust. Applying such real-life knowledge of actors to their screen characters is one of the essentials of American moviegoing, one of the major differences between Hollywood film and all other kinds. So we watch the stars to see, perhaps, how to act if we were in their shoes; and as their personae pit them on opposite sides of any question, Hepburn approves of the engagement and Tracy worries about it and at last gives in.

The film includes one extreme attack on racism, and naturally it is Hepburn who delivers it. It develops that Hepburn's chief assistant at her art gallery is scandalized by miscegenation and, when she dares to offer an opinion, Hepburn tells her off abruptly, brutally, and finally. Given the many little hypocrisies that bourgeois social and business life entails, and given the setting—a middle-class driveway, with the assistant in her car and Hepburn leaning on the door—the moment is revolutionary, a shocker. Hepburn actually fires the woman and throws her out of her life in a devastating, dead-on curse-out that has audiences clapping and cheering—not so much for Hepburn's sentiments as for her intrepidity in tackling issues directly. We get a flash of the Hepburn we've heard of and fear to meet, and we wish we were as tough with people we dislike. Comedy immediately follows, for relief, when Hepburn goes back into the house and Houghton, oblivious of what has happened, says she thinks the assistant is a bigot and should be fired. "How," asks Hepburn, "can you be so hard?"

Tracy was ailing seriously during the shooting and died just after it wound down, leaving Hepburn more the survivor than ever. She had lived through a golden age of talkies, lived through industry upheaval when the studios broke apart, lived through fluctuating tastes in theatre, lived through an adored romance with an admired actor.* When she started out, it was considered intellectual to belittle her. Dorothy Parker made a derogatory assessment† that was quoted everywhere, a sure sign that to be anti-Hepburn was chic. But by the 1970s Hepburn stood beyond criticism. She was an example of what indomitable and inimitable used to mean before they were co-opted by the poets of hype: a remarkable woman. She started by being too Different to be popular and ended by making Different the thing to be.

She was one of the few actors who could sell out on Broadway in a thin vehicle, and her film roles, despite occasional miscasting, kept her acclaim current. She was no one's idea of a great American actress, for there are too many things that she doesn't do well; yet who has tried more of the major American parts? She has filmed O'Neill, Tennessee Williams, William Inge, Philip Barry, Edward Albee, and even braved the ritual of the big-budget star-vehicle musical comedy in *Coco* (1969), on the life of Coco Chanel. The show had a terrible score, a funny but empty book, and made too much of Hepburn's opening Act II uttering her first public "Shit!" Big deal. Cecil Beaton's fashion parades set on a revolving stage were intriguing and Hepburn was a treat, but it's odd that when she left the show, and Danielle Darrieux took over with superior expertise in atmosphere and song, *Coco* died. Hepburn was the show, the star, the experiment; I'll try this, this, and this, she says, and I'll do my best and let's hope it works. She is amateur in one sense: unaware of or unmoved by her limitations. She has also tried the for-

---

*Tracy is one of Hollywood's standout men, still a controversial figure. Some cite his techniqueless brilliance—that "just *do* it"—others cite his mean personality, meaner when he drank. He seems to have been ideal for Hepburn, two sharp blades cutting each other down to size.

†"She ran the gamut of emotions from A to B," reviewing Hepburn's Stella Surrege in *The Lake*.

eign repertory—Jean Giraudoux, in a heavy-handed all-star international *The Madwoman of Chaillot* (1969), not to mention her stage Shakespeare and Shaw and her Greek adventure as Hecuba in *The Trojan Women* (1971).

Talk of survivors! As the queen of a people destroyed by war, Troy's men killed and women carried off as slaves, Hepburn might have been expected to play an archetypal war hater in a piece of great relevance to, among other places, Vietnam. But while Hepburn has the granite and the fire for the role, she lacks the range, the bitter perspective of a figure as big as history. Hecuba is Hannah Arendt in a robe. Hepburn is her own archetype; she doesn't travel. She is much more comfortable in *Rooster Cogburn* (1975), a western with another self-made archetype, John Wayne. It's strange to find such differently aimed people playing with such rapport, but the socialist Hepburn and the free worlder Wayne got along fine. Uh-oh, her fans worried—fans of her moral clarity, that is. Is she actually *tolerant* of the Other Side? But she is not so far from them as one might think. Not long ago, on *60 Minutes,* Hepburn expressed a doubt about the good effects of permissiveness, and the interviewer, one of those television idiots no more knowledgeable than his briefing notes can make him, was clearly surprised. Surely the great Kate did not favor censorship? "Don't be too sure," she said.

No one is sure about her except close friends, yet all America knows her—the trying apprenticeship of the no-quit RKO aspirer, the feast of the Tracy collaboration, the insistence on making sense. Hepburn is one who bent the system to her needs, who stayed herself but was open enough to lighten her tone when she learned that lightness suited her. Heavy parts beyond her capabilities have not hurt her; on the contrary, we try to see it her way. Won't future interest in that *Trojan Women* really boil down to curiosity about Hepburn's Hecuba? No doubt Garbo is more the Hollywood dissident, but Garbo was so compressed that even her astonishing talent was exhausted at a certain point. At this writing, Hepburn is still playing, still surprising. Will she never stop growing? She should stop; she's too old to grow; but that calla lily is in bloom again; yah, she will stop; don't be too sure.

# INTERMISSION:
## *SOME VIEWS OF IT*

Rudolph Valentino looks a mite stunned, but then **Nazimova's** colleagues in her gala silent heyday never did know how to take her. This shot of *Camille* shows how pungent silent acting was—but for comparison we have **Clara Bow**, greatest of the It girls, if only by reputation. Nazimova was of the modern stage, true actress; Bow was a typical Hollywood product, a charisma rather than a talent. Here she is in a "buddy picture," *Wings,* the first movie to win an Oscar as Best. Flanking Clara are the buddies themselves, Buddy Rogers and Richard Arlen. (No jokes about Rogers' name; they also called him Charles.)

**L**ittle **Mary** strikes an attractive mean between the stage-manic Nazimova and the hapless Bow as a stage performer who adapted easily to film. She could act; she *did* act. She also rose to become Hollywood's biggest draw (ever) and a pillar of the industry. Those who regard her as too sweet and saintly will rejoice to learn that she loved her gin. Here she is as tot and adult, in silent and talkie: *Rebecca of Sunnybrook Farm,* typical Little Mary in costume, pranks, and moral uplift; and *The Taming of the Shrew,* with grown-up costumes, wordplay, and an anti-feminist message that Pickford probably thought silly. Still, it's Shakespeare. She looks crestfallen, no doubt because the career and the power—the invincible It of the crowned queen— were beginning to fail. Superb dress, though.

TS PF 71 A

Little Mary recalls us to **Lillian Gish**, in their shared beginnings and lifelong friendship as two stars of Old Hollywood looking on with something less than joy as the usurpers, looters, and starlets of the studio era pushed them aside, forgot them, and made "biographies" without a shred of authenticity. In 1951, something called *Valentino* showed filming on a silent set with the actors working entirely through the script, without a hint of pantomime projection, and the major forces in Valentino's life—Nazimova, Rex Ingram, June Mathis, and Natacha Rambova—never appeared. This is like Oz without the Scarecrow and Tin Woodman. I wonder what Gish thought of Valentino the man. In this shot of *La Bohème*, from Gish's MGM days, Valentino's successor as Great Lover, John Gilbert, chases her around the trees.

Admirers of Louise Brooks's *Lulu* hairdo can here admire its originator, **Colleen Moore**, in *Sally*. Moore is another of the old guard who folded tents in the early 1930s and crept away, for many reasons other than voice problems, most of the reasons being studio tyranny. As the industry reordered itself for the "talkers" (as sound films were once called), bosses thought it high time to destroy entrenched actor power and pull in a new generation with no loyalty to tradition and no experience of liberty or responsibility. You supply the It, kid; we'll do the rest.

Some silent stars hung on—MGM's Big Three, for instance, better known for their talkie work anyway. Here are **Greta Garbo** and **Norma Shearer** in key roles: Garbo as the ballerina Grusinskaya with John Barrymore in *Grand Hotel,* and noble wife Shearer confronting homewrecker **Joan Crawford** in a dress salon in *The Women.* A good trivia question asks whom Crawford played in the film—Crystal Allen. Even more telling is Shearer's character's name—Mrs. Stephen Haines.

1091-248

**C**rawford: talk of Hollywood products! But Crawford is exceptional. A perfected star, in glory, eclipse, and death, is an intimate stranger; whereas Joan Crawford has become somewhat closer to us over the recent years of Revelation. In this one case, we feel we know her. Her It has many parts, so let's examine the elements of Crawford in A Gallery of Early Joan: *serious*, in *Grand Hotel* with Barrymore; *musical*, in *Dancing Lady* with Fred Astaire; *she loves the high life*, with Marc MacDermott in *The Taxi Dancer*; and *the intent lover*, perfectly paired with Clark Gable, again in *Dancing Lady*. Another Joan, of the halfback shoulders and deep-dish lipstick, really belongs to the Warners Crawford of the 1940s. At least, that's when the whole regalia became silly. Those who can't really appreciate a star until she's been wrecked have something to look forward to some pages hence, but for me this is the true Joan, the dancing lady at the grandest of hotels, MGM.

870-27

Now to The Ladies. **Jeanette MacDonald** sings the title song in *San Francisco* in a hat that a banshee might wear to a *briss*, and **Irene Dunne** sings "Make Believe" to Allan Jones in *Show Boat*. Musical ladies. Here's **Myrna Loy**, also in a musical, a revue called *The Show of Shows*, but you'll have to hunt for her (look far right). Typically, for her early years, she's lost in the shuffle in exotic makeup. Nick Lucas stands far left; films like this one shattered his film hopes. How Loy survived was a wonder to Lucas. This is the Chinese Number, "Li-Po-Li."

Any study of golden-age talkie Hollywood takes in a lot of Gable, here with **Constance Bennett** in *After Office Hours*. Gable has big hands. A less dashing but classier Gable was William Powell, below with **Kay Francis** in what is called a weepie, *One Way Passage*. After the ultra-torch actress Francis, it is necessary to clear the color palette with a satiric version of The Lady, **Margaret Dumont**, here vamped by Groucho Marx in *The Cocoanuts*.

Stage Ladies were a must, with their staircase entrances, telephone scenes, diction, great magical doubting pauses, and the rest of the kit. Here are two great ones, pregnant in pause, **Ann Harding** (below) with Clive Brook in *Gallant Lady* and **Helen Hayes** (right) with John Beal in *Another Language*.

Strangely, these gifted women ended in the same weepies that Francis handled, though on Broadway they tried everything from melodrama to high comedy. This is a problem built into not It but Hollywood's idea of It: women's lives are calibrated in romance. No wonder all film was stunned when Gish came back from Italy looking refreshed after having played a nun. No wonder she looked refreshed.

No woman felt the oppression of the love plot more than those who played openly sensual. In *The Blue Angel* **Marlene Dietrich** was the oppressor, can't help it, but here we catch up with her in *Blonde Venus*, with Cary Grant; and believe me, she's paying for it now. Sacrificing all for husband Herbert Marshall, she strikes a deal with Grant, Marshall throws her out . . . a weepie. But anything Josef von Sternberg directs defies Hollywood's genre code, and we do get Dietrich in one of her niftiest costumes, a gorilla suit.

"What kinda notions ya got?" **Mae West** asks of notions salesman W. C. Fields in *My Little Chickadee*. Here was one sensualist who never paid the price—not on screen, anyway. Off it, liberty cost Mae plenty—such as directing her career by her own lights, even the right to work. Note her outfit. Was Mae putting us on or is that her idea of finery? We'll never know.

1037-181

West wrote her own material; her coeval comediennes delivered other writers' lines. Here's **Marion Davies**, too often the bride when she would have made a jaunty bridesmaid, *en carrosse* with Bing Crosby in *Going Hollywood.* Marion, as Louella Parsons used to write when earning the favor of William Randolph Hearst, never looked lovelier. **Carole Lombard** looks pretty good, too, here with Barrymore in *Twentieth Century.* She has been bullied and battered, but she has found the role that will make her one of the most likable stars. If there was ever an actress who proves that It is more a matter of personality than looks—as Mrs. Glyn vainly kept telling the world—Lombard's the one. Plenty of actresses could match her for looks and talent, but who had her guts and fairness and honesty?

West was a concept and Lombard a person; **Eve Arden** was a sequence of sarcastic replies. Here we see her, characteristically, with secretarial tools in a supporting part, in a middle-late Lubitsch comedy, *That Uncertain Feeling*. Melvyn Douglas (right) does a take and Harry Davenport, whose career is so rich it goes back to Gilbert and Sullivan on Broadway in the late 1870s, does his cool grandpa looking on.

Comes now **Marie Dressler** in her glory as just about the biggest box-office attraction in MGM's early talkies. With Garbo in *Anna Christie* she's a sodden tramp of New York harbor; with Lionel Barrymore in *Dinner at Eight* she's a vivacious thespian. One's Eugene O'Neill, the other Kaufman and Ferber; one's life poetry and the other's a vaudeville. In art or corn, Dressler was great. Did she have It? Well, you don't top the lists in Hollywood by just playing on your ukulele, kids.

Four stages in the career of **Katharine Hepburn**: RKO prestige star of fancy flop movies; the clever comeback artist who designs her transformation from elite favorite to box-office star; the MGM Kate of the Spencer Tracy partnership; and the survivor. First, *Alice Adams,* with Fred MacMurray as the society boy Hepburn hopes to charm—the still catches young Hepburn's mannered enchantment. Next, a trimmer talent astonishes Hollywood in *The Philadelphia Story,* with James Stewart as the reporter Hepburn thinks she loves on the eve of her wedding to John Howard; actually, she's still crazy about her first husband, Cary Grant. Next, Spencer and Kate in the usual wrangle, this one from *Pat and Mike.* Lastly, it's Kate and John Wayne in *Rooster Cogburn.* When you're on John Wayne's side in a western you *know* you're a national heroine. Wayne impressed Hepburn; she wrote a piece for *TV Guide* extolling his virility, a novelty, she thought, "in these gay times." She must also have enjoyed sparring with Humphrey Bogart in *The African Queen,* challenging his bum informality with her brittle bluntness.

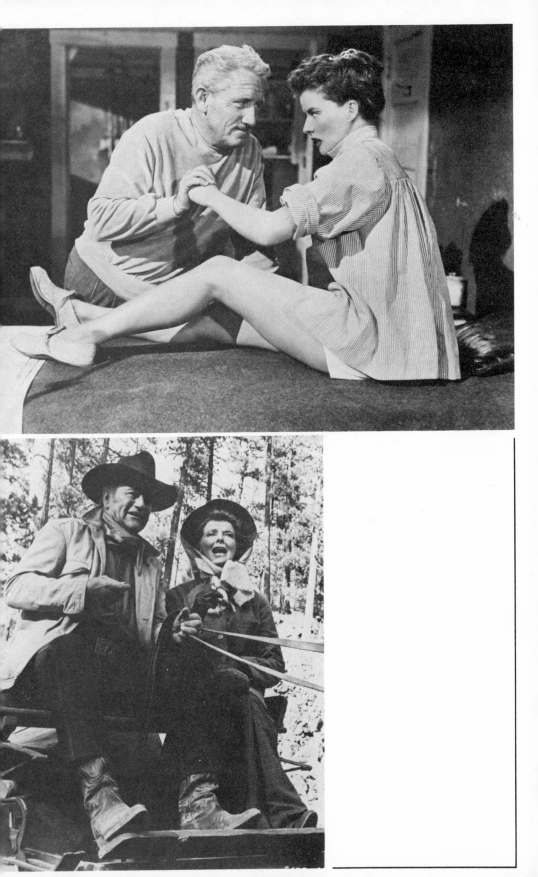

Now the fighters. **Glenda Farrell** and **Joan Blondell** check the employment ads in Warners' favorite period setting, the Great Depression. This is *Gold Diggers of 1937*; note the ironic message on the trash bin to the left. (Trivia question: Who are the two women behind the stars?) "You're a man disgusted with all civilization," **Barbara Stanwyck** tells Gary Cooper in *Meet John Doe*, preparing him for the shutters. She learns disgust, too. The wild surmise on the faces of Natalie Wood and **Rosalind Russell** in *Gypsy* reflects the horror of the vaudevillian backed into the lowest of the low, burlesque. But as Gypsy (Rose Lee), Wood will triumph and free herself from grabby Momma Rose. Ethel Merman was bitter at having lost her stage role to Russell, and Angela Lansbury's fans treasure the 1974 revival. But Russell may be the best of the three—not in singing, certainly, but in being able to render a thoroughly dislikable person without the slightest bid for sympathy.

**B**ette Davis! Above, she's tough in *Bordertown* (with Eugene Pallette and Paul Muni); near right, she's acting in *Of Human Bondage* (at Leslie Howard); top right, she's flirting in *Jezebel* (near George Brent); far right, she's gay as a hatter in *All About Eve* (with Gary Merrill, Celeste Holm, and Hugh Marlowe). One odd thing about her (among many): lately, it's become chic to pronounce her first name as "Bet" rather than as "Betty." Why is this?

Now the kids. Here's Little **Judy** in her neglected first feature, *Pigskin Parade*, a treat about a boondocks college accidentally taking on (and beating) Yale at football, through the discovery of watermelon hurler Stu Erwin. A moment of dismay: coach Jack Haley, his sister Patsy Kelly, Erwin, his sister Judy, perennial coed Betty Grable. Whatever happened to the college musical? Whatever happened to the musical, period? Top right, comes a woman Judy, eight years later, with Tom Drake in the last scene of *Meet Me in St. Louis*.

Meanwhile, **Deanna Durbin** plots with Mischa Auer and Adolphe Menjou in *100 Men and a Girl*. Can it stay pure? **Rita Hayworth**'s before and after says no: Rita chaste with Fred Astaire in *You Were Never Lovelier*. . .

. . . And Rita vavoom singing "Put the Blame on Mame" in *Gilda*. For reference, the last of the ace It girls, **Marilyn Monroe**, does her naive at Arthur O'Connell in *Bus Stop*. Come to say it, O'Connell does a pretty telling naive, too. It meets It.

939-2

Musical women. **Doris Day**, as Jean Kerr (more or less) to David Niven's Walter, sang only one number in *Please Don't Eat the Daisies*. **Liza Minnelli**, here in "The Money Song" from *Cabaret*, with Joel Grey, does more singing on Broadway than in film. **Julie Andrews**, consummate in heroine parts, lived through (and was nearly wrecked by) the suicide of the Hollywood musical in such events as *Thoroughly Modern Millie*, long, dumb, and sloppy. Here Andrews and James Fox are introducing a dance sensation (they hope) called "The Tapioca." Last is **Streisand**, unique in *Hello, Dolly!*, here in the title numbo. Streisand proves what little work Hollywood finds for musical women. She's the greatest singer in the land, and what does she do? Mostly not musicals. Streisand has big hands.

Some contemporary persons now. Michael Sarrazin sleeps on **Jane Fonda**, Bruce Dern glaring on, in *They Shoot Horses, Don't They?* and **Lily Tomlin** possesses John Travolta in *Moment by Moment*. Political films. Fonda's is Marxist microcosm, Tomlin's sexist propaganda: Fonda plays an articulate prole and Tomlin plays (apparently) a man. The story goes that a troupe of Old Hollywood veterans went to *Moment by Moment*, and when Tomlin took this, uh, man in her arms and, like, had him, they just spilled all their popcorn.

For a finish, let's consider what happens to these Old Hollywood stalwarts when they get old. They can be made symbol: **Gloria Swanson** at the fadeout of *Sunset Boulevard:* "I'm ready for my closeup, Mr. De Mille." They can be made mock of: **Eve Arden** as the high school principal in *Grease;* note that she's still a form of secretary. They can be preserved, perhaps pickled: **Lucille Ball** mummified in *Mame* . . .

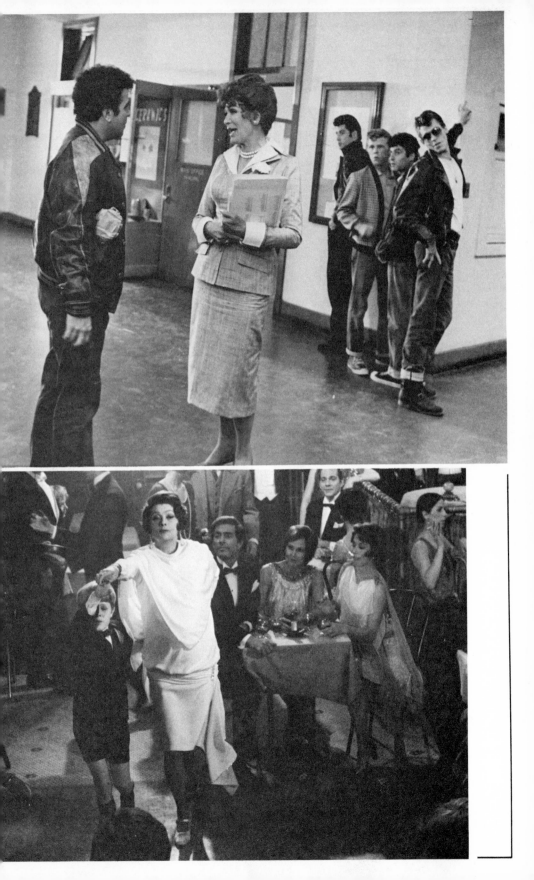

O r they can be freaked: **Bette Davis** in *Whatever Happened to Baby Jane?*—note Joan Crawford dying behind her. And they can be trashed: **Faye Dunaway** as Joan Crawford in *Mommie Dearest*. The question is Did Joan Crawford go to Hell? The answer is yes: and they called it Hollywood.

# 10

# *Fighters*

GLENDA FARRELL
JOAN BLONDELL
ROSALIND RUSSELL
ALICE FAYE
BARBARA STANWYCK

*Did you get two pairs of pants with that suit?*

—GYPSY ROSE LEE
to Alice Faye in *You Can't
Have Everything*

Early in *Golden Boy*, the film version of Clifford Odets' play about a young Italian violinist who turns boxer, a gangster is crowding manager Adolphe Menjou. Indicating Menjou's associate Barbara Stanwyck, the gangster asks, "This your girl?" and Stanwyck answers it for him: "I'm my mother's girl."

This was something new in film, like the screwball heroine distinctly thirties in tone and opinion: the independent woman. Grown cynical about life in which the laws are made and the customs appraised by men, they appear to be the most level-headed and worldly people who have yet shown up in the movies, more aware of how the System works than a cowboy hero, yet as clear as he is in assessing each new face for good or evil intentions.

They were not ideologues. There is no political amazement in their statements. Still, they seem to feel that man in his interminable competitions and paranoia has made life extra tough. American art in the Depression had a gritty realism that we have since lost, an immediacy and a banner-headline violence that connected fiction, theatre, painting, and film to life in the streets. One sees this especially in certain women characters, though midway through the decade censorship muzzled some of the realism. (For four years, women could be prostitutes, for example; by 1934 even the suggestion of this was horror to the expurgators, though the Hays Office accepted "dance-hall girls" and "nightclub hostesses" as euphemistic compromises.) These certain women took men as they came, flat out and a little contemptuously. Men made the Depression, they seem to say, while women are steady, reasonable, and tireless. Men are usually off somewhere yelling and clashing.

This is the attitude particularly of the Warner Brothers city films, from crime drama to romantic comedy. Every block, every tenement room, was filmed in the studio, but the dialogue and action carried the ultra-realistic despair of not making it in places where making it big is all that counts. It was Warners that revived the figure of the gold digger, running it into a whole series of musicals set backstage and on stage on Broadway, imbued with the fanaticism of putting on the show so everyone can get off the breadlines. Dick Powell, Ruby Keeler, Joan Blondell, and Glenda Farrell play youngsters; James Cagney, Adolphe Menjou, and Warner Baxter turn up once each as directors; various Warners comics fill out the scene; and Busby Berkeley stages the numbers to Harry Warren–Al Dubin songs. Not all the films have *Gold Digger* in the title: *42nd Street* (1933) launched the series, and between official *Gold Diggers of 1933, of 1935,* and *of 1937* there were *Footlight Parade, Dames,* and *Stage Struck.* At first there weren't that many gold diggers in these films, but the type began to creep into the series and dominates the 1937 *Gold Diggers* in theme as well as action. Perhaps the Depression was taking too long to go away; or perhaps Warners wanted to spice up the unvaried texture of the films.

Whatever the reason, the gold digger remains one of Hollywood's most politicized characters, though she is looking for security, not ideological freedom. The figure derives from non-musical backstage comedies popular on Broadway in the late 1910s and early 1920s, and it was this figure that Mae West used as the basis for her act. In her savvy one-liners, West was a very "aware" humorist, most keen when dissecting the vanity and larceny of men and the hypocrisy of the social structure. "When women go wrong," she tells us in *She Done Him Wrong,* "men go right after them."

However, West's gold diggers ran counter to the prevailing sentiment that kept women were looking for love under all the fortune hunting; and the authorities actually threw her into jail for subversion, though of course they didn't call it that. In the silent days, it was the sweet-thing gold diggers who turned up in adaptations from Broadway, most notably in *The Gold Diggers* (1923) and *Gentlemen Prefer Blondes* (1928), but the talkies' use of vernacular slang and sass edged sentimentality to the side, for a realistic tone encouraged a realistic point of view. Suddenly, gold diggers were no longer like the heroine of *The Gold Diggers,* who starts out fleecing a snob and then falls for him, or like that of *Gentlemen Prefer Blondes,* the celebrated Lorelei Lee, who lives off the fat of the grand. Talkie gold diggers stood just this side of having to steal to eat.

Tough broads. Warner Brothers, home of Bette Davis and, later, Joan Crawford, was their capital city. But the toughest of them all was Glenda Farrell, who never made it to star status. Farrell played most of the real gold diggers* in the series, resorting to blackmail in *Gold Diggers of 1935* to pinch fatuous millionaire Hugh Herbert for some hush money—not that he did anything. Herbert is too entranced with his snuff box collection to care about sex; but he writes poetry, and Farrell has him sign one of his more effusive concoctions and thus has the makings of a tidy breach of promise suit. Herbert rebuffs her suggestion that they settle it out of court; fine with Farrell. She'll wait and get more. "See you in the tabloids," she says with a smirk as she goes.

Yet Farrell, too, had to show sentimentality when the time came, in *Gold Diggers of 1937*. (Of the breed, only Mae West never softened, and look what happened to her.) At first Farrell is her usual self, a woman of steel who softens only for sisters in trouble. Applying for a job as a stenographer, she interests an employer who tells her that most secretaries lack zip. "*You've* got it," he notes. "And I'm going to keep it," she snaps. But life is hard and Farrell is not too moral about some things; and she embarks on a paid seduction of aged, nerve-racked Victor Moore at the invitation of his partners, who hope he'll kick off so their many embezzlements will not be detected. They aim Farrell at Moore, and as she sails off to earn a few the long way, she sighs mockingly, "It's so hard to be good under the capitalistic system." But when Moore takes a liking to Farrell she melts and reveals the plot against him in one of those "I'm not worthy of you" scenes, and by the fadeout they're a love match. They make an odd couple, the wheezy, vague vaudevillian and the hard candy with the surprise nougat center.

But that is exceptional Farrell. Most of the time she was so tough that she wasn't appreciated till camp collectors of the 1960s rediscovered her many B-budget programmers and began quoting her putdowns. However, one of Farrell's colleagues at Warners, Joan Blondell, managed to hit a mean between tough and sentimental and became much better known than Farrell, though never a big box-office draw. Blondell often teamed with Farrell, because with Blondell in tow Farrell's cracks were funny as well as grim (if only because Blondell laughed at them), and with Farrell in tow Blondell had someone she could open up to. Alone, Blondell could carry a picture, but she seldom got a good one. A child of vaudeville stock, she was initiated into film along with James Cagney for a minor play in 1930 and was set down on the Warners treadmill, making eight films in 1931 and nine in 1932. She never troubled the studio chiefs for better parts and big

*Ginger Rogers makes a stab at it before Farrell enters the series, but it isn't meant seriously and seems more an atmospheric vignette than true fortune hunting. In *42nd Street* Rogers becomes the fancy companion of sugar daddy Guy Kibbee when Bebe Daniels turns on him. In *Gold Diggers of 1933*, she again makes a play for Kibbee, but this time Aline MacMahon is first in line. "Start walking and keep walking," MacMahon suggests, "and if you ever come near him again I'll break both your legs." Haughtily, Rogers replies, "I could easily resent that."

raises and appears not to have cared much about her career in the first place.

Many years later, she wrote a novel, *Center Door Fancy*, with recognizable depictions of her marriages to Dick Powell and Mike Todd and a heroine obviously modeled on herself: highly attractive in the blond, bright-eyed, buxom line, looking for love in a home, and constantly getting sidetracked by the wrong men. At one point in the book, a character tells her she has "no drive to be an actress, really. It's just a job to you that may pay off. . . . It seems you're more pleased with yourself when you've placed a vase of flowers strategically in your room than—than at the sound of applause! . . . Crazy girl, you just want a home and your family."

Blondell was no enigma to Depression audiences. She was honest, cynical, determined. She can take charge. In *Blondie Johnson* (1933) she plays not the gun moll of Chester Morris, lounging in a bed jacket while he pulls off a job, but the leader of the gang, the mastermind. (Both are apprehended, but they'll serve time, repent, and be united.) In *Footlight Parade* (1933), as showman Cagney's secretary, she virtually runs the film, getting Cagney to hire Ruby Keeler out of the typing pool and onto the stage (whereupon Keeler really does say, "Gee, Mr. Kent, that'd be swell!"), forcing Cagney's crooked employers to pay him earnings they had been withholding, and protecting Cagney from gold digger Claire Dodd, incidentally getting off the film's zinger in telling Dodd, "As long as they have sidewalks, you've got a job!" At the film's end, when Cagney has pulled off a spectacular comeback, she cries, "You did it!" and he replies, "You mean *we* did it!" He's right.

Blondell, then, was no gold digger, though she talks her way through a greedy verse of "All's Fair in Love and War," the big finale of *Gold Diggers of 1937*, outlining a plan to take some ancient millionaire for his kaboodle. "A sudden love attack," she says, "and I'd have all his jack." As with Rogers, this is frippery. Blondell wants to work for her living.

But what can you do when they're not hiring? In *Dames* (1934), Blondell resorts to blackmail to fund Dick Powell's show, and her aggressiveness is effervescent but officious. When she learns that Powell's girl Keeler is the daughter of sausage-casing tycoon Guy Kibbee, Blondell scents "a meal ticket coming over the horizon" and tells Keeler, "Beat it, buttercup," to clear the office for a planning session with Powell. Later, she blithely turns up in Kibbee's bed and demands twenty thousand dollars (the show's budget) to vanish. At length he gives in; how much did she want?

BLONDELL: Twenty-five thousand.
KIBBEE: You said twenty thousand the first time.
BLONDELL: Why didn't you pay me the first time?

In essence, Blondell is a warrior against the Depression, sometimes tearfully, bitterly; sometimes with strenuous optimism. In *There's Always a Woman* (1938), a crime comedy in which the butler did it, Blondell plays detective Melvyn Douglas' secretary and wife. Business is slow and Douglas discouraged, so Blondell exercises positivism to keep them going. Here's another "don't let the times get you down" teaming, more buoyant than Blondell and Farrell and also, obviously, convenient for romance. Douglas is always teasing Blondell and Blondell is always cheering up Douglas; and that's how marriage was born. He's a typical vain, arrogant man constantly blowing his style over little things. She's impetuous, resourceful, and constantly in trouble. At a restaurant, whither a case involving Another Woman in Mary Astor's marriage has led her, Blondell is so intent on eavesdropping on a nearby table that at a climactic moment her chair crashes over. Meanwhile, she's holding up her end in a series of tiny quarrels with Douglas—though by the close of the scene, drunk on champagne, they are alone in the restaurant cooing. They must have more in common than they think they do. Earlier, hanging up on a conversation with Blondell at a pay phone, Douglas mutters, "Little gold digger"—then pulls open the change box to see if his nickel came back.

Blondell became so identified with Depression resistance and the gold-digger syndrome that she had trouble retaining even her secondary position in the 1940s. She owed everything to her looks, style, hard work, and to Warners' better writers. Nobody else gave her anything. Nor did the studio build her; she was a working girl, neat. Her thirties marriages—first to a cinematographer and then to Dick Powell—were hardly the sort that create an intrigue of celebrity; and despite her superb figure, she was never a sex star. In short, Blondell had character, which appeals to us today looking back on the time, but no veneer of allure to appeal to them then. So Blondell, too, was typed by time and lost her currency.

By 1940, when Blondell left Warner Brothers to freelance, she was anything but indispensable, playing roles that almost any actress might have tackled—the Constance Bennett character in *Topper Returns* (1941), with John Wayne in *Lady for a Night* (1942), in *Christmas Eve* (1947), so obscure that even trivia buffs can't place it. Only three good chances came her way in the whole decade, *A Tree Grows in Brooklyn* (1944), *Adventure* (1945), and *Nightmare Alley* (1947), and she had supporting roles in all three.

Her Aunt Cissy in *A Tree Grows in Brooklyn,* from Betty Smith's nostalgic novel, was to have been the principal role (originally intended for Alice Faye), but much of Blondell's footage was cut from the release print—astonishingly, as she is without question the best thing in it. Cissy is a vulgar, frivolous version of the characters Blondell had played in the Berkeley backstagers, a mean-streets Auntie Mame, and while such parts always brought out the shtick in vaudeville veterans, Blondell plays her entirely for character, letting the jokes play themselves. Shirley Booth, in the same role in the musical version on Broadway a few years later, went in heavily for shtick, and it's interesting to compare the two on that old question of stage versus film acting. Blondell was not at her best on stage (though she scored a success in *The Effect of Gamma Rays on Man-in-the-Moon Marigolds* Off Broadway in 1972, despite her stated lack of understanding of or sympathy for the part). She was an intuitive performer who took no pains with her portrayals, and thus didn't act her characters as much as feel like them and let it show when the camera turned: magnetism.

Booth, on the other hand, was not at her best on film. She assessed her parts, thought them through, polished them through stumbling rehearsals that would unnerve her fellows till, just before opening night, all the practice would coalesce into a whole person. Moviemaking held her back, with its puny rehearsals and short takes, though she came through with a marvelously wacky Dolly Levi in Joseph Anthony's film of *The Matchmaker*. In the end, both women delivered champion Aunt Cissys, but Booth's was more a variety turn of great style while Blondell's came right off the pages of Smith's book.

Oddly, Blondell gave her best performance in this time of relative neglect, and in her first below-the-title billing in some fifty pictures. This was in *Adventure,* the aforementioned Clark Gable–Greer Garson romance. Blondell plays beautifully with both, an uninhibited tomato with the man and a wise adviser to the woman. She is as exuberant as ever before, but seems more adept, more faceted, as if she finally did take up acting by technique and is now approaching parts in the Shirley Booth manner. *Adventure* really needs Blondell, for while the two stars are in trim, it would have been just another MGM lady-meets-cowboy love tale without Blondell; for unlike a cowboy or a lady she has nothing to prove, just is, and thereby gives the tale a shot of self-belief. Some viewers get so involved in Blondell's part of the show that they start worrying about her more than Gable or Garson, for the urgency that she projected in the Depression *has* survived, has simply been rechanneled.

Unfortunately, by the 1950s there were not even many stars left to support. Blondell returned to the stage (in, among other parts, Aunt Cissy in the *Tree Grows in Brooklyn* musical), made forgotten films, did television work, wrote her novel; and when she turned up, game but poor, as a malt shop waitress in *Grease* (1978), everyone asked, Isn't she dead?

The gold diggers were strictly thirties women, doomed to obsolescence. What of the professional woman, who scorns men's money to make her own? Many actresses turned up as office honchos, but one above all typifies the style, Rosalind Russell. Unlike Blondell, Russell didn't fade down after her first decade; in fact, she had her biggest hit well after, in the 1950s. And when Russell was old, the question was not Isn't she dead? but Why isn't she doing more? Here is one of the great sustained careers, for Russell had a secret weapon: the stage.

She started in theatre, though before she had established herself in New York she had already entrained to the coast for a screen test at Universal. They gave her the typical Hollywood runaround: lure the starlets out by the carload, let them hang around waiting for a call, then *maybe* test *some* of them. At her first test, Russell encountered an unhelpful staff, went through nine takes: nothing. Meanwhile a friend had talked her up at MGM, where she made a splendid test and was offered a contract.

Only one problem: Universal still held first refusal on her option—and Universal decided to sign her.

To understand Russell's dilemma, one must realize that MGM was the top studio, where anyone they were interested in was carefully nurtured, groomed, and developed. It wasn't just the top-okay place to be a star in; it was the place where you *became* a star, because experts managed your development. Universal was the dullest of the major studios, imploded from its former days of silent glory in bread-and-butter genres into a few sound stages' worth of horror pictures. Universal was the place where Uncle Carl Laemmle ruled gently, a Rotarian mogul. Once, a load of extras in costume massed at the front gate to meet him as he returned from a trip abroad to the California sunshine. "Vat a beautiful, beautiful day!" Laemmle cried. "So vy ain't you people out voiking?" Universal was the place where everyone who was related to (or even knew) Uncle Carl could get a job, and in concert these opportunists had run Universal into the ground. Russell had to cut herself free of this horror lot and move to MGM. She showed up for her interview with Carl Laemmle, Jr., wearing a borrowed fiasco of a dress, a dumb hat, vaselined hair, and a suffocating bra.

Russell went to MGM.

"It was lovely," she recalled. They gave her decent little parts in good pictures, which gave her a chance to learn the business. She spoke well, held herself coolly and firmly, so they gave her a lot of what she termed "Lady Mary" roles, with lines like "How can you spend time with *her*? She's rahther vulgar, isn't she?" MGM saw her as another stage dame, and used her as a pawn to hold Myrna Loy in check. It was a typical studio trick: keep the reigning diva obedient by threatening her with a diva-to-be. But who could imagine two women less similar than Russell and Loy? It must have unnerved Russell to see Loy in action—they made a number of films together—and reflect that *that* was where MGM felt she was headed.

From 1934 to 1939 she learned and grew but could not achieve

stardom, though she was excellent in lead roles in two films more popular now than they were then, *Craig's Wife* (1936) and *Night Must Fall*
(1937). In the former, Russell was a housewife in love with her home
rather than with husband John Boles; in the latter Robert Montgomery
was a genial axe murderer. This was not what the public wanted from
MGM. Give them star turns and fashion; and Russell finally did—the
hell with Lady Mary—in *The Women* (1939), making a place for herself
next to (some think before) Norma Shearer and Joan Crawford as Sylvia Fowler, the meanest of the Park Avenue playgirls. In the opening
credits, each of the leads is introduced as an animal, Shearer a doe,
Crawford a tiger, Mary Boland a monkey, Paulette Goddard a fox, and
so on. Russell is a spitting cat. Shearer says, "Sylvia's all right . . . underneath," but it's Sylvia who sends poor trusting Shearer to the man-
icurist who will unwittingly entertain her with her own dish—that her
husband is cheating on her with Crawford.

George Cukor, *The Women*'s director, didn't want Russell, but she
won him over with a versatile audition, playing the part in different
styles. When filming began, however, she adopted a heavy, villainous
manner; to her dismay, he said he wanted something she had tried in
the audition, an exaggerated comic delivery, lines spun out in rapid
fire and hands flapping and pointing and grabbing. He had a point:
Sylvia spends half the story breaking up a loving family and the other
half gloating over the ruins. If Russell played it straight the public
would hate her. So together they made Sylvia Fowler foolish, more
irritating than vicious, and they put her into the silliest high-style
clothes since Grace Moore went to work for Columbia. Partway
through shooting, Russell pulled a rare unprofessional stunt and called
in sick till she was promised star billing with Crawford and Shearer.
She got it, along with the cover of *Life* magazine, and won her status at
last, as a comedienne.

Her next film, on loan to Columbia, ratified her new position, opposite Cary Grant in *His Girl Friday* (1940). This reworking of *The Front
Page* retained much of the original's cynical spirit in its look at the
newspaper and political games on the eve of a condemned man's execution, but instead of two bickering men, editor and reporter, Russell
played the reporter to Grant's editor as a divorced couple who—one is
sure—will recouple by the fadeout.

Hildy Johnson in *His Girl Friday* is essential Roz the career woman,
the capstone of all the thirties comedies about women making it on
their own and one of the few that approve of their doing so. The title
says she's his girl, true—romance was the price a career woman paid in
the movies. But she's her mother's girl in the ease with which she
moves through male turf, never once trying to take advantage of her
gender for special treatment. On the contrary, Russell's Hildy is more

like a man than a woman in some ways. She dresses in a pin-stripe suit, strides through the city room with confident bravado, doesn't trust fiancé Ralph Bellamy with money (he'd only lose it), bribes her way into an interview with the doomed felon, writes copy like nobody's business, and stops a minor character with a flying tackle, anything goes. Fittingly, Cary Grant treats her as if she were Melvyn Douglas or so (which is why, one eventually figures out, she left him in the first place). He thinks it's a buddy film. Russell thinks it's a romantic comedy.

They're both wrong. It's screwball farce, fast and wild and dark. Howard Hawks directed, goading his stars into throwing it off like a charade, overlapping their lines and battling via jest. They respected the script but fooled around a lot between the lines; at one point, sensing that Russell was about to invent some business, Grant looked right at Hawks and asked, "Is she going to do that?" Hawks printed it like so; anything goes.

Now comes the tricky part—for Russell as for Blondell and the other Depression fighters—for the Depression was over and its major elements were forcibly displaced. Betty Grable and Judy Garland would define the forties heroine, out of the offices and back onto the stages. What happened to Russell?

First, she got married, to Frederick Brisson, son of Carl Brisson, a Danish singer who appeared in a few minor movie musicals. It was a fine marriage, lifelong, and as an agent who was turning producer, Brisson was able to assist his wife in instilling some new momentum into her career. In the event, she survived the 1940s, but in few first-class films. Russell was fine as the older not-so-great-with-the-boys sister in *My Sister Eileen* (1942), with Janet Blair as the blond ingenue every male is after, and she put her all into a high-risk venture she felt deeply about, *Sister Kenny* (1946), the life of the Australian nurse who pioneered a radical therapy for polio victims. Russell also copped one of the classic parts of America's stage literature, Lavinia Mannon in the film of Eugene O'Neill's adaptation of Aeschylus, *Mourning Becomes Electra* (1947). Dudley Nichols edited the text and directed; with Michael Redgrave, Katina Paxinou, and Raymond Massey as the other Mannons, it sounded like a valiant project, not popular but reputable and, it was hoped, artistically persuasive. Alas, no one liked it, and the three-hour road-show print was cut by an hour in general release and now appears to be lost.

In all, Russell was still in there, but she needed a smash. She found one not in Hollywood but in New York, playing the older sister again in a musical based on *My Sister Eileen*, *Wonderful Town* (1953). The Leonard Bernstein–Betty Comden–Adolph Green score and some stylish Jerome Robbins choreography distilled a spunky thirties atmosphere—solid vehicle—and Russell proved adept in giving out with what musical comedy takes—solid star. She cooed and bawled "Ohio" (the one that begins "Why, oh why, oh why-o") with kid sister Edie Adams, catalogued "One Hundred Easy Ways to Lose a Man" with vigorous fatalism, taught Brazilian naval cadets the conga while rattling off the names and places of the time ("How do you feel about Harold Teen, Dizzy Dean, Mitzi Green?"), extolled the merits of the new hep in "Swing!" and, with Adams, socked out "The Wrong Note Rag" and became the toast of Broadway. Brooks Atkinson suggested she run for president, and *Wonderful Town* became so identified with Russell's performance that, great show though it was, it began to fail as soon as she left it, replaced by Carol Channing.

Now, how to invest this new fame in her sagging movie career? Doing a film musical may have been a good idea, but *The Girl Rush* (1955) wasn't apt. As a gambler's daughter who inherits a rundown hotel in Las Vegas, Russell sings, dances, and delivers her famous cool put-downs with the half-closed eyes and basso voice, but the Hugh Martin–Ralph Blane score is terrible, the many nightclub routines are grotesque even when they aren't trying to burlesque nightclub routines, and Russell at forty-odd is too old to play a love plot with Fernando Lamas. Worst of all, the film is stolen by Marion Lorne as Russell's aunt, doing her bumbling stutter bit. True, no one bumbles and stutters like Lorne, but this was to be Russell's grand comeback.

Another idea: play someone completely out of mode. At MGM, Russell had been haughty ladies, good-guy debs, incognito princesses, tight-lipped spinsters, and crazies. Now, in the film version of William Inge's play *Picnic* (1955), she played another spinster, but a desperate, sad, and at times strangely uninhibited woman who is much more interesting than either the vagabond stud (William Holden) or the small-town prom queen (Kim Novak) who have the leading roles. It's a part movie stars seldom played: unattractive, crummy, hopeless. A schoolteacher past her bloom, the best Russell can hope for is marriage with an extremely reluctant but bullyable Arthur O'Connell; and the worst that can happen is her life up to this point. To a woman who enacted the spiffiest professionals and socialites, MGM's threat to Myrna Loy, the role was degradation as well as a challenge. Yet Russell digs into it, with no starry peeks from behind the mask to reassure the fans.

Anyway, it wasn't that much of a challenge to Russell, whose acting abilities were too often hidden in cinch parts like those in *The Citadel* (1938), as a doctor's wife, or in *Never Wave at a Wac* (1952), as a wastrel trying to learn self-respect. The former is serious, the latter comic; the former has classy Brits and Tone, the latter oddballs and slapstick; the former indicts corruption, the latter just has fun. The range suggests Russell's versatility, for she is fine in both. Yet the two parts themselves call for no special gifts, and too much of Russell's career had been like that.

In fact, the biggest hit of her life was the cinchiest part of all, that of the scatterbrained but strong-willed Mame Dennis, first on Broadway in 1956, then on screen two years later. One should not underestimate Russell's artistic seniority in this part. Going back to the source, Patrick Dennis' novel *Auntie Mame,* one finds a character harder and meaner than the one Russell played. Jerome Lawrence and Robert E. Lee wrote the play *Auntie Mame* expressly for Russell and put more than a little of the star's screen persona into the mix, ending up with something of an *Auntie Roz.* Moreover, none of the actresses who prominently tried the part in the 1950s—Constance Bennett, Beatrice Lillie, Greer Garson, Eve Arden, and Sylvia Sidney—brought anything like the warmth and dazzle that Russell brought to it. Still, given the circumstances of the play's conception, it was right up Russell's alley, even if she did have to work mightily to keep it in motion.

*Auntie Mame* was the most expensive non-musical production to that date in Broadway's history, with a wondrous Travis Banton wardrobe, a gigantic cast, and so much decor that noisemakers and projections were needed to simulate comic tempo in the lulls while the sets were being changed. The whole thing rested on Russell, as the den mother of the avant-garde who raises an orphaned nephew. In the course of the proceedings she, among other capers, wrecks the out-of-town opening of a play in which she has a walk-on; leads a southern fox hunt despite a total lack of knowledge of horses, foxes, and the south; writes her memoirs; humiliates suburban bigots to discourage their daughter from marrying her nephew; and closes the evening by taking in her grand-nephew to raise, the cycle sentimentally ever turning. One line in the play, "Life is a banquet, and most poor sons of bitches are starving to death!" lost some urgency in the film, adapted by Betty Comden and Adolph Green, who were forced to use "suckers" in place of the no-no phrase. Naturally, this was the version most Americans heard; but, even bowdlerized, it meant so much to Russell that she entitled her autobiography *Life Is a Banquet.* So, yes, Mame is Russell is Mame. Interestingly, when it came time to turn *Auntie Mame* into a musical, Angela Lansbury rivaled Russell with a quite different but comparably unique portrayal, and since it turned out that *Mame* with music is more fun than the songless *Auntie Mame,* it's Lansbury's stint that will remain vivid, though Russell got to preserve her Mame on film and Lansbury was replaced by Lucille Ball in the *Mame* movie.

In any case, *Auntie Mame* was the hit that remade Russell. She was bigger now than ever, and had lived to eat her cake and have it. "I wanted a home, a husband, children, a variety of experience," she wrote. "I wasn't willing to pay the price of superstardom." Her Broadway connection, from *Wonderful Town* to *Auntie Mame,* had kept her fresh—better, a prodigy. She retained the connection in the three films that followed *Auntie Mame,* all adapted from the stage, though in *A*

*Majority of One* (1961) she inherited a role styled for Gertrude Berg—short, dumpy, and Jewish. Russell—tall, slim, and not Jewish—seems precisely wrong, though she did much field work in developing her inflection. The point is not how well Russell can imitate an ethnic sound, but that we know she is as far from Gertrude Berg as Quentin Crisp is from Clint Walker. *Five Finger Exercise* (1962) saw her in a part played on stage by Jessica Tandy—still not right—and Russell then took over Ethel Merman's once-in-a-lifetime part in the movie version of *Gypsy* (1962), the musical on the relationship between Gypsy Rose Lee and her pushy mother.

The outcry, when Russell was announced, was loud in New York. Hollywood shrugged. In her book, Russell tells that her husband was known as "The Wizard of Roz" for his share in her career decisions, but she's not quite correct. Brisson was known as "The *Lizard* of Roz," especially by Merman when she learned she wasn't going to do the *Gypsy* movie. But the sad truth of the matter is that Merman never clicked in film, though she had been in and out of Hollywood since the first days of sound. Very "stage" in all she did, she delivered her parts square on, decreeing more than acting them. Hollywood was afraid of her, and seldom let her play her Broadway roles when scheduling the film versions. Look at it from their side: her *Call Me Madam* (1953), a typical Merman smash on Broadway, did not do good business *nationally* as a film. Came then *Gypsy*, and Warner Brothers said, Let there be Roz.

Russell says she wasn't dubbed, but Lisa Kirk sang at least some of the vocals, and a good thing, too, for as Mama Rose, who favors Baby June (Havoc), then Louise (Gypsy), then learns (in a way) to stand on her own, Russell has everything the character needs, but could not have got through the tunes unaided. *Gypsy* is not *Wonderful Town*. It's a singing show, and Merman carried it, because everyone else in it was a child, a dancer, or Jack Klugman. Merman also acted in *Gypsy*, for the only time in her career, but Hollywood preferred using Russell plus dubbing to worrying about Merman's recognition patterns in Kansas City and Tucson. Warners filmed the show faithfully and Russell is superb, with all the cavalier meanness that the role requires, cheating her father, cheating landlords and restaurant owners, cheating her daughters, cheating her lover, cheating—of course—herself. She waves away objections as she pours tavern flatware into her handbag, exchanges one star daughter for another with desperate thoughtlessness, and sells that daughter to burlesque because mother must have show biz and there's nothing else left. It's an epic part, using an extravagantly characterful score (by Jule Styne and Stephen Sondheim) to travel the years and places without losing concentration. One would think it impossible to cast, with all its singing action (the immensity of the lead part is one reason why the show is seldom done), and when

Russell was announced for it, Broadway bled from old wounds. But Russell triumphed.

It's just as well that she did, for her following films were ghastly: nun comedies, madcap thriller comedies, and even a black comedy that almost no one saw. But *Auntie Mame* had made her a household face, and she retained a strong reputation through the years despite her current work. Why? It was that crazy-nice aunt, who proved in the end more durable than all of Russell's tailored professional women. Mame is timeless. She came along when Russell was passing from the scene and made her, as far as these things go, eternal.

Another of the thirties women who became closely identified with her time had no trouble surviving it, yet she never had a standout hit—never had any ups or downs at all. She started out on the wrong foot in the wrong type, corrected the seasoning, soared to the top, and became one of the biggest stars. This was Alice Faye, a standout Depression fighter for her stirring use of song and dance. Blondell was the gold digger, Russell the professional, and Faye was the show biz kid, playing women who came up from the slums to win fame on Broadway. She was sweet to look at but had an edge; she couldn't dance all that well but moved with sure rhythm; and her acting was passable. This made excellent material for a musical star, but Faye brought something extra, an effortlessly keen hook on a song that socked it high and held it there, vibrating with self-belief. When Faye sang a cheer-up song, it was a pep rally. When she led a dance number, it was bacchanalia. And when she sang her torch songs of lost love, somewhere a fairy died.

The kind of voice that Faye used for singing—low and taut—was relatively new in the 1930s. Even into the 1920s most pop composers continued to favor the operatic or near-operatic soprano; and when sound invented the Hollywood musical, the big women singing stars accorded to the older type on the order of Jeanette MacDonald and Grace Moore, whose lightly plangent lilt outfitted them for princess and diva roles. But Faye's penetrating basso provisioned a vastly different character, a girl of the proletariat, city-tough yet just folks. In real life a daughter of Hell's Kitchen, to the west of the New York theatre district, Alice Leppert turned Faye for the chorus line but rose as a singer with Rudy Vallee's orchestra. She went to Hollywood with Vallee for *George White's Scandals* (1934), took over the lead when the scheduled star Lilian Harvey gave up on Hollywood and went back to Europe, and stayed on when Vallee, too, left.

She had landed at Fox, then in the chaotic last days before it merged with Darryl Zanuck's Twentieth Century Pictures, and Fox built her as a Jean Harlow, with bleached hair, pencil-line eyebrows, and a few man-killer parts. This approach, happily, was abandoned after a while; Faye is too nice to convince as an Other Woman. Better let her describe camaraderie, sisterhood, and commitment to self-realization as a performer. Already, the differences between Faye and Warner Brothers' comparable backstage heroine, Ruby Keeler, are evident. Keeler, too, is nice, but has far more charm than talent and doesn't initiate anything. If a director indoctrinates, primes, and aims her—as Warner Baxter does in *42nd Street* (1933)—Keeler is willing to Go Out There a Youngster and Come Back a Star; but Faye actually produces and writes. She invents her opportunities, whereas Keeler has to be bullied into taking them.

In *Every Night at Eight* (1935), on loan to Paramount, Faye is Dixie Dean, who organizes a girls' trio with her office co-workers Frances Langford and Patsy Kelly. Langford occupies the romantic center of the film with George Raft, but we're so busy enjoying the rise of Faye's trio that *Every Night at Eight* becomes more a success story than a romance, *opera senza amore*. See the girls locked out of their boardinghouse because they can't pay the rent; see them enter an amateur contest and look like the odds-on favorites till Langford faints from hunger; see them surmount each difficulty—together, all for one—and come through at last as radio stars.

Music, throughout, turns the key. Without a song, there isn't all that much to Faye, for music is what she believes in. Countless women sang on film in Faye's era, 1935 to 1945, from Metropolitan Opera stars and tinny legits to belters and outright toneless mouthers, but few made so much of the song as personal metaphysics, and none but Faye made singing the propelling actuation of their films. *Every Night at Eight*'s "I Feel a Song Comin' On" is typical. At first Kelly takes the lead and the other two give out with the indispensable syncopated "dah dah *dah* dah" backup. In the second chorus, Faye takes over solo, in scat blues style, each "la di he, la di ho" defining the articulate incoherence of swing. Faye pulls the scattered parts of swing together, in fact, retaining a connection with the black vocal influence while singing with all-white bands, getting as much out of an uptempo as a torch number, and respecting melody enough to want to diddle it some on the spur of the moment. She's adept, too, in the good old ballad style. "What a woman!" Tyrone Power observes upon hearing her deliver "Carry Me Back to Old Virginny" in *In Old Chicago* (1938). If music can cheer and stimulate, it can also bring us home to basics. Through the years, hot or cold, she keeps telling us what a service song provides. It's good for you. The title tune in *Music Is Magic* (1935) lists its uses, for example in disposing of melancholy: "A little jingaling'll make you jolly!" And what would romancing and dancing be without song?

Faye sounds this note repeatedly, which makes many of her films rather alike. Besides, all of them seem to be backstagers with Don Ameche, Tyrone Power, or John Payne as Faye's love interest (some of the longer ones have both Ameche and Power). But like the gold digger and the professional woman, Faye was in the right time, the first decade after recordings and radio and the musical film had been absolutely acculturated on a national scale beyond considerations of class or region.

Commercial recording dates back to the turn of the century, but the Victrola and its discs were prohibitively expensive. One RCA recording of the quartet from *Rigoletto* (one side, no flip) cost six dollars, and this was in 1907, when they were using real money. Typically, the Victrola and the album of Caruso and Farrar solos were the ne plus ultra of the upper-middle-class household, but not till the late 1920s could everyone afford one. Similarly, radio took the whole decade of the 1920s to creep into the nation's living rooms, and the film musical didn't exist till 1929, when all major theatres underwent the conversion to sound. So not till 1930 was American music a pandemic public thing, with all ears attuned to the same sounds. And the first sound to catch every ear—with a universal visual appeal, a democratic morality, and a rags-to-riches-through-determination story package—was Alice Faye. Communications, the modern electro-automated America (circa 1919–    ), converged, in its infancy, on her.

Faye did not pursue her recording career. Zanuck's stars made few records; anyway, Faye prefers to do one thing at a time. While she made movies, she didn't want to make records. And while she was married, she didn't want to make movies, so in 1945 she left Fox to put in some time as the wife of bandleader Phil Harris. They were busy on radio for years, but she didn't make another film till 1962, a hideous remake of *State Fair*. Faye was greeted like an old friend, and was about the only thing that anyone liked in the film. She and John Payne proved less adept than formerly, however, in a revival of the stage musical *Good News* that toured the country in the mid-1970s. The two old stars could not keep the show going in New York, but they did pull in many thousands of customers on the road.

Faye stayed famous, then. She never strained for a comeback in squalid shlock just because that was all she was offered, nor did she fade from memory just because she wasn't continually in view. Hers was not a strenuous stardom, for Fox churned her pictures out according to set formula. Nor was it an episodic stardom with periods. She started, rose high, and stayed high till she bowed out. Perhaps her distinctly musical identity protected her from the vicissitudes that plagued Blondell and Russell. Who could have been more thirties than Faye, instituting the throaty contralto as a choice American female vocal range and sparring with reluctant producers, egocentric stars, and other interlopers between talent and the Big Break? Yet who was bigger than Faye in the 1940s? No one.

Faye was accessible, just a notch or two above what you could get or be. Women found her impressive and men liked her; she obviously liked them. She goes through an occasional tough-cookie act with a number of men, the "I'm my mother's girl" statement of gender, but unlike some stars, she doesn't think too much of such tactics, preferring to sing numbers like "Whose Big Baby Are You?" and "Are You in the Mood for Mischief?" in good weather and a torch song in bad. She's unpretentious; sexist oppression is too big an idea for her.

On the other hand, Barbara Stanwyck met it head-on, not often, but so fiercely when she did that it made her one of the most enduring of the thirties figures. In many ways, Stanwyck is like a Joan Crawford who never made it to MGM, a star despite her films. Crawford's MGM series is nothing to win a prize on, true, but her vehicles were well produced, all their effects striving to enhance the headliner. But Stanwyck's films, early, middle, and recent, are almost all programmers. Even her A pictures have a B mentality. However, her studios, mainly Columbia and Warner Brothers, countered MGM's glamour with a naturalistic thrust that enabled Stanwyck to speak (or at least look as if she were thinking) of a set of first principles to govern the socialism of gender.

Still, many of her films are a trial. Maybe her trouble was that she was too easy to work with, willing, prompt, unselfish, professional. Directors and actors who shared a set with her compulsively tell interviewers how wonderful she was. "In a Hollywood popularity contest," Frank Capra said, "she would win first prize hands down"; and Robert Preston likened her to a "patron saint of actors." But in Hollywood it's the tough ones who get what they need; Stanwyck got lead parts in backward pictures.

To start with, she missed out on making the film version of *Burlesque,* the backstage weepie that brought her to prominence on Broadway. *Burlesque*'s male lead, Hal Skelly, repeated his role, but the film, renamed *The Dance of Life* (1929), was to be refashioned as a musical, so Paramount gave the part to Nancy Carroll, whom they were very hot on as a likely star for modern-dress sweetie musicals (though she sang and danced only passably and reluctantly).

Stanwyck came west anyway in 1929, for her vaudeville headliner husband Frank Fay was among the many stage people drafted for sound work. However, Fay made a fool of himself as the emcee of Warner Brothers' endless, asinine, and expensive revue *The Show of Shows* (1929), and his film career bogged down while Stanwyck's plodded along. Soon they were living in real life the plot of *Burlesque:* she rose, he fell and drank heavily, and the marriage suffered.

Stanwyck was lucky in hitting off a collaboration with director Frank Capra at Columbia, for her acting was diffuse and he helped her to focus it. They did not begin well—Capra recalls her as "sullen" and "plainly dressed" at her interview and says she stomped out on him— but Fay fought for her and she played the lead in Capra's *Ladies of Leisure* (1930), the tale of a party girl who falls for a gentlemanly heir, is talked out of marrying him by his mother, attempts suicide, and survives to find him grinning at her hospital bed when she awakens. Anyone could have played it, many better than Stanwyck does. But three films later, in *The Miracle Woman* (1932), the Stanwyck-Capra partnership is paying off.

*The Miracle Woman* is a strange film, offered, the credits announce, "as a rebuke" to evangelists who sell The Word "for gold." Stanwyck plays one such, for while she is not a cheat, she works for a crooked promoter. The role calls for the self-communing mission that snake-oil preachers must have, and this Stanwyck cannot style. Nor does she make it clear whether she herself believes in what she does. But there is a striking scene in which she visits her love interest, David Manners, and they play with a mechanical piano and sing "The Farmer in the Dell." It's a brief moment, but Capra seems to have filmed it spontaneously, without a script, and here Stanwyck is compelling. She was one of those one-take actors who progressively lose their concentration; an opportunity for improvisation was just up her alley. The scene is whimsical, giddy, and, as the camera pushes in close to Stanwyck, we sense the unnerving potential of cinema not as art but as infernal machine, nightmare mirror: the camera is sucking up life.

Already, Stanwyck was falling into tough-girl parts. In *Night Nurse* (1931), she at first plays the idealistic, good-humored nurse in contrast to Joan Blondell's crusty pessimism. Stanwyck made *Night Nurse* at Warners, without Capra, and she's a little out of trim, smiling her part instead of acting it. (Blondell, too, is ahead of her prime here, secure only in the wisecracks.) But once the plot gets moving, we see Stanwyck's grit. She is assigned to care for two little girls who are being starved to death. Clark Gable, then a featured player, handles the villainy as Nick the chauffeur, and makes his first entrance—shocking to those who know him only in his King days—in pajamas and an embroidered Oriental robe. Nick runs the house, so to save the girls Stanwyck takes him on—plus a mean housekeeper, the girls' alcoholic mother, and an evil doctor. Bootlegger Ben Lyon helps her, but it's really Stanwyck's fight, and she wins it.

It was Capra who gave her her first top-class entry, *The Bitter Tea of General Yen* (1933), but Stanwyck most successfully defined her emerging character in less ambitious movies. In *The Lady in Red* (1935) she is a professional horsewoman who berates the socialites she associates with for their scummy selfishness. In *Annie Oakley* (1935) she's dynamite with a rifle, better even than her romantic vis-à-vis Preston Foster. (She throws their first match: "I couldn't beat him—he was just too pretty.") In a remake of *Stella Dallas* (1937), she's a vulgar woman who gives up her daughter so she can marry into a nice set.

Stanwyck is athletic, gallant, honest. She was not typed, like Joan Blondell or Jean Harlow, but some things she just couldn't do, as witness *The Mad Miss Manton* (1938), that screwball thriller that Katharine Hepburn almost did. Melsa Manton has Stanwyck qualities—tenacity, temper, intelligence, and leadership. But Stanwyck can't play screwball. If she is to extend her range, *Stella Dallas* is more the thing, for as the loving, loud mother Stanwyck never takes advantage of a fast weep or a bathetic look into the faraway. "All my life," says Stella, "I've wanted to go to the real places and get in with the right crowd." But her tragedy is that she *isn't* a social climber. She's too lazy to refine herself, too genuine to have fun with snobs. Thus Stanwyck holds our sympathy: by not asking for it. The final scene of Stanwyck watching her daughter's wedding from outside in the rain should feel manipulative, but Stanwyck's tact lightens the tone, even when menaced by the cliché of the policeman telling her to move along.

Is she brazen, lawless, an urban rhinestone? This is the Stanwyck image, of the hard-bitten prole who slaps men, cries, then slaps them more. Few of her roles featured this image, but she is recalled for them because no one else did them as well, including Joan Crawford, the second half of whose career might be viewed as an elocution teacher's imitation of Barbara Stanwyck. When she snarled, "I'm my mother's girl," at gangster Joseph Calleia, she snapped a trap on her character that would bounce her into a squad of tough-girl parts in the 1940s— as a cardsharp in *The Lady Eve* (1941), as a stripper in *Lady of Burlesque* (1943), as a rich bully in *The Strange Love of Martha Ivers* (1946). To round off the set, she was killed off in *Sorry, Wrong Number* (1948).

It was Capra who emphasized Stanwyck's resilience and heroism, in the controversial *Meet John Doe* (1941). Some consider this film the peak of Capra's good-versus-evil egalitarian comedies; some call it the worst in a line of rose-colored, self-congratulatory, pretentious psalms, "Capra corn." It is certainly the darkest of Capra's satires, and its story is so dire, so close to uncovering certain truths about how our society operates, that Capra filmed five different endings for it. And none of them works.

Made after the Second World War had begun, *Meet John Doe* is nonetheless saturated with Depression feelings—about unemployment, money-boss fascism, populism, and the quest for individualism in an age turned by machines. Gary Cooper is the protagonist, Edward Arnold the villain, and James Gleason and Walter Brennan the nice-guy commentators, but it is Stanwyck who directs the proceedings. She initiates the plot, as a thirty-dollar-a-week reporter who concocts a letter signed by a John Doe who promises to jump off the top of City Hall on Christmas Eve to protest the world's evils. A bad-times layoff throws Stanwyck out of work, so to reclaim her job she proposes to hire some stooge to impersonate this John Doe and run a series on him. It's wildcat stuff, hot copy, but editor Gleason resists it. "If it was raining hundred-dollar bills," Stanwyck tells him in desperation, "you'd be out looking for a dime you lost someplace!" At length Gleason sees the light. They audition a lot of bums, hire Cooper, and we're off.

Robert Riskin's script and Capra's direction shoot us along so quickly that it's easier to enjoy the action than to think about it, but on repeated viewings one starts to notice that Stanwyck is something of a bad guy here. Her scheme is daffy and charming, but it's also a viciously exploitive scam. Hard times, career momentum, the film's pace and suspense, and Stanwyck's appeal obscure this; and we forgive her in the end because she's solid and fair when we need it most. But early on, she's actually in league with Capra's favorite villain, the newspaper tycoon. Arnold, with his murderous, fat poise, plans to use the expanding network of John Doe clubs as a base from which to shape a totalitarian takeover. "What the American people need," he tells his boardroom cronies, "is an iron hand." Stanwyck is present at this meeting, a fancy dinner, for Arnold has made her his confederate. Earlier, he had asked her what she wanted from life. "Money," she tells him. And he replies, "I'm glad to hear someone admit it."

Few of Stanwyck's colleagues could have played the role; few had the range to encompass extremes of greed and gallantry and make them feel like strains of the same urgency. Stanwyck wants to win, badly, and this in particular the 1930s admired. But she doesn't want to win on Arnold's side, and this, too, is very thirties, very Capra. By the time of the dinner meeting, she's feeling guilty, disgusted, and very much in love with Cooper, who bursts in on the bosses and defies them. Not only is he not jumping off any roof: he's going to unmask the fraud at a huge John Doe rally. Stanwyck, reconstructed, joins him, but Arnold's bravos cut the microphone wires and disrupt the rally. Capra's beloved little people, the salt of the earth but awfully quick to turn on you when the trouble begins, renounce John Doeism and the world is a mess again. Have the bosses won? If they can't use a thing, they kill it.

Dismay and disillusion fill the film at this point. The rally, spectacularly brought off, starts in electric anticipation, grows thrilling and terrible, and collapses in riot; and Stanwyck senses that Cooper can make America whole again only by going through with it. Who is the true protagonist of the story, who the true doer? Stanwyck started the story and now she clinches it, staggering out of a sickbed to the top of a snow-laden City Hall on Christmas Eve to stop Cooper from jumping.

Now, how does it end? Capra tried everything. Cooper jumps, Cooper doesn't, Cooper falls, Cooper is pushed, what? The logical ending, given the forces arrayed against him, is that he jumps: only the supreme act can redeem the corruption of big-money lies. But preview audiences hated that ending, and the one seen today—the last one Capra filmed—finds Stanwyck in charge. She talks Cooper out of jumping by citing "the first John Doe"—Jesus, clearly. It's a silly speech, pietistic and importunately sentimental (also wrong—the first John Doe did jump, so to speak). But by now Stanwyck is so convincing as the chivalrous and intelligent person, Arthur and Merlin together, that she almost convinces us. To top it, she faints. Cooper carries her toward a crowd of John Doe adherents who haven't broken faith, and Gleason takes the last line. "There you are," he tells Arnold. "The people. Try and lick that."

*Meet John Doe* marked the high point of Stanwyck's career and of the Depression women fighters in general, the last charge. Historical flux brought in a change of types, from gold diggers, professional women, and backstage proles to women mainly interested in making love matches for themselves. Wartime meant escapism, displacing the hard-edged thirties women. True, Faye reached the peak of her stardom in the war years, and Stanwyck went on to a notoriety (in a strange blond wig) in Billy Wilder's *Double Indemnity* in 1944. But the ideological urgency that instructed the fighters melted away, and, for instance, after *Meet John Doe* Stanwyck is a tough broad with appetite but no purpose. In *Double Indemnity* she conspires with insurance salesman Fred MacMurray to murder her husband, yet seems uninvolved in both the murder and the inevitable romance with MacMurray. It's not even clear why she turns against MacMurray. "I'm rotten to the heart," she tells him, shooting to kill. "I used you." But it is he who kills her, with a classic salute in the mean *policier* parlance that the 1940s loved: "Goodbye, baby."

The problem was *film noir,* one of Hollywood's distinctive artistic inventions but a genre so bitter and constricted that it sours and strangles everything it touches. Obsessed with greed and sex, longing for violence, and trapped in darkness, *film noir* as an aesthetic was largely devised by German emigrants fleeing Nazism, and they had little interest in limning the idealism and camaraderie of the thirties fighter comedies. But because their art called for strong women, they inherited many of the fighters (or women very much like them) and bent their energy from rebuilding a wrecked world to grabbing at loot and pawing men. Thus, the Stanwyck we see in *Double Indemnity* isn't the woman Capra worked with, but an archon of nearly guiltless evil, a match for any man—not in the good fight but in the bad deal. Typically, in the scene in which MacMurray is to dispatch Stanwyck's husband during a car ride, Wilder closes in on Stanwyck coolly running things at the wheel. She doesn't even bother to look over and see when MacMurray grabs her husband's neck.

This new Stanwyck carries through for the rest of her career. She no longer needs toughness; she just has it. It becomes Hollywood fun. "Don't kid me, baby," says Robert Ryan, pulling Stanwyck to him in *Clash by Night* (1952). "I know a bottle by the label." Before he can kiss her, she socks him. "Peace on earth," he snarls, retreating. And on her exit, she rates his number: "Big mouth, fast dollars." That's all *Clash by Night* gives us, besides a young Marilyn Monroe feeling her way into acting: Stanwyck and Ryan battling over love. Ten years later, in *Walk on the Wild Side,* she was still at it, raging at men and pushing people around. This steamy tale had her as a bordello madam in love with Capucine, and Stanwyck follows through with the premise so honestly that even in the censored television prints the tenderness she feels for her star whore, and the defensive attack she launches on Laurence Harvey when he threatens to take Capucine away, is very evident. But after *Meet John Doe* there is much less to savor in what Stanwyck is given to work with.

Old revolutionaries are always an encumbrance; comes the revolution, who needs them? Stalin's solution was direct: execution. Hollywood's solution was messy: demotion to supporting parts or second-line films. The independent woman, as gold digger, backstager, professional, or, like Stanwyck, all-around ace from criminal to crusader, was essential to the Depression for role-model morale. In such hard times, heroic men were not sufficient; the culture needed heroic women as well. Hollywood moguls became not unlike frightened conscripts on the battlefield shouting, "Mother," as the horror closes in. Yet when the real war came, when men could take care of things themselves, woman was retired or demythologized. The heroes of the wartime movies were almost exclusively male; woman leads contented themselves with putting on shows and riding on trolleys with the boy next door. Is it possible that American women have been decreed, by gentlemen's agreement, useful in leadership roles only in times of disorder, when the very foundation of the societal system is shaking, and relegated to supporting roles in times of order?

The 1930s was a dangerous time. As the years dragged on and the Depression seemed unable to bottom out, people increasingly considered radical alternatives, or at least discussed them, and at times upheaval appeared to wait just around the corner. It would be natural, if a little *misterioso,* for men to appeal instinctively to the mythopoetic character of woman, to the transcendence, forgiveness, and wisdom that we know of from statuary, epic poetry, and folk tales. Men make war: women make peace. Bizarre as it sounds, the employment of women like Blondell, Faye, Russell, and Stanwyck gave the apparently courseless Depression a structure.

But in times of order, these archetypes are not on call. The war years brought our very survival into question, but domestically this was a period of stupendous social integration. With the deaths of close relations on every mind, religion much practiced, ration cards keeping people in line, and all labor strikes suspended, World War II imposed a sense of priority and sequence upon the land. And the constraints were loosened so gradually that the culture in 1949 was not that different from what it had been in 1945.

The woman fighter, as a Hollywood trope, is an officer of much honor and little respect. She's like medicine, badly needed when needed and ignored when not needed. It will be interesting to see if the disorderly 1960s give us more fighters, or merely delight in the toughies left over from *film noir*.

# 11

# *Dame Camp*

BETTE DAVIS

*Who did this to me?*

—SAMUEL GOLDWYN
upon viewing Bette Davis'
screen test

*Who'd you expect, Ann Blyth?*

—BETTE DAVIS
to director Robert Aldrich
on the set of *Whatever
Happened to Baby Jane?*

Bette Davis must be the easiest
imitation going. Just puff densely at an imaginary cigarette, wave your
arms, and emit "Petah! Petah! Petah!" This is true fame: everyone
knows who she is and what she does. Yet when she arrived in Hollywood in 1930, everyone was baffled. She was no one, it was thought;
she could do nothing. And Warner Brothers, where she spent two decades under contract and worked like a slave, tossed her into an appalling number of incompetent films in her first ten years, each one
offering a totally different and unconvincing Davis. It's a wonder she
survived Hollywood at all.

She shall play ingenue, they decided, for want of any other idea, in
*The Man Who Played God* (1932), opposite George Arliss as a pianist who
loses his hearing and turns philanthropist; Davis stands by and understands. No, wait! She has that sophisticated look, the flint and the
spring of the New York partygoer. She shall play sophisticate in *The
Rich Are Always with Us* (1932), in a supporting part as Marbro Barclay,
"the pest of Park Avenue," who watches Ruth Chatterton come to
know George Brent and says things like "I'm not a nice girl" like a hen
trying to crow. Nay, she has hidden her charms. She shall play femme
fatale in *Cabin in the Cotton* (1932), as southern trash who tells Richard
Barthelmess, in the first of the quotable Davis lines, "Ah'd love to kiss
you, but Ah jus' washed ma hayuh." Or perhaps she's a glamour girl.
Let's try her in a blond wig in a fashion setting! She shall play a de-

signer opposite that suave William Powell in *Fashions of 1934*. Wait! She has possibilities as an urban toughie! She shall play with James Cagney in *Jimmy the Gent* (1934), what a team! And, as a playgirl getting a bad name in the papers in *Fog Over Frisco* (1934), she shall die the death.

In fifteen films in about twenty-eight months, Warner Brothers was unable to fix Davis' identity. Typing may be a curse, but it does help to break the ice between performer and public: bad for survival but good for starters. Davis couldn't get typed. All these pictures were terrible, moreover, and she got little help from her co-workers. George Arliss was extremely helpful, virtually breaking Davis in to film technique, but her directors were hacks who didn't know how to talk to actors or couldn't be bothered; and Michael Curtiz, the emigrant Hungarian who directed *Cabin in the Cotton*, vilified Davis on the set in the hearing of all present. "Who'd want to go to bed with her?" he screamed at Darryl Zanuck; movies are about sex.

Nor did Davis' employer Jack Warner know how to develop her. He pushed her into stardom too early in a terrible vehicle, emblazoning her name above the title of *Ex-Lady* (1933) before the public was ready to fill the theatres on her account alone. Nor was this the studio to accommodate a self-willed actress like Davis, who had her own ideas about what suited her. In *Bordertown* (1935), challenged by a mad scene in a courtroom sequence, Davis wanted to express psychosis not through the traditional scream session but subtly, through the eyes. She had to fight for her view of it right up to the front office, where she was told that audiences would not get it without italics. But previews vindicated Davis' approach. If *Bordertown* was a triumph, it was despite Warner Brothers.

Davis was another of the fighters, not a Depression fighter but a studio fighter. None of the five stars in the preceding "fighters" chapter was a truly ambitious pro. Farrell's ambitions, if she had any, were not tested, for she was never given a main chance. Blondell worked, it seems, because even long hours and studio ingratitude were better than what she found at home. Faye retired at her height to enjoy housekeeping; and neither Russell nor Stanwyck was a colleague-trampling role-grabber. But Davis, though she played fair, badly wanted to make it—so much so that when a role came along that promised public amazement and actressy prestige, Davis worked hard to take it, though the character was so unsympathetic that no "sensible" star would touch it. However, it was an honorable project, from W. Somerset Maugham's *Of Human Bondage*, and would give her something film had not yet given: challenge.

Problem was, *Of Human Bondage* was being made by another studio, RKO, and Jack Warner was danged if he'd let another lot reap the profits after he'd done all the building. *Building?* Throwing Davis into one goulash after another? That wig in *Fashions of 1934* makes her look like Nathanael West's design for a marked card. "The day I met Bette Davis I knew she *had to be Mildred*," says John Cromwell, *Of Human Bondage*'s director. "No other actress in Hollywood would have dared face a camera with her hair untidy and badly rinsed, her clothes cheap and tawdry, her manner vicious and ugly." And she plays it all, hilt to blade, using Leslie Howard's foolish love for her Cockney waitress Mildred, playing indifference, stupidity, selfishness, and vanity without redemption. For ultimately Jack Warner did let her go to RKO, adding, "Go hang yourself."

On the contrary, the film made her a star for real, one with a following as well as top billing—and a unique star, despite rather than through her ability to pass in love. *Of Human Bondage* is one of the few films not to have a romance in it. True, most of the action concerns Howard's courtship of Davis. But toward the end, when she rips into the famous "wipe my mouth" speech, one realizes that there is no love in her, and that she has killed his. She disgusts him, he tells her.

DAVIS:  Me? I disgust *you?* You're too fine! . . . You cad. You dirty swine! I never cared for you, not once. . . . It made me sick when I had to let you kiss me. I only did it because you begged me. You hounded me! You drove me crazy! And after you kissed me I always used to wipe my mouth! Wipe my mouth!

And she proceeds to give him a demonstration, from elbow to wrist, before wrecking his flat and slashing paintings and stealing bonds, to sound-track jazz. Reviewers raved but audiences were appalled, making the film famous yet unsuccessful. And Jack Warner said, "See?"

But *Of Human Bondage* saved Bette Davis from ending as a cast-off ingenue, exhausted and bored. It won her an Oscar, though through some mischance that has never been explained she was not nominated that year and had to wait to win the award at the next sitting, for *Dangerous* (1935). *Of Human Bondage* made her fascinating as an actress, maybe a little scary, and launched her reputation as the kind of person you have to go to the movies to see. Like Little Mary, Betty Bronson, Joan Crawford, Marie Dressler, Carole Lombard, and Katharine Hepburn, Davis became her own type. Her nervous verbal attack, her brisk inquisitorial style, and her intensity combined into something Hollywood didn't otherwise have in stock. The smoking and the accent came later; this young Davis doesn't imitate so easily.

Nor was she easy to cast, given the films Warners turned out. Back on the lot after *Of Human Bondage,* Davis went right into the strange nonsense she had been trying to escape. In *Satan Met a Lady* (1936), a remake of *The Maltese Falcon* with Warren William as the detective in a big black hat, a jewel-filled trumpet instead of a falcon, and one of the worst pieces of writing in the history of the alphabet, Davis makes her first appearance eavesdropping on a train in dark glasses. She is mysteriously silent; later, when she speaks, the script is so foolish that both she and William are constantly giggling, turning away from the camera, or trying to bring it off with droll looks. Davis waxed somewhat less droll in a showdown with Warners after *Satan Met a Lady.* She had paid her dues and won her place in the industry, and if Warners couldn't give her parts worthy of her, she was walking, contract or no contract.

Here is where Davis made her name as a fighter. Warner's response did not satisfy her, so she left the country to work in England, and the resulting court battle filled the newspapers. Given the authoritarian structure of the post-talkie studios, it was to be expected that some star would defy them in court; and it's impressive that the most explosive cases involved Warners stars—James Cagney, Olivia de Havilland, and John Garfield besides Davis. She lost her battle (de Havilland won sometime later on virtually the same issue), but Jack Warner, more forgiving than some moguls, lent her the money to pay her court fees and welcomed her back. Besides, he needed her.

Though he had not exploited it well, her fire-and-ice potential could still make her his prestige star, and the scruffy Warners needed all they could get. Doubtless *Marked Woman* (1937), Davis' first film on her return from England, is no one's idea of a prestige picture, but it's topically intriguing, a version of the Lucky Luciano case in which a gangster was sent to prison on the testimony of prostitutes. As already noted, there were no prostitutes in the movies in 1937; they were called (and strongly encouraged to act like) "hostesses." But *Marked Woman* makes it so clear what the hostesses do that a scheduled television showing in 1965 was canceled. That the Catholic Legion of Decency could accept in 1937 (albeit with an "Adult" rating) what was to prove unacceptable in the permissive 1960s (albeit on television) only goes to support what revival-house moviegoers have discovered: Hollywood's thirties output is startlingly rich.

*Marked Woman* gives us Davis as cousin to Blondell and Stanwyck, real Depression grit. She touches all the points, claiming the fighter type for her mixture of ferocity and limp fatalism. She blows hot where other women are patient; she grows calm where others might steam with anger. She is, no question, a born fighter. We get Bette's Loyalty to Her Sisters when she defends a slightly over-the-hill hostess from gangster Eduardo Cianelli's critical eye. Cianelli would fire the woman, but Davis vouches for her. "Smart girl," Cianelli notes. "Maybe too smart," says his henchman. And there's Bette's Gender Independence, when a gent in black tie puts his arm around her and she folds his arms, pulls away, and stares him down. Or Bette's Generosity, when she warns the gent that he's in trouble with the gang and had better skip town. We expect Bette's vulnerability as well, when District Attorney Humphrey Bogart tells her that her sister, involved with the gang, has been killed; but we expect Davis to play the scene better than she does. It's badly written and overacted, oddly flat for all its noise. But Davis has yet to learn how to project vulnerability, while ferocity seems to have come naturally to her. Bravery, too, is a cinch, in her confrontation with Cianelli. She's tough, but he's tougher, and has his bully boy beat her up and carve a cross on her cheek, the mark of the squealer.

Here we leave the *Marked Woman* story and visit the *Marked Woman* set, where we get Bette's Dedication to Art Truth: the makeup man prepared her for the big scene of Cianelli's trial with the daintiest of bandages and, oh, the dearest little bruises, fit for a star. Davis drove off the lot to a doctor, had herself bandaged for real, and returned to corporate consternation. In *Of Human Bondage* she had had to play someone dying of tuberculosis and looked it; now she looked like someone who had been beaten up and marked. Exactly; horrors. "We film this makeup," Davis told them, "or we don't film me today." They filmed her, they filmed her.

Much as one might laugh at *Marked Woman* today as a dated melodrama—what melodrama isn't dated?—it tells us some likable things about Hollywood, and what it was capable of. There are few more abused people than gangland's prostitutes, and *Marked Woman* shows it from this angle of sympathy. Cianelli is as vicious as they come, yet at his trial his lawyer does his best to shred the women's evidence; as Cianelli has enslaved them, his lawyer will defame them, and civil liberty, says Warner Brothers, is something a beast can rent exclusively. Moreover, *Marked Woman* offers no judgment on the morals of "loose" women. On the contrary, they are the heroes of the film. Sisterhood and despair is what we're left with at the close, not man-woman romance. Conditioned by Hollywood practice, we have figured that Davis and Bogart are setups for a love match, but at the end, when Cianelli has been found guilty (and warned that he will lose his chance of parole if any of the women come to harm) and Bogart tells Davis, "We'll meet again," she replies, "I'll be seeing you," as if the words meant "Goodbye forever." And the last shot presents the five prostitutes walking off together into urban fog.

For all its trenchant social polemic, *Marked Woman* was just another programmer, planned to fill theatres for a week and be forgot. What, then, of Davis the prestige star; what of road-show spectacles and highbrow junkets? She very nearly played Scarlett O'Hara in *Gone With the Wind,* at least according to a Hollywood legend that has Jack Warner buying the rights to Margaret Mitchell's novel and Davis stomping out of his office when promised the role, knowing nothing of the book and assuming it was more of the garbage she had been mired in. In fact,

Warner never bought *Gone With the Wind*. Davis *was* a strong contender for Scarlett, along with Katharine Hepburn, Miriam Hopkins, Tallulah Bankhead, and numerous others. But David Selznick, who had bought the book, was planning to produce it as the talkie complement to *The Birth of a Nation*, a sensation of sensations; and with Warners contractees Olivia de Havilland and Errol Flynn likely possibilities for Melanie Hamilton and Rhett Butler, he feared turning his monster into a Warner Brothers festival with the addition of Davis.

Still, Davis played a kind of Scarlett in *Jezebel* (1938), an antebellum southern romance with a selfish heroine, *Gone With the Wind* in a nutshell. Coming out at the height of the PR surrounding Selznick's supposed search for an unknown to play Scarlett, *Jezebel* made an appetizer for the bigger film and won Davis a lot of notice, the cover of *Time* magazine, and a second Oscar. It also gave her a chance to work with William Wyler, a gifted director but a moody and mysterious perfectionist who often kept his notion of perfection from his cast. "Let's take it again," he would say—but not why. *Dark Victory* (1939), a soft-grained weepie capped by Davis' facing up to a terminal illness, concentrated the gathering opulence of Davis as a star; and *The Private Lives of Elizabeth and Essex* (1939), history lavish in Technicolor, imploded this opulence to its essence.

Davis as Elizabeth I is Davis prime, the Davis one imitates, without the cigarette. She has the crazy deep voice, the restlessness, the imperial rage. Her entrance is star-turned, the queen heard unseen as she dresses for a ceremony behind a screen. Moments later she is manifested in all her consequence, superb on her throne at the end of a huge hall hung with shields and tapestries. Still, we don't see her face-on till the camera pans up from her feet past a tumult of robes complete with green ostrich plume to a red-wigged horror of a head. Elizabeth I is a figure scarcely to be imagined, and to produce her Davis resorted to a more effusive style than usual, in musical terms all sharps and flats with abrupt changes in tempo and volume. She tears papers, smashes mirrors, slaps her fist against her waist, staggers around her rooms, raves and sulks, takes umbrage at a look, grabs and snarls and fidgets and grumbles. And of course there's the odd pronunciation, all T: "Rabat, let's be kint, for a momenht."

Robert, Earl of Essex, was Errol Flynn, a curse of Davis' existence; she wanted Laurence Olivier in the part. But doing a historical epic for Warners meant playing with Flynn. As queen of Burbank, where the Warners lot was located, Davis had to pay prices MGM's Crawford and Paramount's MacDonald never even thought of. Crawford had Gable for sex and Montgomery for jest; MacDonald had Chevalier when she made her best films. Davis had Paul Muni, George Brent, Warren William, and Flynn. "He carries himself like a king!" trills one of Elizabeth's court ladies, gazing down on the open pageant of the hero riding through London in triumph. No, Flynn carries himself like a randy doorman, but who else looked good in tights? Anyway, the central business in *The Private Lives of Elizabeth and Essex* is not Flynn's halfhearted adventuring but Davis' incredible commitment to playing a loveless, ugly woman as loveless and ugly. Davis was the great no-glamour star, a handsome woman who couldn't have cared less about how she looked on screen. No, she does care: to appear precisely as the character should appear. In *Of Human Bondage*, in *Marked Woman*, and here in *Elizabeth*, she shatters the wisdom that a star always looks her best.

Davis wants to act, feed the character, look the part. In *Watch on the Rhine* (1943) she shows up in a black traveling outfit that the Wicked Witch of the West would have thought dowdy. Yet at Marion Davies' circus party Davis arrived looking smashing in real clothes and gazed dourly on the freak outfits Davies had laid in for forgetful guests; eventually, Davis allowed herself to be talked into a beard.

This contradiction, uniting Davis the committed actress and Davis the star in a gala gown—a contradiction inherent not in Davis but in the energy of the glamour business—comes to a head in *Mr. Skeffington* (1944), about a vain New York debutante of the 1890s who marries a man she does not love. At first Davis plays the beauty, dashing down a stairway into a crowd of admirers, pitching her voice higher than usual (in *Elizabeth* it was lower), wearing Orry-Kelly's period costumes as if clothes are her life, and flirting and pouting simultaneously. She's like a big jeweled fan. But the film covers some territory, and when husband Claude Rains returns home, having been blinded by the Nazis, Davis has become a grotesque harridan whose hair is falling out in swatches. Rains's blindness heals the plot's wounds, for as he cannot see Davis, can only remember her as she was, he is the only man she can live with. But meanwhile we have undergone an unconventional exercise in stardom: Davis has gone to extremes in two opposing directions, first to beauty, then to horror. Her fans approached *Mr. Skeffington* with caution. Do they love Davis as deb or as witch? Or are the two facets reconcilable? Some treat the film as an "experiment," and tame its wildness by reducing it to a trivia challenge: What is the name of the woman Davis keeps breaking lunch dates with throughout the film, and who played her?*

Camp trivia is an element of the appeal of most old movies, but Davis' seem especially applicable. This is partly because of Warner Brothers' failure to cast her consistently in early films and partly because of her own desire for variety in her work. Touring through the Davis oeuvre, one keeps meeting totally different people with her looks and voice and strenuous accenting, while such rivals as Shearer, Garbo,

*Janey Clarkson. No one played her: she never appears.

and the two Crawfords (MGM and Warners) are inveterate from film to film. (Hepburn varies, but she is always exceptional.) And as Davis is the only one of them who was not precisely a glamour star, she has become the special favorite of camp buffs—for what is camp but beveled glamour?

Davis' best films utterly defeat this view. *The Little Foxes* (1941), for instance, from Lillian Hellman's play, features Davis as a frighteningly unstoppable villain. Moreover, to understand the problem of the "actor's choice" involved in a career like Davis' is to discard camp as disrespectful. *The Little Foxes* set was overshadowed by Tallulah Bankhead's much-admired performance in the stage original, and director William Wyler wanted Davis to try playing the role in a softer grain. This is how Hollywood deals with a villain when the villain is a star. But Davis was convinced that Hellman had written the character with only one reading in mind. Bankhead gave it, and Davis felt artistically compelled to give it, too, though it prompted constant bad-mouth from Wyler and would surely earn her Broadway censure for her having "copied" Bankhead's rendition.

Time has acquitted her, for now Bankhead's portrayal is a memory and Davis' survives vitally. Yet time has also savaged some of Davis' less sturdy vehicles, and even as we admire her work we enjoy the films themselves only with a certain reductive detachment. Take *Now, Voyager* (1942), one of Davis' most revived pictures and a phenomenon in its day for the cheer it brought to women who felt defeated by plain looks or other social handicaps. *Now, Voyager* introduces Davis as a wretched spinster and turns her into a knockout, unseating her domineering mother and proving that shyness can hide a cynosure. Again, Davis stands midway between tropes of actress and star, person and glamour queen. One might approach *Now, Voyager* structurally, as a study in Hollywood's imagism of personality; or metaphysically, for its crude poetry of rebirth and transcendence. But many viewers take it as a feast of trivia:

What is Bette Davis' character's name? (Charlotte Vale.) What *doesn't* she do in her first shots? (Speak.) What are her first words, to psychiatrist Claude Rains? ("Introverted, Doctor!") When Davis has been transformed into a beauty, goes on a pleasure cruise, and Paul Henreid asks her if it's "Miss or Mrs.," what does she reply? ("It's 'aunt.'") What does Henreid say immediately after he lights two cigarettes in his mouth and hands one to Davis? ("Do you believe in immortality?") Who did the cigarette trick first in what earlier Davis movie? (George Brent, for Ruth Chatterton, in *The Rich Are Always with Us*.) Henreid pulls the cigarette stunt a second time; what does Davis say immediately after? ("I hate goodbyes.") What's the name of the little girl whom Davis cares for at Rains's sanitarium? (Tina.) Whom is she supposed to remind you of? (Davis, before her transformation.) What's the last line of the film? (Davis: "Oh, Jerry, don't let's ask for the moon. We have the stars.") And, most insidiously, what's the name of the song, with lyrics by Kim Gannon, that was set to one of Max Steiner's more plangent themes from the sound-track score? ("It Can't Be Wrong.")

It can't be all that right, either, for, persuasive as Davis is, her studio still hadn't resigned itself to her determination to swing wide of the glamour arc. In another adaptation from Broadway, *The Corn Is Green* (1945)—this time in a part created by Ethel Barrymore—Davis plays a schoolteacher coaching a bright Welsh miner for a university scholarship. Davis' character was considerably older than Davis was at the time, and there is no romance between her and the boy; yet rather than herald the film for what it was, Warners' PR tried to sell it as a love weepie. "In her heart of hearts she knew she could never hold him," the posters explained, admitting that Davis was "the screen's most honored actress" but presenting her as a youthful love symbol.

*Of Human Bondage, Jezebel, The Little Foxes,* and Davis' other triumphs of thespian will never freed her from the tyranny of Hollywood marketing. She had escaped typing. There was nothing she was wrong for, and little she couldn't do; she may have been the versatile star of her era. But she couldn't escape the ontology of stardom: a lady dazzles.

Not that Davis' late Warners films were glittering prizes. In *Beyond the Forest* (1949) she plays what the ads described as "a midnight girl in a nine o'clock town," obsessed with leaving the boondocks for Chicago. Davis is dire as Rosa Moline. She commits adultery and murder, caws "What a dump!" at her home, undergoes an abortion, insults everyone on contact—all this not necessarily in any order—and at length dies after crawling to the railroad tracks over a distance not much shorter than the New York Marathon course. *Beyond the Forest,* by general Hollywood agreement, was the worst film ever made, and terminated Davis' seventeen years as a Warners contractee. She endured shooting till a few days before the wrap, then threatened to become suddenly unavailable if she were not released from her obligations to the studio. "To hell with it," she said.

It's typical that the most classic of camp quotations—"What a dump!"—is a Davis line, for Davis is camp's principal victim. First they forced her to be an ingenue, then, when a few decent projects revealed her gifts, they tried to force her to be . . . an older ingenue. Somehow, they couldn't place her. The studio deputy who was to have met Davis' train back in 1931 returned from the station without her because he didn't see anyone with star potential. So, from her oblique angle, trying to push in one direction while her fame dragged her in another, Davis emerged a caricature of what she had never planned to be in the first place: star diva. And the film that made her one followed directly on her escape from Warner Brothers, *All About Eve* (1950).

It might be the film that ruined Davis or the film that made her immortal. It is certainly a masterpiece of a kind and might even be the best Davis movie. But it is also the campiest major production Hollywood ever produced. Joseph Mankiewicz directed from his script, and his mordant literacy suffuses this most backstage of backstagers, entirely about and located in the Broadway milieu, where aging star Davis befriends self-denying waif and fan Anne Baxter and is gradually supplanted by her. It's a pet show-biz psychosis, the fear of being precisely replaced—yet we don't learn all about Baxter's Eve in the end. She is a deceiver, and as we seldom see her alone or with a confederate, she is hidden from us in her disguises.

However, we see much of Davis, as Margo Channing: Davis in costume, Davis in dressing-room cold cream, Davis bitchy and Davis vulnerable, Davis generous and Davis hostile, Davis in Jezebel's rebelliousness, Elizabeth's hauteur, Fanny Skeffington's vanity, Rosa Moline's voracious ire. The imitation is in full swing, with the addition of a throaty growl half Elizabeth and half Tallulah Bankhead, which apparently was the result of medical treatments for a psychosomatic loss of voice. *All About Eve* capped an era for Davis. It was originally thought to have inaugurated a new one for her as her official industry comeback after departing her studio berth, but Davis' Margo Channing uses the best of what Davis had learned over the Warners years, and she was not to make another first-rate film.

So this is the graduation, not the commencement. Moreover, it is Davis' most popular film part, her unique achievement, and her admission at last that manneristic star playing, in certain films, works. Her Margo is an abstract of the hard-boiled stage dame, a composite of every star who irked Mankiewicz, yet, beyond that, a symbolic rendition of the genus diva.

Gertrude Lawrence was to have played it (she disagreed with Mankiewicz on a minor point and was dropped from consideration), and Claudette Colbert was signed, but she hurt her back and had to drop out. The film's producer, Darryl Zanuck, had yet others in mind, most notably Marlene Dietrich. But now that Davis has played it, Margo is played for keeps. The age, the insecure status, the intrigues—who knows better than Davis? Margo should have earned her a third Oscar, but Anne Baxter was nominated as well, so *All About Eve* voters split the tickets, and Judy Holliday took it for *Born Yesterday*. Davis' authority in the part was emphasized when Betty Comden, Adolph Green, Charles Strouse, and Lee Adams made *All About Eve* into an empty musical, *Applause,* in which Lauren Bacall won critical and popular acclaim for a truly nowhere performance. (Ironically, Anne Baxter succeeded her in the part, as Eve succeeds Margo in the film; Baxter was much, much better but still not Margo.)

Why is *All About Eve* so camp? It's Mankiewicz' doing, not Davis'— yet, as the star of the enterprise, Davis is the person we identify as the genius of the place. And that place—backstage Broadway, complete with director-lover (Gary Merrill), playwright (Hugh Marlowe), playwright's Radcliffe wife (Celeste Holm), *mitteleuropäisch* impresario *mit Schlag* (Gregory Ratoff), and reptilian critic (George Sanders)—is replete with put-down, burlesque, and loitering gay aroma, the presiding elements of camp. The put-down lies in the dialogue, which has been quoted ceaselessly at fast-trackers' parties since the film opened. The burlesque inheres in Mankiewicz' observations of the egomania that sustains show biz. ("It's about time," Hugh Marlowe remarks to Davis at a turbulent rehearsal, "that the piano realized it has not written the concerto!") The gay is everywhere subtly, and in one case palpably: Eve. In two scenes, she appears as she is, away from her audience of dupes: once with a woman neighbor to whom she is suspiciously close in an almost squalid way (perhaps because Baxter never smiles in this movie, only makes her mouth pretty when she thinks it politic to do so, and in this scene she smiles) and later with a younger Eve type. This is in the startling finale, when a schoolgirl (Barbara Bates) steals into Eve's hotel room to adopt her as Eve adopted Margo. Like Eve, Bates's character goes by a pseudonym, feigns humility, and lies naturally, as when she tells Eve of the many Eve Harrington fan clubs among Brooklyn high school girls. That's dubious. High schoolers of 1950 formed clubs around movie stars, not stage people. Still, Eve is intrigued and invites Bates to spend the night.

So Bette Davis' most essential role belongs to a camp masterpiece. Sadly, it is in the nature of how camp works that from it there is nowhere to go but plummeting down.* Davis never got another first-rate film after *Eve*. While she did not lack for work, she worked in junk, and it feels characteristic of decline-and-fall that she played a has-been movie headliner in *The Star* (1952), that she played Elizabeth I again in *The Virgin Queen* (1955)—wasn't her first try definitive?—that she played the baglady turned into a duchess in *Pocketful of Miracles* (1961) with less verve than May Robson brought to the same part in *Lady for a Day* some thirty years earlier.

Worse yet, Davis' sportive return to Broadway in the revue *Two's Company* in 1952 did not show her off well. In her opening spot, "Just Turn Me Loose on Broadway," twisting and twirling in an evening gown with four chorus boys, she was game but inappropriate, at one point calling out, "It's tricky," when it clearly wasn't. In a Sadie

---

*Alternatively, one could stay with camp and build a career on it; but this was impossible till burlesque became the dominating comic mode in the 1970s. More of this later.

Thompson takeoff, she was inept. In a country number, "Purple Rose," she was strange. In her eleven o'clock spot, "Just Like a Man," she was saddled with stupid material, literally a song without a tune. Davis had tried musical comedy once before, in a spot in the Warners wartime revue *Thank Your Lucky Stars* (1943). Wending her way through "They're Either Too Young or Too Old" and following it with some jitterbug, Davis was if nothing else putting out for morale. But *Thank Your Lucky Stars* came between *Watch on the Rhine* and *Old Acquaintance*, two of Davis' deftest efforts. Coming after *All About Eve, Two's Company* could only affirm the Imitation, the camp Davis.

And what, then, was *Whatever Happened to Baby Jane?* (1961) but the final nail in the coffin that held the reputation of Bette Davis? As the alcoholic slattern murdering sister Joan Crawford by degrees, Davis was in fine form, but to what end? The film has its cute slashes of frisson, as when Davis imitates Crawford's voice (through overdubbing) to do dirty work on the telephone; or when Davis goes into one of her ancient child-star routines, then catches sight of her blasted face in a mirror and screams; or when Davis serves Crawford a rat for dinner, then cackles obscenely while Crawford goes into hysterics and revolves in her wheelchair. (A homage to Lillian Gish in the closet in *Broken Blossoms?*) But two brief clips, from Crawford's *Sadie McKee* (1934) and Davis' *Parachute Jumper* (1933), recall the actresses' idealistic springtime in the midst of a foul winter; and, anyway, this shocker only led Davis on to more shockers. In *Dead Ringer* (1964), in a dual role, Davis kills her twin sister out of spite. *Hush . . . Hush, Sweet Charlotte* (1964) was more *Baby Jane*, with Olivia de Havilland in for Crawford.

And so it has gone since then. Davis is now more a folkway than an actress, so much so that when she was unavailable for overdubbing her role as the witchlike Widow Fortune in the television adaptation of Thomas Tryon's novel *Harvest Home,* the comedian Michael Greer, famed for his Imitation, taped the lines for her. We fade out on a beldame bristling with umbrage as she confronts a huge fat queen doing the Imitation on a segment of *Laugh-In.* Davis looks like Tennyson watching the Kraken wake.

# 12

# *Maidens and Pinups*

SHIRLEY TEMPLE
DEANNA DURBIN
JUDY GARLAND
ELIZABETH TAYLOR
RITA HAYWORTH
BETTY GRABLE
AVA GARDNER

*Nothing matters like that crazy little Judy.*

—AN AUTOGRAPH
COLLECTOR, 1963

*The trouble is, I'm not an actress.*

—RITA HAYWORTH

*I'm the girl the truck drivers love.*

—BETTY GRABLE

*I never brought anything to this business and I have no respect for acting.*

—AVA GARDNER

Youth and beauty are considered paramount in the inauguration and maintenance of woman stars. But (as the preceding chapters have I hope demonstrated) they are much less significant than such variables as talent, the ability to exploit an exploitive system for one's own ends, and the pressure of contemporaneity. It was neither youth nor looks that got Katharine Hepburn and Bette Davis entree into Hollywood; nor did youth and looks have anything to do with RKO's and Warner Brothers' decisions to build them into stars; nor did advancing age and deteriorating looks have anything to do with their later good or ill fortune.

A great many actors have been hired entirely on the basis of physical charisma, and a great many have been made or broken by considerations of age. The pinup, as a type, suggests a woman whose function is to do little more than look great (for just as long as she can, and no longer); and the maiden, a type halfway between child and woman, obviously depends greatly on youth. Still, there aren't many pinups or maidens who made it big or for long on youth alone. Lana Turner is an exception, with her desultory sense of characterization, her legendary discovery in Schwab's drugstore,* her first notable bit part as a high school Lilith in tight sweater and beret in *They Won't Forget* (1937), and her endless scandals of sex and violence. Turner was nothing but a cutout.

On the other hand, Turner's fellow pinup Betty Grable capitalized on her musical comedy talents, not on her looks. Grable was so essential to the notion of the pinup girl that she made a film by that title—in the title part—but none dares call Grable a cutout. You can't get by on looks in musicals. There are dance numbers to lead, songs to introduce, memorably or else. And Grable was never a glamour star, to moue in fine feathers. One must have talent.

Let's take the maidens first, for they worked even harder than the pinups. It helped to be pretty or vivacious, but the child star phenomenon favored precociousness rather than cuteness, so the kids were constantly putting out. True, certain little boys, such as Jackie Coogan and Jackie Cooper, won a huge if very temporary following entirely on charm. However, their colleague Shirley Temple won hers for her astonishing gifts. Other little girls were bright enough to master lines and choreography; other little girls could sing and tap. But what other little girl had Temple's polish? When Graham Greene somewhat disingenuously discussed the grown-up aspect of the way she carried herself, libel suits resulted, and the Temple side won. But in truth she was practiced beyond her years, not just surprisingly but improbably good.

Kids liked and still like her pictures, virtually all made for Fox, though the saccharine quality of the dialogue combined with Temple's dauntless optimism (under constant fire) makes them heavy going for some. Characterologically, Temple followed the path of Little Mary and Janet Gaynor—all of them made film versions of *Daddy Long Legs,* and each two of the three shared other roles as well—but if Gaynor suppressed the outrage Little Mary often expressed, Temple lost it altogether. Little Mary's and Gaynor's enemies are cutthroats and bigots; Temple's are, at worst, Lionel Barrymore. However, Temple's less dangerous world made an apt setup for musical numbers, which allowed her to do what she did best, and from the mid-1930s through 1940 she was more or less the biggest money in film.

There was no one else like her. Most of her rivals were more kid

* Actually it was a soda fountain across the street from Hollywood High School. The sixteen-year-old Turner caught the eye of a journalist, who introduced her to agent Zeppo Marx, fourth and least of the Marx Brothers. No one seems to like the corrected legend, so the Schwab's myth survives, as does Schwab's; the soda fountain vanished long ago.

personalities than performers, and even the odd exceptions—Mitzi Green at Paramount before Temple and Bobby Breen at RKO during and a little after—were kid singers, while Temple was a cultural symbol. Temple, with a touch of Little Mary and healthy dollops of neatness, good manners, and cunning, dwelled in her own little sphere of poverty versus wealth, authoritarian buttinskys versus indulgent father-figure protectors, and urban blues versus rural exuberance.

Was Temple a role model? She was to parents; the kids were unable to emulate her and almost certainly resisted any coachings in that direction. Besides, Temple functioned as a virtual orphan, motherless and usually cut off from or stronger than her father surrogates. But as entertainer or moral example, she proved the temporary status of the tyke star by failing to survive her adolescence. At six or seven, Temple couldn't make enough movies to satisfy her public. But in 1940, at the age of twelve, she suffered her first box-office failure, and her stardom was snuffed out. She continued to make films throughout the 1940s, but it turned out that the thing she did best was neither singing nor dancing, nor conquering adversity, but being a dynamite little doll. Grown, she was ordinary.

Temple was the last of her kind. Later child actors were seldom genius stars and reverted to the Coogan-Cooper style of cuteness. But then Hollywood had the Temple replacement ready: the maiden. This type combined the innocence of the child with the responsibility of the adult, splitting the difference between the two extremes for the love plots: callow youths, soda-shop dates, and no kissing. The maiden would be older than Temple was when she lost her public, yet younger than Little Mary and Janet Gaynor were when they played kids. Most significantly, she would adopt Temple's musical reverberation—the *singing* character—to more mature circumstances. Temple, typically, was a kid in search of a home. Deanna Durbin and Judy Garland were kids in search of a job.

Both girls started at MGM in 1935, when their outstanding musicality promised great doings, in specialty spots and support if not lead roles. Roger Edens, of MGM's music department, thought Garland's audition "the biggest thing to happen to the MGM musical," with her whipcord belt voice and little-girl glee. Durbin was scarcely less impressive, with her nimble operatic soprano. By comparison, Shirley Temple could sing no opera; anyway, all tunes became tyke anthems in her little mouth. So Garland and Durbin, with their spectacular adult ease, upped the type's performing range while retaining the type's innocence. Garland was fourteen and Durbin fifteen when they made a one-reeler together, *Every Sunday* (1936), about two girls saving threatened free park concerts by lending their vocal talent to them. Showing the resourcefulness that both would exploit later on, Durbin in matchmaking and Garland in putting on the show, the two advertise and talk up the concerts besides performing, and their combination of raw youth and expertise is striking.

They make a nice team, too, with Garland belting out pop and Durbin riding above her in the classical vein. But MGM already had a grownup diva in Jeanette MacDonald, who had launched her extraordinarily successful series of operettas with Nelson Eddy the year before in *Naughty Marietta*. So MGM kept Garland and let Durbin go to Universal, where she became that studio's number one draw in "little miss fixit" comedies built around Durbin's warmth, sparkle, and recklessness. She didn't dance. On the contrary, her stolid musical numbers, centering on the open-mouthed closeup, lent dignity to otherwise surprisingly farcical plots. No matter how much finagling and darting around Durbin resorted to, she could always pause to lead a church choir or deliver a cutting of *La Traviata* on the concert platform.

*Three Smart Girls* (1937), Durbin's feature debut, billed her in the opening credits as "Universal's new discovery" with a breathless invitation to delight, and after an establishing shot of a Swiss lake we get Durbin bang on, sailing with her two sisters in striped T-shirts and sailor caps, Durbin on tiller and coloratura. The plot is quickly provisioned: Durbin's parents have separated, Dad is in New York seeing another woman, and the three decide to join him and break it up. Durbin was originally to have played on equal terms with sisters Barbara Read and Nan Grey, but during shooting producer Joe Pasternak realized Durbin's potential, upped the budget, and expanded her part. She is not exactly the star of the show, but she gets all the fun business as well as all the numbers, and her screen image is already taking form, with its refreshing sides of cynicism and burlesque. She is no goody-goody. "Muffins and milk!" she exclaims at lunch. "That's no food for fighters!" And unlike Shirley Temple, who handled adults with a dear whim, Durbin constantly gets into trouble.

Everyone in a Durbin film is either part of the problem or part of the solution. In *Three Smart Girls* the problem is father Charles Winninger, fortune hunter Binnie Barnes, and her pushy mother Alice Brady. But the solution takes in almost everyone else, from featured players to extras, including a squad of cops and a judge entranced by one of Durbin's lighter classical solos, in Italian, when she opens up in court. Too young for romance, Durbin leaves the love stuff to sister Read (opposite Ray Milland) and concentrates on reuniting her parents and crying for joy in a final closeup.

Only a year later, in *Mad About Music* (1938), Durbin has a fellow, a military-school cadet. But they don't spend much time together, as Durbin is racing around inventing a father, getting composer Herbert Marshall to impersonate him, and running off to see her movie-star mother Gail Patrick in Paris. Naturally, the last scene features Patrick and Marshall making a likely couple. There are the songs, too: the catchy "I Love to Whistle," a pious "Ave Maria," the semi-classical "Chapel Bells," and another pop item, "Just a Serenade from the Heart," for the closing tableau.

By 1940, at $400,000 a film, Durbin was no pretty thing but, like the best stars, something special that came through personably. She was special not because she sang better than a kid should but because she sang better than most singers can: a talent. Still, she was a kid and there's always the problem of growing up gracefully. Universal paired her with Robert Stack in the aptly titled *First Love* (1939), which underlines the Cinderella input into the Durbin style with a closing "and they lived happily ever after"; and *Nice Girl?* (1941) was advertised with a shot of Durbin in slinky black pajamas. But Durbin herself wanted to break out of the rut, not widen it. Universal tried alternating typical Durbin entries, including followups to her *Three Smart Girls* character, with sorties out of type and genre. But these outraged the public.

By 1946, Durbin was twenty-five, one of the two or three most highly paid women in Hollywood, and still an attraction—but definitely not a Smart Girl anymore: a woman. *Because of Him* (1946) finds her tricking actor Charles Laughton and playwright Franchot Tone into giving her a chance on stage. Laughton goes along but Tone balks, which sets up both the career plot and the romance. The music is fine, the cast fine, and one scene in which Durbin harangues Tone with the old chestnut "Goodbye, Forever" in a hotel hallway, down in the elevator, into the lobby, and in the revolving door to the street—the whole thing almost entirely in pantomime except for Durbin's singing—is matchless.

In short, Durbin managed to grow up without losing the musicality, impishness, and dash that made her a star. Nor did her vehicles sag especially, though most of the later ones were not as good as *Because of Him*. Durbin's career ended then, but for an unusual reason: she had tired of Hollywood and left.

Like Durbin, Judy Garland proves how much more goes into stardom than looks. Garland is in some ways the all-basic film personality, familiar to millions for a number of reasons having nothing to do with face and physique. Who more than Garland gathers into one image the whole Hollywood experience at its headiest and gloomiest, fanatic popularity confronting her own greed for emotional breakdowns? And who had more talent than she, or a better showcase for it? Garland, in her heyday in the 1940s, was the best-equipped woman singer-dancer at the studio most expert in musical comedy, MGM. Betty Grable (at Fox), whose period of stardom coincides almost exactly with Garland's, was Garland's only rival, and Grable's collaborators were far less notable than Garland's, who included Mickey Rooney, Gene Kelly, Fred Astaire; directors Busby Berkeley and Vincente Minnelli; and songwriters Rodgers and Hart, the Gershwins, Cole Porter, Irving Berlin, and Harold Arlen.

Yet Garland represents much more than musical comedy expertise: in her numerous breakdowns and comebacks, in her shocking tales of studio-ordered drug addiction, in her early death, and in her openness as a performer that seemed to give away the self in every character. It's no great deal in film to leave a name behind one, but to remain a working *experience* after death is true stardom. Who was Theda Bara? Who was Mary Pickford? Garland survives as they do not: in a theme song that is one of the most enduring melodies in American culture; in a number of classic films; and in a kind of replica of herself, a daughter, whom she left behind to carry on the concerns of vulnerability and vitality and the absurd idealism about the splendor of all-out gut-spilling show-biz performance.

Garland's fans will agree that her talent supports her place in the culture. Some of them would develop that sacramentally, as if her talent—exploited then humiliated then ravaged by worldly ills as it was— were her transcendent gift, to be received ecstatically, the way they touched her hands at the close of her concerts, the faithful pressing to the font for absolution. Death is a cabaret.

Those who are respectful of her talent but more neutral toward her personally regret that her vulnerability has been made into a fetish, especially as it seems to have passed on to her daughter Liza Minnelli by connoisseurs' fiat. The nonbelievers would probably sum up Garland's case as that of a dynamic performer who made a decade of fine musicals, toward the end of it beginning the series of collapses that rendered her unfit to work except irregularly and frequently at less than her best. They regard her tales of irresponsible drug prescription ("They'd give us pep-up pills to keep us on our feet long after we were exhausted, then they'd take us to the studio hospital and knock us cold with sleeping pills") as untrue, her lateness and no-show stunts as entirely of her own making, and her stardom as being less impressive than that of other stars of her level of celebrity. Garland is unique, certainly, they would say, but not stupendous.

Garland supporters could counter this easily. Drugs now regarded as dangerous were relatively easy to obtain in the 1940s, and MGM might well have supplied uppers to fatigued actors and downers to aroused ones without knowingly encouraging a dependence on them.*

---

*There is on record at least one episode of an actor's being destroyed by narcotics at his employers' willing connivance. Silent star Wallace Reid suffered an injury on location, and, rather than let staff and equipment go idle, Reid was shot full of morphine to enable him to complete the location work. By then he had become addicted. Rather than lose the money he could pull in at the box office, his studio fed the habit to keep him active; he died at the age of thirty, his disease made fully public. Because Reid's image was that of the collegiate hero, his death proved one of the shocks of the age.

Insomnia, a problem for Garland's family in general, can disrupt the schedule of someone who is expected on the job at dawn six days a week. And as for Garland's caliber of stardom, does it truly lack texture? Who are the biggest stars? Little Mary, Garbo, Crawford, and Davis are possibly the four that would come most quickly to mind in terms of historical Hollywood; how do they compare with Garland? Little Mary cannot compete on any level, for her films hide away in vaults while *Babes in Arms* or *Meet Me in St. Louis* plays television somewhere in the land every week. Garbo and Crawford are basically one-role stars, entirely defined within a single image. (In Crawford's case, this is actually one image halved: Our Dancing Flaemmchen and Mildred Dearest.) Davis is versatile and imposing, but her long career yields only about ten years of great work, and at that often in disreputable vehicles.

Garland, of them all, is most genuinely legendary, like her or not. Applying that old saw that runs "The story plus X equals the truth," one sees most stars as the story—the image, really—worked into a chain of stories. Because the visual evidence is compelling, the image seems like a full experience of the person. But in fact the persons are actors playing roles, and X—the rest of them that we can't see—stands between the truth and us. But Garland, perhaps alone among great stars, supplied her own X in performance: in the reverberant uncertainty of the little girl roles, in the hyperventilating of some of the numbers in her later MGM's, and in her skillful combination of the uncertainty and a new self-vindication in *A Star Is Born,* her comeback after the break with MGM. This information is too persuasively like a Judy to be merely the actress's projection of her parts. It *is* Judy.

Or so they say. And notice that none of the argument has anything to do with glamour. Garland started as an okay-looking kid with a weight problem, a terrific natural belt, and the commitment to lyrics that the best singers have. She hung around MGM on contract with little more to do than sing, at L. B. Mayer's prompting, for visiting VIPs. Odd that the studio couldn't find a place for her in their musicals; odder still that Garland was originally to have been sent to Universal to play Durbin's part in *Three Smart Girls,* considering how different their repertories were. But it seems that Universal had no intention of running a series of coloratura vehicles until, stuck with Durbin, they made the best of it.

MGM didn't make anything of Garland until she showed her stuff on loan to Twentieth Century–Fox in *Pigskin Parade* (1936), one of the better college musicals. Garland's part comprised a few lines and three songs; the songs make the film. Too, Garland had been successful on radio. So stop waiting for an image to blossom: put the girl in a film and let her do what she does. Seeing the light, MGM slipped Garland into *Broadway Melody of 1938* (1937), a backstager with plenty of accommodation for an assortment of talent. Eleanor Powell races horses, Robert Taylor produces shows, Sophie Tucker runs a boardinghouse and waxes nostalgic over George M. Cohan's Broadway, Judy Garland is her daughter, George Murphy and Buddy Ebsen dance. There's a lot of room in there between the Powell-Taylor romance and putting on Taylor's show for a number of any kind, and Garland supplies the best kind in "You Made Me Love You," with a special introduction, "Dear Mr. Gable," so she can direct the song as a wistfully regretful ballad to the actor's framed photograph. She is also very useful in the grand finale, "Your Broadway and My Broadway," set against an Art Deco rendition of skyscrapers and theatrical marquees, with the chorus in tuxedos (the men in black, the women in white), Garland and Ebsen arriving in a cab before they go into their tap. The number, choreographed by Dave Gould around Powell at her most scintillant, is so good that director Roy del Ruth couldn't stop filming it, and editors unfortunately took out a chunk of Garland's footage to cut the finale to general-audience size rather than musical-comedy-buff taste.

So far Garland is little more than a singer-dancer, and our taste is only whetted. It's sharpened in *Everybody Sing* (1938), in which she takes a lead part as the daughter of a zany theatrical family. Most importantly, we begin to sense Garland's coming significance in her musical bias, for Hollywood musicals of this period are obsessed with balancing popular and "serious" music. *Everybody Sing* makes Garland pop's spokesperson. She opens the film by getting thrown out of school for subverting a class sing of Mendelssohn's "Spring Song" with an updated adaptation, "Swing, Mr. Mendelssohn, Swing!"—the whole class taking up the rhythm and scat lyrics. "Mr. Mendelssohn had his day," Garland explains. "Benny Goodman is here to stay."

Garland's role in *Everybody Sing* is an elaboration of the *Every Sunday* she made with Deanna Durbin. Shall the music of the nation blow hot or sweet? *Every Sunday* recommended compromise, but Garland, the archon of the forties musical, sings hot as a rule. *Everybody Sing*'s "Down on Melody Farm" promotes the rural nostalgia of the lazy river, but it's contemporary in form, and when music isn't, Garland is ready to jazz it—the *Rigoletto* quartet, for instance. She also does a comic number with Fanny Brice in her Baby Snooks character—"Why? Because!"—and takes what on Broadway would be called the eleven o'clock spot posing the classical-pop dilemma one last time. "Shall I sing a melody of birds on the wing?" asks Garland, as if mapping out the borders between Durbin's turf and her own. "Or shall I sing of swing?"

Actually, she sang of everything from a bungalow for three or four or more to a jumping joint; for while the *Every Sunday* short correctly identified Durbin as the little diva and Garland as the jazz baby, the fifteen MGM musicals that Garland made in starring parts emphasized not urban jive but rural sentiment. Those that aren't set on the farm or out west take place in an older, sweeter America, and the contradiction adds strongly to Garland's appeal. She has the moral innocence and the tenacity of the Little Mary era, yet handles herself well in a modern-day challenge. She is one of the few genuinely timeless stars, sure to retain her popularity over the coming decades, because she is one of the movies' few figures who span huge eras. Little Mary helped lead the transition from one-reelers to short features to big-show specials, but time caught up with her when Hollywood began to talk. Janet Gaynor helped lead the transition from silence into sound, reigned triumphantly for all of five years, then faded away even as she made her most popular film. Katharine Hepburn is transitional not historically as these others but intimately, entirely within her personal structure as a character. But who, other than Garland, managed to pull all the traditional virtues out of the deep native past into the postwar era? She is as big as ever over a decade after her death.

These virtues stand in relief as of 1939, the year she became a star, in *The Wizard of Oz* and *Babes in Arms*. Till then, she had been an assistant in other people's pictures; in the *Wizard of Oz* everything happens to her. MGM made an all-out effort on this one, the usual collaboration of visionaries and hacks finding just the look and tone for the trickiest of genres, sentimental fantasy. Everyone else in the film supplies the fantasy. Garland, who dreams the whole thing when a falling window sash bonks her unconscious, supplies the sentiment, made of about equal parts of intelligence, generosity, and audacity.* Not coincidentally, these are the qualities her companions in Oz are searching for themselves: the scarecrow wants a brain, the tin woodman wants a heart, the lion wants courage. It is as if her dream has broken her character into its component actions—and, to round out the reading, she herself wants her home and family: sentiment at its dead center level.

Musically, too, Garland is laying her traces. Harold Arlen and E. Y. Harburg wrote for the *Wizard* a full score of character songs and ensemble plot numbers, and for Garland they planned two pieces, one to display her strangely mature command of a ballad and one to reveal her swing. The ballad, "Over the Rainbow," of course became her motto theme. The swing number, "The Jitterbug," was unfortunately deleted before the film's release, but she recorded it, and back to back with "Over the Rainbow" it makes a fetching set: the yearning girl who understands what tradition and belonging entail and the cutup who knows the value of a good-for-nothing strut.

*Babes in Arms*, Garland's third teaming with Mickey Rooney but the

---

*These are not sentimental qualities of themselves. But Hollywood's exploitation of them to characterize its heroes has sentimentalized them.

first in which they were cast definitively as a couple, keeps the *Oz* Garland on home territory. *Oz* was adventure, with a tornado, fighting trees, narcotic poppies, flying monkeys, and a terror chase through the castle of a wicked witch. The babes are simply putting on a show Right Here in This Barn. But the circumstances that threaten Garland are no less potent than those that threatened her in Oz. The same wicked witch, Margaret Hamilton, is on hand in *Babes,* dispossessed of her magic but given the power to send the babes to the county institution while their vaudevillian parents tour the boondocks in a last glum hurrah.

*Babes* unveils someone even more terrifying than the wicked witch: June Preisser, as Baby Rosalie, who vamps Rooney and gets him to give her Garland's part in his show. "Would you punch me right in the nose if I asked you to understudy?" Rooney asks Garland miserably. But Garland is loyal. "Katharine Cornell did it," she replies through her tears. "I should be proud." She even applauds Baby Rosalie when she goes through some exhibitionistic warm-up exercises at her first rehearsal. Garland's a leader, so the other babes clap along; but how much can she take? When Rooney tries a stage kiss on Baby Rosalie, Garland walks out in a torch tune, "I Cried for You." Yet she returns, briskly informing Rooney, "I may be a sap about the men I pick, but I'm no quitter!" And, as MGM believes that such commitment is bound to carry one through, Baby Rosalie's father pulls her out of the show and the babes wind up not in a barn but on Broadway, revving up patriotism for the coming war with "God's Country," pungent to say the least. "We've got no *duce,* we've got no *Führer,*" Rooney exults. "But we've got Garbo," Garland adds, "and Norma Shearer."

There were *Babes* follow-ups with Rooney and, when Garland was too old to vie with a Baby Rosalie, pairings with Gene Kelly to take Garland's ancient yet new-styled zip into womanhood. There were period shows to place the zip in its primitive context, as when Garland treks into pioneer territory to help run the commercial way stations in *The Harvey Girls* (1946). There were specialty appearances in revues and biographies, to celebrate a stardom so individual it dwarfed everyone else in the films, as when *Till the Clouds Roll By* (1946), the unlife of Jerome Kern, suddenly wakes up and lives when Garland does a bit as Marilyn Miller. That the zip was ailing badly by the time of *The Harvey Girls* did not hurt Garland's story: the X of tantrums, paranoia, drug mania, and schizophrenic viciousness was unknown to all except those who worked with her and (by report) the rest of the film town. Yet, when she wasn't falling apart, she was a pro of pros, picking up songs, dance steps, and lines with amazing speed and adding to the planned action her own jabs of show-biz muscle. She made her co-workers hate her for her lateness, her dressing-room dawdling, her muttered terrors, then would suddenly spark up out of nowhere and electrify them with her efficient brilliance. Never was a person so adept at a job and so loath to do it adeptly.

Husbands began to come and go, Liza was born—she appears briefly in the last scene of *In the Good Old Summertime* (1949)—and a seemingly ideal Garland vehicle, *Annie Get Your Gun,* so defeated her resources that the spark went out and production was shut down, later to be resumed with Betty Hutton. Somehow, Garland pulled herself together for *Summer Stock* (1950), a return to the *Babes* idea but with grownups (Gene Kelly, Eddie Bracken, Phil Silvers, and Marjorie Main) and with the new postwar MGM tone, soggy where the *Babes* series has grit, and pokey where *Babes* snapped. Yet the sentiment is a little tired, ground out, as if MGM were so certain about musical style that it doesn't bother improvising anymore. At times, the vitality is just loud.

*Summer Stock* is a fetid sausage of a musical, one of the few putting-on-the-show films in which you hope they don't. *They* are a theaterless city troupe invading Garland's Connecticut farm with dishonorable intentions toward her barn. It seems that sister Gloria de Haven invited them up; she wants to be an actress. All through the 1940s, Garland had played people driven to make it in show biz, but the drive is less enthusiastic now than desperate. In the *Babes* films, Garland wants to succeed because Mickey Rooney does and she admires him: what he wants is what she wants. In *Easter Parade* (1948) with Fred Astaire, she's getting a little independent. Her head is turning. In *Summer Stock,* we experience her ambition more than her need for love, as if she has had to modernize her virtue further, liberate it. She can still move us with romantic vulnerability in the ballad "Friendly Star," but now her love song is more about what she wants than, as in the *Babes* ballads, what she can't get. Because now she can, must. At *Summer Stock*'s climax, sister de Haven vanishes just before opening night and Garland goes on in her place. When de Haven turns up at intermission, repentant, Garland refuses to relinquish the role. She likes being on stage. She wanted it and took it.

But there can be no room for Garland at MGM anymore. From their side, she has become unreliable, shooting up the cost of each picture by a fortune. From her side, she no longer needs a boss, can't even tolerate one. MGM released Garland, and she made a bold turnabout, leaving film temporarily to try her hand at concerts. First in London, then New York, she was a sensation, at once suggesting and disproving the idea that she was through. No one whom MGM fires is not through. But anyone who can give what Judy gives in a one-person show is just getting started. She is the first person since Jolson to blow entire audiences away, and she does it not through the insane helter-skelter of the compulsion to be loved, as Jolson did, in a diarrhea of art. She does it through the insane concentration of the compulsion not to need love. She even sings Jolson's songs—"Rockabye Your Baby with a Dixie Melody" and "Swanee." And sings them better than Jolson.

She was that good, no question. But she was a mess. She blamed it on her mother, who pushed her around; on L. B. Mayer, who pushed her around; on numerous others. For years, her problems were hidden from the public; now she was talking and much of what she said sounded unbelievable. Her wonderfully layered virtue of American grit decomposed even as the talent itself firmed up for her biggest triumph, for Warner Brothers, in *A Star Is Born* (1954), the reinvention of Garland as movie star. When Oscar time neared, popular opinion was certain Garland would take it, but Hollywood voted against her. She had washed out at MGM, bad-mouthed the business to journalists, and was reportedly still bratting it up on the *Star Is Born* set, wasting time and money. Hollywood loves a comeback, but the town had a score to settle with Judy Garland. They gave the Oscar to Grace Kelly for a walk-on part in *The Country Girl:* she walks on and walks through.

*A Star Is Born* was Garland's last good hitch in movieland. She did three later roles (her voice is heard in another two), but by then the troubles had wilted her zip. Still, she was supplying her X on screen, playing wrecks as she was a wreck. Her legend erupted as a bad smell out of an old egg. Yet take one view of Garland in her prime, in *The Wizard of Oz* and *Meet Me in St. Louis,* and the virtues capture one all over again. If she was a product of MGM, she at least profited in the parts MGM gave her, parts that co-opt our understanding of who she might be behind the story. When the truth came out, as Garland told it, it was a horror show. But what are you going to believe—what you've heard or what you can see? Baby Frances Gumm's innocence is more riveting than the exhaustion and pain the many Garland biographers detail. And it is riveting because so much talent lies behind it.

Durbin walked, Garland went cockeyed, but Elizabeth Taylor held on to become perhaps the ultimate in movie stars. As role model? No, that was Little Mary or Rosalind Russell. As fashion plate? No, except for the jewelry. Lilyan Tashman, Joan Crawford, Shirley Temple, and Diane Keaton made bigger waves in dress. As actress? No. Then as what? As star itself. Elizabeth Taylor is the Mae Murray that worked.

Not that Taylor ever made the emotional investment in stardom that Murray did. Taylor seems more to co-exist with fame than to dwell within it. But, on the other hand, fame loves Taylor as it has loved few before her; and everything in her personal life fascinates the public— much more so than her films themselves, which since about 1976 have been obscure addenda to her career. Taylor is a star in the old-fashioned sense of the Hollywood-raised, studio-nourished, much-married, money-spending headliner who has at least three or four films in her dossier that a great many people liked and continue to enjoy in revival. But she is also a new-style celebrity in that what she is is more important than what she does. It's not even certain that Taylor represents anything anymore, the way that Stanwyck represented womanly guts and generosity or Jean Harlow represented good-natured promiscuity. Taylor doesn't have to do anything to stay famous. She is stardom itself, neat.

Unlike Durbin and Garland, Taylor had no adaptable talent that anyone knew of when she started out, some five years after the two older girls. Durbin was Universal's creature of opera and Garland MGM's musical comedy gem, but Taylor was put into *Lassie* films, trivial adolescent romances, a *Little Women* remake. One film stood out in this period, *National Velvet* (1944), from Enid Bagnold's novel about a girl who wins, loves, and trains a horse, then rides him in a derby disguised as a boy. Taylor did have a talent, it turned out: riding. She also had a winsome beauty well beyond the bounds of her years. "Her eyes are too old," complained a casting director at Universal, where she made her first film in 1942 at the age of ten. "She doesn't have the face of a kid." Yet in *The Nation* James Agee claimed to have been "choked with the peculiar sort of adoration I might have felt if we were both in the same grade of primary school." He thought her beautiful, but not an actress. "She seems, rather, to turn things off and on . . . but without much, if any, of an artist's intuition, perception, or resource."

*National Velvet* settled Taylor in at MGM as a kid on the rise, and there was little question that she would wear the teenage years well, for she had never been a tyke and therefore had nothing to lose. On the contrary, womanhood completes her. In *Ivanhoe* (1952), the would-be Fitzgeraldian *The Last Time I Saw Paris* (1954), and *Giant* (1956), Taylor looked fine and turned the moods on and off skillfully, as Agee noted. She was sometimes miscast, making an amusingly WASPy Rebecca in *Ivanhoe* or a hopelessly modern Lady Patricia in the Regency-period *Beau Brummell* (1954). But in *Raintree County* (1957), as the psychotic femme fatale who takes Montgomery Clift from sweet Eva Marie Saint, Taylor began to exploit a mean and sexy streak that was to give her something of an identity for her next few films. She would bedevil some choice romantic men stars of her generation—after Clift, Paul Newman in the adaptation of Tennessee Williams' *Cat on a Hot Tin Roof* (1958), then Laurence Harvey in a version of John O'Hara's *Butterfield 8* (1960), in which she plays what we presume to be a high-class hooker (the whitewashed script makes it hard to tell without consulting O'Hara). Actually, Harvey is crueler to Taylor than she is to Clift or Newman, but the film didn't read that way, for sometime before it was released came the sensational collapse of the Debbie Reynolds–Eddie Fisher marriage, the immediate cause being the Elizabeth Taylor–Eddie Fisher romance.

It's difficult to recapture today the shock those headlines made then, and the sudden change they made in Taylor's perceived character. Try to imagine troubleshooting little Deanna Durbin growing up to play man-eater parts and appear to carry her roles into her private life, and one glimpses something of the Taylor aura in its middle era between child actress and famous woman. Let's not rehearse the arguments for and against—the "poor little Debbie" on one hand and the "you can't break up a good marriage, only a bad one" on the other. Let's just remark that, as a curious exhibit of how differently the two sexes were encouraged to act in the 1950s, adultery, divorce, and remarriage not only didn't hurt Taylor's career but spurred it. Adultery, divorce, and remarriage destroyed Eddie Fisher.

One reason why Taylor triumphed despite the exposure of her personal life is that her evolving persona really needed a little scandal; it was as if one couldn't understand *Butterfield 8* without knowing who Eddie Fisher was (MGM obligingly cast him in the film), and, understanding *Butterfield 8,* one began to enjoy Taylor all the more. Hollywood was so glad she had at last keyed her work to an image that she was handed an Oscar for *Butterfield*—over two great dames (Greer Garson and Deborah Kerr) and two rival sensualists (Shirley MacLaine and Melina Mercouri). This is what is called sweeping the field.

Another reason for Taylor's support is her constant battles with illness, some quite serious, though one has the feeling that if Taylor were in London and someone were to sneeze in Tibet, she'd come down with strep throat. Taylor isn't the first star to have hospital glamour as well as other kinds, but in the studio days getting sick meant raising expenses and sabotaging schedules and answering to moguls. Taylor's stardom became most effective after the structured studios had dissolved into freelancing parlors, and there was no continuity of career to answer for. Bette Davis had even worse luck than Taylor in staying healthy; virtually every film she worked on found her fighting some disability. She fought, and showed up, and worked: because you had to. In the 1930s and '40s, alienate one producer and you might alienate all his allies and sycophants and wake up the next morning doing an ice-skating musical at Republic with Vera Hruba Ralston. In the age of Taylor, however, alienate one producer and you could always find another—the teams had split apart.

As a sensualist, Taylor could play some choice vamp roles, recycled, but could also be counted on to delay shooting with medical layoffs and unaccountable latenesses. *Cleopatra* (1963), then, was inevitable, with Taylor in the Theda Bara–Claudette Colbert role, an unprecedentedly expensive and mismanaged production, and a new high in star salary with Taylor's cool million and ten percent of the gross. (Oddly, the project originated as a vehicle for Susan Hayward, with Stephen Boyd to play Marc Antony and Peter Finch Caesar.) Unlooked for benison was Taylor's romance with Richard Burton, her Antony (with Sybil Burton in the role formerly played by Debbie Reynolds and

Eddie Fisher moving to the back row of the chorus), for it gave the film extra publicity: Come see Liz and Dick in ancient times! Yet their love scenes generated little heat; *Cleopatra* is decorous rather than dynamic. The New York press generally reviewed the production budget rather than the movie and gloried in their pans, but such was the interest in Taylor's latest *amour fou* that the film did decent business and eventually recouped its negative cost of $31 million.

Too much stateliness was *Cleopatra*'s problem, also the problem of other Taylor-Burton teamings. But *Who's Afraid of Virginia Woolf?* (1966), from Edward Albee's four-character play about a lurid all-night party of college professors and wives, was properly ferocious. Taylor moved from vamp to bitch in nasty hair and boozy growls, and won praise (and a second Oscar) for a taut portrayal that many had thought beyond her capabilities. She played a comic version of the part in *The Taming of the Shrew* (1967), with Burton as Petruchio, and now was at her peak: solid fame, substantial vehicles, fine performances and trusty collaborators, especially in Franco Zeffirelli's colorfully florid staging of the Shakespeare with a cast of West End repertory stalwarts. It's Taylor's best role *and* best film.*

After it, however, she made a series of duds. *Boom!* (1968), also with Burton, from Tennessee Williams' *The Milk Train Doesn't Stop Here Anymore,* could have been a savvy little shocker, with Taylor as a retired courtesan visited in her Italian villa by a beautiful man known to café society as "the angel of death." Paul Roebling originated the role on Broadway in 1963 opposite Hermione Baddeley, and when he walked on stage in his lederhosen, whole sections of the audience began to moan and scream. Casting Burton in the part was a Hollywood cheat, turning a sexy poetic joke into fanzine gossip: Come see Liz and Dick in Capri! An excursion to Las Vegas with Warren Beatty in *The Only Game in Town* (1970) was talky. *X Y & Zee* (1972) with Michael Caine reclaimed the Taylor shrew in a tired triangle. *Hammersmith Is Out* (1972), Faustian black comedy with Burton, was if nothing else daring, but it was nothing else. *Identikit* (1974), an Italian film, was scarcely released in America at all, and *The Blue Bird* (1976), a fairytale spectacle made in Russia by George Cukor with a flashy international cast, laid a great big Fabergé egg. (Noting the film's "co-production" status as the combined efforts of Soviet and American diplomats, staff, and performers, *Time* magazine called it "probably the first movie in history made because a country was available.") In 1940, the same tale had finished off Shirley Temple as a bankable star. Taylor simply rose above it.

In fact, the fate of her films seemed to have no connection to her

---

*The two don't always coincide. Judy Garland's best performance is perhaps that in *A Star Is Born,* but surely *Meet Me in St. Louis* and *The Wizard of Oz* are better films.

standing as a Hollywood star. Trying to separate Durbin and Garland from their work is pointless, but Taylor is far more the newsmaker than the actress. Flop after flop, she remained top-okay for reporters and readers. She and Burton, divorced in 1974, remarried while *The Blue Bird* was being processed, and the usual spectacular jewelry changed hands for the event. Shortly thereafter they split again, and the columns filled with her dates. There were rumors that she might try the stage. There was the trip to Iran at the invitation of the Ambassador to the United States, Ardeshir Zahedi. As the Italian press had vilified her during *Cleopatra,* so did the Iranians now. One magazine described her as a "fattish, short, big-busted woman with poor makeup, and totally out of fashion." (True, she'd be so much more stylish under a *chador.*) Then came the courtship of John Warner, to become Taylor's sixth husband, simultaneously with Burton's own remarriage, which tied up that chapter in Taylor's history nicely.

What of Taylor the actress? The question is beside the point, but Taylor did get to the stage at last in 1981, in a revival of Lillian Hellman's *The Little Foxes,* and by then her metamorphosis from inhabitant of Hollywood to denizen of the great world was complete. Critics and public reviewed the performance in the light of her screen career, picking out reminiscences of *Virginia Woolf* and *Secret Ceremony* in her Regina Giddens, but they treated the event far more as a confident star turn than as a questionable adventurist lark, however questionable it may have been. Film stars have bombed on Broadway. Nancy Carroll, Gloria Swanson, and Paul Newman and Joanne Woodward, among others, had scarcely learned their lines before the closing notice was posted. But Taylor was not permitted to bomb: Come and see Liz live as a bad guy! It was too rich to miss, and Taylor herself had such a good time she celebrated by dumping Warner, taking *The Little Foxes* to London, and preparing to form a repertory company.

Taylor's crossover from child star to bitch temptress reveals Hollywood's approach-avoidance to sex that informs kid and vamp avatars alike. In the 1930s, sexy women really were sexy. In the 1940s, the all-basic pinup Betty Grable was more sanitary than salacious, and the kids were graduated into womanhood with as much of the sprite about them as possible, as if Hollywood were blunting the difference between innocence and worldliness. Time was when a woman was a woman, and a kid—Little Mary Pickford, for instance—stayed a kid for as long as possible. But by the 1940s, the two extremes were mixing, sharing properties.

Consider Rita Hayworth. Here was one of the most beautiful women in film history, and the only beauty queen as such at her studio, Columbia, so one would expect her to have played many a siren. On the contrary, she mostly played heroines of musical comedy, the most innocent of genres, and when she did play sensual, she was out of her league, not actress enough to convince as a fatale. Yet that was the point: let a Nice Girl play a Bad Woman, and the Nice will forgive the Bad. Whether through an actress's charm, skill, or clumsiness didn't matter.

Hayworth was grace itself when she moved, but she was a dancer entirely, taking her character cues from music. (She couldn't sing and was invariably dubbed.) Partnered by Fred Astaire in *You'll Never Get Rich* (1941) and *You Were Never Lovelier* (1942) and by Gene Kelly in *Cover Girl* (1944), Hayworth inflamed the notion of the chaste beauty with an erotic glow. Her supple line—her tact, really—made her perfect and remote even as her looks beguiled intimately, the profile of Diana shaded by Venus. But, taken from musicals to exploit her allure, she lost access to what made her allure so telling. In *Blood and Sand* (1941) she plays the grandee who dallies with bullfighter Tyrone Power, taking him from wife Linda Darnell with an amused rapaciousness. Hayworth had just broken through to stardom. Though she was on loan to Fox, where presumably no one had any intention of building her up just so Harry Cohn could reap the profits, still *Blood and Sand* was a certifiable event: a Technicolor remake of a Valentino classic with Fox's biggest draw and touches of prestige in the use of Rouben Mamoulian to direct and Nazimova as Power's mother.

So this was no quickie, sink or swim. Yet Hayworth is horribly wrong, trying to project sophistication by grimacing or showing jaw. In confrontation with Darnell, mistress versus wife, Hayworth takes on a scene that was trite even before sound came in; and not only has she nothing new to bring to it, she doesn't even know the clichés. Darnell asks, "Shall I be frank?" and Hayworth replies, "Please do," with so little *take* that Shirley Temple might have read the line with more womanly oomph. Later, when Hayworth drops Power for his successor as star torero, Anthony Quinn, Hayworth gets an opportunity to dance a little. But: with Anthony Quinn?

Some women stars were so good in musicals that they were content to specialize—Eleanor Powell, for instance. But then Powell was at MGM, so richly supplied with specialists that each of them could pursue his calling at his ease. As Columbia's Big Lady, Hayworth had to adapt. She was a star in the general sense of projecting a unique image that carried her beyond questions of acting technique or collaborative support, but she was a star also in the economic sense of staking films with her appeal regardless of their quality.

Anyway, that image was complex, touching base with the maiden and pinup tropes and carrying as well its own erotic elegance. About one of her several scraps with Cohn, Hayworth complained to a reporter that her boss was obsessed with "the image he was going to make me till I was ninety." However, that image varied considerably from film to film. *Cover Girl* brought out the neighborhood sweetheart in Hayworth, as a small-time dancer in Brooklyn who turns down a career in fashion and a ritzy marriage to stay with her small-time impresario Gene Kelly. But *Gilda* (1946) brought out the sexpot in Hayworth. This bias on the image was most persuasive, for the kinky love-hate affair of Hayworth and Glenn Ford and Hayworth's heated striptease to "Put the Blame on Mame" has made *Gilda* the most fondly recalled of Hayworth's films. Her sweetheart side was overwhelmed, and Hayworth became known as "America's Love Goddess." "Few women," wrote Winthrop Sargeant, "have more willingly and deftly submitted to becoming the passive material out of which a myth can be created."

Musicals could add little to this myth. Musical heroines observed innocence, egalitarianism, and monogamy, while Gilda is worldly, sybaritic, promiscuous, a tease, and a louse. And Gilda was the new Hayworth. So Hayworth played a rota of Gildas—in *The Loves of Carmen* (1948), again with Ford; in *Salome* (1953); in *Miss Sadie Thompson* (1953). Meanwhile her personal life had harmed her image, as it does so often in Hollywood careers. Her mating with Orson Welles, who was regarded as an arrogant washout of the high kulcha, was interesting and if nothing else gave us *The Lady from Shanghai* (1948), written and directed by and starring Welles in a funhouse concerto grosso, with Hayworth again on siren. But Hayworth divorced Welles—"I couldn't take his genius twenty-four hours a day any longer." She then made liaison with Aly Khan, a millionaire of extraordinarily textured Eastern stock she met in Cannes while taking some months off to let her famous long (dyed) red hair grow back from the nasty clipping Welles gave it for *The Lady from Shanghai.*

The Khan episode made Hayworth one of the most famous people in the world, but a technicality about Khan's divorce and the birth of Hayworth's daughter by Khan some six months after the wedding brought upon Hayworth the rebuke of authority figures from the Pope to the *Hollywood Reporter.* Somewhere in the middle belongs Harry Cohn, who despaired of ever clearing his protégée's image but did, to his credit, continue to release her films. Perhaps he understood that the sanitized kid-women and pure-sexy pinups of the 1940s were not to survive anyway. In the 1950s, to fight television, Hollywood was to promote woman's sexuality as it had never dared do in the past. Not coincidentally, this is precisely when Hayworth went into her dance of seven veils.

She also went into decline. Her image was not so much sullied by scandal as confused by it. What was a Rita Hayworth picture now? Once it was a lithe musical, later a sexy melodrama. But by the time she played the San Francisco matron who takes up with Frank Sinatra in *Pal Joey* (1957), highly expurgated from a stage musical with a Rodgers and Hart score, Hayworth wasn't even doing Rita Hayworth pictures anymore: *Pal Joey* was a Frank Sinatra picture. Nor did Hayworth get to show what musicals used to inspire in her. Her big number, "Zip," had her re-enacting the put-on strip she had introduced in *Gilda,* and otherwise she floated in and out of the action trying to look tough. *Pal Joey* as Columbia filmed it is not unlike an American version of *Blood and Sand* with Kim Novak in the Linda Darnell part, by which simile Hayworth has come full circle, back in an unsuitable role as a sophisticate. *Blood and Sand* and *Pal Joey* enclose some golden and some ashen years of a shockingly wasted career, and the remainder of it is sad. There were further movies, but few of them are decent and some really horrendous. Anyone for a screening of, for instance, *The Naked Zoo* (1971)?

Hayworth, for all her once-in-a-blue-moon beauty and dazzling dancing, typifies the Hollywood star as commodity, with no encompassing viewpoint on her possibilities, only reactions to specific projects. While good vehicles came her way, she had no cause for complaint— but no foundation on which to plan, either. So when damaging vehicles trapped her, she was helpless. The public retreated from her for doing in life what she had been doing in her films, and as her better-known marriages to outsiders and has-beens dismayed industry feelings, Hayworth's later years made a kind of goof stardom without affiliation—no clear image, no important billing, no sure public, not even a guarantee that her foreign pictures would be released domestically.

Hayworth's fellow forties pinup Betty Grable might have suffered comparable setbacks, but she settled down at a studio where formula musicals were a given. Thus she was encouraged to do what she did well and her typing underwent no evolution. Like Hayworth, Grable started as a dancer, working the Hollywood lots for years without finding a niche, then burst forth as a top star in musicals. Unlike Hayworth, Grable was a beauty in a good-natured, everyday rather than a spectacular sense. Hayworth inspired; Grable was liked, and that protected her. While Hayworth fell victim to the postwar sexual hypocrisy that kept demanding more and more flesh of its pinups and then turned away in revulsion when it got what it wanted, Grable hoofing in her shlock musicals and grinning over her shoulder in her one-piece bathing suit upheld the established decencies. She indicated eroticism, never inhabited it. Had Grable been in Hayworth's shoes at Columbia, she would never have made *Gilda.*

Blond spunk, Betty hit Hollywood under the guidance of a determined mother just when sound had arrived and pretty dancers were needed to swell the chorus lines of the many musicals. The Depression, too, had just arrived, and everyone was looking for work, so though Grable had no trouble landing jobs, she got lost in the lines, despite mother Lillian's legendary aggressiveness in bearding impresarios in and out of their lairs. Perhaps Grable's difficulties stemmed from her all-around talent. She sang well enough, danced well enough, played her characters (when she got one to play) well enough, but did nothing distinctively. Most of Hollywood's musical stars got ahead by capitalizing on a supreme gift—Eleanor Powell's or Fred Astaire's dancing, say, or Lawrence Tibbett's or Judy Garland's singing. There were exceptions, of course. Maurice Chevalier possibly and Ruby Keeler certainly got further on their charm than on his singing or her dancing. Still, a B average gets one nowhere in Hollywood; better to flunk a few subjects and catch one A, for casting is crude, type at first sight, and one has to bowl them over pronto.

Grable didn't. Whether in quickie trifles or major productions, she does her little bit and vanishes. Take *Whoopee!* (1930), Samuel Goldwyn's faithful filming of a smash Ziegfeld musical western built around Eddie Cantor. Goldwyn took most of the original cast, set them up on stagey locations, trimmed the original script, arranged for Technicolor cameras, and announced his big deal with a flourish. And whom do we first encounter after the credits are over? Grable. Hurry music accompanies a long shot of two groups of riders dashing through the desert, joining where their roads converge, and dismounting in a theatrical plaza for an opening number. One of the men delivers one of the tightest expositions in the history of narrative art:

"We've ridden twenty miles today to see Sally Morgan and Sheriff Bob Wells get married!" The gang screams, "Whoopee!" And Betty takes stage.

"What a wild man you are, Bill!" she cries.

"Wild enough to tame you!" he responds.

She asks, "Oh, yeah?"

He answers, "Yeah!"

And she's into the verse ("Oh, a cowboy's a wild man, but oh, what a mild man . . ."), going on to rope him like a dogie while the mob takes the chorus, all then forming a conventional geometry to go into the dance, choreographed by Busby Berkeley in his first Hollywood assignment. Berkeley shapes a few of the oscillating patterns and overhead kaleidoscope shots he was to perfect in the Warners backstagers a few years later; and it's a fine, joyous, artificial opening. Yet Grable gets lost in it and is not seen again for the rest of the film.

Similarly, she catches every eye in a number in the Astaire-Rogers vehicle *The Gay Divorcee* (1934), flirting with Edward Everett Horton and coaxing him to try a step or two; but once the number finishes, Grable is out of the picture. She didn't even rate name billing. When she was mentioned, it was usually for idiotic college musicals in which the boys do nothing but play football, the girls do nothing but plan proms, and the faculty consists of Martha Raye. Grable would have at the most a glancing relationship with the story line; she was on hand to lead the coeds in the dance numbers, and she became a joke in the columns of hip reviewers.

That was the 1930s for Grable, till she gave up on pictures and took a featured dancing role in the Broadway show *DuBarry Was a Lady*. As with Hepburn in *The Philadelphia Story* and Rosalind Russell in *Wonderful Town*, making a splash on Broadway reads in Hollywood as Ripe for Comeback, and back they come, reprieved or, in Grable's case, Discovered at last. This time, having no specialty came in handy. Twentieth Century–Fox's Darryl Zanuck needed someone to take over in *Down Argentine Way* (1940) for Alice Faye, stricken with appendicitis, and he wanted the replacement slugged in with as little rearranging as possible. A distinctive performer might have pulled the part out of whack, but Grable fitted in nicely, singing, dancing, and charming as Faye might have done. Now, Faye was a superior singer and Grable the better dancer, and while both projected as breezy, uninhibited blond urban proles, their personalities were quite different in small ways that in the aggregate made them unalike. But this was convenient for Zanuck. The two could trade off leads in his big musicals, making for a fine novelty. They could also appear together with success in the still-useful threesome ventures, with yet a third blonde ringed in between them. Best of all, one could be used as a threat against the other in the event of prima donna trouble.

So Grable joined the Faye series, taking over as the main feature when Faye retired in 1945. The forties Fox musical retained the loose backstager structure of those of the 1930s, but wartime exigencies and the passing of Depression politics called for less emphasis on gold digging and unemployment paranoia in favor of nostalgic or exotic settings, Technicolor, and Carmen Miranda. Though Grable and Faye worked side by side as sisters in *Tin Pan Alley* (1940), and though Grable played a role or two that Faye might have been more comfortable in, she lent her personal fruit-and-cream style to the series, and by the late 1940s the big Fox musical had become the big Grable musical, less class-conscious, less screwy, and less disjointed than the big Faye musical of the late 1930s had been. Faye belted out determination and spun lamentation, romanced amiable juveniles, and shared the numbers with a host of specialty acts. Grable sang less characterfully, so the songs didn't matter as much in her films—and, frankly, weren't as good. But Grable had bigger, sexier males to play opposite and fewer vaudevillian intrusions to work around. Faye's films, if they had a theme, were about survival. Grable's films were about love.

Take *Wabash Avenue* (1950), prime late-middle Grable: Henry Koster directing in Technicolor, five second-rate songs, the beer halls of old-time Chicago for locale, sets and costumes without a trace of verisimilitude, Victor Mature for kiss panels, Phil Harris as Mature's rival,

James Barton as a comic drunk, Margaret Hamilton as a crusading saloon trasher, and, for a plot source, a Grable vehicle from seven years earlier, *Coney Island.* Grable, as pinup, was always on an intimate footing with her audience, but to watch Marlene Dietrich run through "What Am I Bid for My Apples?" in *Morocco,* strolling through a nightclub to make satiric passes at both sexes, and then to watch Grable singing "May I Tempt You with a Big Red Rosy Apple?" in *Wabash Avenue* is to learn how little erotic content a pinup could have. *Morocco,* of course, came out before the Production Code rearmament of 1934 strangled the sex out of the movies. Still, sixteen years later, one of the nation's leading cheesecake stars is behaving about as cakily as Squirrel Nutkin's Little Mary hand puppet.

A homegrown gal, Grable does not bear the foreign harlot's sexual license. The young Dietrich lived on men; Grable dances. In *Wabash Avenue,* she does the shimmy in one number, a Dixieland strut in another, and goes on to a fan dance, a parasol dance, and a fifth turn as a Dutch girl in braids (though the song trills of Copenhagen). And when Victor Mature makes the indicated move, Grable is wild. Mature, manager of the club where Grable performs, finds her in a costume with enough feathers to fill a hundred pillows. He pulls the feathers off, she backs away, he chases her, and is virtually stripping the woman when they fall onto a couch, when he takes his first kiss. She is stunned: "What'd you have to do that for?" When Mature points out that they both did that, Grable slaps him hard. If he kisses her again, she'll kill him if she has to hang for it, and "I'll hang happy."

Grable was the quasi-virgin pinup, closer to Garland than to Hayworth, even if the postmaster general felt driven to ban her famous bathing suit still from the mails. Grable was a family pinup, a wife and daughter, and thus very close to the wrapped-up tone of her times. Other women were degraded in *film noir,* but Grable mostly made musicals like *Wabash Avenue,* putting on the show, resenting and then romancing arrogant men, and sticking by her pals in trouble. When, occasionally, Zanuck tried to expand her in unusual projects like *That Lady in Ermine* (1948), a Continental satire begun by Ernst Lubitsch and finished by Otto Preminger, Grable and her public were alike unhappy.

As for stardom, Grable enjoyed it but didn't let it run her life. A highly private person who held things back even from close friends, she was ebullient and silly in company and seldom took her movies seriously. She referred to *Meet Me After the Show* (1951), another backstager no better than it should be, as *Eat Me After the Show,* and *The Farmer Takes a Wife* (1953) became *The Farmer Takes a Dump.* Yet she understood the ceremonies of stardom, as when, on the set of *How to Marry a Millionaire* (1953), she told Marilyn Monroe, "I've had mine, honey. Go get yours." This was a generous salute. Grable had been having serious troubles with Zanuck: his dictatorial guidance annoyed her and her independence incensed him. There had been suspensions and hard words, and Monroe was clearly intended to take over Grable's position as maximum leader of the big Fox musical. Yet when her number was called, Grable went quietly.

It's strange that two such counteractive outlines as those of the maiden and the pinup could overlap, but that's how different the 1940s are from the 1930s. Try to imagine Irene Dunne or Jeanette MacDonald trading roles with Marlene Dietrich or Jean Harlow. Yet Grable could easily have played many of Judy Garland's parts, and vice versa, while Rita Hayworth encompassed the two extremes of type within a close space of time, from *Cover Girl* to *Gilda* in two years. It took Elizabeth Taylor longer to make a comparable jump, but consider the distance traveled—from *National Velvet* to *Cat on a Hot Tin Roof*!

The 1920s was the age of bunk, the 1930s that of inquiry. What were the 1940s? At war with itself, the decade feared what it needed and celebrated the commonplace, and therefore its key images are often ambiguous or contradictory. No era was more comfortable with child-women than the 1940s, yet at the same time audiences delighted in *film noir* heroines with a kiss of death.

One woman stands out for her consistency in this time, Ava Gardner. Here was a sex star who was a full-grown woman playing roles of erotic allure. Refreshingly, she regarded her image, her films, and Hollywood in general as rubbish. "I'm just a plain, simple girl off the farm," she once said—but when she entered a room, she was the only one who wasn't impressed. Her looks and voice were special, unplaceable, and she could enact regional American natives or women of the most exotic nationalities, people of education or of none, victims and monsters, with aplomb. She could suggest anything just by showing up, for her appearance and bearing were such that the audience, thus imaginatively goaded, filled in the rest for themselves.

Gardner was born in Grabtown, North Carolina, groomed at MGM, and unveiled most noticeably as a *noir* rat in *The Killers* (1946), an expansion of Ernest Hemingway's short story, ensnaring and doublecrossing Burt Lancaster. She went on to play the goddess of love in *One Touch of Venus* (1948), a redemptive damozel in *Pandora and the Flying Dutchman* (1951), a jazz-age loser in *The Snows of Kilimanjaro* (1952), also from Hemingway: figures of myth. MGM didn't know it, but Gardner was to be the last in her line, the final studio-made glamour package with the secrets of Garbo and the earthiness of Crawford.

Gardner was willing to experiment, as when she played Julie Laverne, the suffering half-caste "second heroine" of *Show Boat* (1951). A sentimental musical was the last place one expected to see Gardner (especially as Lena Horne was so much righter for the part), but she did a creditable job, doing her own singing on "Can't Help Lovin' Dat

Man" and "Bill" and bringing them off, unlike most non-singers, as if she understood how a musical works and why the songs are there. She is also at her ease in the impromptu shuffle dance that follows "Can't Help Lovin' Dat Man." For some reason, MGM decided to overdub Gardner's vocals with Annette Warren; meanwhile, the record album had come out with Gardner's tracks intact, and they survive to argue for the honesty of her portrayal. Heaven knows, this third film *Show Boat* needed a little honesty to counter the fatuous grandeur of the main love team (Kathryn Grayson and Howard Keel) and the frivolous fun people (Joe E. Brown and Marge and Gower Champion).

Gardner obviously cared about *Show Boat,* for when she didn't care about an assignment she walked through it. Still, this only added to the experience of watching a giant personality coming through in a set of experiences. Gardner was one of the most broadly based of stars, known less through her roles than through her marriages (to Mickey Rooney, America's number one adolescent male; to Artie Shaw, who cultured her up; to Frank Sinatra, just moving into his Mean Man phase), and through friendships that turned a wheel of mirrors, shifting reflections too fast to follow. She was wanton; no, she was bored; then she was sensitive; no, she's bored again—but so intensely she might be playing the story of Garbo. Garbo materialized in her roles; Taylor materialized in her publicity; Ava Gardner disappeared into her roles and publicity combined. By the time she made *The Barefoot Contessa* (1954), the public was convinced it was her own story. Maybe it was, for Gardner had become her own myth, as the star who didn't care.

*The Barefoot Contessa* is Joseph Mankiewicz' assault on the international movie world, centered on the discovery, rise, rebellion, and death of a star not unlike a Spanish Gardner. The cast are almost all creeps—megalomaniacal producers, the servile PR man, Riviera sycophants, movieville partygoers on the make in their cups. Humphrey Bogart, a good-guy screenwriter and Mankiewicz' mouthpiece, is the best thing in the film, his famous toughness now defeated and a threat to creeps only in his comparative truth telling. His sympathetic comments help form our reading of the saga of Maria Vargas (Gardner), who strolls barefoot into stardom and eventually drifts into marriage with a count (Rossano Brazzi) who murders her. Originally her role was to have gone to a true Vargas, freshly discovered, but none seemed right. Nor did anyone who was established. Maybe no one could act it: it's all telling, no showing. In the event, Gardner doesn't extend herself, as if she's letting the audience's belief in stardom work for her. This is her *Camille,* her *Stage Door,* her *A Star Is Born,* her *Mildred Pierce,* the fable of who the star is. *The Barefoot Contessa* bears no witness to the facts of Gardner's life; other than her village childhood and her contempt for filmmaking, she has little in common with Maria Vargas. But stardom attracts wonder so romantically that the portrait is biographically persuasive.

One was not persuaded: Gardner. Her choice of films after *The Barefoot Contessa* seems to bear out her grudges against Hollywood, with drivel like *The Little Hut* (1957), *The Naked Maja* (1959), and Dino de Laurentis' offensive epic *The Bible* (1966) sandwiched between conventionally decent events like *The Night of the Iguana* (1964), from Tennessee Williams' play. This is one of Gardner's best efforts, probably because director John Huston troubled to bring out her bawdy humor—her, as he put it, "random, gallant, wild openness." As a hotel proprietor going happily to rot in Mexico, Gardner had a part few would be as comfortable in as she is. (Bette Davis originated it on Broadway, in an act of supreme will.) With Richard Burton as Gardner's vis-à-vis and Elizabeth Taylor in attendance on the set, *The Night of the Iguana* was from shooting to premiere what Hollywood calls an event.

Sadly, Gardner's career has since relaxed into big-money disaster films like *Earthquake* (1974) and others even less mentionable. She never thought she was much of an actress, so perhaps she feels best served by shlock, though it is notable that, in anything, she disdains exploitive prurience. "I made it as a star dressed," she once said. "If I haven't got it dressed, I don't want it." She does what she likes, living quietly in London and finding things to do that interest her far more than moviemaking ever did.

It is inevitable that women stars whose type strongly depends on youthful innocence or on prime post-deb beauty cannot pursue lifetime careers at the top. Ironically, however, none of the women in this chapter simply got old. Durbin got bored. Garland got impossible. Hayworth got an unmanageable image. Grable got replaced while she was still in her prime by an impatient boss ready with the "next" Grable. Taylor and Gardner are still devastating lookers and still active.

It is not a question of age, or of cooperation with or resistance to the system, or of quality of vehicles, though all these variables apply in some measure. It is not a question of looks, especially, for this glamour thing is subjective as a critical or historical topic and redundant anyway because all stars are, by Hollywood standards, interesting to look at. Talent is the gauge, the answer to the question Who will win? It is what tells us why Katharine Hepburn and Bette Davis are compelling in their early films despite their roughness or miscasting; it is what makes a tour through Rosalind Russell's or Barbara Stanwyck's careers intriguing despite the numerous dull entries; and what makes Colleen Moore's many flapper comedies insightful long after the political structure of the flapper was dismantled. Talent is enough, even in Hollywood. Every woman in this chapter, maiden or pinup, made it on something bigger than looks, and lost it—those who did—through something more debilitating than physical decline.

Looks used to be enough, especially when Elinor Glyn said you either had It or you didn't and everyone took her to mean sex appeal. Glyn meant charisma, the basis of character projection in film, the occult valor they look for in the screen test. But Glyn was speaking of silent It, totally different from the It of the talkie. Some silent stars were nothing but an image in motion, and they were the ones who died when sound moved in to comprehend a more creative image. The talkie It does more, works harder. It's talent. But the memory of one true charisma dies hard, and was still active in the 1950s, when the greatest of the pinups had her day. She looked so terrific that some assumed she had no talent at all; and either she didn't care and it didn't matter and she never knew what hit her, or she did care and it killed her: depending on which legend one chooses to believe.

# 13

# *The*
# *Ultimate*
# *in It*

MARILYN MONROE
JAYNE MANSFIELD
KIM NOVAK

*I hope they don't do that to me after I'm gone.*

—MARILYN MONROE
after reading the script for
*The Jean Harlow Story*

Twenty years after talkies changed the form—therefore the content—of the movies, Billy Wilder looked back on the essence of silent It in *Sunset Boulevard* (1950), displaying It as a rotten, murderous solipsism. The public looked up at the screen as if through a window into glamour—but on the other side, glamour was looking into a mirror, at itself. The public was the unseen accessory that capitalized the act of self-love. Wilder demonstrates that glamour is not self-satisfying, though it lives for itself: it only works when conveyed in its imagistic It to the public. Glamour is a tree falling in a forest. No one there, no sound. And for his star, to show who glamour was, Wilder revived the prototype of golden-age glitter, Gloria Swanson.

The perfect choice. Swanson was the first of the really big glamour queens, so seldom seen in the talkie decades that she could be mistaken for the character she played, Norma Desmond, who lives on memories of her glory and waits through the dead decades for her second chance. *Sunset Boulevard*, then, is true fiction: forgotten star hires penniless writer to edit her comeback script, takes him as her lover, and shoots him when he walks out on her. She is insane. When her mansion fills with policemen and reporters, they can put her under arrest only by letting her think that she's playing a big scene for the cameras. "All right, Mr. De Mille," she says, revving up the fire-and-ice ducts, "I'm ready for my close-up." The film fades out on hysteria and self-love slinking up to the camera, closer, closer.

Is this Hollywood glamour?—or just silent glamour? By 1950, a great many moviegoers had no experience in silence, and might well have assumed that things were different in the old days. They were. Wilder makes this clear by intertwining an imagery of death and the grotesque with his references to silence. Besides the corpse of the writer, which opens the film, there is Swanson's pet chimp, also a corpse; the names of departed stars; a bridge game among a few survivors (most notably Buster Keaton); the writer's job (*ghost*writing); a New Year's Eve party for just Swanson and her writer, complete with band; and silent film itself, which haunts the action not as a lost art but as whiffs of decayed candy. Those outstanding historical adversaries Swanson and Erich von Stroheim had made their peace over the *Queen Kelly* fiasco (we even get a tantalizing glimpse of the film) and appear here as mistress and husband/servant/bodyguard. But Hollywood was at war with its past.

Not all the old glamour was neurotic or gone with the wind. Lillian Gish, having survived the decades on stage, returned to Hollywood irregularly as of the late 1940s, and turned in one of her best performances in *The Night of the Hunter* (1955), a bizarre, not easily describable piece directed by Charles Laughton in clear homage to the aesthetic and moral principles of D. W. Griffith. If Hollywood has an Off Broadway, *The Night of the Hunter* is its exhibit A, and it's a strange place to encounter the former Griffith belle and MGM heavyweight draw, now something like an aged Little Mary, clucking at her brood of orphans and toting her shooting iron with efficient bustle. If Gish is what's left of the old silents, then Wilder's savage comedy is merely one opinion, not a general one.

But wait. Gish was always an outsider, even in MGM. It was Swanson who led the film colony, set tone, defined the star's portion. Grab anyone living in America in 1925 or so, ask "Who's a movie star?" and chances are better than okay he'd name Swanson. "Why are you so late?" Swanson asks William Holden, the writer, when they meet. "Why have you kept me waiting for so long?" Twenty years, and the ghosts haven't stopped walking. "You used to be big," Holden tells her. "I am big," she snaps. "It's the *pictures* that got small." And she's good, her arms folded or waving at the ceilings, eyes blank in shades or glowing bitterly, mouth snarling and purring as she poses. Her best role, perhaps. But she's mad: glamour is mad. Mae Murray thought *Sunset Boulevard* bizarre. "None of us floozies was ever *that* nuts," she remarked. Yet she was the biggest nut of all. "So they opened their big mouths," Swanson tells us, "and out came talk, talk, talk! *We* didn't need dialogue—we had faces." Translation: Talent was extra to silent film.

The purpose of silence was to show beauty to every eye. Film made beauty immortal. Yet how brutally the beautiful died: Wallace Reid, Florence Lawrence, John Gilbert, Jean Harlow, Lupe Velez, Carole Landis, James Dean . . .

And Marilyn Monroe. In her, glamour as narcissism reaches its summit. Because the studio system virtually died at about the time that she did, some think of her as the last movie star in the sense of glamour commodity, corporate sexual property, thing. But as she was not the first sex symbol, she was not the last. And despite some reasoned attempts to view her as an archetypal victim of men's power games or at least as an individual pathetically trying to free herself from oppressive generalities, most of Monroe's problems were of Monroe's making.

More books have been written about her than about any other star, yet the record is not clear. Often, her reports vary widely from those of numerous involved parties and bystanders, and they can't all be lying.

So whom do we believe? Certainly the outlines of the tale, as generally known, are true: she was born to an unmarried woman with a genetic history of mental illness. Her father had no interest in her (until she became rich and famous, of course). She was shunted from orphanage to foster homes, married very young and unsuccessfully, and grew up, as so many did, dreaming of redeeming her bad fortune by going Hollywood. And so she went.

Legend expands this. It is generally believed that she was sexually molested by older men in her youth, and the facts of her death, such as they are, are veiled in the possibility of murder. It looks like suicide, but certain irregularities in the investigation suggest a cover-up—says rumor, to protect one of the Kennedys. However, more important than Monroe's early brushes with evil and the circumstances of her death is the question of whether she had talent or was just a pinup. She was spectacular to see, and would surely have had some sort of movie career, but the top stars almost always have something more to offer than a glorious appearance or a cute way. If film calls for a distillation of self rather than the projection of imaginary characters (the Gable approach; and Gable was King), that is still technique of a sort; and, yes, you either have It or you don't. Monroe had It; how well did she use It?

In her earliest films, a model with no acting experience at all, Monroe has tiny parts, the kind that are often snipped out in editing. Her first lead role, however, comes in her third film, for Columbia, *Ladies of the Chorus* (1948), a shortish B-budget musical, horrendous in every aspect: stupid-showgirl-loves-aristocrat plot, wretched songs, insipid leading man, risible finale wherein the aristocrat's mother says she was a showgirl once, too. Monroe is inadequate, though not ghastly. Two years later, she got a walk-on, but a prominent one, in the last Marx Brothers comedy, *Love Happy* (1950), slinking into detective

Groucho's office to enlist his help. It seems that men are following her.

The parts got larger, though she has little better than the same sort of walk-on in *All About Eve* (1950) as George Sanders' date at Bette Davis' welcome-home party for Gary Merrill. Mankiewicz sets Monroe off elegantly. The part itself is dumb blonde at its purest, all style and no content (Sanders introduces her as "a graduate of the Copacabaña School of Dramatic Art"); but where in *Love Happy* she was an absurd vision of no reference to the story, in *All About Eve* she is an element of the theatre world, and moves with flair. She's learning, and her walk-on days are over. By 1953, a promising property in the Twentieth Century–Fox inventory, Monroe takes her first challenge in *Niagara* (1953), as Joseph Cotten's wife, scheming to become his widow. That same year Monroe broke into stardom with a solid vehicle, *Gentlemen Prefer Blondes,* from Anita Loos's linchpin twenties satire via its latest incarnation, a Broadway musical with Carol Channing as gold digger Lorelei Lee.

The Channing show made much of the original's twenties setting. Fox updated the film, threw out most of the Jule Styne–Leo Robin score, and handed Monroe (as Lorelei), Jane Russell (as her sidekick), and an assortment of admiring men to Howard Hawks, so canny at improvising with Lombard, Hepburn, and Russell. How he dealt with Monroe is not clear, but hers is a finished performance in characterization, choreography, and It. Loos wrote Lorelei as a dope; Monroe plays her as intelligent but uneducated, shrewd rather than bright. While Jane Russell is out looking for romance with or without a bank balance, Monroe seeks security. Typically, her big number is "Diamonds Are a Girl's Best Friend" while Russell's is "[Ain't there] Anyone Here For Love?" Lorelei tells Russell, "I want you to find happiness and stop having fun." Yes, it does make sense. She means: "I want you to stop ignoring the future and find a wealthy man to keep you comfortable."

At times Lorelei shoots wide of the mark. Arriving at the pier preparing to cross the Atlantic, Monroe asks, "Pardon me, is this the way to Europe, France?" But "I can be smart," she says, "when it's important." She can, in fact, reason out the politics of gender and reveal the morality behind her exploitation of men far better than they can reason theirs of her. "A man being rich is like a girl being pretty," she tells us: two different forms of power. If Monroe could have taken Lorelei's advice, she might have realized that she was not a victim of the patriarchal studio but one of its potential humiliators. Jane Russell was bigger than Monroe at the time, and took top billing, but *Gentlemen Prefer Blondes* made Monroe the woman to watch in Hollywood.

Few other newcomers have been given such an appropriate part for their first big one and so little competition from the rest of the cast. Russell is fun, sure. But when a late plot turn finds her standing in for Lorelei in court and breaking into "Diamonds Are a Girl's Best

Friend," vamping and yelling all over the place, we realize that Monroe has style. And the men are horrors. Monroe's fiancé, Tommy Noonan, is a sissy; his father, Taylor Holmes, is a grouch; Russell's beau, Elliott Reid, is devious; and Monroe's pet flirt, Charles Coburn, is silly and vain. Note that they have all the qualities that sexist folklore commonly ascribes to women. In some ways, *Gentlemen Prefer Blondes* is shockingly feminist, however inadvertently.

One reason Monroe is good in these showgirl parts is her exhibitionism. She liked to wear clothes that showed off her figure. She posed for a camera with casual abandon and tossed off sexy little movements of leg and hip in the dance numbers with aplomb. *Photoplay* singled her out as Hollywood's debutante of the year, more or less, and she dressed for the awards banquet to show off the reasons why, in excruciatingly tight gold lamé with a décolletage as rich as a jeweler's window. If Monroe had had a sense of humor, one might guess that she had meant to spoof the idea of glamour, but she was probably just trying to look her best in her own way. Surely this was the wrong place—and the wrong era—for such a demonstration. (Joe di Maggio, her boyfriend and later her second husband, refused to accompany her in her costume; columnist Sidney Skolsky stepped in for him.) Worse yet, when Monroe walked in, Hollywood's gentlemanly elite behaved like a troop of randy boy scouts. Emcee Jerry Lewis, bound as always by his exquisite good taste, jumped up on a table and did his celebrated imitation of a gorilla in rut.

A few days later, Joan Crawford had her say on the matter in an interview with Bob Thomas. "There's nothing wrong with my tits," she raged, "but I don't go around throwing them in people's faces." Thomas, of course, couldn't print that. What he did print was fierce enough: "It was like a burlesque show," says Crawford. "Apparently Miss Monroe is making the mistake of believing her publicity. . . . She should be told that the public likes provocative feminine personalities; but it also likes to know underneath it all the actresses are ladies." Thomas thinks Crawford was motivated more by jealousy than anything else. But when she says, "Those of us in the industry just shuddered," she seems to be denouncing Monroe as an inauthentic star, lacking the true glamour that Hollywood and its public agreed upon long before as acceptable, practicable, and self-reinforcing. But isn't that the glamour that stinks of illness in *Sunset Boulevard*? Anyway, wasn't cleavage and availability what Hollywood wanted from Monroe? If she had attended the banquet in the nude, it would have been the first absolutely moral act committed in Hollywood.

By 1955, Monroe was ready to reign as one of the world's famous women and the most resonant of sex symbols. In *The Seven Year Itch* (1955), she is treated as the essential erotic object in a film that won its popularity entirely as a daydream for the nation's frustrated men. The film says, What if you were a paunchy, aging husband who packs wife and child off on vacation, with the summer to yourself? What if the most dazzling blonde who ever drew breath moved into the apartment above yours? What if you invited her down for a drink and she said:

MONROE: Why, thanks! I'd love it!

It's a brainless, boring film, smut for idiots, and, amazing to report, it was the work of Billy Wilder, from a stage hit. Tom Ewell plays the husband engagingly enough; who couldn't? Monroe is what makes it go, right from her entrance carrying groceries and an electric fan, into a dallying ass shot as she goes up the stairs. On her second appearance, looking down on Ewell in his garden, she appears to be nude and explains that she keeps her underthings in the refrigerator. Later, out on a walk with Ewell, she exults and preens as steam blows up under her dress from a sidewalk grating. (Again, di Maggio, watching the location filming in New York, was disturbed by the excesses of sex-symbol imagism but helpless to interfere.) Never has the course of the sex hunt run so smoothly as it does for Ewell with Monroe. From reel to reel, she is nothing but a tasty on a tray.

However, for her work as Cherie, the tank-town "chantoosie" of *Bus Stop* (1956), Monroe was saluted as a comedienne of imagination and point. Her little nobody's dreams of being a somebody are cogently expressed, her lack of talent deftly revealed in an amusingly terrible "That Old Black Magic"—anyone can sing badly, but it's tricky to sing just badly enough—and her climactic acceptance of a humble if pleasant future as a cowboy's wife is believable. Yet, on the arch of success, Monroe was personally on the decline. She was already impossible to work with—late, angry, blowing countless takes on the simplest lines, ignoring director Joshua Logan to confer with her acting coach, and ruthless with her colleagues. There was no question of firing her, though, for she was making Fox a mint. And she must have fascinated her employers just as she did the public. Monroe was an innovation in Hollywood's no-fault glamour complex in that she was the most glamorous of all yet, apparently, couldn't believe it herself. In *Bus Stop,* the manager of the club where she sings calls her "an ignorant hillbilly." Arthur O'Connell says she's "just a gal who works in a saloon." Cowboy Don Murray thinks she's "an angel." It's Murray who's right, by the laws of romance. Yet Monroe had a bad time either being or acting an angel.

The acting problem is relatively easy to understand, for by this time Monroe had undertaken study at the Actors Studio with Lee Strasberg in hopes of becoming a Serious Actress. The Method, which Strasberg derived from Stanislafsky, had stirred an idealistic young generation of stage actors in the late 1940s, most remarkably represented by Marlon Brando's Stanley Kowalski in *A Streetcar Named Desire*. Here was the antidote of the tired grand manner left over from the days of James O'Neill and Mrs. Fiske, with its opulent entrances and Big Moments. Nazimova, of course, had led the trend away from artificiality, but she had her entrances and her Moments even so. Method actors went all the way, often getting so inside their roles as to be unaware of the theatre, of an audience. These weren't plays anymore, but life experiences. Exactly, for Method discipline deals with an actor's personal history, his or her emotional memory. That's where the problem came in for Monroe, because, as many commentators have noted, someone with her painful past would be digging into long-buried traumas in every scene. If she really was a totally unloved and sometimes molested child, then her workdays must have been harrowing. It would also explain her lateness as a reluctance to face up to her past. After all, love and sex were her demons, yet love and sex were what her parts were made of.

Then why didn't she play other kinds of parts? With her power, and her own production company (formed after *Bus Stop*), she could have played anything that Hollywood could tackle. But this Hollywood couldn't tackle anything but love and sex with someone like Monroe in the picture; there just isn't any other kind of Hollywood. So her work was destroying her, and it communicated in a craze to those who shared that work.

On the other hand, she may have been a creep, lazy, selfish, and opportunistic. Certainly her close relationships follow the opportunist's pattern of joyful acquaintance, profitable association, and abrupt departure when all the gains are taken in. Arthur Miller, Monroe's third husband, might be seen as a sometime Monroe chattel, the intellectual archon she adopts to support her highbrow ambitions. Yet he was blamed for using her when he made the character Maggie in his play *After the Fall* (beautifully played by Barbara Loden) a reasonable facsimile of Monroe.

Laurence Olivier, in *The Prince and the Showgirl* (1957), calls her "an unruly child," and this seems the closest epithet so far. How else to explain her being stupid and empty one hour and insightful the next? No one could credit her aspirations—her stated hopes of playing Grushenka in *The Brothers Karamazof* or the tomey books she carted around—for she was often vague, even non-verbal. *The Prince and the Showgirl* might have emancipated her in a cultural sense, for it was a spiffy project, filmed in England, with a script by Terence Rattigan (from his play) and directed by co-star Olivier.

Had Monroe applied herself, she might have won respect as a professional. Instead she played her tricks, alienating the British press, disregarding Olivier's direction to consult with coach Paula Strasberg, so slowing up progress on the set that everybody aged ten years, and then apologizing to the company on the last day, explaining that she had been ill. To be just, the press was hoping to dislike her and Olivier's approach to acting was pre-Method and could never have suited Monroe. Still, she's a selfish goof-off. On *Some Like It Hot* (1959), she took so long to warm up in her love scene with Tony Curtis that by the time she was on he was exhausted, at less than his best; and Jack Lemmon stood there and stood there while Monroe flubbed the line "It's me, Sugar" forty-seven times. Yet at other moments she would rattle off a long scene effortlessly, character and timing in trim. She might have said, "I can turn it on or put it on hold."

Some Like It Hot's co-author and director, Billy Wilder (one of the few directors willing to tackle her twice), asked "whether Marilyn is a person at all or one of the greatest du Pont products ever invented. She has breasts like granite; she defies gravity; and she has a brain like Swiss cheese—full of holes. . . . She arrives late and tells you she couldn't find the studio and she's been working there for years. There are certain wonderful rascals in the world, like Monroe, and one day they lie down on an analyst's couch and out comes a clenched, dreary thing. It's better for Monroe not to be straightened out. The charm of her is her two left feet." On the other hand, he said also that not till filming was over and Wilder fully recovered from the ordeal could he look at his wife "without wanting to hit her because she is a woman."

The fascination with Monroe's paradoxes was dimming among moviemakers, but for the public she was worth the trouble. *Some Like It Hot* is an American comic classic, and Monroe gives a superb performance. In terms of plot, the film belongs to Curtis and Lemmon as musicians who flee Chicago in drag with an all-girl band to hide out in Florida from gangsters (who of course turn up in the band's hotel for a gangsters' convention). However, once Monroe enters to a jazzy muted trumpet as Sugar Kane, the band's ukulele-banging vocalist—"jello on springs," Lemmon comments—the eye never leaves her. She plays herself: that is, she plays the person people know of from her legend. A dumb blonde, naturally, easily hurt, humiliated by the collapse of her foolish dreams, a clumsy liar, an inefficient gold digger. In the band, as in life, she can't obey even the simplest rules, is always late, and makes some odd liaisons. Curtis, in stolen yachting togs and a devastating Cary Grant imitation, impersonates a millionaire, and Monroe makes a play for him, assuring him that she's a society girl who joined the band for a lark. Society got dull, with the limp dances, banal watering places, "and always the same four hundred." Curtis pretends that he has no libido, and Monroe gives him a kissing lesson that remains one of the funniest erotic hits in film. It would be interesting to see what it looked like at about take five, when Curtis was going for it and Monroe not yet trying.

However she behaved on the set, she *is* the film. Even her songs are autobiographical: "Running Wild" for tone, "I Want to Be Loved by You" for theme, and, her plans in disarray, "I'm Through with Love." And, however she felt as a person, as star and actress she had reached the summit. In the stage musical *On the Twentieth Century* (from the same source as the Lombard-Barrymore film), a movie-hating stage wizard assaults his former protégée's screen success as a round of shallow flamboyance. "Shopgirls ape you," he taunts, and in their dreams "farmhands rape you." Everyone wants to touch base with the stars.

But Monroe's stardom was so rich that every studio could produce a Monroe and the lode might still yield indefinitely. The 1950s were dumb-blonde years for Hollywood, even as the competition from television forced moviemakers to investigate adult subject matter that television couldn't treat. Suddenly (the trend had actually started in the 1940s, but it looked sudden) movies about or touching on bigotry, drug addiction, and official corruptions of all kinds had become almost common. Yet here was Hollywood auditioning every sexy blonde it could find in hopes of contracting workable Monroe imitations.

It is a tribute to Monroe's talent that no worthwhile successor could be found. Apparently what she did wasn't as easy as it looks, and looks aren't everything. Yet some of the Monroe spinoffs became prominent. Columbia's Kim Novak, for instance, was one of the top box-office stars even while Monroe was at her height in the late 1950s. She was nothing at all like Monroe in effect, it turned out—stiff on the set and sure of herself off, where Monroe was liquid love in a film and a mess elsewhere. Novak had great eyes, but her face sat as still as a mask. She got started the same way Monroe did, the way all would-be Monroes did in the early 1950s, the era of the starlet, once defined by Ben Hecht as "any woman under the age of thirty not actively employed in a brothel."

The starlet overturned the traditional Hollywood codes for talent-plus-looks or talent-despite-looks, for the starlet was nothing but looks, a woman with no training or experience as an actor who had simply aroused a photographer's interest. On the basis of the stills sessions, she became someone, with a new glamaglitta name and possibly an agent. She attended parties. She met producers. Columnists told of her. She had reduced the acting profession to a pinup of herself. Monroe's was a nude pinup, prone against red velvet. Later, when a blackmailer threatened to expose the faux pas, her studio decided to go with it, leaking the accusation themselves so Monroe could touchingly confess and leave it to the public to support or reject her. Full support. It was the age of the pinup, *così fan tutte.*

Novak had no past to bother her, and she took splendid stills, but she managed to cooperate with the PR people without helping them much. A Columbia publicist reports that she left most of the questions on her PR file blank. "She filled in her name, address, phone number, agent, and the fact that she likes to ride a bike." Nor was she thrilled to lose her name, Marilyn Novak. She conceded on her given name, but wouldn't deny her family. Not much to work with. Still, they took it and built her exhaustively—grooming, fashioning, publicizing. She even turned up in a few movies.

Here the lack of training told on her. Novak was frosty, uncomprehending, dull. She wasn't a dumb blonde, which is lucky, for only a comedienne—from Jean Harlow through Judy Holliday to Goldie Hawn—has made the type work. Rather, Novak played romantic women—a smalltown prom queen in *Picnic* (1956), a naive showgirl in *Pal Joey* (1957), a witch who must turn mortal to love in *Bell, Book and Candle* (1957). She had important co-stars—Tyrone Power, Frank Sinatra, William Holden, James Stewart, Fredric March. She did *Vertigo* (1958) with Alfred Hitchcock, and lucked into the historic *Kiss Me, Stupid* (1964) controversy, when a smutty but hardly revolutionary sex comedy by Billy Wilder caused the righteous hosts to threaten a bluenose boycott for the last time in Hollywood history.

Three years after *Kiss Me, Stupid*, any hopes of monitoring the movies for too much honesty would have come to nothing, but in 1964 this satire on bed switching, with Novak as the hooker, Polly the Pistol, was a test case. Even the defiant Wilder called some actors back to reshoot scenes. It's ironic that Monroe never had this problem, for if Novak is sexy mainly because the script informs us so, Monroe really styled sex for her audiences, here vulnerably and there masterfully, for serious and for fun.

By the late 1960s, Novak had lost her status. Zero Mostel takes the top billing in *The Great Bank Robbery* (1969), a western spoof with familiar faces in the genre parts: Clint Walker as the sheriff, Claude Akins as a brutal outlaw, Elisha Cook, Jr., as his fawning sidekick, Akim Tamiroff and Larry Storch as bandidos. Novak, as Mostel's partner in crime, is much livelier than before but still no actress, overplaying or missing the sense of things. She's funny in her scenes with Walker, because she has finally come up against an actor who's even stiffer than she is. After she pulls Walker close and paws him wildly, she asks, "D'ya like it?" and he replies, "Just 'cause I talk slow don't mean I'm peculiar." Later, when Mostel urges her to take Walker on a picnic to clear the coast for a scheme, she says, "What if he attacks me?" and Mostel replies, "That's a chance he'll have to take."

In the film's general air of burlesque, Novak's part is clearly meant to lampoon the fifties pinup, but it doesn't quite come over, because the trope died out too fast. Monroe's imitations, in fact, killed it, with their putrid starlet cynicism. Even Novak, still somewhat employable, pulled out of the business in the late 1970s except for an occasional turn (including an amusing bitch-in with Elizabeth Taylor in the Agatha Christie mystery *The Mirror Crack'd* at the top of the 1980s).

However, one other in this line, not so much a competitor as a replica of Monroe, never gave up. Stardom was so dear to her that she would appear in Italian muscleman quickies and even porn—anything with a camera aimed at it.

This was Jayne Mansfield, a coarse, pixilated version of Monroe. Starlets aspire to stardom above all, but Mansfield aspired to Monroedom, and was snapped at a New York first-night party in 1955 ogling her idol. Perhaps Mansfield only meant to study the matrix, but in the photograph she looks as if she'd like to gobble her up (Monroe herself seems startled); and while the two did not speak, Mansfield spent the time watching and measuring. She was in a way the biggest Monroe fan.

Mansfield's films are grotesque, crummy jokes exploiting her over-blown figure (40-18-36), her risibly quivering mouth, her clopping walk and squealing sounds, her pestering need for attention. Her imitation of Monroe was so preposterous that Broadway couldn't figure out if she was kidding or for real when she played a Monroe type in George Axelrod's spoof of stardom *Will Success Spoil Rock Hunter?* in 1955. She was if nothing else funny, and moved on to Hollywood for *The Girl Can't Help It* (1957), an insulting one-joke comedy, the joke being the effect of Mansfield's endowment on men. Even the milkman's stock bubbles out of the bottles, and ice melts.

Director Frank Tashlin filmed Mansfield as if he had never seen a woman's breasts before, and Mansfield giggles through the action as if any lead part is ipso facto a tribute. Later that same year she repeated her *Rock Hunter* role, and now she was the toast of cinema. But the fun angled in at an odd tangent, for it was Monroe's studio, Fox, that sponsored these Mansfield fribbles, thereby doubling the spoof, canceling it out, making all Hollywood an infinite burlesque without values. If Fox believes in the dumb blonde love goddess enough to make Monroe its top star, how can it also turn out cheap rip-offs of its own star program? It's like learning that Giuseppe Verdi directed the *Il Trovatore*-wrecking finale of *A Night at the Opera.*

Mansfield had every reason to think she had made it, for by the close of 1957 she appeared with Cary Grant in *Kiss Them for Me,* was dominating the columns, and had attached another point of sex stardom by pairing off with Mickey Hargitay, formerly one of the boys in Mae West's nightclub act. But this was the end of the line; Mansfield's stardom proved even shorter than Betty Bronson's. A Fox western in 1959 completed her contract. Her next opus was *The Loves of Hercules* (1960), an Italian bomb with Hargitay, and the following films, till her death in an automobile accident, were unmentionable garbage.

There were no alternate Monroes to be had. If the talentless Novak and the deluded Jayne Mansfield are the most famous of Monroe's doppelgängers, imagine what the failures were like. What separated them from Monroe? Gall? Will? Luck? What was glamour, now that it was becoming democratically but indiscriminately open to all? What would Marshall Neilan have listed as the essentials for stardom if he could see what was turning up in movies in the 1950s? In Florence Lawrence's day, when stardom was invented, glamour depended on intimacy, on the contact between movie personalities and the audience. All the public needed to know was a name. By the 1920s, glamour was beauty; the public was awed by rather than comfortable with stars. In the 1930s, glamour was wit; the public was charmed. By the 1950s, glamour became fame, and not necessarily anything else. People who had nothing to give could dream of coming in, hanging around, and taking it. For if stardom had been the preserve of the elect, the stories that these stars took part in telling were about sharing and working for something. The movies were made by processes of discrimination, but the movies *taught* egalitarianism. If one saw and believed enough movies, one could, like a starlet, expect that stardom was a civil right. Fame had become its own means and end.

Old Hollywood—the retirees of the Griffith, late silent, and early talkie years—looked balefully upon those who displaced them. As Swanson says, "*We* had faces." What they thought of the starlet syndrome is an open guess, but one thing that must have struck a loud chord of recognition among them was Monroe's passing in 1962, for mysterious deaths were as much a part of the Hollywood structure as swimming pools and cover marriages. Glamour, too, belongs to that tradition, as does talent. The two used to work hand in hand, each taking up whatever slack the other let fall, so that in the 1920s you had, say, a Swanson for glamour and Little Mary exercising her talent; or Janet Gaynor and George O'Brien providing the glamour in *Sunrise,* while director Murnau developed the film artistically.

But by the 1950s, glamour didn't need talent, maybe didn't want it. The question of talent obscures the certainty of beauty and fame. When Paramount screened *Sunset Boulevard* for a group of Old Hollywood notables, the veterans cheered the film and raved over Swanson, probably seeing it as her comeback vehicle and a likely success that would vindicate their tradition. But Little Mary Pickford was nowhere to be seen when the lights came up. Someone told Swanson that Pickford was too "overcome" to stick around. Perhaps Pickford was saddened that she hadn't taken the part herself. It was offered to her before it went to Swanson. But perhaps she, more than the rest, saw what *Sunset Boulevard* said about the business that Pickford had made her life's work. It says glamour is a goon.

# 14

# Comics II

JUDY HOLLIDAY
AUDREY HEPBURN
MADELINE KAHN
MISS PIGGY
LILY TOMLIN
GOLDIE HAWN

*After so many drive-in waitresses . . .
here is class.*

—BILLY WILDER
on Audrey Hepburn

*Mary Jean, nobody's going to pay good
money to see people from the
neighborhood.*

—LILY TOMLIN'S MOTHER
to young Lily

American comedy went dumb in the 1950s; no one has yet explained why. From the screwball 1930s through the more farcical 1940s of Preston Sturges and others, we come to the dead 1950s, when "sex comedies" (usually about not getting it: "no-sex comedies") abounded, and neither viewpoint nor social instincts informed the films Americans went to for fun.

As comedy ailed, so did comics. An American idea of the comic in the 1950s was Jerry Lewis, who does spoofs of the handicapped. I don't think this is funny.* The comedians we knew of in the 1930s—the dada vaudevillians like the Marx Brothers, the satirists like Mae West, the character comediennes like Carole Lombard—this collage of backgrounds and experiences and approaches to craft faded away.

An actress like Judy Holliday stood out, for almost alone she upheld character comedy, the kind of performing that gets far more out of a keenly observed line of text than a prefabricated yok. A highly cultivated and intelligent woman with a zany streak and an unfortunate tendency to carry slightly more weight than was conducive to show-biz success, Holliday found her niche in cabaret, where zaniness outranked physique. Partnered by Betty Comden and Adolph Green, among oth-

---

*Of course, Jerry Lewis also does charity television craze-ins, called "telethons," *for* the handicapped. I think this is funny.

ers, Holliday took the act to Hollywood, where Darryl Zanuck signed them to serve his loosely plotted musicals with specialty larks.

However, the gang's humor was too New York for the audiences that thronged to the Faye-Grable-Haver vehicles. Their first try was *Greenwich Village* (1944), a project with an unappetizing title, second-rank stars (Carmen Miranda, Don Ameche, Vivian Blaine, and William Bendix in the leads), and an insufferable score. It was their last. Fox snipped out almost all the Holliday-Comden-Green footage, used Holliday in tiny parts in two other films, and dropped the whole matter.

It's too bad that Fox couldn't see Holliday's potential, because she spent five years establishing herself on Broadway before she returned to film, and only got eight good movie roles before she died in 1965. But at Zanuck's lot the women were either conventional heroines like Grable or Haver or novelties like Miranda. All the more surprising, then, that Holliday made her breakthrough in the most conventional of types, the dumb blonde: Billie Dawn in Garson Kanin's play *Born Yesterday* (1946). Replacing an insecure Jean Arthur at the last minute, Holliday set a pattern for this character that held for decades, with its crackpot voice range from squeak to bellow, its silly platinum permanent, its one-of-a-kind accent (midwestern Brooklyn comes closest), and prize put-down: "Do me a fava? Drop dead!" This Billie Dawn is the ideal setting for a gifted actress, though Kanin had quite some time talking Columbia's Harry Cohn into letting Holliday do the film version. Cohn gave in, and Holliday triumphed.

In the Hollywood fashion, Holliday won the Best Actress Oscar, a high-paying contract with Cohn, and the right to play dumb blondes for the rest of her life.

No way. Holliday didn't so much turn down dumb blonde parts as turn them around to show her daffy, intelligent side. Her first film after *Born Yesterday* wasn't even a comedy. In *The Marrying Kind* (1952), Holliday and husband Aldo Ray, on the brink of divorce, tell their problems to a sympathetic judge (a woman, by the way). The two definitely belong together, but his career frustrations, the death of their child in a swimming accident, and working-class claustrophobia have soured them. The judge helps them put their house in order by the end, but the real work is done by the two leads, her cynical innocence and his awkward tenderness matching them as two unalike but perfectly balanced bookends.

Obviously, *The Marrying Kind* was a change for Holliday in form and tone. But the succeeding *It Should Happen to You* (1954), the second Kanin-Cukor entry in which Holliday is caught between a plutocrat and an egghead, might well have sent Holliday back into Billie Dawn territory. No—again Holliday found a precise individuality in the character. Her Gladys Glover is the kind of woman whom dull people call oddball. Noting that the southwest curve of Manhattan's Columbus

Circle sports a huge billboard for rent, she rents it and has her name painted on it. Why not? Jack Lemmon, in his first film, plays her dull boyfriend, the egghead, flabbergasted by her profligacy. "What sort of a fruitcake are you?" he screams. What business is it of his? "Why do you have to be *above* the crowd?" he goes on. "Why not part of the crowd?" She is rightfully scornful, and ups the stakes when plutocrat Peter Lawford offers her six signs in exchange for her one. He has a thing about the southwest curve of Columbus Circle. Naturally, the Gladys Glover signs attract comment, and Holliday becomes famous. For what? Well, Kanin points out, you don't have to be famous for something. Famous is itself enough.

What could have made a dandy screwball satire on fame sags half-way through on a "make love not fame" tangent so Holliday and Lemmon can form a couple. Holliday was better served by *The Solid Gold Cadillac* (1956), from the Kaufman-Teichmann stage hit about a little old lady who takes over a big corporation run by crooks. The role was revamped for Holliday, but again she defeated the Billie Dawn suggestions with wackiness merged by good sense. On one hand we get Holliday, company liaison with the stockholders, dictating a letter to a southern "colonel" in Dixie mushmouth. On the other, we get Holliday calmly disarming the practiced racketeers of the board and rousing the stockholders to oust them.

The rest of the story goes progressively limp. Holliday went back to Broadway in a third-rate musical, *Bells Are Ringing*, carrying the piece to glory and doing the film version with Dean Martin. But further Broadway stints flopped, her film offers all called for retreads of her previous parts, and she had not quite finished working on the lyrics to a musical version of Anita Loos's play *Happy Birthday* (Gerry Mulligan was doing the music) when cancer took her at the age of forty-three. Her victory over dumb-blonde typing is exemplary, especially given the era's fondness for the character; but she conquered it in pleasant but hardly irreplaceable films that weren't as good as *Born Yesterday*. A tragic waste.

Directly contradistinctive to Holliday was Audrey Hepburn, light of touch where Holliday was earthy, a cosmopolitan gamine. Hepburn is contradistinctive to all Hollywood, to her very time and place; she is too subtle a soul to tolerate Hollywood's heavy hand. Yet she thrived. She set style, not only in her Givenchy clothes but in her slim, gently accented poise. She seemed like the waif of eight countries raised to nobility, and there is a touch of romance in her background. Part Belgian and part Irish-English, young Hepburn was schooled in Holland, lived there during the German occupation, saw some action in the anti-Nazi underground, became a model and then a Broadway deb in Anita Loos's adaptation of Colette's *Gigi*, in 1951. Hepburn was so unlike the starlets who were flooding Hollywood in the 1950s that her confident presence instantly created a new type of ingenue—mischievous, educated, impeccable. Pictures that were dying to be done but couldn't be cast because all the newcomers were bum suddenly found backers—always with the proviso that Hepburn take the indicated role.

Frank Capra had spent years trying to produce *Roman Holiday,* a droll romance about a runaway princess who falls in step with an American reporter. It was the kind of thing Hollywood could have made with one camera and a costume trunk in the 1930s. Capra himself brought off a classic version of the premise in *It Happened One Night* with Clark Gable and Claudette Colbert. But Capra couldn't find the cast, and he sold the property to William Wyler, who caught Hepburn on the western end of the *Gigi* tour, paired her with Gregory Peck as the journalist, and unveiled *Roman Holiday* (1953) to the public's delight and the industry's amazement. A Best Actress Oscar was the least of Hepburn's rewards.

The most was a spate of parts conceived or tailored specifically for Hepburn—variations on the runaway princess, the Cinderella, the innocent on a fling. In *Sabrina* (1954), she was a chauffeur's daughter who charms the Long Island estate set; in *Funny Face* (1957) she was the bookworm who becomes a fashion model; in *Green Mansions* (1959) she was a forest sprite. There were earnest excursions, too, as Natasha in King Vidor's *War and Peace* (1956); as a nun who breaks her vows to fight the Nazis in *The Nun's Story* (1959); as one of the two women destroyed by slander in *The Children's Hour* (1961), the second filming of Lillian Hellman's play and the first to deal with the homosexuality in the original story.

Both Holliday and Hepburn were limited performers in that their physique, voice, and style worked best in certain kinds of stories and settings. But notice how varied Hepburn's films were compared to Holliday's. Both were supreme comediennes, yet both had to move out of their natural state to keep working, Holliday to the stage and Hepburn to non-comic parts.*

There was so little charm in the 1950s that Hepburn had to supply more than her share. She brightens *Funny Face,* a musical about glamour, by showing how unaffected genuine chic must be. Fred Astaire plays a photographer and Kay Thompson a Voguish magazine editor eager to freshen the layouts. A brainstorm: set the models against highbrow decor. Hunting for, as Thompson puts it, "one of those sinister places in Greenwich Village," the fashion gang invades a bookstore, heartlessly wrecking the place and ignoring the protests of the clerk, Hepburn. In one shot, she is asked to pose with a model, holding up

---

*Even here Hepburn's knickknacky delivery, every line an *object,* lightens the atmosphere. *Charade* (1963), a violent thriller with Hepburn, Cary Grant, and some vicious heavies, reads as suspense but plays, because of Hepburn, as a comedy.

some books for the intellectual touch. The model displays her lifeless poses while Hepburn stares incredulously and finally asks, "What*ever* are you doing?" This anti-glamour girl has more glamour than all starlets put together: dignity, a mind. Astaire, the first in the film to see Hepburn's visual potential, cites her "character, spirit, intelligence," when insisting that Thompson try her out. Thompson, ruled by conventional rules for glamour, considers Hepburn dubiously. "The bones are good," she admits.

It's always more than bones, or Hedy Lamarr would have been the biggest star in Hollywood history. Talent was selling cheap these days, and made something like a last stand in Hepburn, for the actress worked completely outside the It rituals. Her class wasn't an act; Hepburn carried her poise everywhere she went, though she occasionally happened into shlock. *Paris When It Sizzles* (1964), a romantic comedy about a written-out screenwriter (William Holden) getting help from his typist (Hepburn), was so dumb it was kept on ice for two years before being released. It's typical of its day, a premise of possibilities (we see the script enacted, film-within-film, as the two leads concoct it) that are never realized. Sample joke: Holden is a vampire chasing Hepburn around his laboratory-cave, and the camera settles on his table of appurtenances—including Heinz steak sauce. Worse than anything in the film itself, in the way of consumeristic star marketing, is the credit "wardrobe and perfume by Hubert de Givenchy." Perfume? Were the producers contemplating the release of specially treated smellovision prints?

Hepburn is too well liked to be blamed for her poor films, because the good ones are special. Consider *Breakfast at Tiffany's* (1961). Directed by Blake Edwards from George Axelrod's script—the whole taken from Truman Capote's longish short story—*Breakfast at Tiffany's* felt like the northeastern sophisticate's rebuttal to the repressively middle-American texture of fifties culture. In the 1950s, the exceptional events in film were fast flops and the genre programmers the hits. So, after a decade largely made of Biblical spectacles, schoolboy sex jokes, and westerns, a comedy about a hooker moving along New York's fast track—and a comedy as deft as it claims its protagonist is—was a knockout. Or is she a hooker? Men she has abandoned in the wee hours at some club are always pounding at her door by dawn, yet we never see her actually make a rendezvous. Indeed, she seems a bit shocked when she sees Patricia Neal leaving George Peppard money in the nest Neal has rented for kept boy Peppard. Says Hepburn, "I must say, she keeps late hours for a decorator."

She's a child. Capote called her Holly Golightly and wrote of her ambiguously. The movie retains the contradictions in her personality, and who but Hepburn could have played them so nicely? Beautifully dressed outside, she'll answer the door in a man's dress shirt, eye-patches, and earplugs. She's frail, but she can whistle for a taxi. She lives well on a mere hundred dollars a week to commute to Sing Sing to carry cryptic messages between a gangster and his lawyer. She has access to the rich and famous, yet befriends an unknown writer, Peppard. She says, "I can't think of anything I've never done," yet her pleasures are simple, her escapades dear—like stealing a Halloween mask from a five-and-dime—and her only intense relationship is with a brother she hasn't seen in years. "Is she or isn't she?" agent Martin Balsam asks Peppard at a bash at Holly's. Is she or isn't she what? A phony. Balsam says she is—and she isn't. She's "a real phony."

She's a professional orphan—no ties, no rules. She won't admit to owning anything, or being owned, and not only walks out on her own party, but helpfully points out the location to police who have been summoned by a neighbor's complaint. Capote had her fleeing the Peppard character at the end, fearful of touch, but in the film Hepburn and Peppard unite, to a last reprise of the theme song, "Moon River." Surely, any other actress would have made the moment gooey—too willing to love, too understanding. Hepburn's natural cool matches the remoteness of the glow in "Moon River," the sound of which is *Breakfast at Tiffany's* in miniature: lyrical, serene, too suspicious of sentiment to have more than a "huckleberry friend," yet, in the end, tearfully sentimental. This is Holly and Hepburn at once, and the reluctant willingness explains why she seemed so fresh in each part, no matter how often one had seen her before. It was not her poise. It was her curious way of slipping into romance with as many misgivings as enthusiasms.

She's a moon calf, a comedienne of delicate eccentricities, too often wasted in Serious Roles of no genuine importance, so that in King Vidor's somewhat less than Tolstoyan *War and Peace* she is not so much the best thing in the film as the least worst. In *My Fair Lady* (1964) she is too able to be called wrong for the part, yet she can't be right for it. Besides having no voice for one of the American musical's most dashing parts, Hepburn's persona—and perhaps talent—is too chic to suggest the Cockney guttersnipe; and her transformation into a lady of style, on which the whole action turns, went for nothing, because Hepburn already is that lady. Most importantly, projects like *War and Peace* and *My Fair Lady* obscure Hepburn's eminence as a comedienne. Casting her in epic lit and musical comedy suggests that she is an all-purpose star, the kind who is supposed to be special in anything because glamour counts more than anything in the first place. But Hollywood was short of good women comics at this time, which is why Holliday and Hepburn, with their instincts for character rather than laffs, seem adventurous and genuine in comparison with their successors, who have come upon a scene largely endowed with nothing but a taste for spoof.

Thirties story comedy relied heavily on satire, *commenting* on its topic from a point of view; screwball comedy is the prime example. But fifties comedy approached its topics without a viewpoint, prodding for gags. This approach produced as its major event the sex comedies that Doris Day made for Universal and Fox, starting with *Pillow Talk* in 1959. The next stop, in broader decline, threw away the topic altogether, leaving only a setting as the basis for jokes of all kinds. In short: burlesque. With Woody Allen and Mel Brooks the reigning comic geniuses, American film comedy is not about anything, though it uses everything, or anything that happens along. It has its occasional subjects—Allen's Jewish paranoia, or Brooks's obsession with battle-axe women. But these are mere reference points, not developed themes. The cartoon style and lack of character content in these films give few opportunities for acting. The performers become vaudevillians with specialty stunts, or farceurs hamboning whole parts out in caricature deliveries.

In an increasingly unlettered and opportunistic culture, racist, sexist, take-the-loot-and-run burlesque has become extremely popular, and if it has a definitive woman star, that would be Madeline Kahn, a fixture of the Mel Brooks stock company and queen of spoof shtick. Kahn is a sharp comedienne, but she is limited by her audience's low cultural penetration; there is so little that most people have read or heard, that only the most flagrant allusions will register with them. Accordingly, Kahn deals in lavish clichés—Dietrich, MacDonald-Eddy operetta, nineteenth-century grand opera.

Yet when Kahn began her career, she was regarded as a talent with a very wide range—on Broadway. An operatic soprano voice with a keen top made her more than a comic; a Cunegonde in *Candide,* a Musetta in *La Bohème,* and a je ne sais quoi in the absurdist musical *Promenade* promised the musical stage a star to defeat type, redefining the old roles and helping to invent new ones. But the musical was ailing, and there weren't that many opportunities even for Kahn. Also, perhaps her experience in the Danny Kaye vehicle *Two by Two* (1970), soured her on Broadway. This adaptation of Clifford Odets' play *The Flowering Peach* followed the exploits of Noah and his family on the Ark with a dull book, a terrible score (music by Richard Rodgers), and very little for Kahn to do other than top her second-act spot, an execrable waltz entitled "The Golden Ram," with her high C.

Kahn tried Hollywood. But the film musical was in even worse shape than the Broadway kind, and the one Kahn made, Peter Bogdanovich's *At Long Last Love* (1975), was even worse than *Two by Two.* At that, the film, with a trove of Cole Porter songs set into a bungled screwball atmosphere, reserved the legitimate numbers for the romantic leads, leaving Kahn with the camp. "Find Me a Primitive Man," hot and kinky as written, was outfitted with jungle honk into a lampoon of nightclub vulgarity, all the libido mugged out of it. But then Kahn had already established a camp identity, first in Bogdanovich's *What's Up, Doc* (1972) as Ryan O'Neal's dowdy fiancée in a wig that looked like an enchanted cottage, and then in two Mel Brooks entries, *Blazing Saddles* (1974) and *Young Frankenstein* (1974), doing a Lola-Lola number, "I'm Tired," in the first and warbling "Ah! Sweet Mystery of Life" in the second while the monster made love to her.

Kahn's whole part in *Blazing Saddles* is nothing but a Lola-Lola stunt. As Lily von Stupp, Kahn puts on the throaty Dietrich laugh and the lisp; when bad guy Harvey Korman wants Kahn to "seduce and abandon" Sheriff Cleavon Little and asks, "Can you do it?" Kahn replies, "Ah haha! Is Bismarck a hewwing?" Some of this is undoubtedly funny, but the relentless Jewish jokes are stupid—if Brooks weren't Jewish one would think him America's leading anti-Semite—and Korman's calling Kahn a "Teutonic slut" is not a misfired joke but the outburst of a naughty little boy irritating the grownups with a no-no word.

*Blazing Saddles* gave Kahn, if nothing else, a film's worth of shtick. For *High Anxiety* (1977), an Alfred Hitchcock lampoon, Brooks neglected to assign Kahn a charade cue, and she relates to the action as fully as a crosstown bus rider relates to the bus: getting on, riding, getting off. Toward the end, eluding the police at an airport, Brooks and Kahn show up disguised as a Lower-East-Side-of-New-York Jewish couple. But she's not as adept at this turn as he is. Her accent is terrible; she even looks unhappy and bewildered. She wants to do *her* shtick, not his.

Oddly, Kahn had already done a beautiful job in a real part, all lampoon aside, in *Paper Moon* (1973), the film that justified Peter Bogdanovich's high reputation and won little Tatum O'Neal an Oscar as Addie Pray, the larcenous sidekick of a Bible Belt con man (Ryan O'Neal) in the Depression. Kahn played a small part in the film's center as Trixie Delight, the baby-talking hooker whom the con man picks up. Figuring herself Kahn's rival, Tatum at one point pulls a sit-down strike, a serious threat in a road picture. Nothing can move her—until Kahn picks her way up a hill on her bitty spike heels in her pathetic finery to intimidate, bribe, and at last beseech the little girl not to ruin this gig for her. It's a poignant, smartly underplayed passage, the only honest thing the character says in the whole picture. Kahn got an Oscar nomination for her role, too.

Why has Kahn had only Mel Brooks and the Brooks protégé Gene Wilder to guide her since? Probably for the same reason that one of the biggest of today's woman stars is so much a spoof that she isn't even human: Miss Piggy. One of the few television stars to negotiate a successful film career, Miss Piggy epitomizes the freak who through sheer will power overwhelms the conventions for beauty and talent. As designed and worked by Jim Henson's astonishingly nimble Muppeteers, Miss Piggy is oversize, pushy, disloyal, untalented, and unreasonable. She is a true child of the communications age: she has heard of nothing but stardom, so that's what she wants. No one, in any medium, would give it to her ordinarily; so on the *Muppets* television show, she comes on fighting, inventing a romance with the Muppet chief, Kermit the Frog, demanding and sometimes usurping heroine parts and specialty spots, and imitating the poses of stardom's folklore (most notably in a Muppets calendar in which she and Kermit appear in stills adapted from the resonant tropes of Hollywood's past).

The Muppets have made two films, setting the creatures' various personae into full-length narratives spiced with human celebrity cameos. In *The Muppet Movie* (1979), purportedly telling how the troupe got together in Hollywood, Miss Piggy surfaces at a small fair as "Miss Bogen County." Spotting Kermit in the crowd, she sings "Never Before" and suffers a dream vision of their love affair. The whole thing is burlesque, Miss Piggy's voice utterly defeated by the song's range (actually, her raspy instrument would have trouble with "Who's Afraid of the Big Bad Wolf?") and the vision ridiculing summer-afternoon-on-the-river idylls.

As with Brooks and Allen, the humor is detached in the modern style, functioning outside of narrative involvement rather than from within it. It's reminiscent of how the Marx Brothers worked, with direct address of the audience and a running report on the experience of making the film. Carole Lombard, Katharine Hepburn, and Jean Harlow played people; the Muppets play performers bemused or regaled by the quirks of their own production. Thus, the second time someone in *The Muppet Movie* asks, "Why don't you try Hare Krishna?" Kermit says, "Good grief, it's a running gag." It is not an accident that Madeline Kahn and Miss Piggy have become prominent in the same era; this is the age of spoof.

But spoof works well for an entire career only when writing can sustain it imaginatively (as it does for the Muppets), *and* when the artists have control of the producing apparatus (as Henson does) to keep their concepts free of incursions by the money bosses. Studio rule destroyed Buster Keaton (who allowed himself to be talked into a deal with MGM), hampered the Marx Brothers (when they left Paramount for MGM and Irving Thalberg kept trying to film musicals around them, as if they weren't complete in themselves), and disendowed Mae West. Now that most contracts are one-shot deals, most actors are their own bosses, so the unique comics should be thriving. The case of Lily Tomlin suggests that they are.

Countercultural stand-up comedy of the 1970s depended heavily on burlesque, and thus Tomlin got her start on television's *Laugh-In*, with her caricatures of Ernestine the telephone operator and Edith

Ann, the little girl in the rocking chair. Tomlin built up a repertory of more fully developed characters, no longer stand-up sketches but acting vignettes, virtually one-act plays. These characters carried Tomlin through her transition into one-person shows—Mrs. Beasley the suburban homemaker, tending to her laundry duties as the pilgrim tours a shrine; Sister Boogie Woman, a preacher; Crystal, the paraplegic hang-glider; a baglady who knows where the extraterrestrials are hiding; or the nameless pathetic girl who spends an urban ethnic-class prom talking about boys with her friend Margo. Tomlin's aesthetic touches on burlesque, yet she has more in common with monologuists like Ruth Draper than with the Steve Martins and Mel Brookses as she invests her characters with strengths that transcend their disabilities, whether cultural, physical, or emotional. As Tomlin must have been in her youth, they are marked by the whimsical intelligence that most people dislike or suspect. These characters see too clearly; they are too smart for their good. To defend themselves, they dream.

Soon enough it was clear that Tomlin was not a comedienne but an actress, for in her film roles she has laid these characters aside. In *Nashville* (1975) she played the leader of a gospel chorus dealing with the temptation of adultery. In *Moment by Moment* (1978) she played a traditionally romantic role with a modern edge. In *Nine to Five* (1980) she played the mildly embittered office worker disposing of a parasite boss. Not till *The Incredible Shrinking Woman* (1981) did she play a cartoon, as a housewife who goes by the book and develops an allergy to the products of Mrs. Beasley's world and begins to diminish physically, her affliction exploited by the media, the Corporation, and even her adman husband.

None of these parts steals from the others. In *Nashville* Tomlin is cool, a musician who has learned to expend life's potentially destructive energies in her work, leaving her home life secure. In *Moment by Moment* she went over to the other side, still cool but open to experimentation. *Nine to Five* calls for someone altogether different in style, archly commentative, cynical, loyal to her friends but something less than warm. "Welcome to the front lines," she says dryly, showing newcomer Jane Fonda around the office, adding, as the company spy approaches, "Uh-oh, here comes General Patton." *The Incredible Shrinking Woman*, a simplistic fantasy, made Tomlin a foil for the special-effects jokes (a champagne bottle as big as a pagoda, a horror trip into the underworld of the garbage disposal) and marketing greed.

There is little Tomlin cannot do. Many comediennes are limited by their autograph shtick, but Tomlin has none. (Anyway, she is a comic only in the sense that she writes and performs material that is often funny; this has nothing to do with her film roles.) Her approach to the highways of fame is radical. She gives wonderfully offbeat interviews with no personal sensationalism, approaches talk shows with no adherence to their set tempo and ersatz Topics, and once walked off one because she disliked the tone of the talk. Tomlin shouldn't have made it. Yet she has achieved what most artists hope to achieve and what few, in the popular arts, have successfully done: made the audience face itself. Her housewife is not a spoof; Mrs. Beasley *is* a housewife. Sister Boogie Woman is a preacher who has crossed the line that divides earthly hip from bizarroland. The baglady, too, is genuine, a seer of big-city paranoia. It's not that Tomlin's characters are so real they're funny, or so funny they're real. It's that they're real.

This stylized duplication of what it's like to be human and oddly gifted fed Tomlin's universally admired performance in Robert Benton's thriller *The Late Show* (1977). As the title implies, the film presents a congeries of the private-eye conventions we've learned from television's repertory of old movies: the Los Angeles location, with its obsessive car travel and oddball climate; the guarantee of twist frisson; the idealistic detective working around the useless police; the shady minor characters. But Benton recreates the genre, in that his detective (Art Carney) is too old for the violence (thus the *late* show) and the lead woman, a favorite spot for such as Mary Astor, Veronica Lake, and Gloria Grahame, is a mildly screwy sort (Tomlin) unlike anyone of any genre. These two must play the first Los Angeles citizens in all the movies who don't own cars. Tomlin wants to hire Carney to find her stolen cat, Winston, and though he rejects the two-bit offer he is pulled into the case anyway, which of course involves much more than a stolen cat. *The Late Show* revives another piece of the old-school detective thriller, the story line that is clearly told and exciting to follow but which *no* one, not for a hundred dollars, could correctly retell upon leaving the theatre.

The film has style. Tomlin could have taken the easy way and done one of her characters, but she's clearly impressed with the chemistry written into the script to meld her with Carney. They're both somewhat hard-edged people, but in his case it's because he has been living in a mean world and in hers it's because she has been living in her own. She spills out clichés ("I just could never learn to play the Hollywood game") and inventions ("Not only is this car a toilet, but you're the attendant") fluently mixing the day-to-day with the imagined; and because he's a realist, they fascinate each other. "That's just what this town has been waiting for," says Carney evenly—a lesser actor would bluster—"a broken-down private eye . . . and a fruitcake like you." *The Late Show* was what the industry had been waiting for: a thriller with class. Benton is sensible and striking. How neatly he handles the last scene, wherein Tomlin and Carney sit on a bench waiting for their separate buses. Will they make a couple? She has her doubts: "I have to keep up my side of the conversation and your side of the conversation." He has his doubts: "Would it kill you once in a while to wear a damn dress?" A bus pulls up, pauses, moves on. The bench is empty.

Tomlin exemplifies the independent star of the post-studio years. No one planned her, developed what she had. She did it herself. Similarly, she has resisted typing, playing a variety of characters that are nothing like those of her private stock. Tomlin's fellow alumna of *Laugh-In*, Goldie Hawn, also has taken advantage of Hollywood's present willingness to accommodate stars on their terms. On *Laugh-In*, Hawn was the dumb blonde, bollixing up the simplest lines and never coming out of the giggles. It was one of the show's popular features, and to keep it fresh the others, unseen behind the camera, would bait Hawn with gags so her laughter would ring out naturally.

Hawn's first successful film roles, in *Cactus Flower* (1969) and *Butterflies Are Free* (1972), simply expanded her *Laugh-In* persona. *Cactus Flower* introduces Hawn mailing a farewell note, turning on the gas, and settling down on the bed in her negligee, a whimsical way to die. And when her neighbor saves her life, she cries, "Oh, boy, I really blew it!" She got an Oscar for *Cactus Flower*. But when she tried to break out of the type, as in *The Sugarland Express* (1974), she could not draw her *Laugh-In* fans.

In a studio-dominated Hollywood, Hawn might have been locked into dumb blondes forever after, but the *actor*-producer has the initiative rights in today's Hollywood, not the producer. Management, up to the highest echelons, has the stability of a house of cards. (Compare that to the staying power of Carl Laemmle, L. B. Mayer, Jack Warner, Samuel Goldwyn, or David Selznick, virtually presidents for life of their corporations.) A solid draw, which Hawn has become, can plan her own projects, such as *Private Benjamin* (1980), and while on that one Hawn forgot to wire down such niceties as getting the final cut, she had in essence become her own boss.

This is to the good, for, like Tomlin, Hawn is no cartoonist. If Judy Benjamin came off as a curiously ambiguous revision of the dumb blonde in a feminist outlook, Hawn has fine potential; as far back as in *The Sugarland Express* she was in top form in a quite serious part. This was Steven Spielberg's first feature film, based on a real-life incident. Hawn breaks her convict husband William Atherton out of jail, they kidnap law officer Michael Sacks, and the trio sets off for the small Texas town where Hawn and Atherton's baby has been placed in a foster home. Here is a Hawn unknown to *Laugh-In*—emotional, tense, determined. Everything matters. Telling Atherton of her travails among the bureaucrats who took her child away, she breaks down, still talking but incoherent. Pulling herself together, she closes with, "I want my baby back. Now, are you going to help me or not?" It's only the start of one of the movies' great historic turnabouts in type, successful because Hawn reveals a lot of person: swooning at the romance of fame when townspeople celebrate her quest as her group and a tailing parade of squad cars glide through the Texas towns; panicking when thugs attack them in a parking lot; giving way to exuberance and then hysteria as she nears her destination and realizes that the Sugarland house is empty and she is caught in a police trap.

*Cactus Flower* was a cinch, given Hawn's whimsical charm, but *The Sugarland Express* was a challenge, not only for an actress but a certain kind of actress who can convince in Spielberg's highly naturalized pastoral, with the fawning townspeople apparently played by real townspeople, and all sorts of touches—an argument over whether Hawn should use the loo on a stop for gas—that would defeat a mere personality projector.

Still, Hawn's fans prefer her in farce, as witness the success of *Foul Play* (1978). Ostensibly a thriller about a plot to assassinate the Pope in San Francisco during a performance of *The Mikado, Foul Play* is mainly a vehicle for the burlesque chemistry of Hawn and Chevy Chase, a graduate of the pseudo-intellectual *Laugh-In* of the 1970s, *Saturday Night. Foul Play* compares interestingly with *The Late Show,* where the violence is realistic and matter-of-fact. In *Foul Play,* everything is a numbo, a gala set piece—Goldie attacked by a scarfaced creep and saved, mysteriously, by an albino stranger with outer-space eyes; Goldie leaping to temporary safety from a fire escape onto a moving car; Goldie and Chevy, bound, doing reaction shots as Burgess Meredith trades karate chops with villain Rachel Roberts. ("She was one tough old mama," observes Meredith after he dispatches her into a grand piano.) Or compare car chases. In *The Late Show,* Tomlin and Carney follow and then flee the bad guys in a hair-raising scene filmed at night, more a sensation of fear than a view of it. In *Foul Play,* Hawn and Chase run a slapstick demolition derby in a last-minute race to the opera house to save the Pope, with ethnic banter, constant changes of vehicle, full-view daytime shots of the San Francisco hills and the smashing-motor messes, and cute one-liners. It's fun, but it does nothing for character.

In all, Tomlin and Hawn prove that burlesque isn't the only mode of comedy that works today, but they did it by defying their origins on *Laugh-In* (Tomlin entirely; Hawn, now and then) to assert themselves as actresses. It is as much as saying that comedy will limit them. Strange: comediennes of earlier eras found comedy more expansive than playing character. But earlier comedy had a world view, or literacy, to back it up. Now comedy has a funny hat and Nazi jokes.

# 15

# *Musical Women*

DORIS DAY
JULIE ANDREWS
BARBRA STREISAND
LIZA MINNELLI
BERNADETTE PETERS

*Your strength is in your simplicity.*

—CHARLOTTE GREENWOOD
to Doris Day

*People are always behind you when
you're struggling. . . . When you reach
the top, some of them resent you and try
to tear you down.*

—BARBRA STREISAND

*Give me Julie Andrews any day.*

—AN ELECTRICIAN
after the taping of *Color Me
Barbra*

*Be yourself. The world worships the
original.*

—INGRID BERGMAN
to Liza Minnelli in *A Matter
of Time*

Movie genres come and go. The
weepie, a staple of the 1920s and '30s, began to fade in the 1940s,
enjoyed a resurgence in the 1950s, and faded again in the 1960s.
Screwball comedy rose and fell in the space of a few years in the late
1930s. Science fiction had a heyday in the 1950s as B-budget programmers, went into decline in the 1960s, and now has returned as go-for-
broke spectacle.

The musical, except for a brief period of unpopularity in the very
early 1930s, became a Hollywood staple, practiced by experts in the

studio years, but the dispersal of the studio technicians in the 1960s made the musical an expensive proposition, like putting a circus together from scratch each time out. Subsequently, public apathy to most of the big-budget musicals of the late 1960s shattered the form. The experts retired or moved on to stage and television, or went straight in melodrama and comedy. Strangely, none of them seems to miss the musical particularly. Also strangely, all the big musical stars of the post-war years have been women. Maybe not so strange; the most enduring stars of Broadway's musicals, except for men comics, have all been women. Still, why? What's womanly about the musical?

Doris Day's musicals, in fact, were largely tomboy vehicles, emphasizing her energy more than anything else. Originally aimed at the dance, young Doris Kappelhoff suffered an injury that turned her to singing. She made a hit with everyone on her debut, featured in *Romance on the High Seas* (1948), the first of a series of seventeen films at Warner Brothers that veered between nostalgia and backstage contemporaneity. Most of these films are bad in a mediocre way—not boring, not stupid, not even all that dated, just empty, styleless. Those with a Hollywood setting have people like Jack Carson in them, and most of the others include the likes of Gordon MacRae and Gene Nelson. Everyone makes the best of it, but there's no tension in these films, nothing to say in dance, nothing to sing of that hasn't been sung to death by superior talents. These aren't musicals; they're films filling a song-and-dance quota.

Across town at MGM, Debbie Reynolds and Jane Powell inherited the traditions laid down by Judy Garland and Deanna Durbin, respectively, as putting-on-the-show belter and semi-classical soprano in domestic comedy; and while their films are generally unexciting (except for Reynolds' *Singin' in the Rain* and Powell's *Seven Brides for Seven Brothers)*, the MGM know-how in musicals gave them, if nothing else, a sound structure to work in.

At Warners, the only one who knew how in musicals was Day. When her professional name was first suggested to her, back in her band-singer days, she thought it phony, but honesty is one of her salient qualities and—she's wrong—the name sounds honest. To Doris herself it suggested a burlesque queen, as in "The Gaiety Club is proud to present the Voom Girl, Miss Doris Day!" But it's brisk and sunny and plain-speaking, as she is. Without Day, Warners would doubtless have had to give up on musicals altogether, for her zip secures them.

Take *On Moonlight Bay* (1951) and its sequel, *By the Light of the Silvery Moon* (1953): period midwestern settings (note old song titles), turn-of-the-century standards for the scores, source supposedly Booth Tarkington's *Penrod* stories (though none of Tarkington's irony survives). Rosemary de Camp and Leon Ames are Day's parents, Billy Gray (later Bud on *Father Knows Best)* is her younger brother, Gordon

MacRae is the boy more or less next door, and all this has reminded some of *Meet Me in St. Louis*. (*By the Light* even uses *St. Louis'* seasonal narrative frame.) But Minnelli's masterpiece is fancy and wild. This Warners pair is small-scale, tame. Day gives it what edge it has—in her bounciness doing chores, her enthusiasm for marriage and sulking when MacRae wants to wait, her reluctant good will for the plop who courts her, her ingenuity in art (she rearranges a song he wrote, improving it vastly), or her amusing sabotage of what she mistakenly thinks is a liaison between her father and an actress.

Day isn't a charmer, though she has charm, nor a romancer, though she's a fine-looking woman. What she is is candid. For once we get the impression that the star hasn't been developed as a new drug might be, nor is playing herself, but has found roles that match her admirable qualities. Day is good company, so much so that her best part in the Warners series, the delight of Day buffs, is that of *Calamity Jane* (1955), which runs against these qualities in a kind of inside joke. As the frontier heroine who never heard of a dress, Day plays vulgar and dopey, two things she isn't, supplying a new kind of musical comedy fantasy: looks real, but isn't. Naturally, Calam must learn to wear frills and trap her man, belle-style, and there is one hideous miscalculation in the shooting of the film's big tune, "Secret Love," in which Day falls completely out of character to meander through the woods on a hit parade. Still, the fun is distinctive, for Day captures coarseness as professionally as she styles her signature qualities of honesty and vitality.

By the time she left Warner Brothers, Day was well known but not indispensable, though her Babe in *The Pajama Game* (1957), the only major cast substitution amid a troupe of Broadway veterans, was prominent. Babe brought out Day's tenacity, as a union activist in love with management honcho John Raitt, for there is nothing false about her refusal to court him while labor problems await settlement. Unfortunately, soon after *The Pajama Game* Day launched her famous cycle of sex comedies at Universal, limiting her persona to that of the fastidious spinster.

New York smuggies never tire of making Doris Day cracks. It is these films—*Pillow Talk* (1959), *Lover Come Back* (1961), *That Touch of Mink* (1962), and so on—that are responsible. Yet consider the anomalies in Day's real life. Day is likable, loyal, and a pleasure to work with, yet she marries bad-risk men, first a musician who beats her, then a hustler who takes over her business affairs and wins the contempt of everyone in Hollywood. "You don't get too close to a guy like that," said James Garner, Day's vis-à-vis in *The Thrill of It All* (1963) and *Move Over Darling* (1963). "Just good morning, no conversation, and keep your hand on your wallet." She plays independent women—women, even, suspicious of powerful men—yet she let her second husband employ, underpay, and browbeat her brother, exile her son to military school, and dissipate her fortune. She is the national ideal of the person who rejects promiscuity as repellent, yet she has been linked—falsely, of course, but still—with such characters as Frank Sinatra, Glen Campbell, and Jimmy Hoffa. Moreover, her white-bread image has some gritty accretions, such as her father's remarriage, late in life, to a black woman after a lifetime of conventional white racism. Day is a Christian Scientist and loves dogs. Yes. But strange things have happened to her.

The Universal boudoir comedies may be the strangest, for they doted on a woman flabbergasted by the notion of premarital sex, whereas Day had established a character more concerned with larger moral issues. In *It Happened to Jane* (1959), she is a lobster breeder in Maine who takes on the corporation in the person of public-be-damned railroad tycoon Ernie Kovacs. There's a telltale note in that Day resolutely segregates the male lobsters from the females. (How do they breed?) She also keeps one male lobster as a pet, and she is forever grabbing him as he sneaks into the females' pen. So perhaps Day herself had set up *Pillow Talk,* first and best of the Universals. The film acts as if it were capping an improvisation rather than inaugurating a routine. Decorator Day is virtuous, unselfish, reasonable. Songwriter Rock Hudson is seductive, selfish, sloppy. Thelma Ritter is a maid with an endless hangover. Tony Randall is Day's would-be fiancé and the plot's peg in that he is to finance Hudson's musical.

The elements are in place; now, the procedure. We have hip: Randall offers Day a car as a present, she refuses it, and a cop tells him to move it. "My analyst," muses Randall, "will never believe this." "Neither will mine," says the cop. And we have gender banter. Says Randall, "If there's anything worse than a woman living alone, it's a woman saying she likes it." We have farcical overkill: Hudson has been abusing his share of Day's party line, so he has to disguise his voice when they meet; he pretends to be a Texan. And we have counterpoint: as they part after the first date, Hudson tells us in voice-over, "I'd say five or six dates ought to do it," while Day is thinking that she has met Mr. Right.

*Pillow Talk* is entertaining. But Day went on to remake it too many times. *Lover Come Back* has Hudson and Day all over again, and while *That Touch of Mink* switches over to Cary Grant, it so overdoes the Day primness that the series' one joke—sex—stales. There are funny moments when, on a trip to Bermuda with Grant and dreading the coming seduction, Day becomes paranoid. She fears everyone Knows About Her. To show her state of mind, a raft in the hotel pool, a horse-drawn carriage, and an elevator all turn into huge beds. But, at the crucial juncture, Day's ruses are a little much. When "I forgot my toothbrush!" and "I have an uncle who's a socialist!" fail her, she breaks out in a rash.

The series went on, with James Garner, Rock Hudson again, Rod Taylor, and Richard Harris trading off the leads, and there was one novelty in *Move Over, Darling,* a remake of *My Favorite Wife* (with Day, Garner, Polly Bergen, and Chuck Connors in the roles originated by Irene Dunne, Cary Grant, Gail Patrick, and Randolph Scott), in that Day tries to forestall not her own sexual encounter but Bergen's, Garner having remarried because he thought wife Day was dead. By this time, the late 1960s, the Day boudoir farce had become a laughingstock, though Day's drawing power kept them in the black. Sadly, she took little part in the boom in adaptations of Broadway musicals that dominated these years, making only *Jumbo* (1962), perhaps the smallest of the big musicals. For someone who was, at the start, instantly familiar, Day has lately become oddly unavailable. Whatever became of her?

If nothing else, Day at least recreated herself when she abandoned the musical. Julie Andrews has not been able to do so; the sweet exuberance of *Mary Poppins* (1963) and *The Sound of Music* (1965) suited her better than her later non-musical roles, which seem determined to prove that she's human and only emphasize her starchiness. Andrews needs music; it loosens her up. *Mary Poppins,* her debut compensation from Walt Disney for missing out on Jack Warner's *My Fair Lady,* lacked the tartness of P. L. Travers' storybook nanny, and *The Sound of Music* is depressingly nice. The stage show had kids and nuns, but the movie added puppets; at that, the puppets (the Baird marionettes) give the best performances after Andrews herself.

*Thoroughly Modern Millie* (1967) presented Andrews with a fine opportunity, but the film as a whole is slow and silly. Andrews' part, that of a diligently self-reconstructing Modern of the 1920s, has bite and canny fun. But Andrews was at less than her best in *Star!* (1968), not exactly based on the life of Gertrude Lawrence. A signet of the Gershwin and Coward styles in musical comedy and the all but irreplaceable heroine of *Lady in the Dark* and *The King and I,* Lawrence was a difficult person, to put it mildly, and the film glossed her over. *Star!*'s Lawrence is flamboyant, rebellious, unreliable, bitchy, and somewhat destructive, which is halfway there,* but way beyond what Andrews can convincingly project. In the numbers, of course, she's the top. But there is no getting around the miscasting in her dialogue scenes. Here is this impeccably fine-lined woman trying to slum, and it doesn't take.

Can Hollywood give one of its treasurable musical talents so little?

---

*A more closely observed copy of Lawrence is to be found in Kaufman and Hart's *The Man Who Came to Dinner.* They called her Lorraine Sheldon.

Andrews' career started out with the right choices and good breaks that make legends instructive listening fifty years after. At eighteen she crossed the Atlantic to play the heroine of *The Boy Friend* in its Broadway premiere, wowed critics and folk, went on to Eliza Doolittle in *My Fair Lady*—in which part she has never been equaled, much less surpassed—and held the center of what was at the time, 1957, the most successful television special, Rodgers and Hammerstein's *Cinderella*. Another television outing with Carol Burnett was also a triumph.

Besides talent, Andrews had something few of her coevals did, tact, and this made her an intellectual's choice musical comedy heroine as well as a popular figure. But the times have been running against Cinderella types. *Mary Poppins* and *The Sound of Music* were flukes, unrepeatable—not that Hollywood didn't blow uncountable millions trying to repeat them. When the dust cleared on the account books, Andrews was, in a way, the scapegoat. She started it. So she paid, getting bad press for a fine performance in *Darling Lili* (1970), making only one film in the next eight years, plus her part in *"10"* (1979). At that, she might not have worked at all if she hadn't married Blake Edwards, *Darling Lili*'s director. What does a woman have to do to get noticed in this culture, bare her breasts? Andrews duly did, in *S.O.B.* (1981). Shame.

Still, many Hollywood careers run in cycles, and Andrews has lately risen high again in *Victor/Victoria* (1982), as a woman impersonating a female impersonator in Paris in 1934. Edwards has come quite some way from the suave *Breakfast at Tiffany's*—to idiotically pointless slapstick and no sense of locale or era. But Andrews is in trim. Now that a few hits are backing her up, how about letting her tackle *Lady in the Dark?*

If Andrews lost power, Barbra Streisand has gained it, steadily, in well-planned moves from Off Broadway anonymity to Broadway notice in a small part to a series of hit Columbia albums of top-class show and cabaret material through a Broadway musical smash and some dazzling television specials on to Hollywood, rock, disco, and total control of her destiny. Besides being one of the few bankable draws in a big-budget film, she is a symbol of Oscar-Grammy-Emmy, woman-boss, *molto*-clout stardom, to the point that her personal appearance anywhere can cause a riot, even among industry insiders. The smell of the fame on this woman is awesome, and she made it on two things that devotees of clout admire above all: raw talent and brute arrogance. "I am a cross," she has said, "between a washerwoman and a princess."

No one, when she started, could have seemed less likely, with her Erasmus Hall High looks and heavy accent, in her outlandish thrift-shop madeovers, singing her way-out tunes of show biz and camp. She would have got nowhere but for the enthusiasm of some Broadway pros—composer Harold Rome, director Arthur Laurents, composer

Jule Styne, director Garson Kanin—and the coaching of some friends, unknown Broadway applicants like herself. The friends found her the songs and helped her shape an act; the Broadwayites saw the talent behind the rude ignorance and hired her, wrote for her, gave her discipline and polish.

Only one of nine leads in her first Broadway show, *I Can Get It for You Wholesale* (1962), Streisand as secretary Yetta Marmelstein became the show's major asset. Sheree North was better known, Elliott Gould had a bigger part, Marilyn Cooper got the show's big ballad, "Who Knows," and Lillian Roth and Harold Lang were show-biz alumni of some celebrity. Yet Streisand took it. Her second-act comedy spot, "Miss Marmelstein," regularly provoked more applause than anything else in the musical, and its star-is-born promise has passed into Broadway lore with the suggestion that this one number made her.

In fact, she was all over the show, leading chorus numbers and tackling solo verses with the assurance of big talent. She opened the evening, after a fraught ballet of life in Manhattan's garment district, with a comic telephone scene and led off the first song, "I'm Not a Well Man," a duet with her boss. She also led the show's most imposing number, a chorale in a disjointed rhythmic pulse called "What Are They Doing to Us Now?"; and she put no little energy into the hectic Sousa-like "Ballad of the Garment Trade." Miss Marmelstein was a cameo part as written, but it was built up in rehearsals into a solid supporting role, more song than lines—which is just as well, for Streisand was then an uncouth actress, experimental but without a practiced actor's perspective.*

Laurents, who directed the show, contributed to Streisand's development by controlling her worst instincts (and by talking producer David Merrick out of firing her). Garson Kanin, who directed *Funny Girl* on Broadway, may have been her most formative influence in the same way. *Funny Girl*, on the life of Fanny Brice, was to be the ultimate in star vehicles, with such heavyweights as Anne Bancroft, Mary Martin, Carol Burnett, and Shirley MacLaine considered before producer Ray Stark, Brice's son-in-law, was persuaded to go with Streisand. No one can doubt that she was far righter for the part than these others. (Mary Martin as Fanny Brice? How about Sandy Dennis as Madame DuBarry? How about Sonny Liston and Pat Suzuki as Nicholas and Alexandra? How about Warren Beatty and Diane Keaton as John Reed and Louise Bryant?) But Streisand was not ready to take on a big show by herself: eleven numbers solo or nearly; a complex character who is a

---

*Lehman Engel, who conducted *I Can Get It for You Wholesale*, recalls in his autobiography that, night after night, Streisand begged him for a chance to do "Miss Marmelstein" her own way, as opposed to the routine she and Laurents had worked out that was convulsing audiences. Twice Engel gave Streisand her head in the number; both times the audience sat through it in silent confusion.

romantic clown, an ambitious fanatic, and a tragic heroine; plus the make-or-break pressure with all Broadway eyes upon the project, ears taking in delicious reports of impending disaster as *Funny Girl* struggled to find itself in tryouts. Nothing, in all Manhattan, makes choicer dish than a big flop musical.

Then as now, Streisand had endless energy and determination, rehearsing long after her colleagues were ready to quit. It has been said that only a newcomer crazed for the big chance would have taken on the exhausting *Funny Girl* part, but on other hand Streisand simply didn't know any better. No one told her that no previous part in musical comedy history took this much out of anyone. Ignorance and talent. She didn't know enough to defend herself from exhaustion, and she had resources enough to pull the part off. Nor did she know anything of Brice; she dragged it out of herself. Perhaps she played herself; she said as much at the time. With her extraordinary instrument for the numbers, her comic bamboo tuned and trimmed by Kanin (and by Jerome Robbins, called in to take over the production shortly before the New York opening), and her energy running on full, she gave, truly, one of the most astonishing performances Broadway had ever seen—before she tired of the eight repetitions a week and began walking through it.

No matter. Stark had intended the show as little more than an audition for a film, and while Mimi Hines took over for Streisand on Broadway, the main funny girl went off to Hollywood to shoot the show with William Wyler.

She also did the film versions of *Hello, Dolly!* (1969) and *On a Clear Day You Can See Forever* (1970) and was obviously the great hope of the movie musical. However, only *Funny Girl* (1968) was a hit. *Hello, Dolly!* drew critical fire for its showy budget and what was perceived as a bogus heroine, too young for the role and too derivative in style. Furthermore, tales of the star's growing arrogance, at a minimum on *Funny Girl,* were rife on *Hello, Dolly!* She was said to be backseat-driving director Gene Kelly out of his wits, impossible to co-star Walter Matthau, and heedless of the rest of the cast and crew. Yet seeing her in the title number, dancing with the waiters and clowning with Louis Armstrong, is to see a rare talent in top form—and more: to see someone who knows how to do what the Hollywood musical traditionally did in a time when the musical was suffering amnesia.

Still, to this point Streisand had been playing what she was, a Jewish song-and-dance comic. For *On a Clear Day* she switched over into WASP glamour, framing it within her familiar persona by playing a woman with telepathic powers who, under hypnosis, recalls an earlier life as an adventuress in Regency England. So, as Daisy Gamble in straight hair and plain clothes, Streisand did her shtick with the accent and the nasal cracks and the ungainly posture. As Melinda Tentrees in the Vanity Fair flashbacks, she wore Cecil Beaton's high fashion and played sensual diva, doing lascivious things with a goblet as she stared across a dinner party at her future lover. Melinda is a cook's daughter *en masque* as a lady—more or less what Streisand was herself, the washerwoman-princess. In pulling these two worlds together, Streisand was effecting her transformation from a strictly New York phenomenon into a national attraction.

She would also cut loose of the musical identity to play non-singing roles in her next three films, *The Owl and the Pussycat* (1970), *What's Up, Doc* (1972), and *The Way We Were* (1973). One thing she did not lose in the transformation, her abrasive manner. As a hooker in *Owl*, she screamed most of her lines. In *What's Up, Doc?* modeled on *Bringing Up Baby*, she broke screwball's cardinal rule—to wit, don't push—and subverted the whole enterprise. In *Bringing Up Baby* Katharine Hepburn plays Cary Grant's golf ball and drives off in his car; in *What's Up, Doc?*, Streisand wastes a hotel room. (Not that Ryan O'Neal is any help. His sense of style comprises saying things like "I don't know—I wish I did, but I don't" slowly and distinctly.) And in *The Way We Were* Streisand played a self-righteous Jewish leftist who falls in love with apolitical golden boy Robert Redford. But lo, while returning emphatically to the New York idiom, Streisand grew almost serene over the course of the story, putting the abrasiveness temporarily behind her.

*The Way We Were* has become one of the most popular movies of its decade. It is cited as the ultimate sortie in the Streisand campaign for national acculturation through pairings with WASP avatars. With Redford down, the war is won. Actually, Streisand's catalogue of romantic partners is more varied than legend reports, taking in Omar Sharif, Walter Matthau, Yves Montand, and George Segal as well as O'Neal, Redford, and, in *On a Clear Day*, Jon Richardson. Anyway, given Streisand's assertive character, it might be argued that she isn't working her way through the male glamour stars: *they* are lining up for a chance to test their chemistry against hers. True, Redford was reluctant to do *The Way We Were* and reportedly put off making Streisand's acquaintance till the eleventh hour. But she has top billing.

However one views the power of the pairing, it's enticingly anomalous. At college, where they meet, she's penniless, openly sensitive, a crusader, and the campus butt. Redford is well heeled, closed, self-oriented, and the campus king. He's a track star; she's president of the Young Communist League. He's suave, joking his enemies into retreat; she screams "Fascist!" at hers. And he sits and waits and gets what he wants: she has to woo him. "The trouble with some people," he tells her, "is they work too hard." But she wins him. They even manage to come to terms on her political militancy, moving to Hollywood so he can write films, though eventually the HUAC hearings unbuckle her and the marriage collapses. This, too, adds to our understanding of

Streisand. From one angle, she's too New York for a decent guy, raucous and grabby. From another angle, she's too good for him, her good intentions martyred on the reckless California beaches. It's viewer's choice.

Viewer's choice, too, tells us what Streisand is like to work with. Some of her colleagues have raved, congratulating her collaborative imagination. Others describe an insufferable buttinsky who wants everything her way. It's hard to take Hollywood quotations seriously. In planning, on the set, and in the home stretch when everyone is fighting for a flattering final cut, there is tension even among the more affable moviemakers. Afterward, if the film is a hit, the glow of success often melts away the memory of trouble, and talk is sweet. Moreover, a smart movie person wants to stay on everyone's good side: you never know who might be in charge of your next break. So who can tell what temper is showing when someone makes a statement, or what diplomacy is being established? In Hollywood, they say, divide everything you hear by nine.

So the reports on Streisand contradict each other. Frank Pierson, who directed Streisand's remake of *A Star Is Born* (1976), published a disgusted report on her behavior in *New York* and *New West* magazines* that has become the general view of the actress-producer-songwriter. (She composed the music, to Paul Williams' lyrics, for *Star*'s theme song, "Evergreen.") Some had held the view since 1966, when Rex Reed wrote a hostile piece for *The New York Times*, picturing her as an insolent clod. "Three and a half hours late," Reed tells, "she plods into the room, plotzes into a chair with her legs spread out, tears open a basket of fruit, bites into a green banana, and says, 'Okay, ya got twenty minutes, whaddya wanna know?'" Yet Reed, too, recanted later, apologizing to Streisand for what he seemed to admit was a willful hatchet job.

No one in Hollywood's history has had such a conflicted profile. Perhaps Garson Kanin has most demonstrated the contradictory feelings Streisand excites in her collaborators. His public statements about their work on *Funny Girl* have been judicious and admiring. But his novel of 1980, *Smash*, appears to tell of *Funny Girl*, and it's a horror show. All the names are changed, but the parallels are fetching. The musical in the novel is *Shine On Harvest Moon*, on the life of Nora Bayes, a vaudevillian of the generation preceding Fanny Brice's and like Brice a tough Jewish singer and comic. Certain people involved in staging *Funny Girl* are unmistakably recreated, and certain details only an expert could spot recall *Funny Girl* with precision. (One example: the complicated history of a number Kanin calls "Big Town," which

---

*Co-star Kris Kristofferson, too, had hard words about the experience, though around premiere time he took a more agreeable stance.

displeases the woman playing Bayes because it gets a big hand for two supporting players, recalls similar problems with *Funny Girl*'s "Who Taught Her Everything She Knows?") There are a few red herrings. *Smash*'s set designer seems to be modeled on Boris Aronson, who didn't design *Funny Girl*. Still, the reader gets the feeling that, at a distance of fifteen years, Kanin is setting the *Funny Girl* record straight. And in his version, Star—as he calls her—is the devouring maw of show biz itself, nothing but exploitation and narcissism. Is Streisand the Star? One thing's sure: if Streisand were an epoch, she'd be interesting times.

Part of her attraction lies in her complex persona, layered in film after film as she shed early habits, changed form, grew powerful. She can play aggressive and smooth at once, as in *A Star Is Born,* balancing the two in a score as volatile ("The Woman in the Moon") as plangent ("Evergreen"). She can raise the feminist question, in *Up the Sandbox* (1972), turning away from it at the story's end to affirm a career as a housewife. Or she can kid the abrasiveness, in *The Main Event* (1979), a second O'Neal teaming, with Streisand in top-man position as a businesswoman who becomes boxer O'Neal's boss and lover. When she refuses his offer of marriage, he moans, "I feel like a one-night stand." As singer, she can leap from her Broadway repertory into rock, making her first album in the contemporary sound, *Stoney End,* a milestone in that it solemnized the end of Kern-Romberg-Rodgers-Gershwin-Arlen as lucrative names in the American recording industry.

Meanwhile, she complicated all this by turning over (some of) the reins of her corporation to Jon Peters, the owner of Hollywood hairdo salons who suddenly turned recording and film producer. The industry was outraged. The vanity of it sounded like Streisand, but the amateurishness did not. Sneering at "that hairdresser," the press furiously watched its savaging of *A Star Is Born,* the first Streisand-Peters venture, go for nothing as film and recording both grossed what insiders call Very Big Numbers. The film wasn't amateurish at all, though except in the songs it's hardly worthy of Streisand. (One great moment: a groupie with a tape machine tries to wangle an interview with Streisand, finds Kristofferson alone, and beds him. Streisand comes upon them in the act, and as she stands there trembling with hurt and rage, the girl snaps on the recorder and extends the mike to Streisand. "Okay," she tells her. "Go.")

If there is anything to jeer at in the Streisand-Peters partnership, it is not that Peters had never produced a film before, but that his cultural ignorance precluded his being able to comprehend Streisand's force in musical comedy, the gift that makes her unique. Lesley Ann Warren, Peters' ex-wife, says that when they attended Streisand's Los Angeles concert in 1967 he had never heard of her—yet this was long after her first albums, television specials, and the stage *Funny Girl,* all big news in the world of American popular art. Is someone as uninformed as this an appropriate artistic partner for Streisand? With the partnership lately disbanded and the movie musical attempting a comeback, it will be interesting to see what part Streisand takes in the revival.

Another star who would benefit from such a comeback is Liza Minnelli, always at her best in a numbo, a smash singing–dancing spot. Famous by right of birth, Minnelli is one of today's pre-eminent disco personalities, a fixture in the schedules of any New York nightspot with claims on hot. "Liza was there" is a buzz term meaning "The party was elite." This puts a certain emphasis on her film work. Everything she does is made to feel like cabaret, like a turn in the spotlight, fast and dancey with lots of Attitude. Disco doesn't add to; it takes from, and this can put a punk on one's persona.

Minnelli's films are an odd bunch, admired cult items like *Charlie Bubbles* (1967), unadmired commercial flops like *Lucky Lady* (1975), and only two musicals, Bob Fosse's *Cabaret* (1972) and Martin Scorsese's *New York, New York* (1977). *Cabaret* is a classic, and a rare case that subdues Broadwayites' complaint that Hollywood substitutes smoother people for the grainy New York originals when adapting musicals. (Irene Dunne for Helen Morgan in *Sweet Adeline,* for instance; or Ginger Rogers for Clare Luce in *The Gay Divorcee;* or Red Skelton for Bert Lahr in *DuBarry Was a Lady;* or Shirley Jones for Barbara Cook in *The Music Man.*) No one missed Jill Haworth, *Cabaret*'s stage Sally Bowles, for Minnelli has the stand-and-deliver number down cold—Dietrich with her chair in "Mein Herr," slinky depravity in "The Money Song," direct-address love ballad in "Maybe This Time," and all-out socko in the title song.

It was noted that Minnelli was too brilliant to play a third-rate talent like Sally Bowles; but, hell, musicals need Minnelli. The others stand and she delivers. Besides, it was interesting to see the Garland clique in disarray, finding the pretender to the legend in the sort of anti-romantic, commentative piece that Garland could never have played. Garland's It was compulsive, "I am what you see." Minnelli keeps the X that fills out the story to herself.

When *Cabaret* was new and Fosse and Minnelli were the toasts, it looked as if she would be the next musical star, the one they would revive the form for. But, as with Day, Andrews, and Streisand, the issue died. Minnelli tends to sing, at least briefly, in her films. *Lucky Lady* allots her, in a cabaret setting, Kander and Ebb's "While the Getting Is Good," which sounds like something they might have written for *Chicago,* especially in Ralph Burns's raunchy scoring. But when she made a film with her father, a master of the MGM musical, it was a bald terror, *A Matter of Time* (1977). A Cinderella weepie in which faded "countess" Ingrid Bergman coaches chambermaid Minnelli in high living, *A Matter of Time* dribbled and dragged. Director Minnelli badly flubbed the central scene in which Bergman dresses Minnelli for her first night as a courtesan. As tradition requests, the Cinderella has her back to us so, when the transformation is completed, she will turn around and thrill us with the magic. "There, look at yourself!" Bergman cries, and we prepare—but father Minnelli shows us his daughter staring into a crooked mirror and she appears anything but dazzling. The film keeps on making such wrong choices. Old-time movie fans, the sole audience for this fare, were particularly offended by the botching of a genre that Hollywood used to turn out in its sleep. *Films in Review*, a buffs' magazine usually highly composed in tone, called the picture "a turd."

Minnelli does get to sing in it, though. "Do It Again," an old Gershwin tune, performed (complete with its verse) in Louis XV underthings against a jazz band at the end of a costume party, has the confidence that tells us why Hollywood needs Minnelli. Other musical comedy people in her class of expertise are not stars in the Hollywood sense; they're mostly thespians working in New York, hopelessly unbankable. Who besides Minnelli could have played her role in *New York, New York*, with its big-band resuscitations and dream numbo, "Happy Endings"?*

The part was Minnelli's by family heritage, perhaps, for while *New York, New York*'s bite of the past glommed up the kind of musicals neither Garland nor Vincente Minnelli worked on, they *might* have done it (with Gene Kelly in Robert de Niro's part), if with a more positive finish. But the part was Minnelli's by more than that: by commitment. One gets the feeling that she'd make three musicals a year if they'd let her, though again her disco ebullience would limit her characterological range.

One of the New York musical comedy people normally excluded from important lead roles in musicals was recently given a top chance: Bernadette Peters. She has done some non-musical films, including a tasty comic bit in Burt Reynolds' prison film *The Longest Yard* (1974) and leads in burlesques with Steve Martin and Andy Kaufman. Yet her performance in *Pennies from Heaven* (1981) is so distinctive that it is likely to go down as a major event in the reinstitution of the American musical.

Peters is utterly of the genre. With her silent-era bee-stung look, her early-talkie era song-and-dance moxie, and her contemporary naturalist acting style, she can delve into tradition while she renovates it. This is especially strategic in a film that sets out to reconstruct *and* revise the Hollywood musical. Unfortunately, Peters is the only one involved in *Pennies from Heaven* who is capable of such synthesis. Sce-

---

*"Happy Endings" was cut from the original release print, but was reinstated in the rerelease to chime in with the gathering musical comeback.

narist Dennis Potter tells of a sheet music salesman (Steve Martin) in the 1930s who believes the optimistic hokum of popular song even as life keeps proving that pop is a lie. Potter thinks he's working in commentative cliché, but his banalities are inert, plain cliché. He can't even borrow a fake life from our recollection of old musicals, because no musical was this stupid. Old movies were stimulating. They were recipes for self-confidence, whether in putting on the show, getting out of Cinderella rags and on to the ball, or conquering the hazards of Oz. Potter wants to shatter this complacency, but must he humiliate us to do it?

When Vernel Bagneris as a badly downtrodden vagabond black uses the title song to wipe away Depression clouds and unveil the silver lining, we accept his view as the film's view, conditioned by decades of such characters in such song spots to take heart from a positive philosophy. We know—tradition and the moment tell us so—that, whatever happens, Bagneris will somehow get along, always sad and always hopeful. So when Potter has him grab a pretty blind girl and rape her to death, he isn't only challenging the narcotic optimism of popular art, he is smashing an intimacy, a decency, a trust basic to the movies. Worst of all, Potter can't even follow through with his own premise. Circumstantially implicated, Martin is charged with the crime, found guilty, and sentenced to hang. But Potter finds he has written himself into a corner. He doesn't dare end with the hanging of Steve Martin, so he closes with Martin walking off the gallows to join Peters in a perverse let's-get-rhythm! finale. Actually, the film doesn't have an ending, just a few last-minute bad intentions.*

As inept as Potter is director Herbert Ross. Apparently he considered several formalistic possibilities without settling on one, and *Pennies from Heaven* is a battle of modes. Ross uses old recordings for the track. Okay, but will the singers mouth to reasonable facsimiles of their voices, or take any voice at all, including transsexually? Will the songs be keyed to character and plot, or run against them? Will they comment on the action in dream states, or take part in the action, forward it? Each succeeding choice negates the last choice, till one no longer has any confidence in what the film thinks it's doing. And where does that leave Peters?

The casting of Martin further weakens a troubled project. The dubbing procedure spares us his unlikable vocal production, and he underwent extensive training in tap and ballroom. But he's no actor. That burlesque grin nabs the eye like a clown's painted mouth, and he scarcely seems aware of the story line, running vapidly through the

---

*Potter also has not settled on a time of action. At the start, 1934 is flashed on the screen. But we also see a huge wallboard advertising Carole Lombard in *Love Before Breakfast,* and when Martin and Peters visit a movie house they encounter *Follow the Fleet.* The two films were released in 1936.

speeches that are supposed to define his vision as an entrepreneur in pop music. Martin is more assured in his love scenes with Peters, but then he can work to the snickers of his following of eleven-year-olds. As for his dancing, no matter how nimbly Martin moves, he can't pull it off, because he doesn't know why it's there. Has he ever seen a musical? He goes into his dance obediently, not exuberantly, not because his character needs dance. He works hard, but in the end all he has proved is that anyone can learn to tap.

What is right about *Pennies from Heaven* is a few numbers which manage that modern translation of the old forms that the film as a whole does not. At least Peters is in two of them. "Love Is Good for Anything That Ails You" radically affirms the blending of tradition and innovation: a white schoolroom of grinning kid musicians led by a slinky Peters in Berkeleyesque geometry. But does Peters get to sing? No, we're dubbing from the past, remember? She gets to dance with Martin in an Astaire-Rogers homage laid on the "Let's Face the Music and Dance" set with the "Top Hat" chorus line. This is more radical yet, for its authenticity almost suggests to 1981 what it must have been like in the 1930s to experience these dance romances for the first time. For once in this hateful collage, the authors' need to believe in something outvoted their delight in destruction. But again now, where does that leave Peters? She centers *Pennies from Heaven,* much as Bing Crosby, Eleanor Powell, Deanna Durbin, and Doris Day do their vehicles. Peters isn't the whole show by any means, but she is the absolute element, the one who in look, motion, and tone can bridge the eras, rooting the recomposed style in its foundation and following its contemporary reach right up to the minute. She has the unaffected, quaint plain charm of Ruby Keeler, but a spectacular one. She doesn't get by because she is; she works for It. If the musical does indeed come back, she will be essential.

But can the musical come back in times when Hollywood's energies are devoted more to smashing the public's self-image than reinforcing it? The musical is conventionally positive, life-affirming. But today's movies—under the cover of striving for honesty—are often the work of ghouls intent on sharing their self-hatred with the public. Contempt for innocence, delight in degradation, and debasement of all values outside the solipsism of hip have become imperatives of moviemaking. Within that world view a musical can treat a blind girl as if she were a rag doll prop in a fraternity hell-night skit.

# 16

# *Persons; or, All Women Are Whores*

INGRID BERGMAN
RAQUEL WELCH
BO DEREK
SALLY KELLERMAN
DIANE KEATON
JANE FONDA
MERYL STREEP

*You are going to be the first "natural" actress.*

—DAVID O. SELZNICK
to Ingrid Bergman, 1939

*[Jane Fonda] may well be the only revolutionary with her own public relations man.*

—*LIFE* magazine

*Today you have sex symbols without sex personality.*

—MAE WEST, 1970

*I've got to do something outside of Manhattan, outside of 1981, outside of my experience. Put me on the moon.*

—MERYL STREEP
to her agent

Into the strait maze of studio stardom came Ingrid Bergman, on a direct path, saying no. No, she would not change her name. No, she would not change her looks; she would not even wear makeup. No, she would not play the same character in every film. And no, she would not let her employer tell her how to run her personal affairs. Yet Bergman was not a militant rebel battling management for the crusade of it. She just didn't see any wisdom in taking other people's advice against her own good judgment.

This is the behavior of an individual, not a star. Stars, though distinctive as a rule, function within a system of fixed coordinates for typing, marketing, offscreen profile, and so on. Yet Bergman, who began her Hollywood career when the studios ran the industry, survived into a post-studio era, when the personally reachable moguls and the community of craftsmen-collaborators had broken up into impenetrable ghouls taking meetings between the lines of coke. Bergman resists. A new era begins with her, though of course no one knew it at the time (Bergman least of all), and though the reasons for the New Hollywood of the 1980s are based on economics, politics, and cultural drift, not actors' independence.

Bergman's entree into acting is standard classic: orphaned and large for her age, she retreated from her coevals' teasing into dreams of escape in the theatre and, as Garbo before her, enrolled in the academy of Stockholm's court theatre. From there she went into Swedish film, and her weepie *Intermezzo* (1936) caught the attention of David Selznick's scout Elsa Neuberger in New York. The producer sent Kay Brown to Sweden to fetch Bergman, who—not surprisingly, but Brown was surprised—turned out to have a doctor husband and a young daughter. Bergman was willing to try Hollywood, as it must have seemed a childhood fantasy made real, and Selznick decided that for her debut she would remake *Intermezzo* virtually shot for shot. As *Intermezzo: A Love Story* (1939), the film was a hit. Bergman's role, as the other woman in violinist Leslie Howard's marriage, could only work for the American public of that era if the woman shows sufficient horror of adultery. Bergman does. "I'm ashamed," she tells Howard. "And I hate being ashamed."

Hollywood bemused Bergman. Everyone was short, afraid of each other's power, and callous toward those below them in pecking order. When Selznick was unhappy with *Intermezzo*'s photographer, Bergman pleaded for him. Perhaps another could make her look a little better, but was that a reason to fire a man? The very scope of Hollywood floored her. "In Sweden, the film crew and technicians added up to about maybe fifteen," she recalled in her memoirs. "In America there were sixty to one hundred." Selznick spent as much time filming and retaking Bergman's entrance—a simple walk into a living room—as they would spend on an entire scene in Europe. At that, Hollywood didn't see as much in Bergman as Selznick did. "The general topic of conversation," says Bergman of her first Hollywood shindig, "was that David Selznick had just bought himself a nice big healthy Swedish cow." But Selznick's belief in Bergman was vindicated by a handsome box-office take and popular acclaim, despite a very soft pedal on the PR. Selznick's staff kept Bergman's image chaste, remote from the public and the industry alike. She played admirable women in her next two films—both on loan to other studios—to Selznick's profit. At the third she balked.

This was to be *Dr. Jekyll and Mr. Hyde* (1941) for MGM, with a miscast Spencer Tracy as the courtly doctor who concocts an elixir to unleash his latent sadistic streak as "Edward Hyde." Director Victor Fleming was set to film the tale with Bergman as Jekyll's genteel fiancée and Lana Turner as the barmaid whom Hyde debauches. Bergman wanted to play the barmaid, and, after testing her, Fleming okayed the switch (Turner took over the fiancée role) and talked Selznick into it. Bergman probably wasn't thinking of expanding an image, as she never plotted in Hollywood calculus. She was attracted by the acting challenge.

She met it nobly, achieving a *louche* sensuality in her early scenes and a despair later, when the vicious Hyde takes control of her. Tracy meets her as Dr. Jekyll, protecting her from a footpad in a dark street, and seeing her home. Inside, he tells her to open her blouse. Why? "I'd better have a look at you," he says. Despite his professional briskness, she figures it's a come-on, and grins at his mannered approach. When he tells her that he's a doctor, she laughs.

Bergman had been hailed on her debut as fresh. They meant "clean." She tried the erotic at some risk, especially as Fleming made *Dr. Jekyll* clammy, lurid, unbecoming to all involved. Again, Bergman was breaking rules she wasn't even aware of: in Hollywood, you play type. But in Sweden, stage and screen actors (who were interchangeable, anyway) played whatever seemed interesting, regardless of age, coloring, or mood. By Hollywood rules, Dr. Jekyll might have trapped Bergman in a *Gilda* snare.

Yet her next picture has proved to be a giant of romantic Hollywood, *Casablanca* (1943), on loan to Warners. The studio had a knack for either inaugurating or capping a tradition, and while it was being shot *Casablanca* sounded like strange music. It had started as a play called *Everybody Goes to Rick's*. Unproduced, the script was sold to film and handed over to Julius and Philip Epstein to be prepared for Ronald Reagan as the expatriate American café owner, Dennis Morgan as a freedom fighter, and Ann Sheridan as the woman caught between them. Somewhere along the way, Howard Koch was pulled in to make sense of the jumbled script, Michael Curtiz assigned the direction, and Humphrey Bogart, Paul Henreid, and Bergman were put into the leads. All this happened at once, at the last minute, and the actors found themselves on a set without a center. Whom does Bergman truly love, her noble husband Henreid or her erstwhile flame Bogart? Is Bogart a secret idealist or a saloon owner who doesn't give a damn whom he pays his protection money to? Is Casablanca a place of Nazi ruthlessness or of French expediency, with a dash of wit? What to play, whom to play to?

Curtiz didn't know, and Koch was too busy finishing each next day's rewrites to tell. So the actors let their instincts lead them into a locus classicus of the adventure, the love story, the moral parable, all in one. Most of Hollywood's most enduring hits excel as only one of the three. Even *The Wizard of Oz* and *Gone With the Wind* cover only two (the *Wizard* has no love story and *Gone With the Wind*'s parable runs thin early on). *Casablanca* does it all. This explains its staying power: it's so rich in material one has to go back again and again to control it all. Then, too, the actors are in full possession of some highly gratifying parts, naturalistically complex. Perhaps they were simply covering all possible bases in their confusion. Whatever the reason, they nourish the thriller, spark the romance, and effect the allegory.

Yet what could be simpler than *Casablanca?* Everybody goes to Rick's Café Américain, including the woman he loved in Paris, now married to an anti-Nazi activist. "Of all the gin joints in all the towns in all the world," muses Bogart, "she walks into mine!" And what a look they share at the remeeting—so the love plot is off and away. The setting crawls with adventure, in its hustlers, police shakedowns, visits to fixers. Yet the morality is not facile. "I stick my neck out for nobody," says Bogart. However, suave French detective Claude Rains points out in Bogart a sentimental streak. Thus the love story (with Bergman) and the moral parable (with Henreid) come together, adventurously, when Bogart takes the chance to speed them off together. Henreid must escape to fight for good, and Bergman must go with him because he needs her. At first, Curtiz couldn't see ending the film with Bogart giving up Bergman, or vice versa. He planned an alternate finish, obedient to the force of the Bergman-Bogart romance. But after shooting the separation, with its moral underpinning supporting the adventurous bravura, Curtiz realized he had ended the film perfectly.

By the time World War II was over, Bergman had made herself one of Hollywood's most popular heroines, first rate in all sorts of roles from costume-piece victimized wife in *Gaslight* (1944) to nun in *The Bells of St. Mary's* (1945) to costume-piece adventuress in *Saratoga Trunk* (1946) to modern-day whore-for-a-cause in *Notorious* (1946). However, the Hollywood approach to film was tiring her. Too many of these movies are alike, artificial and stagy, without the concentration of live acting before an audience. So when Bergman saw Roberto Rossellini's *Rome, Open City* (1945) and experienced the vitality of the Italian neorealist cinema, she was transfixed. Hiring part- or all-amateur casts, filming in real streets and houses instead of studio replicas, and concentrating on tales of the peasant and urban working classes, neo-realists like Luchino Visconti, Vittorio de Sica, and Rossellini amazed those tired of Hollywood's lying polish.

Bergman was one such. More than that, as a principal victim of the polish—a purveyor of it as well—she saw Rossellini as a redeemer. In her memoirs, she says, "Deep down I was in love with Roberto from the moment I saw *Open City*," sensing that the man who could reclaim her career as an actress could also reclaim her stultified love life. Her marriage had proved as limiting as her work, and it was she who contacted Rossellini and asked to work with him. He reciprocated, they got together, she made her acquaintance with neo-realism, and they did have an affair. But the alliance did not work out as Bergman had expected. For one thing, the films she made with Rossellini are among the worst films ever made. For another, the affair itself provoked the most explosive scandal since the American press tried Fatty Arbuckle for murder in 1921.

The artistic problem is simple: Rossellini was not a great director, far from it. *Open City*, a look at Rome under Nazi occupation, scored the key international success for neo-realism for its riveting honesty, but most of the film's power comes from its literally documentary footage and the performances of professionals Anna Magnani and Aldo Fabrizi. Rossellini's later entries, reverting to purely amateur casts, are embarrassingly primitive, for he had no ability or interest in developing his performers. De Sica could cast his *Bicycle Thieves* (1948, released in the United States as *The Bicycle Thief*) with people who had never acted before and bring out absorbingly realistic portrayals from them. Rossellini simply turned a camera on his amateurs, getting neither realism nor portrayals. What he got, Bergman discovered when she made the first of her Rossellini cycle, *Stromboli* (1950), was a gabble of village noises (in dialect) of no reference to plot or character.

Bergman played a displaced person who marries an Italian fisherman and finds herself a hated alien among his isolated island people. She also found herself the only person in the production who cared about communicating with the audience, including Rossellini. "You can *have* these realistic pictures! To hell with them!" she cried when she had had her fill of watching the Stromboli folk giggle and chatter and hang around on camera. "These people don't even know what dialogue is; they don't know where to stand; they don't care what they're doing. I can't bear to work another day with you!" Somehow or other the two made their peace, but the completed *Stromboli* vindicated Bergman's apprehensions: a boring, paceless film whose only point of interest is Rossellini's lengthy one-take shooting of the Stromboli fishermen making a tuna catch.

*Stromboli* was a gigantic international failure, but the artistic problem was as nothing next to the social problem, for in leaving her husband and daughter for Rossellini and bearing the first of her three children by him before she and he were married, Bergman brought upon herself the rage of the film community, of moralists and opportunists of all kinds, of politicians, columnists, and just about every big mouth in the Western world. Says Bergman, "I thought I would have to give up acting—to save the world from disaster, I mean—for it seemed that I had corrupted everybody in the world."

In these days when prominent actresses who bear children out of wedlock are an acceptable novelty, it is hard to understand how Bergman could have been so badly treated. Perhaps her very appealing image prompted the hysteria. Bergman, remember, was fresh—spiffy, just, graceful. Bergman's following felt betrayed. Had they understood who Bergman was, they should have relished her independence. But they had seen her in her costumes, in her nun's habit, or in the glamour fashion of the all-truth flame who loves Humphrey Bogart but pays her dues to loyalty in *Casablanca*. The story plus X equals the truth; Bergman revealed the X, so they vilified her.

Shocking. But to some extent the outrage was not public opinion but newspaper gossip posing as consensus. While the bonfire consisted largely of the usual screaming censors, doing unto others in their fashion, it was partly stoked by Hollywood, furious that Bergman had broken the behavioral code. To work in the movies is to assent. How dare the woman do what she wants? Worst of all was the press coverage, gleefully chasing her down wherever she went. The Bergman story virtually called the paparazzo into being. Journalists disrupted the premiere of *Vulcano* (1950), directed by the UFA and Hollywood veteran William Dieterle and starring Rossellini's neglected wife, Anna Magnani, when news spread that Bergman was just giving birth to Robertino Rossellini.

They pulled every stunt imaginable to sneak cameras into the hospital. (*Life* got the closest, as far as the shut door to Bergman's room.) They pleaded and finagled for photos of the demoted madonna with her child. That failing, they concocted one, in the style of the old *New York Evening Graphic*'s "composograph": a photo of a woman and a baby in the maternal bed with Bergman's head superimposed in the appropriate spot. The creeps.

There was pressure but no need to ban *Stromboli*—the film flopped without outside assistance. For six years, Bergman lived in Europe, an unmentionable. Then the time came to film *Anastasia,* a melodrama in the old-fashioned Big Moment style that had shattered the cool of the Western cultural capitals. It tells of émigré Russians in Berlin in the 1920s trying to pass off as the last of the Romanofs a young woman who turns out to be just that. Fox had bought the screen rights, director Anatole Litvak wanted Bergman, and Kay Brown (the woman who had traveled to Sweden to bring Bergman to Selznick in the first place) took a hand in "rehabilitating" the fallen image among the Fox honchos.

Actually, Hollywood needed Bergman badly. This was the mid-1950s, now, and the production of ersatz glamour had outrun the pursuit of talent. There weren't many women—if there were any—who could play Anastasia with Bergman's beauty and authority. The character is a miniature of the Hollywood star, groomed and coached by experts to project a certain image to a public; but unlike most stars, Anastasia throws it all away for personal reasons at the apex of her success—exactly as Bergman herself had done.

Bergman needed Hollywood, too, for the Rossellini episode had hurt her artistically. Fox ultimately thought it expedient to forgive Bergman, and the industry celebrated her return by voting her Best Actress for *Anastasia*. Yet Bergman remained her own self and made no recantation. Indeed, the part in effect affirmed her right to go her own way publicly and privately.

This independence marks Bergman as much as her talent does, even if her films in this comeback period suggest more the starry foofoo of a "movie movie" than the work of a pro obsessed with challenge. Anything she touches is given dignity, even such botches as *The Visit* (1964), a spineless reduction of Friedrich Dürrenmatt's moralistic black comedy that so disappointed the Swiss playwright that he boycotted the film's premiere in Geneva—a momentous act, as Geneva gets few premieres.

Bergman's elegance even transcends such paradigms of Hollywood flash as *The Yellow Rolls-Royce* (1965), a "sequence-film" in the new mode of doing a *Grand Hotel* spaced out to different places and times. *The Yellow Rolls-Royce* is Hollywood's idea of class—lush location shots; an all-star lineup with Continental cachet (Jeanne Moreau); the unveiling of a new heartthrob (Alain Delon—a wave crashes on the beach when he scores with Shirley MacLaine); British author and director (Terence Rattigan and Anthony Asquith); gala incidental score—and no bite whatsoever. Well, not until Bergman struts into the final sequence as a briskly reactionary American plutocrat who aids an anti-Nazi Yugoslavian (Omar Sharif) in the early days of World War II. Bergman knows the piece is hoke, but she doesn't play hoke, despite such encouragements in that direction as an idiot yapping lapdog, a formidable wardrobe, and a sudden change of politics. She even makes the inevitable romance with Sharif seem improvisational. At his tender look, she tells him, "No sentimental gush!"

Bergman is like Audrey Hepburn in her womanly poise, like Lillian Gish in her unquestionable commitment of talent, like Katharine Hepburn in her independence and timelessness, and like Bette Davis in her ability to be interesting in the worst of films. And, sure enough, many consider her the last of the stars, the retrospective final chapter of a handbook on moviemaking that listed as its first imperative "Stimulate, don't discourage." Actually, she is less the last star than the first person in the modern sense. How can anyone be the last star when procedures for sculpting and marketing an image are as vital as ever? Even after Monroe's death, Fox was hunting for another starlet to turn into a sex symbol. And did not that studio find one such in Raquel Welch?

However, while Welch is an outstanding looker, she has no image to invest in the It. What does she represent? As sex symbols, Theda Bara was a devourer; Clara Bow complaisant; Mae West cynical, aggressive, and promiscuous (in other words, a man); Rita Hayworth treacherous; Marilyn Monroe ambiguous, veering from predatory through tolerant to magnanimous. Welch is sex itself, but nothing more. She has made all sorts of films, yet registers nothing but the stupendous build proclaimed (no, decreed; for glamour has declined to the vocative) in the ads for *One Million Years B.C.* (1967). What is Raquel? *Fantastic Voyage* (1966) was science-fiction, *Bedazzled* (1967) zany comedy, *One Hundred Rifles* (1969) racial western, *Myra Breckinridge* (1970) miscarried satire of sex and Hollywood, *The Wild Party* (1975), a cult-film homage to the Fatty Arbuckle case with some musical comedy spliced in.

Welch has made every kind of film but a good one. (*Bedazzled* is the exception, but she does little more in it than breathe.) She is a starlet made good, not an actress. Taking over as Lauren Bacall's replacement in the Broadway musical *Woman of the Year* in late 1981, Welch worked hard, extending herself far more than Bacall did and revealing a pleasant singing voice. Yet it was a nowhere performance. Bacall walking through the part was nonetheless Bacall, exercising imagistic muscles just by showing up, while Welch has nothing to draw on but her sex celebrity.

Starletism—the plain marketing of looks as glamour and glamour as talent—ran out of control in the 1970s. It found its apex in Farrah Fawcett-Majors, the first actress who was nothing but a poster. Majors won prominence in television, but couldn't make it in film. Isn't there a lesson there? Yet the starlet plan remains the dominant one, as if they are looking for Monroe's It and not Monroe's talent. As if Monroe had no talent; maybe they don't think she did. Once, actors won Hollywood contracts on the basis of stage work. Now they earn parts in open casting calls run like beauty contests.

So if Farrah didn't make it, Brooke Shields did. A baby model, she grew up to play the girl raised in a bordello and sold to a painter in Louis Malle's *Pretty Baby* (1978) at the age of eleven. She became a favorite of gossip journalism for her television ads for Calvin Klein jeans, for the shots of a nude photo session that her mother permitted her at the age of ten, and for her dazzling percentage-point deal for the huge hit *The Blue Lagoon* (1980), still in her mid-teens. Compare the activities and parental guidance of Brooke Shields with those of Shirley Temple, and one gets a fix on the difference between then and now. Then, talent was It; and now It is money, sex, and fame. Do mothers urge their daughters to emulate Shields as they once used little Shirley as an example? Do women find inspiration in the work of Raquel Welch? The all-out application of starletism, ironically, has made the truly talented stand out, for the comparison devastates. Try to imagine Ingrid Bergman posing in the nude, at any age. Yet Bergman was no prude. It seems that glamour in this disco age is narcissism. Maybe it always was. But the studios kept it wrapped, sublimated. *Sunset Boulevard* revealed it. Now it's in the open.

Glamour is fame. Talent, personality, even It—these are not elements of glamour anymore, except among holdovers from earlier times like Bergman, or among the few gifted actors who are employed by uncorrupted directors and who then break through on the force of charisma. Cliff Gorman once told of a visit that glamour paid him. It's a telling tale. Gorman had suddenly become hot (Broadway hot, local but very fulfilling) for his portrayal of Lenny Bruce in the play *Lenny*. Nightly, the famous made their way to his dressing room to welcome him to their company and make a fast column or two. One night it was Welch's turn. "She's coming! It's Raquel!" they shouted up the stairway, and a suite of henchpersons and photographers burst into Gorman's room. They shot Welch, they shot Gorman, they shot Welch and Gorman, and they left. "She's going! It's Raquel!" and she was gone. She hadn't said a word to Gorman; no one had. He says he felt as if he'd been raped.*

The PR machine, which runs glamour, has made it difficult for important movie actors to retain their integrity. This has been a problem in the movies ever since Carl Laemmle invented Florence Lawrence's streetcar accident, and almost everyone but Katharine Hepburn and Ingrid Bergman has had to compromise to work. PR was not an aspect of life in Hollywood: it was sustenance. PR lies sourced the personal legend, PR teams protected the innocent and guilty alike from legal troubles, PR narratives turned into screenplays and gave some actors their biggest hits. But before and during the studio years, a habitually moviegoing public devoured all the films that Hollywood could produce. The disintegration of the production-exhibition monopolies in the 1950s left fewer films to fill fewer theatres, and people became habituated to television. Now most people go to movies irregularly, to

---

*Glamour must take it as well as dish it; that's the PR dues. When Dick Cavett interviewed Welch on television in 1980, the questions averaged out to an age-eight level with a strong smell of attack. Raquel learned a lesson that night: there is only one PR, and everyone in it is junk.

certain films, increasingly to Big Films. Big cost, big stars, big story. PR no longer works for an industry. It works for a few Big people.

This is the main reason why there are fewer big women stars today than there were in the studio years: there aren't as many lead roles to cast as there formerly were (because there are fewer films in the first place), and men, who still run the industry, mostly make films about men. This, combined with the concentration of glamour upon starlets of both sexes, has put some unlikely persons in the Big seats, people who can be glamorous despite their films: because they haven't the talent to make good ones.

Bo Derek may be a prime example. She is one of the biggest stars and an abysmal actress. She is also the most spectacular-looking woman in film history, and when she was cast as an uninhibited yet elegant young bride in *"10"* (1980), she capped the appetites and anxieties of an age. The notion of sexual liberation had been ground into a cliché without meaning. Woody Allen styled it as a party he couldn't get invited to, *Laugh-In* made it into doodles, novelists tried it for metaphor, hippies made it dreary. In *"10"* Bo Derek shows it to be an intelligent choice. It's a challenge as well: only the self-assured dare. Strangely, the movie doesn't seem to approve of her.

*"10"* is obsessed with sex. Everyone in it is getting into or out of an affair, Dudley Moore plays a composer working on a musical comedy called *Dreamboat,* and a running gag treats the use of telescopes for neighborly voyeurism. Further, Moore's first sight of Derek, on a Mexican beach, seriously applying suntan oil, her hair furrowed and capped in beads, is critically handled. We are meant to pursue her along with him. And he can have her: he saves her husband from drowning, gains entree, and spends an evening alone with her. "Did you ever do it to Ravel's *Bolero?*" she asks him. "My uncle turned me on to it." The moment, with its jab of taboo in the incestuous reference, recreates the atmosphere of forbidden fun that sex used to have.* Yet Moore can't face up to Derek's ethic of have it and enjoy it. *"10"* is a satire that's afraid of romance: you can't get the girl. Moore leaves chaste, disgusted by Derek's openness, her lack of hip problems. *"That's* your problem," Moore tells her.

The film's author and director, Blake Edwards, sends Moore back to his girlfriend Julie Andrews and clearly means for us to recoil from Derek's honesty. Who can live up to such an ethic? Edwards asks. Who can be so free? But she is persuasive; and the film—because of its disapproval of her—is false. Moore was crazed for her and should have accepted the invitation. Of course he would return to Andrews. It is she, not Derek, that one would spend one's life with. But why turn

---

*Doing it to *Bolero* is an old joke. Lorenz Hart used it in a lyric to one of the songs in *Pal Joey* in 1940.

down a pleasant hour with Derek? The trouble with *"10"* is that it doesn't know what it wants. Moore proposes to Andrews, but she turns him down "because we spend too much time arguing, and not enough making love." Yet surely marriage impends. The last word is sounded—as Moore and Andrews sink to the floor to the strains of, yes, *Bolero*—by Moore's neighbor, outraged by what he sees through the telescope. Some trade. He gives Moore hardcore, and "you reciprocate with PG!"

"Bo isn't really an actress," says her husband. "She's a happening." True. She's the personification of the beauty and peace that two decades of liberation couldn't find. A California girl, of course, a show-biz fluke who fell into the territory when an agent spotted her visiting friend Ann-Margret in Las Vegas. Derek is one star who isn't typed by time, but *for* it, chosen to set an example: be cool and do it to Ravel's *Bolero*. Her husband, John Derek, is an actor graduate of late-studio Hollywood who turned to photography and to marrying women beautiful enough—and willing—to do *Playboy* pictorials. He has been accused of "managing" Bo, but he only directed and photographed *Tarzan, the Ape Man* (1981). Bo produced it.

Really. She fired workers who weren't working, rerouted the emplaning of animals to the location in Sri Lanka, superintended everything from casting to catering, survived a lion attack, brought the project home on time and in budget ($6.5 million or so), and had her little joke in the logo before the opening credits: her company is Svengali Productions, and we see a huge cartoon Bo working the strings of a tiny puppet John.

There is a slight feminist overlay in the dialogue. But in major respects the film is a remake of two earlier *Tarzan* films, with heroine Jane meeting the jungle lord while searching for her lost father. The Dereks had hoped to bring out the erotic content latent in the tale— tropical heat, gala bods, no clothes, jungle zuzu. Again, it's Bo as liberator, archon of the equilibrium of good sex. If everyone were free . . . But everyone doesn't look like Bo Derek. Liberation will be slow, anyway, for an advance guard of prudes forced the Dereks to snip some of the Tarzan-Jane romantic footage, taking all the sport out of the picture. In any case, the critics mashed the film before word of mouth could protect it.

It wasn't bad. The script was poor; at one point, Bo likens her adventure to a story and says, "I don't know whether to laugh, or to cry, or to turn the page. Gosh! I hope it has a happy ending." The line is, uh, weak, and Bo does nothing to fortify it. But the story pacing is okay, the decor intriguing, the disparaged slow-motion sequences actually rather amusing (though a battle with a snake goes on too long), and the plot sturdy if twice-told. The casting, too, was right. Richard Harris as Bo's long-lost father is insufferable, but for once his character was supposed to be. The Tarzan, Miles O'Keeffe, is fine in what little the Dereks allotted him (such as no lines). Bo is Bo. *Tarzan, the Ape Man* will probably score a big success on television, and the Dereks will be turning down a hundred spinoffs.

The sudden rise of Bo Derek is indicative of the way things are now in the movies. On the basis of the one part in *"10"*—not literally but effectually her first film role—Derek and her partner became instantly prominent, with the power to choose and oversee their own vehicles. Why? It's partly in the nature of stardom as construed today; but, also, the culture needed Bo Derek in the 1970s as specifically as it needed Clara Bow in the 1920s and Monroe in the 1950s—to affirm certain revolutions in the nation's sex life which, without these symbols, are unofficial and vulnerable to counterrevolution. None of these last three women has an actor's calling. They are beauty contest winners who go on—happenings, as John Derek notes. It is interesting that Clara Bow was virtually an employee of her studio, that Marilyn Monroe had to make some twenty pictures before a few consecutive winners gave her autonomy, but that Bo Derek made both eminence and independence on one role. It is not because she is more adept than the others, or a better horse trader. It is because stardom moves fast now, and stardom is Big.

The word "stardom" itself has become debased through overuse, rendered meaningless. Hack journalists routinely apply it to anyone who acts; hype is so ingrained that almost everyone who writes on film writes PR. Like glamour, stardom has redefined itself over the years. In the 1910s stars were people you knew by name; in the 1920s they were actors with enough It and fans to carry a film. This held through the studio decades. But by the 1960s the word "star" was being used loosely enough to cover anyone who played a lead in any movie, or anyone who had anything remotely principal to do in anything from midwestern salad-bar dinner theatre to offbeat city cabaret. If any jerk or crazy is a star, what's Elizabeth Taylor? Ah: a superstar.

Ironically, some who have the charisma and talent and uniqueness of the old-time star can be ignored in the riot of overspeak, for there are just so many advertisements, big breaks, and puff-piece interviews to go around. One non-star who has earned recognition is Sally Kellerman, a most contemporary actress. Kellerman embodies the exhaustion of getting over the 1960s, her crooked smile, burned-out throat, and itchy free-associative monologues all trying to convalesce on mellow. Kellerman's problem is bad luck. Except for *M\*A\*S\*H* (1970), she keeps getting into weird films that no one sees. Even a Broadway excursion, in *Breakfast at Tiffany's* (1966), with Mary Tyler Moore as Holly Golightly and Kellerman standing in for Moore and playing a minor part, was a bomb. Not a cultist's flop, like *The Grass Harp*, or a short-run artistic success, like *She Loves Me*, or a stimulating objet trouvé by prominent showmen, like *Pacific Overtures*. A big, loud, stupid, dumb bomb. Yet Kellerman's duet with Moore, "The Home for Wayward Girls," was a neat moment.

Kellerman's neat. No one's like her, and if her films were hits, they'd be spinning off Kellerman roles for imitations to fill. But her films are not hits, partly because of Kellerman's contemporaneity. Most moviegoers don't want to come out of the 1960s; they either weren't of age then or don't want to recall it even to resolve its conflicts. *M\*A\*S\*H* is a fluke, about the only Robert Altman film that made a big profit and one of the few films of a purely sixties celebration that has advocates outside the hip city centers.

Look at the other Kellerman films: *Brewster McCloud* (1970), *Slither* (1973), *Rafferty and the Gold Dust Twins* (1975), *Welcome to L.A.* (1977). Who but a dedicated movie buff places the titles? And look at the roles Kellerman plays: a mad boy's guardian angel in *Brewster,* a speed freak in *Slither,* a kidnapper in *Rafferty,* a realtor making a play for a client in *Welcome to L.A.* Somehow, a grotesque family-fare musical slipped in there, the remake of *Lost Horizon* (1973), but Kellerman's career was already so offbeat that nothing could hurt her. Nothing helped, either. Familiar to millions as "the one who played the tough nurse in *M\*A\*S\*H,*" Kellerman can take on all sorts of parts, as for example the heroine of Public Television's adaptation of Dorothy Parker's story *Big Blonde*. It's a twenties tale, of that brittle Parkerian pathos, and Kellerman is right there with it, a jazzy romantic turning fatalist in a bad marriage. The set whimsies of the pot generation are laid aside for a precise re-creation of era and kind. Kellerman's adaptability, from Altman to Parker, is noteworthy. So why isn't she a star? "Please let me always be drunk!" cries the big blonde, Hazel Morse. "Now, that's no kind of prayer!" her maid comments. "Who's praying," Kellerman retorts, "to what?"

Kellerman is the most seventies of actresses, but who took the fame for the time? Diane Keaton. Here is a talent less adaptable, though Keaton's switchover from Woody Allen comedy *(Sleeper,* 1973), into epic melodrama *(The Godfather,* 1972, 1974), into Woody Allen seriocomedy *(Annie Hall,* 1977) on to artiste *(Looking for Mr. Goodbar,* 1977) is impressive, and was ultimately vindicated by strong work at the top of the 1980s.

Keaton's range within the Allen films alone is wide. At first, in *Play It Again, Sam* (1972), she is little more than a foil. By the time of *Love and Death* (1975), a sendup of Russian literature, she is one of the company farceurs, blithely airheaded, most forceful when the issues are most vague, like an emigrant midwesterner in New York who has adapted its forms but not its content. She is Allen's odd man in, not daffy exactly but the sort of person to whom daffy things happen. Keaton turns this quality over on its serious side in *The Godfather,* wherein she alone of the principals questions the tribal imperatives of the Mafia family. Odd again.

For many, *Annie Hall* was the height of Keaton, as much her vehicle as Allen's. (Even the title is a tribute, Hall being Keaton's family name.) In Allen's oeuvre it is a kind of *Brideshead Revisited*, the satirist's sole romantic foray and the expansion of his personal symbols. Telling how Allen courts and wins Keaton in New York, then loses her to California, *Annie Hall* pulls in every possibility in the handbook of film—directorial involvement, directorial detachment, farce, horror, parallel constructions, non sequiturs, animation, *Verfremdungseffekt*, fantasy, shots in all shapes and tempos. It's an ethnic-cultural joke elaborated into a national identity parable. Apparently, Allen mixed a brew so rich he went beyond the limits of workable structuring and had to depend heavily on the selection process of editing. But the result is a gem so bright it made Keaton the diva of the age, a trend setter in fashion, an industry heavyweight complete with Oscar, and a critic's darling.

She is to love. Allen opens the film alone against a blank background, speaking into the camera of his love for Annie. We then see them in *his* element, a Thalia showing of *The Sorrow and the Pity*. Later, in bed, Keaton wonders how she'd stand up under torture, and Allen tells her, "The Gestapo would take away your Bloomingdale's charge card, you'd tell them everything." In her dress shirt and tie, vest, baggy pants, and floppy hat, Keaton is a ne plus ultra of the WASP style. She comes from Chippewa Falls, Wisconsin, has a "Grammy" who gave her the famous tie (Allen's grammy didn't give presents—"she was too busy getting raped by Cossacks"), and orders pastrami on white with lettuce, tomato, and mayonnaise. Fitzgerald's Daisy's voice was "full of money." Keaton's voice, when Allen meets her for the last time in Los Angeles, is full of tofu. She tells him, "You're like New York City." He broods on art and politics and cannot hold her.

Indeed, she moved on, out of burlesque. But by then so had Allen. If *Annie Hall* marked the synthesistic perfection of the jokes he had been telling for a decade, Keaton's role in it was characterological rather than generical; and in *Interiors* (1978) they both abandoned comedy altogether. *Manhattan* (1979) returned them to surer ground; some think it Allen's masterpiece. But while it is hard to imagine Allen working out of his frame of Zabar's-angst comedy, Keaton successfully emerged from her *Annie Hall* persona in *Reds* (1981).

Here was a solemn event, Warren Beatty's major work. Running slightly under four hours, and costing over thirty million dollars, *Reds* is history, romance, spectacle, melodrama, and a political statement. Beatty produced, co-wrote, directed, and appears in it, so *Reds* is virtually his. Yet isn't there something of an oxymoron in the phrase "Warren Beatty's major work"? With *Splendor in the Grass* (1961), *Promise Her Anything* (1966), *Bonnie and Clyde* (1967), *Shampoo* (1975), and *Heaven Can Wait* (1978) behind him, Beatty is something less than a thoroughbred in art. He has done just enough not to be a Hollywood flimsy, and as a certified McGovernite he is top-okay politically. The subject he chose—John Reed, Louise Bryant, the Village bohemian set of the 1920s, and their involvement in the Russian Revolution—is fascinating. But for all the challenge and harmony that Beatty and Keaton find in the central love story, *Reds* has weight without authority and panorama without insight. It is not a Hollywood bio in the old style of, say, *Night and Day*. The story is scrupulously researched, the point of view fair, and the times recreated. A special platoon of Reed's and Bryant's contemporaries, including Adela Rogers St. Johns, George Jessel, Rebecca West, and Scott Nearing, recall the subjects at intervals throughout the film, sitting against a black background.

Still, the problem of capturing people and politics in one film has not been solved. *Reds* is not a political story, but it is about political people, and here the script and the acting fail. The secondary characters, such as Emma Goldman and Max Eastman, are mere quotations; only Grigori Zinovyef has been brought off, and that because he was nothing but politics, a self-made cipher. Jerzy Kozinski plays him well. In general, there is indication of political obsession rather than a feeling for it.

*Reds* is not the great opportunity for Keaton, though she and Beatty both won wide acclaim. Keaton's Annie Hall was most funny when her love relationships were most fragile, most troubled, and this quirk in her persona undercuts her fragile, troubled romance in *Reds*. There is always a trap in being perfectly cast in a unique part, as with Betty Bronson as Peter Pan or Bette Davis as Margo Channing; one keeps thinking that Keaton will say, "La-di-da." Critic Stanley Kauffmann saluted Keaton's "fire and determination and *fullness*" and declared her "the legendary Louise whom Jack [Reed] needed." The very notion of a *Reds*, unthinkable on several counts in previous decades, is exciting and the film is engrossing. Beatty is a director of take upon take, and Keaton is a great preparer, and this care shows in the work. But it may be that Keaton was far better served by *Shoot the Moon* (1982), small and simple.

*Shoot the Moon* has been described as a look at the disintegration of a marriage, but the marriage is already shattered when the film begins. What we see is the disintegration of a separation, through the husband's inability either to break away cleanly or accept the emotional turmoil he has created. Albert Finney as the husband has the trickier part, but Keaton's wife is a gem, feeling her way through suburban calamity as if she were making a cautionary tale at Hera's express commission. *Shoot the Moon* opened shortly after *Reds,* and the comparison between these two Keatons is taking, as both deal with a stormy marriage complicated by a second man, Eugene O'Neill in *Reds* and, in

*Shoot the Moon,* a man who builds Keaton a tennis court while Finney moves in with his girlfriend. In *Reds,* Keaton is so busy summoning up Bryant's ambition and passion that historicity overcomes her: she is not an epic personality. (That may be *Reds'* singular fault—epic characters cast with intimate actors.) In *Shoot the Moon,* Keaton is mother, wife, lover, the pieces snugly fitted. Bo Goldman's script and Alan Parker's direction suit the Keaton style, though they go way off in a restaurant scene that has an implausibly rotten pianist-singer and an even more implausible yelling match between Finney and Keaton. It is the household Keaton who is most resonant here, on home turf made foreign by the destructive complexity of the love relationship. Keaton is natural with her four daughters, running the line between support and distraction very convincingly.

If *Shoot the Moon* reveals Keaton at her most accomplished, *Reds* is interesting for its view of her as a fighter, the thirties woman figure whose life victories were not won exclusively in reference to man-woman romance. Keaton rose to prominence in a sheltered position, Woody Allen's girlfriend playing Woody Allen's girlfriend. But it is notable that in her first bid for attention as an important actress, in *Looking for Mr. Goodbar,* she played a sexually promiscuous woman who paid for her independence with her life. The final scene, in which she virtually goads her last pickup into murdering her, makes a connection between sex and violence that would have offended moviemakers of the 1930s. Menace was not erotic then, except in some relatively harmless outbursts from Gable and Cagney. Even there, the effect was more that of the tough guy than the mean lover. Gable and Cagney pushed women around; they didn't murder them. And what is notable about Keaton's ritual of passage in *Mr. Goodbar* is that all of today's actresses are expected to undergo something of the sort. Can an actress have stature if she doesn't play a whore? (Even Bergman made that trip, decades ago, in *Notorious.*)

There were no successors to the thirties fighters. Women have gone from "my mother's girl" to "my boyfriend's girl" in three decades, passing through Marilyn Monroe, Raquel Welch, and other sex symbols who lack the moral structure of earlier symbols. Achieving personal independence from men (the studio moguls), women have lost characterological independence (to the pronounced sexual harassment of PG). As censorship has given way, movies have got sexier. But no principles govern the revelations. In a disco age, glamour is sex; and no one wants to subvert the rituals of glamour, for glamour precisely produces income. The more glamour, the greater the profits.

There is one fighter left, Jane Fonda. But some of the causes she fights for are despicable, and at that she came into fighting from out of shlock and baby-doll nudity. She has Ingrid Bergman's pioneer work in the star's personal revolution to thank for her rehabilitation as a national heroine after a few years of industry boycott, and she got into acting in the first place as Henry Fonda's daughter. But Fonda has resisted the *film noir* legacy that types strong women as cheats, maniacs, killers, and whores—imitation bad men. It is fitting that she gave her finest performance in *They Shoot Horses, Don't They?* (1969), a Depression-era film of uncompromising social opinion.

In form the story takes the *Grand Hotel* microcosm to a dance marathon. But there are no golden-age clichés. The marathon manager, Gig Young, closes the film with "The dance of destiny continues . . ."—much as Lewis Stone closed MGM's *Grand Hotel* with his "People coming, going . . ." But *Grand Hotel*'s irony took energy from the adventures of seeing Garbo, Crawford, Beery, and the two Barrymores in one film. *They Shoot Horses,* despite a familiar cast, works on a different angle of commentary. "Will fortune reward her pluck and spirit?" Young asks his audience when Fonda temporarily dances alone, having quarreled with her partner, Michael Sarrazin. "Will she make it?"

She can't. She has lost the ability to believe in fairness, charity, and luck. She has lost it because there aren't any. Directly contradicting the old Hollywood truism that determination makes a winner, *They Shoot Horses* even explodes that favorite American dream—breaking into the movies. Fonda tried that, but Central Casting closed her out. She couldn't even get seduced into a part, and comments on Hollywood's peculiar sexual orientation: "I think I've been letting the wrong sex try to make me." If *Grand Hotel* was about the richness of the movies, where Beery speaks to Crawford and Crawford speaks to Barrymore and Barrymore speaks to Garbo and Garbo speaks only to God, *They Shoot Horses* is about the cruelty of capitalism. As the marathon applicants are checked in, aged sailor Red Buttons likens them to cattle on a boat. No, says Fonda—they feed cattle. And there's her face for the first view in the film, angry, hopeless, early old. Buttons comes back, "They kill cattle," and Fonda replies, "That puts them one up on us, doesn't it?" It's a pregnant exchange, for Buttons is virtually slaughtered, exhausted to death; and Fonda really would rather be dead than live so meanly.

James Poe and Robert E. Thompson wrote the screenplay from Horace McCoy's novel, the kind that could be sold to the movies in the 1930s but not filmed then. Too bitter, too honest. Warners could have cast it and the Warners writers could have adapted it, but the outlook is so bleak Warners probably couldn't have released it. Except for a prelude of a horse sporting in a meadow and being shot, and a few glimpses of Michael Sarrazin's arrest and trial for the murder of Fonda, at her request, the film's action is limited to the marathon and its horrors. It isn't just slow dancing for several days. It has talent spots, tiny rest-and-food breaks, (unplanned) sexual jousting, and elimination races. "You don't need to be number one as you amble down life's highway," exults Young. "But—*don't! be! last!*" Other lines also suggest a symbolism that connects the marathon to life, especially when Fonda learns that the big money prize she has been shooting for is a hoax. She quits; that's the end. "Maybe the whole damn world is like Central Casting," she tells us. "They got it all rigged before you even show up."

Some said the 1969 Oscar contest was rigged so Fonda couldn't win. Her politics were uninformed, strident, and anti-establishment in the extreme. Many assumed that Word had gone out against her before the voting. Any acting citation that passes over a performance of the strength and clarity of Fonda's in *They Shoot Horses* is hurting itself more than it's hurting Fonda. Still, the winner, Maggie Smith for *The Prime of Miss Jean Brodie*, gave a competitive performance. Besides, the acting Oscars prefer to go not to unique talents but to dues-paying stars who turn in image-defining portrayals. There have been exceptions, such as Anna Magnani for *The Rose Tattoo* or Simone Signoret for *Room at the Top*. But generally the awards have favored regulars who outdo themselves—Norma Shearer, Ginger Rogers, Jennifer Jones, Joan Crawford, Loretta Young, Elizabeth Taylor. This is hardly a list of all-time acting greats.

Anyway, Fonda won as Best Actress for *Klute* (1971) two years later, when her radicalism was even more pronounced. Her talent and the force of her image were too impressive to ignore. Her radicalism was even more impressive, for its propagandistic self-righteousness, its elitism, its apparent love of everything that hates America and hatred of everything that likes it. She teamed up with some of the most destructive career radicals of the time, purging every operation they joined of those who disagreed with them. The most flagrant instance in point was the FTA (Fuck the Army) show, a revue Fonda organized with Donald Sutherland to tour Army bases with politicized entertainment.

Successful at first, the tour degenerated into doctrinal infighting. James Skelley, a former Navy officer who helped found the anti-war Concerned Officers Movement in the late 1960s, noted the show's opportunism with disquiet. "There was very little attention paid to the question of GI rights," he said. "Most of the activity was aimed at converting GIs into active revolutionaries." At one cocktail party after an FTA performance at a coffeehouse outside Fort Lewis near Tacoma, Washington, "The GIs were excluded. I mean, the [Shelter Half coffeehouse] staff locked up the place. It was them getting their kicks rapping with celebrities, while the GIs were sent on their way." Stiffer and more widely quoted disgust was sounded by Country Joe McDonald, a singer with imposing credentials in the jug band, folkie-protest Berkeley acid scene. McDonald called Fonda "totalitarian" and quit the FTA show. At the same time, Fonda's former political mentor Fred Gardner published an article in *Second Page*, a San Francisco newsletter, indicting the FTA show for its "missionaries and fakes." The show "does nothing but advertise organizations and projects that have utter contempt for soldiers."

What happened to FTA was happening all over the parts of The Movement in the early 1970s. Young opportunists of the 1960s, egged on by the exploitive media, co-opted the old revolutionaries' decades of hard, serious work with trashy PR episodes, contempt for history, and enthusiastic internecine wars. Complicating the scene was feminism, another new reading of an old revolution, and one with almost as many combative splinter groups as it had spokesmen. Moreover, Fonda had married Tom Hayden, of leading leftists perhaps the most hated—by leftists. Abbie Hoffmann has dubbed Hayden "our Richard Nixon," and a recent favorite insiders' joke, credited to Gore Vidal, runs, "Tom Hayden is starting to give opportunism a bad name."

When Fonda and Sutherland filmed *Steelyard Blues* (1972) with some of the FTA crew, they inevitably reflected the skewed morality of the radical left world view. "A smug game for rich stars to play and for kids trying to be hip to laugh at," wrote Pauline Kael. "It's a show-business vice that the stupidly romantic artists who banded together to make this movie should have so little sense of reality and of their own privileged status that the pickpockets and other petty miscreants are considered nonconformists and friendly 'outlaws,' while the people who work for a living—the straights—are a piggy, vindictive, stupid lot." *Variety* set a precedent in euphemism by declaring the film "strictly for selected audiences."

Undeterred, Fonda set out to express her views in film. She made a pilgrimage to Jean-Luc Godard, master of the Brechtian style in cinema. But *Tout Va Bien* (1972), meaning "Everything's Fine," a study of a workers' factory takeover, left Fonda out of the creative process. Godard and his co-author, Jean-Pierre Gorin, were not eager for actors' input. Moreover, they put together a short called *Letter to Jane* (1973) in which they impeached her revolutionary procedure. A second try, filming Ibsen's feminist classic *A Doll's House* (1973), was similarly dissatisfying, as Fonda and FTA veteran Nancy Dowd edited David Mercer's adaptation and director Joseph Losey resisted their contributions. Fonda learned what many women's rights advocates could have told her: you can't make feminism with a man.

The radicalized Fonda struck some movie buffs as a wildly ironic comment on Hollywood history. Could such a father produce such a daughter? The Lincolnesque Henry gave the central performance in John Ford's *The Grapes of Wrath* (1940)—one of Hollywood's most important films and the very heart of New Deal positivism. Jane gave the central performance in Sydney Pollack's *They Shoot Horses, Don't They?*— one of the most important films of new Hollywood and the heart of

Marxist critique. If this is revolutionary, it is also dedicated to artistic and human values. But *Steelyard Blues, Tout Va Bien,* and the FTA show were revolutionary in the vein of new-left fascism. Here Jane left Henry and tradition behind. (This is not to mention Jane's brother, Peter, of *Easy Rider* and other nouvelle vague of the counterculture.) Buffs of old Hollywood were bewildered.

In fact, Jane Fonda had long been a controversial figure. Back when she was involved in such frippery as *Tall Story* (1960) and *Period of Adjustment* (1962), her statement that marriage was "obsolete" was prominently quoted. Such remarks made waves. Such movies as *Walk on the Wild Side* (1962) and *The Chapman Report* (1962), sexually outspoken, marked her for daring or, if one disapproved, for turpitude. A billboard advertising *Circle of Love* (1965) displayed her nude on a bed. This was Hollywood treachery, not Fonda's idea; still, no one forgave her. In early 1970, Rex Reed wrote an interview piece that emphasized Fonda as pot smoker. Another storm. So even before her politics moved leftward, Fonda was a culture shocker. By the time of *Steelyard Blues,* there were more than a few in the industry who would gladly have seen her name on a blacklist. Her films of the early middle 1970s were all made abroad, *The Blue Bird* (1976) as far afield as Russia.

Now comes rehabilitation. *Fun with Dick and Jane* (1976) teamed Fonda with George Segal in a satire, *Julia* (1977) was high-gloss melodrama, *Coming Home* (1978) a weepie, *Comes a Horseman* (1978) a modern western, *California Suite* (1978) a Neil Simon comedy, *The China Syndrome* (1979) a thriller. And so on. These were films in a Hollywood vein, major productions in familiar genres, all hits or respectable failures. The strong showing of *Julia* in particular largely silenced those who regarded Fonda as a traitor to her country.

Yet Fonda has had her way, for while making films that reach the average moviegoer, she has used each to stress a different aspect of Amerika the Beast. *Fun with Dick and Jane* attacks corporate crime and says our society is so corrupt that the only way to survive is to steal. But this is a big-budget Hollywood star special. Like the millionaire rock stars who harped on capitalist greed, it deals a stacked deck. *Julia,* based on Lillian Hellman's story, revives the lie that the popular-front "anti-fascism" of the 1930s was humanitarian; any mention of humanitarianism stinks when used in reference to Hellman and other admirers of Stalin's Gulag. *Coming Home* is more insidious in its romantic triangle, Fonda at the center, that rejects the Vietnam veteran who came back whole (Bruce Dern) in favor of the Vietnam veteran who came back in pieces (Jon Voight). Is Fonda saying that the only good man is a broken man, metaphorically castrated? *The China Syndrome* opened a national dialogue on the dangers of nuclear power, its argument strengthened just after it opened by the Three Mile Island disaster. Here at least there is a legitimate attack to be launched. But the issue stands in bad company. As the old protest song runs, "Which side are you on?"

How a fair-minded gem like the aforementioned *Nine to Five* fell into the pack is a mystery, though in the end this is more Lily Tomlin's and Dolly Parton's film than Fonda's by the passive nature of her part. *Nine to Five* offers an antidote to the sanctimonious intolerance of post-1960s radicalism. The film says, Assert yourself and neutralize your enemies. For once, we have a story that doesn't need a love plot to hold interest; women here are concerned with their work. They kidnap their vulture of a boss and take over the office, instituting a more reasonable salary program, a relaxed dress code, a day-care center, hiring advantages for the handicapped, and flexible schedules. And they let the boss try life on the other side, trapped in a house all day with soap operas to divert him. Amid a number of films of feminist inquiry, about escaping the pressures of heterosexual courtship and forging a career, *Nine to Five* made the neatest statement.

Comes the revolution, of course, there will be no reasonable salary program or flexible schedules, and Fonda will be answering to a central committee for having made *Barbarella*. Yet for the time she must be regarded as the only American woman star who successfully combined a political crusade and a movie career. She at length made public rapprochement with her father, teaming up with him and that other golden-age symbol, Katharine Hepburn, for *On Golden Pond* (1981), a sentimental domestic comedy like unto those of the Old Hollywood, when every movie carried a tacit G rating. As with Ingrid Bergman, Fonda has been thoroughly re-established in the industry, along with husband Hayden, who appears to have reversed himself on his earlier radicalism. Appearing with Jane in 1979 on *Meet the Press*—so reports Richard Parker in *The New Republic*—"Tom announced that he was in favor of free-enterprise capitalism and the unconditional survival of Israel, that he had never been a Marxist or even a revolutionary, and that he had opposed the use of violence in the 1960s—a great surprise on all counts to those who knew him."

Rarely does a star ally herself so closely and publicly with a husband who is not an actor. But politicians are actors today; this, too, has diluted the Old Hollywood recipe for glamour. Actors are less like actors than they used to be, more available to scrutiny outside of their roles. But those in other professions are more like actors than they used to be; everyone who appears on television becomes a performer by the nature of the medium. Fonda and Hayden have conquered the middle-American animosity they inspired in the 1960s. But they have done it the way actors do everything: through their roles and their PR. The entire system is not only rotten; it is a play, a movie, a trick show. Experience is processed. Thereby, it is not objectionable but perversely sensible that Fonda, as Bergman before her, has seen the same people who once denounced her now just as enthusiastically laud her, because she earns them all that nice, delicious money.

This suggests that Hollywood has not changed all that much over the years. Fonda's political stardom is innovative, and neither *They Shoot Horses* nor *Klute* could have been made in bygone days. But Fonda's later successful films, like *Julia* and *Coming Home,* are in form and tone respectful of American cinema traditions, and the profit motive in the rehabilitation of the outlaw actress reminds us of many a historical incident of Old Hollywood. The feuds. The comebacks. And if the industry's slant on the meaning and use of glamour has changed over the years, actors still have to have It. Feminists claim that today's film exploits women as no mogul ever did. But men, too, are exploited. When a large percentage of films deal with murderers, rapists, thieves, and cheats in a protagonistic manner, then all humanity, all society, is degraded.

What is new for woman is the collapse of the typing machine and the freedom to pursue acting projects outside the industry. In the studio years, stage actors who joined film were not generally permitted to return to the stage unless their careers (and therefore their usefulness to the studio) were floundering. Then, they'd seek reinvention on Broadway. Today, the practice of contracting actors one picture at a time allows them to mix movie work with guest spots in theatre, from Shakespearean repertory to avant-garde experiments. This allows the dedicated thespians to renew their art with stimulating reconnaissance. Genuine actors—the antidote to starletism—have worked in the movies from day one. But by the 1920s, the contract system and the functions of stardom demanded that these actors renounce the stage. Now, those who need the balance of the two can take it. This is certainly new.

Meryl Streep might be the definitive figure in this matter. By the mid-1970s, she was for many New York theatregoers the definitive young actress, distinguished by her command of technique. Many young stage actors impress with their ability to summon character emotionally and realistically. But in role after role they play that same character. Streep worked a lot, and every time one saw her she was somebody else. She had not only concentration but craft. She could even vary her style, as repertory artists do.

Streep modified her technique to suit movie It, less self-protected than that of the stage. But her native gift for stepping entirely into a role, as if closing a curtain behind her and thou shalt not peek in, has allowed her to play quite an assortment of parts. The films themselves don't seem that various. They are all more or less serious, with no excursions into genre, no song-and-dance or *noir* ambiance to master. Yet Streep herself changes completely from part to part. In *The Deer Hunter* (1978) she is insular, ethnic working class, assigned from birth to serve selfish or inscrutable men. In *Manhattan* (1979) she is art-class demon, leaving Woody Allen for a woman, brusquely cutting past him in a street scene while he pleads for sympathy. In *The Seduction of Joe Tynan* (1979) she is professional class, southern, tactful, and flies her own plane. In *Kramer vs. Kramer* (1979) she is an adman's housewife, tearful and unsteady. In *The French Lieutenant's Woman* (1981) she adds two new systems of information to her dossier, in a double role as the helplessly vacillating heroine of the film within the film and the more casually unreachable actress who plays her.

Most of today's stars plume themselves on such variety of person, but most of them must depend on traditional Hollywood indications of character, via costume, say, or by "doing" long silences between lines. Even gifted actors can lose their gifts in the relatively limited span of character that film allows them. Dustin Hoffman, Streep's husband in *Kramer vs. Kramer,* was in his youth a little toast of Off Broadway for the conviction he brought to bizarre parts. The movies assigned him one part, that in *The Graduate,* which he has played ever since.

This will not happen to Streep, though women are even more limited than men in character span. She keeps in contact with her calling rather than with her profession as others have structured it. When Pierre Trudeau came backstage at Joseph Papp's Public Theater to congratulate Streep on a performance, she thanked him. When he asked her for a date, she said no. Congratulations make sense; formal PR recognition by the disco elite does not. "Why," she asks, "do famous people only want to meet other famous people?"

To use each other. That's how glamour works. Then Streep has no glamour. She will not materialize at the Places, will not nob with the Faces. Hers is fascinating, but not a star's face. It's an actor's face. It changes from role to role. It was hard in *Manhattan,* a lot of nose; sweet in *The Deer Hunter,* moist; devious, twice over, in *The French Lieutenant's Woman.* Does she have It? She has stage It: talent. What's the X in her story? She'll never tell you. She is remarkable as much for what she doesn't do as for what she does. She doesn't like PR; that's remarkable. She could play the lead in *The Ingrid Bergman Story,* comes the time.

Old Hollywood and the veteran buffs are not happy. Today's movies are loathsome and filled with villainy. One leaves depressed. They are so unlike what they used to be that a term had to be devised to distinguish the old-time entertainment from the new, insistently: a *"movie* movie." Every biography that is published seems planned specifically to deface another idol. One book tells us that Errol Flynn spied for Hitler. Others will tell of sexual cosmopolitanism. Poor Joan Crawford, savaged in *Mommie Dearest,* turns up as an aggressive lesbian in the latest Bette Davis bio. Myrna Loy refuses to read such books. She probably doesn't think too much of the latest movies, either. They have Persons now but they had Faces then; they had It. *Interview* magazine asked Faye Dunaway what her favorite movies were, and she cited one, *Casablanca*. It has, she says, "all the elements: intrigue, mystery, glamour."

Aren't they the same thing? They were once. Now there is only intrigue. The mystery has been exposed and the glamour is for rent. Don't ask Marshall Neilan for an updated list of the Great Essentials for Stardom. Ask Pierre Trudeau or Raquel Welch next time they come backstage to welcome you into popular history. Ask them for a reading on the rise and fall of It. When was It most potent? At MGM in the early 1930s, perhaps, when Garbo and Crawford were at their zenith—doesn't *Grand Hotel* have more It than any other film ever made? When did It lose its drive? When Garbo retired? When Crawford faded? When Crawford died? Or when Crawford's legend was revised by her daughter Christina?

We hate stars; that's how you know that It is over. The all-basic elements of public interest and producers' engineering that date back to Florence Lawrence and Theda Bara are still dynamic. But the stories about the stars—the films themselves—don't give us the admirable, emulatable characters they used to. Under the guise of a profound naturalism, moviemakers present deceit, greed, egotism, and debauchery as behavioral norms. Moviemakers don't claim that these are the major human qualities, no. But we are used to the movies as the American mythology, the tales of love, of ambition, of heroism, the tales of how to live. Going to the movies was the Great American Secular Rite. The stories told us how to aim for utopia and It told us what utopia would feel like when we got there. Now the movies tell us that we cannot get there from here; no kind of It can make that lesson anything but depressing. Stars didn't die for our sins; they *lived* for them, to teach us to overcome deceit, greed, egotism, and debauchery. We loved stars then, learned from them (in their stories, that is, not in their lives). Today's stars have little to teach us that we want to learn.

Those who were looking for woman producers, directors, writers, or actors to redeem the current scene as woman's character in general helped redeem the Great Depression (as fighters and screwballs) are bewildered. The feminist 1970s were supposed to open the culture somewhat, instruct the mythology. There are many woman producers and directors and writers. Yet, except in a very few films, women have not been able to assert themselves. Most of their projects fail to find financing; some that are made cannot secure a major release. So Hollywood's women stars go on playing whores, and that's another reason why It died. For if It was sex appeal as well as charisma, It nonetheless withheld certain information. It's tact was alluring. Garbo and Crawford were sexier than the actresses of today, yet they never needed skin shots and hot lines in the modern style. You either have It or you don't.

It was what held the mythology together, made the tales of love and death a consolation for what you couldn't get in real life. You could know Garbo; you could be Crawford. Now the mythology is offensive. The men are still allowed to be Beowulf, sort of, but the women are all Grendel's dam. Old Hollywood says these people aren't fun, aren't pretty. They had faces then, remember. Actually, what these people aren't is vital, clear, true. Once, the word "Hollywood" meant an adventure of strong men and interesting women. Now, who knows what Hollywood is? and the women aren't especially interesting. I ask you, who is writing these scripts, who directing them?

We'll have to take our utopia in the beyond. In heaven, Katharine Hepburn coaches the tennis team, Joan Crawford works for the Resistance, Lillian Gish heads the NEA, Margaret Dumont gives the parties, and Gracie Allen is the policeman. In hell, Lillian Gish coaches the tennis team, Katharine Hepburn gives the parties, Margaret Dumont heads the NEA, Gracie Allen works for the Resistance, and Joan Crawford is the policeman.

# A Selective
# Bibliography

Marjorie Rosen's *Popcorn Venus* (Coward, McCann, 1973) and Molly Haskell's *From Reverence to Rape* (Holt, 1974) are essential reading. The two authors chose the same subject—to quote Haskell's subtitle, "The Treatment of Women in the Movies." Yet while both are comprehensive and strong on detail work, they do not overlap. Rosen is the more informal in style, especially alert to shifting patterns in the culture, and a committed Hollywood buff; Haskell writes in great reasoning chapters of paragraphs, so to speak. Rosen, then, is something of a guide and Haskell something of a teacher. Both are eminently readable. One after the other, in either order, makes for true penetration.

The Eden Press (at Box 51, Saint Albans, Vermont 05478) has brought out Sumiko Higashi's *Virgins, Vamps, and Flappers: The American Silent Movie Heroine*. This is careful work, perhaps the one book on Hollywood you read without finding a single mistake. Typing technique was originated in the second decade of the silent period, so those making a feminist inquiry should hear what Higashi has to say. I think, however, that she would have made a stronger case if she had investigated the serial heroines, exceptional in their day.

The basic element of research in this territory is the biography. Those written with the cooperation of or even wholly by the subjects themselves have the advantage of personal witness and opinions. The silent era is rich in such work. Most useful is *Lillian Gish: The Movies, Mr. Griffith, and Me* (Prentice-Hall, 1969), written with Ann Pinchot. Like Gish, it is clear, fair, and true. Colleen Moore's *Silent Star* (Doubleday, 1968) never comes to grips with the content of the films that made her one of the biggest stars of her day. It also lacks an index, which makes it more a reading than a research experience. Buffs like it, however. *Swanson on Swanson* (Random House, 1980) is exhaustive and forthright. Swanson not only knows where the bodies are buried, she tells.

Most fascinating and least fully examined of them all is Little Mary. There have been a number of biographies besides her own *Sunshine and Shadow* (Doubleday, 1954), but her chroniclers have for the most part reworked material from this one book, and she doesn't have much to say for herself. How these people can go rattling on about what they said to Mr. Zukor or who came to dinner, and never put down more than an idle phrase or two about their work—the characters and stories that made them influential—is a puzzle. Perhaps the best of the Little Mary lot is Booton Herndon's *Mary Pickford and Douglas Fairbanks* (Norton, 1977). Nothing to startle either the committed or the unconvinced, but good reading and some fresh material. Charles Higham, who has not done a Little Mary book, had the closest encounter with her. He actually got to Pickfair, and was settled in a public room, where Mary *telephoned him from her bedroom* (italics mine). She didn't say much to him, either. Well, if it's not a sighting, at least it's contact.

Unlike Pickford, Joan Crawford has come forth to the life; she *is* the movies. Her own volumes, *A Portrait of Joan* (more or less told to Jane Ardmore; Doubleday, 1962) and *My Way of Life* (Simon and Schuster, 1971) are the dull black-and-white prints. Bob Thomas' *Joan Crawford* (Simon and Schuster, 1978) is bold and bright. The Technicolor spectacular, however, is Roy Newquist's *Conversations with Joan Crawford* (Citadel, 1980). A small book, handsomely and unpretentiously produced, it reveals Hollywood—glamour and horror—as no other work has done. Crawford knew what it was like to be promising, to hold the top, to slip and remount, and to crash to Skid Row; she knew Gable, Mayer, Little Mary and Doug, grips and gaffers; she heard the rumors and starred in a few; and she lays it out here. It's a compelling monologue, given structure by Newquist's apt questions; and not unlike a last report on the deathbed, all debts paid out. No matter how you feel about Crawford personally, you may find yourself admiring her by the end.

Now it's all talkies. Warren Harris' *Gable and Lombard* (Simon and Schuster, 1974) is lively. Charles Higham's *Marlene* (Norton, 1977) is the best of the Dietrich books. Rosalind Russell's *Life Is a Banquet* (Random House, 1977) is made extra readable by the assistance of Chris Chase. Katharine Hepburn is said to have been outraged by Garson Kanin's *Tracy and Hepburn* (Viking, 1971). But this is a loving portrait, candid but more respectful of Hepburn's privacy than other authors would be. Kanin begins, "Katharine Hepburn is tall—not as tall as she thinks she is, but tall." He may have lost her right there; I get the impression that she doesn't take to criticism or correction well. But better Kanin than Christina Crawford, eh? For the full life story, try Gary Carey's *Katharine Hepburn* (Pocket Books, 1975).

Of this middle-era Hollywood group, Bette Davis has been the best served, in two vital entries. Whitney Stine's *Mother Goddam* (Hawthorn, 1974) is nicely detailed and has the extra advantage of Davis' running commentary, elaborating and occasionally contradicting Stine's report. As with Crawford in the Newquist interview, Davis' recollections and opinions reveal a far more likable woman than we have known from the parts she played. Special credit to Michaele Vollbracht's cover drawing of Davis in one of her *Now, Voyager* "after" outfits, with a pin sporting the Warner Brothers insignia affixed to her blouse. Arresting. (Mother Goddam, by the way, was the name of the Hong Kong brothel keeper first played by Florence Reed in the play *The Shanghai Gesture*. In the movie version, she was renamed Mother Gin Sling.) Charles Higham's *Bette* (Macmillan, 1981) hacks away at a few idols in the contemporary manner, but respects Davis. He dismisses Stine as a "fan" and Stine's book as "a record of names, dates, and places." This is graceless, also misleading. Otherwise, Higham does his usual good job.

Another biography enriched by the subject's own musings is Alan Burgess' *Ingrid Bergman* (Delacorte, 1980)—and Bergman is more interesting than most stars in terms of personality and career. Someone should do one of these running-commentary jobs on Jane Fonda; it would be interesting to hear her own views on the many several controversies that surround her. Till then, two fine works await the curious. Thomas Kiernan's *Jane* (Putnam, 1973) emphasizes her political involvements. Gary Herman and David Downing's *Jane Fonda: All American Anti-Heroine* (Quick Fox, 1980), with its bizarre publishing imprint, page-crowding photos, and come-hither cover design, looks like a rip-off, but the authors are literate and insightful. They also treat the films themselves in greater detail than most authors do.

Of those who trafficked in musicals, there are few imposing volumes to be cited. An exception is *Rainbow* (Grosset and Dunlap, 1975), Christopher Finch's authoritative review of Judy Garland's life and career, superbly produced with photos no one else has used—a book to treasure. Doug Warren's *Betty Grable* (St. Martin's, 1981) is subtitled "The Reluctant Movie Queen," which suggests a thesis on stardom. But Grable is less rich in affirmations and contradictions than most of her colleagues, and nothing like a Garbo of the musical. How much, then, can one say? Also, she tended to make the most formula-oriented films of her day, from thirties college romps to forties backstagers, so Warner is hard pressed to keep a character in focus. He comes through nicely; but his queen rules a very minor kingdom. Doris Day does not "speak" into A. E. Hotchner's *Doris Day* (Morrow, 1975) in the Davis-Bergman manner, but just about everyone else she knew does. It's worth a look.

Barbra fans will already be familiar with James Spada's *Streisand: The Woman and the Legend* (Doubleday, 1981) for its tasty pictorial display. However, Spada seems to be something of a fan himself. (This is his second book on Streisand.) He neither gushes nor protests too much, but something in the way of critical detachment is lacking, about the woman if not the legend. René Jordan's *The Greatest Star* (Putnam, 1975) is welcome, then, for its considered judgment calls. Aficionados of show biz must investigate Garson Kanin's *Smash* (Viking, 1980), the novel based—I think—on the original *Funny Girl* production. *Is* that Streisand? In one scene Kanin has his protagonist, the director, reasoning with his Star. When he tells her that she's learning and improving, she replies, "Don't butter me up, buster. I'm not a piece of toast." And when he begins an illustrative story involving the tryout of *As Thousands Cheer* and taking in the likes of heavyweights Irving Berlin, Moss Hart, Hassard Short, Clifton Webb, Marilyn Miller, and Ethel Waters, Star says, "Some show. I never heard of any of them." If that isn't Streisand in tone, diction, and level of show-biz expertise, I'm Marilyn Miller.

More generally, Arlington House has brought out a huge line of career study compendiums. Unfortunately, while these provide good research material, they rather drone on. Those who want to see for themselves might try James Robert Parish and Don E. Stanke's *The Leading Ladies* or *The Hollywood Beauties* by Parish, Stanke, and Gregory W. Mank (are these real names?). Norman Zierold's *Sex Goddesses of the Silent Screen* (Regnery, 1973) deals with Theda Bara, Pola Negri, Mae Murray, Clara Bow, and, gone and forgotten by all but Zierold, Barbara LaMarr. Michael Bruno's *Venus in Hollywood* (Lyle Stuart, 1970) deals with foreign stars who worked in America as sexual icons, from Negri and Vilma Banky to Sophia Loren. Racy and amusing.

Charles Affron's *Star Acting* (Dutton, 1977) is an enticing novelty: Gish, Garbo, and Davis caught in some seven hundred frame enlargements—not stills, but duplicates of the film itself. (Affron even reproduces a view of Garbo's *Anna Christie* entrance in the different costume of the German-language version.) The author uses the pictures to discuss the three women's different styles; also, "how we perceive star acting in context." Alexander Walker treats the same subject from a different angle, with a few stills, in *Stardom* (Stein and Day, 1970), a classic of its kind. A dud of this kind is Richard Dyer's *Stars* (British Film Institute, 1979), much like a Ph.D. thesis with its greed for quotations of commentators famous and obscure and its ideological buzz words. Dyer is pretentious and boring; ironically, he is an avid critic of other writers' styles in his book reviews.

Lastly, there is Kevin Brownlow's *The Parade's Gone By* (Knopf, 1968), one of the three or four best books on Hollywood ever published, sumptuous, comprehensive, precise. A recollection of the silent age, it deals heavily with only three of the present book's subjects, Farrar, Swanson, and Pickford. But Brownlow has caught the panorama of Hollywood in its infancy, adolescence, and early maturity so beautifully that the book has become the primary study for anyone who wants to know how American film works, in any era. The title comes from an adventure of Old Hollywood veteran Monte Brice, an all-arounder who survived the decades to watch the filming of *The Buster Keaton Story* in 1957. They were getting everything wrong—the bio facts, the techniques, the people. When he told them, they shoved him aside. "You're an old man," an assistant informed him. "The parade's gone by." Brice had seen the future, and it doesn't work.

# Index

*Adam's Rib*, 154, 155, 156
*Adventure*, 103–4, 165
*Alice Adams*, 147–48; also *Intermission*
*All About Eve*, 191–92, 193, 223; also
    *Intermission*
Allen, Gracie, 137–38, 139, 284
Allen, Woody, 238, 240, 269, 272–73
*Anastasia*, 265–66
Andrews, Julie, 245, 249–50, 269–70;
    also *Intermission*
*Anna Christie*, 76, 127; also *Intermission*
*Anna Karenina*, 80
*Annie Hall*, 273, 274
Arden, Eve, 123, 138–39, 284; also
    *Intermission*
Arthur, Jean, 96, 111–12, 233
Arzner, Dorothy, 12, 135
Astor, Mary, 144, 164
*At Long Last Love*, 238–39
*Auntie Mame*, 170
*Awful Truth, The*, 65, 151


*Babes in Arms*, 200, 202–3
Bacall, Lauren, 191
*Back Street*, 160
Ball, Lucille, 135–37, 138, 139; also
    *Intermission*
Bankhead, Tallulah, 187, 189, 191
Bara, Theda, 1, 3–10, 18, 19, 23, 31,
    36, 39, 51, 52, 53, 67, 71, 106, 107,
    116, 124
*Barefoot Contessa, The*, 217–18
Barrymore, Ethel, 96, 190
Barrymore, John, 64, 80, 87, 88, 96,
    127–28, 129, 144–45; also
    *Intermission*
Barrymore, Lionel, 47, 87, 96, 127,
    195; also *Intermission*
Baxter, Anne, 191–92
*Because of Him*, 198

Bennett, Constance, 9, 61, 63, 64, 83,
    84, 100, 132, 164, 170; also
    *Intermission*
Bergman, Ingrid, 154, 245, 256–57,
    260–66, 268, 275, 287
Bern, Paul, 114
*Beyond the Forest*, 190
*Big Street, The*, 135
*Bill of Divorcement, A*, 144–45
*Birth of a Nation, The*, 47–48, 50, 187
*Blazing Saddles*, 239
Blondell, Joan, 103, 161, 162–65, 174,
    176, 180; also *Intermission*
*Blonde Venus*, 108, 111; also *Intermission*
*Blood and Sand*, 23, 210
*Blue Angel, The*, 106–8
*Blue Bird, The*, 208–9
Blythe, Betty, 5
*Bohème, La*, 51; also *Intermission*
Boland, Mary, 71, 138, 167
Booth, Shirley, 153, 165
*Bordertown*, 183; also *Intermission*
*Born Yesterday*, 191, 233, 234
Bow, Clara, 26–29, 44, 63, 74, 85, 271;
    also *Intermission*
Brady, Alice, 130, 197
*Breakfast at Tiffany's*, 236–37, 250
*Break of Hearts*, 147, 153
Brenon, Herbert, 10, 18, 22, 53
Brent, George, 94, 187; also *Intermission*
*Bringing Up Baby*, 99, 102, 143, 150–52,
    153, 253
*Broadway Melody of 1938*, 200–201
*Broken Blossoms*, 48, 49, 50
Bronson, Betty, 17–18, 24, 36, 61, 184,
    230
Brooks, Louise, 11, 41
Brooks, Mel, 238, 239, 240
Burke, Billie, 127
Burns, George, 137–38
Burton, Richard, 207–8, 215

*Bus Stop,* 225
*Butterfield 8,* 206, 207


*Cabaret,* 256; also *Intermission*
Cabin in the Cotton, 182, 183
Cactus Flower, 243
Cagney, James, 112, 161, 162, 163, 183,
    185, 275
*Calamity Jane,* 247
*Camille,* 80
Canova, Judy, 138
Capra, Frank, 80, 175–78, 235
Carey, Gary, 150, 287
*Casablanca,* 262–63, 265, 283
*Charade,* 235
Chatterton, Ruth, 94, 95, 98, 100, 109,
    139
*China Seas,* 113
*Christopher Strong,* 145, 153
*Citizen Kane,* 133–34, 135
*Clash by Night,* 179–80
*Cleopatra,* 207–8
Colbert, Claudette, 32, 96, 191, 207,
    235
Collier, Constance, 139
*Coming Home,* 279
*Conquest,* 81
Cooper, Gary, 8, 27, 96, 99, 108, 109,
    111, 146, 177–79
*Corn Is Green, The,* 190
*Cover Girl,* 139, 210
Crawford, Joan, 9, 23, 58, 61, 69, 71,
    74, 83–92, 98, 102, 107, 109, 113,
    139, 142, 144, 146, 152, 156, 167,
    175, 184, 189, 193, 200, 205, 224,
    276, 277, 282, 283, 284, 286; also
    *Intermission*
*Critic's Choice,* 136–37
Cukor, George, 63, 80, 81, 113, 128,
    144–45, 153, 155, 167, 208


*Dames,* 163
*Dance, Girl, Dance,* 135
*Dark Victory,* 187
Davies, Marion, 70, 133–35, 139; also
    *Intermission*
Davis, Bette, 9, 90, 109, 142, 146, 156,
    182–93, 200, 207, 266, 282, 287,
    288; also *Intermission*
Day, Doris, 238, 244, 246–49, 256, 284;
    also *Intermission*
*Deer Hunter, The,* 281–82
De Havilland, Olivia, 187, 193
De Mille, Cecil B., 11, 12, 17, 30–32,
    42, 93–94, 220
Derek, Bo, 269–70
*Desert Song, The,* 100

*Destry Rides Again,* 110
*Devil Is a Woman, The,* 108
Dietrich, Marlene, 46, 61, 74, 79,
    105–112, 113, 115, 118, 120, 123,
    152, 215, 216, 238, 239, 286; also
    *Intermission*
*Dinner at Eight,* 113, 127–28; also
    *Intermission*
Dodd, Claire, 98, 163
*Double Indemnity,* 179
Douglas, Melvyn, 82, 100, 164
*Down Argentine Way,* 214
Dressler, Marie, 81, 125–28, 130, 136,
    139–40, 184; also *Intermission*
*Dr. Jekyll and Mr. Hyde,* 262
*DuBarry Was a Lady,* 135–36, 256
Dumont, Margaret, 102, 284; also
    *Intermission*
Dunaway, Faye, 83, 283
Dunne, Irene, 93, 100–101, 150–51,
    216, 256; also *Intermission*
Durbin, Deanna, 196–98, 200, 205,
    218, 246


*Easy to Wed,* 136
*Ella Cinders,* 25, 26; also *Intermission*
*Everybody Sing,* 201
*Every Night at Eight,* 173


Fairbanks, Douglas, 9, 43–44, 49,
    55–56, 86
Fairbanks, Douglas, Jr., 86, 101
*Farewell to Arms, A,* 96
Farrar, Geraldine, 16–17, 32, 36, 53,
    83
Farrell, Charles, 58–59, 61–62, 65
Farrell, Glenda, 161–62, 164, 183; also
    *Intermission*
*Fashions of 1934,* 183–84
Faye, Alice, 160, 164, 172–75, 180,
    183, 214
*Female on the Beach,* 90
Fields, W. C., 120–21, 133, 137; also
    *Intermission*
*Flaming Youth,* 25–26
*Flesh and the Devil,* 74–75
Fonda, Henry, 61, 135, 136, 276,
    278–79, 280
Fonda, Jane, 260, 275–80, 287; also
    *Intermission*
Fontanne, Lynn, 65, 69, 70–71, 96–97,
    142
*Fool There Was, A,* 4, 5, 8
*Foreign Affair, A,* 111–12
*Foul Play,* 244
Francis, Kay, 6, 95, 109, 153; also
    *Intermission*

*French Lieutenant's Woman, The,* 282
*Funny Face,* 235–36
*Funny Girl,* 252, 254–55
*Fun With Dick and Jane,* 279

Gable, Clark, 8, 58, 69, 70, 76–77, 80,
    86, 88, 100, 103, 113, 132, 146,
    167–68, 176, 201, 222, 235, 275;
    also *Intermission*
Garbo, Greta, 9, 69, 72–83, 84, 87, 91,
    98, 102, 107, 108, 109, 111, 113,
    123, 127, 130, 142, 146, 152, 159,
    188, 200, 216, 217, 276, 283, 288
*Garden of Allah, The,* 109–10
Gardner, Ava, 194, 216–18
Garland, Judy, 62, 103, 168, 194,
    196–97, 198–205, 213, 215, 218,
    246, 256, 287; also *Intermission*
Garson, Greer, 83, 93, 102–104, 170,
    207
*Gay Divorcee, The,* 213, 256
Gaynor, Janet, 57–65, 71, 195, 196,
    202, 231
*Gentlemen Prefer Blondes,* 223–24
Gilbert, John, 13, 15, 27, 54, 67, 68,
    74–76, 79–80, 84, 111, 112, 155,
    222; also *Intermission*
*Gilda,* 211, 212; also *Intermission*
*Girl Rush, The,* 169
Gish, Lillian, 9, 37, 46–56, 61, 67, 69,
    74, 112, 142, 146, 221, 266, 284,
    285, 288; also *Intermission*
*Gold Diggers of 1935,* 162
*Gold Diggers of 1937,* 162, 163; also
    *Intermission*
*Golden Boy,* 160
*Gone With the Wind,* 186–87, 263
Gordon, Ruth, 72, 155
*Go West, Young Man,* 119–20
Grable, Betty, 101, 168, 194, 195, 198,
    212–16, 218, 233, 287; also
    *Intermission*
*Grand Hotel,* 80, 87, 127–28, 276, 283;
    also *Intermission*
Grant, Cary, 8, 58, 100, 117–18, 122,
    125, 143, 146, 150–51, 153, 156,
    230, 235, 253
*Grease,* 165; also *Intermission*
*Great Bank Robbery, The,* 229
*Greed,* 20–21
Griffith, D. W., 1, 2, 25, 37, 39, 40, 41,
    43, 45, 46–51, 53, 54, 56, 112, 221
*Guardsman, The,* 96–97
*Guess Who's Coming to Dinner,* 157–58
*Gypsy,* 171; also *Intermission*

Hamilton, Margaret, 19, 120–21, 203, 215

Harding, Ann, 68, 94–95, 99, 100, 152;
    also *Intermission*
Harlow, Jean, 112–15, 118, 123,
    127–28, 132, 144, 172, 206, 216,
    222, 229
Hawks, Howard, 129, 168, 223
Hawn, Goldie, 229, 243–44
Hayes, Helen, 96; also *Intermission*
Hays, Will H., 35, 119, 133
Hayworth, Rita, 194, 209–12, 215, 216;
    also *Intermission*
Hearst, William R., 70, 133–35
*Hello, Dolly!,* 252; also *Intermission*
*Hell's Angels,* 113, 114
Hepburn, Audrey, 232, 234–37, 266
Hepburn, Katharine, 23, 58, 99, 100,
    109, 139, 141–59, 184, 187, 194,
    202, 253, 266, 268, 280, 284,
    286–87; also *Intermission*
*High Anxiety,* 239
*His Girl Friday,* 167–68
*Holiday* (Griffith), 95, 99
*Holiday* (Cukor), 95, 152
Holliday, Judy, 154, 156, 191, 229,
    232–34
Hopkins, Miriam, 99, 187
Horne, Lena, 216
*How to Marry a Millionaire,* 215

*Idiot's Delight,* 70–71
*I'm No Angel,* 118–19
*In Old Chicago,* 173
*Intermezzo: A Love Story,* 261
*It,* 29
*It Happened One Night,* 151, 235
*It Happened to Jane,* 248
*It Should Happen to You,* 233–34

*Jezebel,* 187, 190; also *Intermission*
*Joan the Woman,* 17
Johnny Guitar, 89, 90
Jones, Shirley, 256
*Joy of Living,* 101
*Julia,* 279

Kael, Pauline, 278
Kahn, Madeline, 238–39
Kanin, Garson, 141, 155, 233, 251,
    254–55, 286, 288
Kauffmann, Stanley, 274
Keaton, Diane, 205, 251, 272–75
Keeler, Ruby, 161, 163, 173, 213, 259
Kellerman, Sally, 271–72
Kerr, Deborah, 207
*Kiss Me, Stupid,* 229

*Klute*, 277, 281
*Kramer Vs. Kramer*, 282

*Lady From Shanghai, The*, 211
Laemmle, Carl, 2–3, 9, 13, 67, 166
*Late Show, The*, 242–43, 244
Lawrence, Florence, 2–3, 9, 10, 19, 24, 63, 222, 268
Lawrence, Gertrude, 191
*Libeled Lady*, 114, 136
*Lion in Winter, The*, 156, 157
*Little Foxes, The*, 189
*Little Minister, The*, 146
*Little Women*, 145–46, 148, 149
Lombard, Carole, 70, 98, 99, 100, 125, 128–33, 140, 150, 184, 232, 258, 286; also *Intermission*
*Looking for Mr. Goodbar*, 275
Loos, Anita, 12, 71, 223, 234
Loy, Myrna, 99–100, 166, 282; also *Intermission*
*Letty Lynton*, 87
Lubitsch, Ernst, 44, 46, 52, 66, 68, 80, 82, 97, 99, 215

MacDonald, Jeanette, 7, 53, 58, 70, 97–98, 172, 197, 216, 238; also *Intermission*
McLaine, Shirley, 207
Macpherson, Jeanie, 12
*Mad About Music*, 197–98
*Mad Miss Manton, The*, 149, 177
*Magnificent Obsession*, 100–101
*Male and Female*, 31–32
*Mame* 137; also *Intermission*
Mamoulian, Rouben, 79, 80, 97, 210
*Manhattan*, 273, 282
Mankiewicz, Herman, 133–34
Mankiewicz, Joseph, 154, 156, 191–92, 223
Mansfield, Jayne, 230
March, Fredric, 64, 69, 80, 88, 99, 100, 131, 140, 148, 229
*Marie Antoinette*, 70
Marion, Frances, 12, 126
*Marked Woman*, 185–86, 188
*Marrying Kind, The*, 233
*Mary of Scotland*, 148–49
*Mata Hari*, 78–79
Mathis, June, 12
*Matter of Time, A*, 256–57
Mayer, L. B., 14, 16, 52, 54, 66, 67, 68, 70, 71, 75, 85, 88, 92, 102, 112, 114, 115, 128, 153, 205
McCambridge, Mercedes, 89
*Meet John Doe*, 177–79; also *Intermission*

*Meet Me in St. Louis*, 200, 205, 208, 247
Merman, Ethel, 135–36, 171
*Merry Widow, The*, 13–15
*Mildred Pierce*, 88, 91, 139
Miller, Ann, 139
Minnelli, Liza, 199, 204, 245, 256–57
*Miracle Woman, The*, 176
Miranda, Carmen, 214, 233
*Moment by Moment*, 241; also *Intermission*
*Mommie Dearest*, 84; also *Intermission*
Monroe, Marilyn, 115, 180, 215–16, 220, 222–31, 267, 271, 275
Montgomery, Robert, 69, 88, 95, 125, 167
Moore, Colleen, 25–26, 27, 29, 36, 44, 45, 50, 63, 71, 218, 285; also *Intermission*
Moran, Polly, 126, 127, 136
*Morning Glory*, 143, 145, 146, 148, 150
*Morocco*, 79, 108, 215
*Mourning Becomes Electra*, 168
*Move Over, Darling*, 247, 249
*Mr. Skeffington*, 188
*Mrs. Miniver*, 102
Murray, Mae, 11, 13–16, 24, 51, 83, 135, 205, 221
*My Fair Lady*, 237, 249
*My Little Chickadee*, 120–21; also *Intermission*
*My Man Godfrey*, 125, 130–31, 151
*Myra Breckinridge*, 123, 267

*National Velvet*, 206, 216
Nazimova, Alla, 21–23, 36, 51, 52, 53, 78, 210, 226; also *Intermission*
Negri, Pola, 33, 35, 53, 74, 109
*Never Wave at a Wac*, 169
*New York, New York*, 256, 257
Neilan, Marshall, 41, 42, 45, 52, 55, 67, 78, 112, 126
*Night After Night*, 117
*Night of the Iguana, The*, 218
*Nine to Five*, 241, 280
*Ninotchka*, 82–83
*Nothing Sacred*, 131, 132, 140
*Notorious*, 263
Novak, Kim, 169, 228–30
*Now, Voyager*, 189–90

O'Brien, George, 57, 59, 231
*Of Human Bondage*, 184, 188, 190
Olivier, Laurence, 79, 95, 226–27
*On a Clear Day*, 252–53
*One Touch of Venus*, 139, 216
*On Golden Pond*, 280

*Orchids and Ermine,* 26
*Our Dancing Daughters,* 85, 86, 89

*Pajama Game, The,* 247
*Pal Joey,* 211–12, 229
*Paper Moon,* 239
*Paris When It Sizzles,* 236
Parsons, Louella, 56, 68, 81, 84, 133
*Pat and Mike,* 154–55; also *Intermission*
*Pennies From Heaven,* 257–59
Peters, Bernadette, 257–59
*Philadelphia Story, The,* 153; also
    *Intermission*
Pickford, Mary, 2, 9, 37–56, 60, 62, 65,
    67, 71, 86, 112, 122, 135, 142, 184,
    195, 196, 200, 202, 209, 231, 286,
    289; also *Intermission*
*Picnic,* 169, 229
Piggy, Miss, 239–40
*Pigskin Parade,* 200; also *Intermission*
*Pillow Talk,* 238, 247, 248
Pitts, ZaSu, 19–21, 23, 102
*Platinum Blonde,* 113
*Pollyanna,* 41, 43
*Poor Little Rich Girl, The,* 41–42
Powell, Eleanor, 201, 210, 213
Powell, Jane, 246
Powell, William, 95, 99, 129, 130, 132,
    183
Power, Tyrone, 23, 70, 173, 210, 229
*Prince and the Showgirl, The,* 226–27
*Private Lives of Elizabeth and Essex, The,*
    187–88

*Queen Christina,* 79, 80, 111
*Queen Kelly,* 34, 221

*Rain,* 87
*Rainmaker, The,* 156
*Random Harvest,* 102, 103
Raye, Martha, 138, 213
*Rebecca of Sunnybrook Farm,* 40, 42; also
    *Intermission*
*Reckless,* 114
Redford, Robert, 253
*Red Mill, The,* 133
*Reds,* 273–74, 275
Reynolds, Burt, 6, 257
Reynolds, Debbie, 206, 207, 246
*Rich Are Always With Us, The,* 94, 182
*Roberta,* 101
Rogers, Ginger, 101, 139, 149, 154,
    162, 256, 259, 277
*Roman Holiday,* 235
*Romola,* 50–51

Rooney, Mickey, 198, 202–203, 204,
    217
*Rooster Cogburn,* 159; also *Intermission*
*Rosita,* 44
Russell, Jane, 223
Russell, Rosalind, 71, 89, 92, 113,
    165–72, 174, 180, 183, 205, 218,
    286

*Sadie Thompson,* 33
*Safety in Numbers,* 33
St. Johns, Adela Rogers, 63, 93, 274
*Salome,* 22
*Saratoga,* 115
*Satan Met a Lady,* 184–85
*Scarlet Empress, The,* 108, 120
Selznick, David O., 62–63, 64, 110,
    114, 260, 261–62
*Seven Sinners,* 110–11
*Seventh Heaven,* 58, 59, 60
*Seven Year Itch, The,* 224–25
*Sextette,* 123–24
*Shanghai Express,* 108, 113, 118
Shearer, Norma, 53, 61, 67–72, 74, 80,
    81, 83, 91, 95, 102, 107, 167, 188,
    277
*She Done Him Wrong,* 117–18, 122
Sheridan, Ann, 262
Shields, Brooke, 267–68
*Show Boat,* 216–17
*Show People,* 135
*Six of a Kind,* 138
*Solid Gold Cadillac, The,* 234
*Some Like It Hot,* 227–28
*Song of Love,* 156
*Sound of Music, The,* 249, 250
*Sparrows,* 40, 45
Springer, John, 92
*Stage Door,* 139, 143, 149–50, 152
Stanwyck, Barbara, 109, 132, 160,
    175–80, 183, 206, 218
*Star!,* 249
*Star Is Born, A* (Wellman), 62–65
*Star Is Born, A* (Cukor), 200, 205, 208
*Star Is Born, A* (Pierson), 254, 255
*Steelyard Blues,* 278, 279
*Stella Dallas,* 176–77
Stewart, James, 110, 229
*Strait Jacket,* 91
*Strange Interlude,* 69, 95
Streep, Meryl, 12, 260, 281–82
Streisand, Barbra, 62, 245, 250–56, 288
*Stromboli,* 264–65
*Student Prince, The,* 68–69
*Suddenly Last Summer,* 156, 157
*Sugarland Express, The,* 243–44
Sullavan, Margaret, 64, 100

*Summer Stock*, 204
*Sunny Side Up*, 61–62, 65
*Sunrise*, 59–60, 74, 106
*Sunset Boulevard*, 220–21, 231, 224, 268; also *Intermission*
*Susan Lenox: Her Fall and Rise*, 76–77
Swanson, Gloria, 9, 30–35, 36, 38–39, 52, 54, 60, 93, 209, 220–21, 231, 286, 289; also *Intermission*
*Sylvia Scarlett*, 148, 153, 156

Talmadge, Norma, 52–53, 67
*Taming of the Shrew, The* (Taylor), 55, 56; also *Intermission*
*Taming of the Shrew, The* (Zeffirelli), 208
*Tarzan, the Ape Man*, 270–71
Taylor, Elizabeth, 157, 205–209, 216, 218, 229, 271, 277
Taylor, Robert, 81, 101, 105, 132, 154, 201
Temple, Shirley, 6, 62, 130, 195–96, 205
"10," 250, 269–70
*Tess of the Storm Country*, 40, 41, 43
Thalberg, Irving, 51, 52, 53, 66–70, 97, 113, 240
*That Touch of Mink*, 248–49
*There's Always a Woman*, 164
*They Shoot Horses, Don't They?*, 276–77, 278, 281; also *Intermission*
*Thin Man, The*, 99–100, 151
Thomas, Bob, 224
*Three Smart Girls*, 197, 198, 200
*Tin Pan Alley*, 214
Tomlin, Lily, 232, 240–43, 244, 280; also *Intermission*
*Topper*, 100
*Torrent, The*, 73
Tracy, Spencer, 8, 112, 114, 153–59, 262
*Tree Grows in Brooklyn, A*, 164–65
*Trojan Women, The*, 159
Turner, Lana, 195
*Twentieth Century*, 129, 131; also *Intermission*
*Two-Faced Woman*, 72, 82–83, 88

*Vagabond Lover, The*, 126–27
Valentino, Rudolph, 6, 12, 33; also *Intermission*

Velez, Lupe, 70
*Visit, The*, 266
Von Sternberg, Josef, 44, 46, 79, 105–112, 120
Von Stroheim, Erich, 14–15, 20–21, 33–34, 112, 221

*Wabash Avenue*, 214–15
*Walk on the Wild Side*, 180
*Watch on the Rhine*, 188
*Way Down East*, 48–50, 61
Wayne, John, 8, 110, 159, 164
*Way We Were, The*, 253–54
Weber, Lois, 12
Welch, Raquel, 267, 268, 275, 283
Welles, Orson, 133–34, 211
West, Mae, 114, 116–124, 135, 136, 137, 145–46, 152, 161, 162, 232, 267; also *Frontispiece* and *Intermission*
*Whatever Happened to Baby Jane?*, 90, 91, 182, 193; also *Intermission*
*What Price Hollywood?*, 63–64
*What's Up, Doc?*, 239, 253
White, Pearl, 24, 26
*White Sister, The*, 50–51
*Whoopee!*, 213
*Who's Afraid of Virginia Woolf?*, 208
Wilder, Billy, 111–12, 179, 220–21, 225, 227, 229, 232
*Wind, The*, 51–52
*Wings*, 29; also *Intermission*
*Wizard of Oz, The*, 202–203, 208, 263
*Woman of the Year*, 153–54, 155
*Woman Rebels, A*, 149
*Women, The*, 71, 87, 167; also *Intermission*
Woodward, Joanne, 209

*Yellow Rolls-Royce, The*, 266
Young, Loretta, 277
*You Were Never Lovelier*, 210

Zanuck, Darryl F., 62, 172, 174, 191, 214, 215, 233
*Ziegfeld Follies, The*, 102–103
Zukor, Adolph, 39, 42, 43, 48